SOUTH CAROLINA
BIOGRAPHICAL
DICTIONARY

SOUTH CAROLINA
BIOGRAPHICAL
DICTIONARY

PEOPLE OF ALL TIMES AND PLACES
WHO HAVE BEEN IMPORTANT TO THE HISTORY
AND LIFE OF THE STATE

—◆—

SOMERSET PUBLISHERS, INC.
521 Fifth Ave., 17th Floor
New York, N.Y. 10175

Copyright 1994 © by Somerset Publishers, Inc.

Library of Congress Cataloging-in-Publication Data

South Carolina biographical dictionary : people of all times and
  places who have been important to the history and life of the state.
      p.   cm.
   ISBN 0-403-09933-1 : $79.00
   1. South Carolina--Biography--Dictionaries.
CT259.S68   1994
920.0757--dc20
   [B]   94-25945
                                                               CIP

LIST OF PERSONS

ADAMS,
 JAMES H.
AIKEN,
 DAVID WYATT
 WILLIAM
 WYATT
ALLSTON,
 ROBERT F. W.
 WASHINGTON
ALSTON,
 JOSEPH
ANSEL,
 MARTIN FREDERICK
ASHMORE,
 HARRY S(COTT)
 JOHN DURANT
 ROBERT THOMAS
AYLLON,
 LUCAS VAZQUEZ DE
BARNWELL,
 ROBERT
 ROBERT WOODWARD
BARUCH,
 BERNARD MANNES
BASS,
 CHARLOTTA SPEARS
BEE,
 BARNARD ELLIOTT
BELLINGER,
 JOSEPH
BENET,
 CHRISTIE
BENNETT,
 THOMAS
BERESFORD,
 RICHARD
BERNARDIN,
 JOSEPH LOUIS CARDINAL
BETHUNE,
 MARY MCLEOD
BLACKWOOD,
 IRBA CHARLES
BLAIR,
 JAMES
BLANCHARD,
 FELIX A(NTHONY)

BLEASE,
 COLEMAN LIVINGSTON
BONHAM,
 MILLEDGE LUKE
BOWEN,
 CHRISTOPHER COLUMBUS
BOYCE,
 WILLIAM WATERS
BOYD,
 JULIAN P(ARKS)
BRATTON,
 JOHN
BRAWLEY,
 WILLIAM HUGGINS
BREVARD,
 JOSEPH
BROOKS,
 PRESTON SMITH
BRYSON,
 JOSEPH RALEIGH
BULL,
 JOHN
BURKE,
 AEDANUS
BURT,
 ARMISTEAD
BUTLER,
 ANDREW PICKENS
 MATTHEW CALBRAITH
 PIERCE MASON
 SAMPSON HALE
 WILLIAM
BUTTZ,
 CHARLES WILSON
BYRNES,
 JAMES FRANCIS
CADDELL,
 PATRICK HAYWARD
CAIN,
 RICHARD HARVEY
CALDWELL,
 PATRICK CALHOUN
CALHOUN,
 JOHN CALDWELL
 JOSEPH
CAMPBELL,
 CARROLL A. JR.

LIST OF PERSONS

FULMER,
   HAMPTON PITTS
   WILLA LYBRAND
FURMAN,
   RICHARD
GADSDEN,
   CHRISTOPHER
GARDEN,
   ALEXANDER
GARY,
   FRANK BOYD
GASQUE,
   ALLARD HENRY
   ELIZABETH HAWLEY
GEDDES,
   JOHN
GERVAIS,
   JOHN LEWIS
GETTYS,
   THOMAS SMITHWICK
GIBSON,
   ALTHEA
GILDERSLEEVE,
   BASIL LANNEAU
GILLESPIE,
   JOHN BIRKS "DIZZY"
GIST,
   WILLIAM H.
GOLDSTEIN,
   JOSEPH L(EONARD)
GORRIE,
   JOHN
GOSS,
   JAMES HAMILTON
GOURDIN,
   THEODORE
GOVAN,
   ANDREW ROBISON
GRAYSON,
   WILLIAM JOHN
GREGG,
   WILLIAM
GRIFFIN,
   JOHN KING
GRIMKE,
   ANGELINE E.
   SARAH MOORE
GUERARD,
   BENJAMIN
HAGOOD,
   JOHNSON

HAMILTON,
   JAMES, JR.
   PAUL
HAMLIN,
   TALBOT FAULKNER
HAMMOND,
   JAMES HENRY
HAMPTON,
   WADE
HARE,
   BUTLER BLACK
   JAMES BUTLER
HARLEY,
   JOSEPH EMILE
HARPER,
   ROBERT GOODLOE
   WILLIAM
HARRELSON,
   KENNETH SMITH
HARVEY,
   WILSON GODFREY
HAYNE,
   ARTHUR PERONNEAU
   ROBERT YOUNG
HAYNSWORTH,
   CLEMENT FURMAN
HENEGAN,
   B(ARNABAS) K(ELET)
HENRY,
   EDWARD LAMSON
HEYWARD,
   DUNCAN CLINCH
   EDWIN DUBOSE
   THOMAS, JR.
HIGBE,
   WALTER KIRBY
HINES,
   JOHN ELBRIDGE
HITCHCOCK,
   THOMAS, JR.
HOGE,
   SOLOMON LAFAYETTE
HOLLAND,
   KENNETH LAMAR
HOLLINGS,
   ERNEST FREDERICK
HOLMES,
   ISAAC EDWARD
HUGER,
   BENJAMIN
   DANIEL ELLIOTT

LIST OF PERSONS

viii

LIST OF PERSONS

JOHN LANNEAU
THOMAS SANDERS
MCNAIR,
ROBERT EVANDER
MCQUEEN,
JOHN
MCSWAIN,
JOHN JACKSON
MCSWEENEY,
MILES BENJAMIN
MEANS,
JOHN H.
MIDDLETON,
ARTHUR
HENRY
MILES,
WILLIAM PORCHER
MILLER,
STEPHEN DECATUR
THOMAS EZEKIEL
MITCHELL,
THOMAS ROTHMALER
MOORE,
THOMAS
MOSES,
FRANKLIN J.
MOTTE,
ISAAC
MOULTRIE,
WILLIAM
MOWRER,
PAUL SCOTT
NAPIER,
JOHN LIGHT
NESBITT,
WILSON
NICHOLLS,
SAMUEL JONES
NOBLE,
PATRICK
NORTON,
JAMES
NOTT,
ABRAHAM
O'CONNOR,
MICHAEL PATRICK
ORR,
JAMES LAWRENCE
OSCEOLA
OVERSTREET,
JAMES

PARKER,
JOHN
PATTERSON,
ELIZABETH J.
JAMES O'HANLON
JOHN JAMES
PEACE,
ROGER CRAFT
PERRY,
BENJAMIN F.
WILLIAM HAYNE
PETERKIN,
JULIA
PETIGRU,
JAMES LOUIS
PICKENS,
ANDREW
FRANCIS W.
PINCKNEY,
CHARLES
CHARLES COTESWORTH
THOMAS
POINSETT,
JOEL ROBERTS
POLLITZER,
ANITA LILY
POLLOCK,
WILLIAM PEGUES
PULITZER,
JOSEPH
RAGSDALE,
JAMES WILLARD
RAINEY,
JOSEPH HAYNE
RANSIER,
ALONZO JACOB
RAVENEL,
ARTHUR, JR.
READ,
JACOB
RHETT,
ROBERT BARNWELL
RICHARDS,
JAMES PRIOLEAU
JOHN GARDINER
RICHARDSON,
JAMES B.
JOHN PETER
JOHN SMYTHE
ROBERT CLINTON
RILEY,
CORINNE BOYD

ix

LIST OF PERSONS

JOHN JACOB
RICHARD WILSON
RIPLEY,
ALEXANDRA
RIVERS,
LUCIUS MENDEL
ROBERT,
HENRY MARTYN
ROBERTSON,
THOMAS JAMES
ROGERS,
JAMES
ROPER,
DANIEL CALHOUN
ROSEN,
ALBERT LEONARD
RUSSELL,
DONALD STUART
RUTLEDGE,
EDWARD
JOHN, JR.
JOHN
SAWYER,
FREDERICK ADOLPHUS
SCARBOROUGH,
ROBERT BETHEA
SCOTT,
ROBERT KINGSTON
SEABROOK,
WHITEMARSH BENJAMIN
SHAW,
ROBERT GOULD
SHELL,
GEORGE WASHINGTON
SHEPPARD,
JOHN CALHOUN
SHUBRICK,
WILLIAM BRANFORD
SIMKINS,
ELDRED
SIMMS,
WILLIAM GILMORE
SIMPSON,
RICHARD FRANKLIN
WILLIAM DUNLAP
SIMS,
ALEXANDER DROMGOOLE
HUGO SHERIDAN, JR.
JAMES MARION
SINGLETON,
THOMAS DAY

SMALLS,
ROBERT
SMITH,
CHARLES A.
ELLISON DURANT
O'BRIEN
WILLIAM
WILLIAM LOUGHTON
SNYDER,
JOHN WESLEY
SPRATT,
JOHN MCKEE, JR.
STACKHOUSE,
ELI THOMAS
STOKES,
JAMES WILLIAM
STOLL,
PHILIP HENRY
SWEARINGEN,
JOHN E(LDRED)
TALBERT,
WILLIAM JASPER
TALLON,
ROBERT MOONEYHAN, JR.
(ROBIN)
TAYLOR,
JOHN
JOHN CLARENCE
THOMPSON,
HUGH SMITH
WADDY, JR.
THURMOND,
STROM
TILLMAN,
BENJAMIN RYAN
GEORGE DIONYSIUS
TIMMERMAN,
GEORGE BELL, JR.
TIMROD,
HENRY
TRAPIER,
PAUL
TRAVIS,
WILLIAM B.
TROTTI,
SAMUEL WILDS
TUCKER,
STARLING
TURNER,
HENRY MCNEAL
VANDERHORST,
ARNOLDUS

VESEY,
  DENMARK
WADDEL,
  MOSES
WALLACE,
  ALEXANDER STUART
  DANIEL
WATSON,
  ALBERT WILLIAM
  JOHN BROADUS
WEST,
  JOHN CARL
WESTMORELAND,
  WILLIAM C(HILDS)
WHALEY,
  RICHARD SMITH
WHITE,
  JOSH
WHITTEMORE,
  BENJAMIN FRANKLIN

WILLIAMS,
  DAVID R.
  RANSOME JUDSON
WILSON,
  JOHN
  JOHN LYDE
  STANYARNE
  WOODROW
WINN,
  RICHARD
WITHERSPOON,
  ROBERT
WOFFORD,
  THOMAS ALBERT
WOODWARD,
  JOSEPH ADDISON
YARBOROUGH,
  CALE
YOUNG,
  EDWARD LUNN

A

ADAMS, JAMES H., (1812-1861) — forty-first state governor (D) of South Carolina, 1854-1856.

He was born in Minervaville, South Carolina, the son of Mary Howell Hart Goodwyn and Henry Walker Adams. His parents died when he was an infant, and he was raised by his maternal grandparents.

Adams attended Captain Partridge's Academy in Norwich, Connecticut, and received an A.B. degree from Yale College in 1831. His political career began with an interest in the nullification issue; he was a member of the South Carolina Nullification Convention in 1832-1833. After an election to the South Carolina House of Representatives in 1834, he served until 1837, and was elected again in 1840-1841 and 1848-1849. He then became a member of the South Carolina Senate in 1850, holding this office until 1853, and was also a presidential elector in 1852.

Adams was elected governor of South Carolina in December 1854. After the passage of the Kansas-Nebraska Act by the U.S. Congress, and the subsequent fighting in "Bleeding Kansas," State politicians were strongly concerned with the issue of slavery expansion to the territories. By the mid-1850s, distrust of abolition was almost universal in South Carolina. Adams proposed to reopen the African slave trade, advocating it on humanitarian grounds, and as a means of rooting out the atrocities known to exist in connection with illegal traffic of slaves.

After his term, Adams ran for the United States Senate, but was defeated in the election. He retired to private life for a short time, but returned to public life to become a member of the South Carolina Secession Convention in 1860-1861. Formally declaring his views that South Carolina should withdraw from the Union, he was a signer of the South Carolina Ordinance of Secession. In 1860, he was joined by James L. Orr and Robert Barnwell as peace comissioners to negotiate the transfer of federal property in South Carolina to State control.

Adams died in July 1861 in Richland County, South Carolina. He was married to Jane Margaret Scott in April 1832. The couple had 11 children.

AIKEN, DAVID WYATT, (1828-1887) — (father of Wyatt Aiken and cousin of William Aiken), a U.S. Representative from South Carolina; born in Winnsboro, Fairfield County, S.C., March 17, 1828; received his early education under private tutors; attended Mount Zion Institute, Winnsboro, and was graduated from South Carolina University, at Columbia, in 1849; taught school two years; engaged in agricultural pursuits in 1852; during the Civil War served in the Confederate Army as a private; appointed adjutant and later elected colonel of the Seventh Regiment of Volunteers; relieved from service by reason of wounds received on September 17, 1862, at Antietam; member of the State house of representatives 1864-1866; secretary and treasurer, Agricultural and Mechanical Society of South Carolina, 1869; member, executive committee, National Grange, 1873-1885, and served as chairman, 1875; delegate to the Democratic National Convention at St. Louis in 1876; elected as a Democrat to the Forty-fifth and to the four succeeding Congresses (March 4, 1877-March 3, 1887); chairman, Committee on Education (Fortyeighth and Forty-ninth Congresses); was not a candidate for renomination in 1886, being an invalid throughout his last term; died in Cokesbury, S.C., April 6, 1887; interment in Magnolia Cemetery, Greenwood, S.C.

AIKEN, WILLIAM, (1806-1887) — thirty-six state governor (D) of South Carolina, 1844-1846.

He was born in Charleston, South Carolina, the son of Henrietta Wyatt and William Aiken.

Aiken attended private schools, and graduated from South Carolina College in 1825. After traveling extensively, he operated a rice plantation in Jehossee Island near Charleston.

He was elected to the South Carolina House of Representatives in 1838, and held this office until his election to the South Carolina Senate in 1842, which he served through 1844.

Aiken was elected govenor of South Carolina in December 1844. During his term, he directed his efforts primarily toward economic development and railroad construction. By 1845, fifteen cotton mills and three woolen mills were operating in South Carolina. The State Legislature also chartered the Graniteville Manufacturing Company with a capital of $3,000,000, which became the beginning of large-scale manufacturing growth in the State.

After leaving gubernatorial office in 1846, Aiken retired briefly from public life, then was elected to the United States House of Representatives in 1851, serving until 1857.

Aiken was married in February 1831 to Harriet Lowndes. He died in Charleston in September 1887.

AIKEN, WYATT, (1863-1923) — (son of David Wyatt Aiken), a U.S. Representative from South Carolina; born near Macon, Ga., December 14, 1863; reared in Cokesbury, Abbeville (now Greenwood) County, S.C.; attended the public schools of Cokesbury and of Washington, D.C.; official court repolcter for the second South Carolina judicial circuit and, later, for the eighth circuit; volunteered as a private in Company A, First South Carolina Regiment of Infantry, during the war with Spain; later appointed battalion adjutant by Governor Ellerbe, and acted as regimental quartermaster during the greater por tion of his senice; was mustered out in Columbia, S.C., November 10, 1898; elected as a Democrat to the Fiftyeighth and to the six succeeding Congresses (March 4, 1903-March 3, 1917); unsuccessful candidate for renomination in 1916 and again in 1918; lived in retirement until his death in Abbeville, S.C., February 6, 1923; interment in Melrose Cemetery.

ALLSTON, ROBERT F. W., (1801-1864) — forty-second state governor (D) of South Carolina, 1856-1858.

He was born in All Saints Parish, South Carolina, the son of Charlotte Anne and Benjamin Allson.

Allston attended John Waldo's School in Georgetown, South Carolina, and graduated from West Point Military Academy in Georgetown, South Carolina in 1821. He was appointed a Brevet Second Lieutenant, Third Artillery, and served with the Coast Survey Corps.

After resigning his commission in 1822, Allston became a planter and scientific agriculturist, joining his family's estate. He reclaimed a neglected territory on the Pee Dee River, he built canals and embankments, and became a major rice planter.

Allston was actively involved in local politics from an early age. He was a member of the Building Commission, the Prince Frederick Church, the Georgetown Library Society, the American Association for the Advancement of Science, the St. Cecelia's Socety, and the South Carolina Historical Society. He was also a trustee of South Carolina College, and the president of the Waccamaw Indigo Society.

From 1824-1828, he was Surveyor General of South Carolina. He was elected to the South Carolina House of Representatives in 1828, serving until 1832, and had a seat on the South Carolina Senate from 1850 to 1856. He was a presidential elector in 1852.

Allston was elected governor of South Carolina in December 1856. At this time, the issue of secession had reached major proportions, and South Carolina became divided into three contending political factions: the Democrats, who hoped to reach settlement within the existing political structure, the Nationists, who sought establishment of a Southern party to defend states' rights, and the "Know Nothings," who stressed nationalism, Protestantism and native Americanism. Although those stressing secession had a strong following, the 1857 Dred Scott decision by the U.S. Supreme Court, which appeared to support Calhoun's doctrine of states' rights, weakened the position of calling for immediate withdrawal from the Union.

Allston left office in 1858. He served as a presidential elector of the Confederate States in 1861, and was a member of Soldiers' Board of Relief.

Allston's agricultural pursuits resulted in his earning a silver metal at the Paris exposition of 1865 for his scientific methods of rice cultivation, and a gold metal in 1856. He also advanced methods for raising livestock by importing breeds of sheep, cattle, and horses to improve native breeds.

Allston was married to Adele Petigru in 1835. He died in April 1864 in Chicora Wood, his family estate near Georgetown, South Carolina.

ALLSTON, WASHINGTON, (1779-1843) — was an American artist whose paintings were distinguished by their highly dramatic content and romantic treatment of light.

Born in Brook Green Domain, South Carolina on November 5, 1779, the son of Captain William and Rachel (Moore) Allston, Washington Allston was graduated from Harvard University in 1800. The next year he sailed to England to study at the Royal Academy under Benjamin West. In 1803, he went to Paris and then on to Italy, where he studied the old masters and formed a close friendship with Samuel Taylor Coleridge and Washington Irving. In 1808, he went to Boston, returning to England three years later with his pupil, Samuel F.B. Morse. He lived in England until 1818. During this time he created his finest paintings. Among these were a portrait of Coleridge and "The Agony of Judas", which he considered his best work. However he destroyed this painting for fear that it would be misunderstood.

Allston's canvases were distinguished by their highly dramatic content and a characteristically romantic treatment of light, while his color was often compared to that of Titian. He eventually earned the name of the "American Titian." Also during these years, Allston published a book of verse, *The Sylphs of the Second Season with Other Poems*, in 1813. He later published *The Paint King* and *The Two Painters*. In 1841, he published *Monaldi*, a romance illustrating Italian life, and in 1850 a volume of his *Lectures on Art and Poems* was printed.

In 1818, Allston returned to the United States and established a studio in Boston, later moving to Cambridgeport, Massachusetts. Among his major works of his last years were "Moonlit Landscape", "The Flight of the Florimell" and "Belshazzar's Feast," a huge painting that he had begun in 1817 and, despite his almost continual work, he left unfinished at his death. None of the works of this period seemed to fulfill the promise of his youth, but he had nonetheless a secure position in American art.

Washington Allston married Ann Channing in 1809. After her death, he was remarried to Martha Dana in 1830. He died in Cambridgeport on July 9, 1843.

ALSTON, JOSEPH, (1778-1816) — ninteenth state governor (D-R) of South Carolina, 1812-1814.

He was born in All Saint's Parish, South Carolina, the son of Mary and William Alston.

Alston had a privately tutored education, and also studied at Princeton University. After studying law in the offices of Edward Rutledge, he established a practice and helped manage the family plantation. He became a member of the lower house of the South Carolina Legislature in 1802-1803, and again in 1805, serving until 1812.

Alston was elected governor of South Carolina in December 1812. He assumed office during the War of 1812, when the State was in constant fear of attack by the British Navy. The South Carolina militia had been called to duty; however, many of the men were resentful of being placed under discipline of the Regular Army's "Articles of War." Disorder became so great that, in August 1813, Alson disbanded the militia and demanded that the Legislature grant him adequate control over the troops. Though the order was revoked, his action made him extremely unpopular in the State, and Alston left public office in 1814.

Other events that took place during Alston's administration were the survey and land fixing of the boundary line between the two Carolinas, and the establishment of a State bank in Charleston.

Alston was married in 1801 to Theodosia Burr. The couple had one child. He died in Charleston, South Carolina in 1816.

ANSEL, MARTIN FREDERICK, (1850-1945) — Sixty-forth state governor (D) of South Carolina, 1907-1911.

Born in Charleston on December 12, 1850, the son of John and Frederika (Bowers) Ansel. He studied law under James H. Whitner and was admitted to the South Carolina

Bar in 1870. He began a law office in Franklin, North
Carolina and worked there for about four years. In 1876,
he moved his practice to Greenville, South Carolina. He
was married in 1878 to Ophelia Spreight who lived until
1895. Three years after that, in 1898, he married Mrs.
Addie (Hollingsworth) Harris. He was the father of three
children.

Ansel was elected to the State House of Representatives
and served from 1882-1888. He was solicitor of the
Eighth Judicial District of South Carolina from 1888 to
1901. He ran for the Democratic gubernatorial nomination in 1902, but was defeated. Four years later, in 1906,
he ran again, and not only received the nomination but
also won in the general election, running unopposed.
During his tenure in office, the state liquor dispensary
system was abolished in favor of a state-wide prohibition
giving counties the option of retaining dispensaries on a
local level. Also during his administration, state funding
was provided for high schools, a Confederate Veterans
Home was founded, as well as the State Health Office, the
State Insurance Department, and the Audubon Society.
Ansel was reelected to the governorship in 1908. He
retired from office in 1911 and returned to practice law in
Greenville, where he died on August 23, 1945.

ASHMORE, HARRY S(COTT), (1916-?) — author,
editor, was born in Greenville, South Carolina on July 28,
1916. He attended Clemson College, earning a B.S. degree in 1937. He also attended Harvard University on a
Nieman Fellow during 1941-42.

Ashmore worked as a newspaper reporter in Greenville,
South Carolina between 1937 and 1940. During 1940-41,
he was a political writer for the *Charlotte News* in Charlotte, North Carolina, and served as that paper's associate
editor from 1945 to 1947, eventually becoming editor.
During the latter year, he moved to Little Rock, Arkansas
to work as editorial page editor for the *Arkansas Gazette*,
and then moved up to executive editor in 1948, a position
he held until 1959. From 1960 to 1963, he was editor-in-
chief at *Encyclopaedia Britannica* in Chicago, and in the
latter year, became a consultant for that firm.

Between 1960 and 1968, Ashmore was chairman of the executive committee for the Santa Barbara Organization Center for the Study of Democratic Institutions; in the latter year, he became its president.

Ashmore's books include: *The Negro and the Schools*, 1954; *An Epitaph for Dixie*, 1958; *The Other Side of Jordan*, 1960; *The Man in the Middle*, 1966; (with William C. Baggs) *Mission to Hanoi*, 1968; *Fear in the Air: Broadcasting and the First Amendment*, 1973. He also contributed articles to several periodicals.

Ashmore has received a number of honors, including the prestigious Pulitzer Prize for editorial writing in 1968, during the time he was working for the *Arkansas Gazette*.

Ashmore served in the United States Army between 1942 and 1945, attaining the rank of lieutenant colonel and receiving a Bronze Star and two oak leaf clusters. He is married to Barbara Edith Laier and the couple have one daughter.

ASHMORE, JOHN DURANT, (1819-1871) — (cousin of Robert Thomas Ashmore), a U.S. Representative from South Carolina; born in Greenville District, S.C., August 18, 1819; attended the common schools; studied law; was admitted to the bar but never practiced; engaged in agricultural pursuits; member of the State house of representatives 1848-1853; comptroller general of the State 1853-1857; elected as a Democrat to the Thirty-sixth Congress and served from March 4, 1859, until his retirement on December 21, 1860; chairman, Committee on Mileage !Thirty-sixth Congress); during the Civil War was elected colonel of the Fourth South Carolina Regiment, but resigned before the regiment was called into service; engaged in mercantile pursuits in Greenville, S.C.; died in Sardis, Miss., December 5, 1871; interment in Black Jack Cemetery, near Sardis, in Panola County.

ASHMORE, ROBERT THOMAS, (1904-   ) — (cousin of John Durant Ashmore), a U.S. Representative from South Carolina; born on a farm near Greenville, S.C., February 22, 1904; attended the public schools of Greenville; was graduated from Furman University Law School, Greenville, S.C., in 1927; while a student engaged in agricultural work, retail sales, and as a substitute rural mail carrier; was admitted to the bar in January 1928 and engaged in the practice of law in Greenville, S.C.; solicitor of Greenville County Court 1930-1934; solicitor of the thirteenth judicial circuit of South Carolina 1936-1953; during the Second World War, while on official leave from duties as solicitor, volunteered for service in the United States Army in December 1942, serving in this country and overseas until discharged from active duty in May 1946, as a lieutenant colonel in the United States Army Reserve; promoted to colonel in 1955; elected as a Democrat to the Eighty-third Congress to fill the vacancy caused by the death of Joseph R. Bryson; reelected to the Eighty-fourth and to the six succeeding Congresses (June 2, 1953-January 3, 1969); was not a candidate for reelection in 1968 to the Ninety- first Congress; resumed the practice of law; member of the board, South Carolina Appalachian Regional Planning and Development Commission (later South Carolina Appalachian Council of Governments), 1970 to present, and chairman, 1970-1972; is a resident of Greenville, S.C.

AYLLON, LUCAS VAZQUEZ DE, (c.1475 - 1526) — was a Spanish explorer.

Born in about 1475 in Toledo, Spain, Lucas Ayllon was one of the group who came to Hispaniola (Santo Domingo) in 1502 with Governor Nicholas de Ovando. He was made a judge of the supreme court of Hispaniola.

Intrigued by the reportedly rich lands to the west and north, he formed a partnership with the clerk of the Audiencia of Hispaniola and, in 1520, sent a ship captained by Francisco Gordillo to sail northward until they could reach land. Ayllon did not accompany the ship. The sailing party landed in in 1521. They took possession of Indians living there and brought 150 back to be used as slaves. On their return, they were brought before a commission which freed the slaves and ordered their return to the homelands.

Ayllon obtained a grant of the new land. He fitted another vessel and, in 1526, sailed with 500 colonists and the Indians, with the intention of returning them to their home. Landing at the mouth of the Santee, they sailed

northward to the Chesapeake and, on the site of James-
town, founded the settlement of San Miguel de Guandape.

Many of the colonists contracted swamp fever and died,
including Ayllon who died on October 18, 1526.

B

BARNWELL, ROBERT, (1761-1814) — (father of Robert
Woodward Barnwell), a Delegate and a Representative
from South Carolina; born in Beaufort, S.C., December
21, 1761; educated in the common schools and by private
teachers; volunteered for service in the Revolutionary War
when sixteen years of age; received seventeen wounds in
the battle on Johns Island, S.C.; finally recovered and
served as lieutenant with his company at the siege of
Charleston in 1780; at the fall of that city was sent aboard
the prison ship *Pack Horse,* but was released in the
general exchange of prisoners in June 1781; was for many
years president of the board of trustees of Beaufort College; Member of the Continental Congress in 1789; member of the convention of South Carolina for the adoption
of the Federal Constitution in 1788; elected to the Second
Congress (March 4, 1791-March 3, 1793); declined to be
a candidate for renomination in 1792 to the Third Congress; member of the South Carolina house of representatives 1787-1788, 1790-1791, and 1794-1801, serving
as speaker in 1795; member of the South Carolina senate
in 1805 and 1806, serving as president in 1805; died in
Beaufort, Beaufort County, S.C., October 24, 1814; interment in St. Helena's Churchyard.

BARNWELL, ROBERT WOODWARD, (1801-1882) —
(son of Robert Barnwell), a U.S. Representative and a
U.S. Senator from South Carolina; born in Beaufort,
Beaufort County, S.C., August 10, 1801; attended private
schools in Beaufort and Charleston, S.C., and was
graduated from Harvard University in 1821; studied law;
was admitted to the bar and commenced practice in Beau-

fort, S.C., in 1824; member, State house of representatives 1826-1828; elected to the Twenty-first and Twenty-second Congresses (March 4, 1829-March 3, 1833); was not a candidate for renomination in 1832; president of South Carolina College (now the University of South Carolina) at Columbia 1835-1841, when he resigned; appointed to the United States Senate to fill the vacancy caused by the death of Franklin H. Elmore and served from June 4 to December 8, 1850, when a successor was elected and qualified; was not a candidate for election; member of the Nashville convention in 1850; commissioner to the Federal Government from South Carolina regarding the secession of that State in December 1860; delegate to the convention of the seceding States in Montgomery, Ala., his being the deciding vote in the South Carolina delegation which carried the State for Jefferson Davis and made him President of the Southern Confederacy; member of the Confederate States Senate 1861-1865; chairman of the faculty of the University of South Carolina 1866-1873; conducted a private girls school in Columbia, S.C.; died in Columbia, Richland County, S.C., November 5, 1882; interment in St. Helena's Churchyard, Beaufort, S.C.

BARUCH, BERNARD MANNES, (1870-1965) — was a financier and public official who was widely known as an advisor and confidante of every president from Woodrow Wilson to John F. Kennedy.

Born in Camden, South Carolina on August 19, 1870, the son of Simon and Belle (Wolfe) Baruch, Bernard Baruch graduated from the College of the City of New York in 1889 with an A.B. degree and soon after entered a Wall Street brokerage firm. Baruch also received honorary LL.D. degrees from several colleges: Williams College, 1923; University of South Carolina, 1925; Johns Hopkins, 1933; Oglethorpe University, 1933; College of Charleston, 1935; The Citadel, 1937; and the College of the City of New York, 1947. He received an honorary D.C.L. from Union College in 1937.

Baruch's successful management of stock dealings enabled him to open his own office in 1903 and within 10 years he accumulated a large fortune. In 1916, President Woodrow Wilson appointed him, over the protests of several congressmen and senators who objected to Baruch's reputation as a financial speculator, to the advisory commission of the Council of National Defense. He advanced to the chairmanship of the War Industries Board in March of 1918. After World War I, he was a member of the Supreme Economic Council at the Versailles Peace Conference and also served in numerous other advisory capacities on economic matters.

Although Baruch thereafter held no major administrative post — not even during World War II when he was active in government economic and industrial mobilization work — he was widely known as a friend, advisor and confidante of every United States president from Wilson to John F. Kennedy.

In 1946, Baruch represented the United States on the United Nations Atomic Energy Commission. He presented to the commission a proposal for the international development and control of atomic energy that, although developed largely by Dean Acheson and David Lilienthal, became known as the Baruch Plan.

Baruch published two volumes of his memoirs, *Baruch: My Own Story* in 1957, and *Baruch: The Public Years* in 1960. In 1964, he presented his papers to the Princeton University library as a nucleus for the collection of the Center for Studies in Twentieth-Century American Statecraft and Public Policy.

For many of his later years, Baruch was a familiar sight in Washington, D.C. where he particularly favored a bench in Lafayette Square, opposite the White House. It was there that he presided as a popular sage and regularly received mail deliveries.

Bernard Baruch married Annie Griffen on October 20, 1897. The couple had three children. He died in New York City on June 20, 1965.

BASS, CHARLOTTA SPEARS, (1880?-1969) — civil rights reformer, was born in Sumter, South Carolina, the daughter of Hiram and Kate Spears. She grew up in the reconstructed South, but left before her twentieth birthday to join her brother in Providence, Rhode Island. There she found work in a local newspaper and began to learn that business.

The cold climate proved unhealthful, and in 1910 she moved to Los Angeles, and got a job working for *The Eagle*, a local L.A. newspaper. Within two years the paper's owner died, and she managed to purchase it from his heirs. Charlotta renamed it the *California Eagle*, and embarked on a course of social activism. Her efforts were strengthened by the arrival that same year, 1912, of Joseph Bass, a Kansas newspaperman, who became her managing editor, and then her husband. In the years before World War I the *California Eagle* crusaded against D.W. Griffith's *Birth of a Nation*, and helped establish the interracial Progressive Educational Association.

Following the war, the paper took on the Ku Klux Klan, and won a court fight when the Klan sued for libel. The turbulent 1930's brought a host of new causes and the Basses helped defend the Scottsboro Nine, supported labor union organizing, and fought discriminatory hiring by the railroads. In 1934 her husband died, but she continued to run the paper and write for various social causes. In 1940 Ms. Bass served as western regional director for Wendell Wilkie's presidential campaign, and in 1943 became the first black grand jury member for the Los Angeles County Court.

1945 brought an end to World War II, but civil rights remained an embattled front in America. Her newspaper campaigned against lynchings that plagued the South in 1946, and soon became embroiled in the "McCarthyism" repression of the late 1940's. These events led her to abandon the Republican party in 1948, and become a supporter of Henry A. Wallace. After the 1948 election she traveled extensively in Europe, and took part in a call to ban the atom bomb. Returning to the United States, she was chosen by the Progressive Party for its vice-presidential candidate in the 1952 elections, the first black woman to run for that office.

Bass retired from the *California Eagle* in the early 1950's. Over the the next several years she prepared her biography *Forty Years: Memoirs from the Pages of a Newspaper*, which was published in 1960. Through retired she continued to help her community by establishing a library for neighborhood youth in her home in

Los Angeles. Charlotta Spears Bass died on April 12, 1969.

BEE, BARNARD ELLIOTT, (1824-1861) — Confederate soldier who pegged General Thomas J. Jackson with the nickname Stonewall.

Born in Charleston, South Carolina, Bee moved with his family to Texas in 1845, when he was 11 years old. His father was an expatriate, but Bee was still accepted to West Point as a cadet "at large." He graduated in 1845, and was commissioned to the 3rd Infantry. Returning to his adopted state he fought under General Zachary Taylor in the Mexican War. He fought battles at Palo Alto and Resaca de la Palma, then left for a short time for recruitment duty. He was later returned to the front and served under General Winfield Scott at Mexico City, Chapultepec, and Cerro Gordo, where he was wounded. He received two brevets for gallant and meritorious conduct. He was also presented with the sword of honor from South Carolina for his patriotic and meritorious conduct during the war.

The rest of Bee's Union service was in the frontier, where he was promoted to lieutenant in 1851, and then was appointed captain of the 10th Infantry. He resigned from the Union March 3, 1861, and was commissioned a major of infantry in the Confederate Infantry. On June 17 he was appointed brigadier-general under General Joseph E. Johnston's army. His inexperienced brigade was forced to face the heaviest part of the fighting at Bull Run, and Bee saw that they were terrified. "Let us determine to die here, and we will conquer," he told his men. "There is Jackson standing like a stone wall. Rally behind the Virginians!" The men followed Bee's orders, and they stood their ground. The Union forces were held back long enough for the defense to be organized in the rear. Eventually Bee lost almost all of his field soldiers and he was seriously injured on the front. He died the next day, July 22, 1861. That one sentence gave Jackson the nickname by which he has been known through history. Bee, who was a great soldier and had a strong capacity for leadership, is known more for that statement than anything else.

BELLINGER, JOSEPH, (1773-1830) — a U.S. Representative from South Carolina; born at Bellinger Plantation in Saint Bartholomew Parish, Ashepoo, Colleton County, S.C., in 1773; planter and owner of "Aeolian Lawn" plantation; member of the State house of representatives 1802-1809 and of the State senate from Barnwell District 1810-1813; elected as a Republican to the Fifteenth Congress (March 4, 1817-March 3, 1819); was not a candidate for reelection to the Sixteenth Congress; died at Charleston, S.C., January 10, 1830; interment in the Bellinger private burial ground, Poco Sabo Plantation, Ashepoo, S.C.

BENET, CHRISTIE, (1903-1951) — a U.S. Senator from South Carolina; born in Abbeville, Abbeville County, S.C., December 26, 1879; attended the common schools, the College of Charleston, the University of South Carolina at Columbia, and the University of Virginia at Charlottesville; studied law; was admitted to the bar and commenced practice in Columbia, Richland County, S.C., in 1903; solicitor of the fifth judicial circuit in 1908; attorney for the city of Columbia 1910-1912; three times secretary of the Democratic State committee; appointed as a Democrat to the United States Senate to fill the vacancy caused by the death of Benjamin R. Tillman and served from July 6 to November 5, 1918, when a successor was elected; unsuccessful candidate for election in 1918 to the Senate to fill the vacancy; chairman, Committee on National Banks (Sixty-fifth Congress); resumed the practice of law; member and later chairman of the board of regents of South Carolina State Hospital 1915-1946; during the Second World War served as chairman of the War Finance Committee for South Carolina and was serving as chairman of the Alien Enemy Hearing Board for the eastern district of South Carolina at time of death; died in Columbia, S.C., March 30, 1951; interment in Elmwood Cemetery.

BENNETT, THOMAS, (1781-1865) — twenty-third state governor (D-R) of South Carolina, 1820-1822.

He was born in Charleston, South Carolina, the son of Anna Hayes and Thomas Bennett. His father was owner of a rice and lumber mill.

Bennett joined into a partnership with his father in the mills at an early age. He also had a career in the banking business, becoming director of the Planters and Merchant Bank of South Carolina in 1810, and director of the Bank of the State of South Carolina in 1819. He held a number of public positions in Charleston from 1812 on, among them Intendant of Charleston 1812- 1814, Commissioner of Free Schools, and Commissioner for Purchasing Debt of the State from Surplus Funds.

Bennett was elected to the South Carolina House of Representatives in 1804, serving through 1806. He was a Representative again in 1808-1810, and 1812-1818, and was Speaker of the House his last four years. In 1819, he was elected to the State Senate, and held that position until 1820.

He was elected governor of South Carolina on December 7, 1820. During his tenure, the slave issue intensified greatly. On December 20, the State Legislature passed a law prohibiting emancipation of slaves without permission of the Legislature, and forbidding free blacks to enter South Carolina unless he or she had lived in the state during the previous two years.

In 1822, while Bennett was still governor, Denmark Vesey, a freed black, inspired a slave rebellion by explaining to blacks that they had been freed by the United States Congress, and that their masters were holding them illegally. Vesey planned an uprising for the night of June 16, at which time the adherents were to seize enough wealth to enable them to escape to Santo Domingo in the Caribbean. His plot was betrayed, however, and the conspirators seized. The principal blacks were tried before a court constituted for the purpose, and thirty-five conspirators, Vesey among them, were hanged. Four white men also were indicted as privy to, and participators in, the conspiracy, and were sentenced to fines and imprisonments.

Although the conspiracy was unsuccessful, it instilled a fear of further slave rebellions and provoked many white Southerners to strengthen their opposition to abolition.

After his gubernatorial term ended, Bennett served in the South Carolina Senate from 1837 to 1840.

Bennett was married to Mary Lightbourn Stone in 1801. He married a second time to Jane Gorden in 1840. He died in January 1865, and was buried in Charleston.

BERESFORD, RICHARD, (1755-1803) — a Delegate from South Carolina; born near Charleston, St. Thomas and St. Denis Parish, Berkeley County, S.C., in 1755; educated in South Carolina and in England; studied law at the Middle Temple in London; was admitted to the bar in 1773 and practiced in Charleston, S.C.; engaged in planting, with extensive estates in Berkeley and Colleton Counties, S.C., and in England; took an active part in the Revolution, serving under General Huger in the Georgia campaign in 1778; was captured at the fall of Charleston in 1780 and imprisoned at St. Augustine ntil 1781, when he was exchanged; member of the State house of representatives in 1781; elected by the State general assembly a member of the privy council in 1782; elected Lieutenant Governor in January 1783, but resigned shortly afterward, having been elected to Congress; Member of the Continental Congress in 1783 and 1784; resumed planting; later engaged in literary pursuits; published the Vigil in Charleston in 1798; died in Charleston, S.C., February 6, 1803.

BERNARDIN, JOSEPH LOUIS CARDINAL, (1928-   ) — is the archbishop of Chicago.
Born in Columbia, South Carolina on April 2, 1928, the son of Joseph and Maria M. (Simion) Bernardin, the young Joseph Bernardin attended the University of South Carolina to study medicine. After three semesters, he turned his attention to the priesthood. He received a B.A. degree in philosophy from St. Mary's Seminary in Baltimore in 1948. He received a M. Ed. from Catholic University in 1952 and was ordained as a priest in the Roman Catholic Church in 1952.
Bernardin was an assistant pastor in Charleston from 1952 until 1954, when he became vice chancellor of the diocese. He was promoted to chancellor in 1956, to vicar general and diocesan consultor in 1962, and to administrator, or executive assistant to the bishop, in 1964. In 1966, he was consecrated a bishop and assigned as

auxiliary to the late Archbishop Paul F. Hallinan of New Orleans.

In 1968, Bernardin went to Washington D.C. as the full-time general secretary of the National Conference of Catholic Bishops and the NCCB's social action agency, the United States Catholic Conference. He remained in Washington until 1972, when he was appointed Archbishop of Cincinnati, a city with a population of 529,000 Roman Catholics in a total population of 2,670,000 in southern Ohio. His episcopal versatility was demonstrated within his first two months, when he called for an end to the American bombing in North Vietnam and then, several weeks later, participated in an ecumenical service in the White House on the occasion of President Richard Nixon's second inauguration.

During his 10 years in Cincinnati, Bernardin became known as a man who asserted himself as the ultimate authority in local church matters, but who sought the counsel of rank-and-file clergy and, to a lesser degree, laity, in his decision making. In controversies, including the local drive for the admission of women to the priesthood, he held the Vatican's opposition while allowing all parties to express their opinion. He settled one dispute between ultra-conservatives and progressives by leaving the choice of religious curricula in parochial schools to the individual parishes. On the other hand, he dared the wrath of supporters of financially troubled schools by boldly endorsing a tax increase for equally strapped public schools. He was also a charitable man who regularly spent holidays saying Mass in prisons and for migrant workers. Toward the end of his tenure, he established a $500,000 emergency fund for the poor and indigent.

As president of the National Conference of Catholic Bishops, Bernardin tended toward the liberal side on such contested issues as the Pentecostal renewal within American Catholicism, which was viewed by some bishops as a threat to hierarchical authority. Regarding women's rights he insisted he was committed to equality. On the controversial subject of birth control, he was oblique, saying that Catholics have "the obligation to follow a correctly formed conscience." On abortion he was firmly Pro-Life.

During his presidency, the National Conference of Catholic Bishops also voiced opposition to capital punishment; approved a "Pastoral Plan of Action in the World Food Crisis" that asked Roman Catholics to fast at least twice a week; and struck down the penalty of excommunication for those who divorce and remarry, although they retained the exclusion from the sacraments of penance and Holy Communion. After leaving the presidency, Bernardin became chairman of the bishop's committee on war and peace. The committee drafted a proposed pastoral letter refusing to legitimatize nuclear war.

On July 10, 1982, Pope John Paul II named Bernardin the new Archbishop of Chicago. He was formally installed as leader of the archdiocese of Chicago during a candlelight prayer service in Holy Name Cathedral on August 24, 1982.

BETHUNE, MARY MCLEOD, (1875-1955) — was an educator whose efforts on behalf of education and improved racial relations brought her to national prominence.

Born in Mayesville, South Carolina on July 10, 1875, the daughter of Samuel and Patsy (McIntosh) McLeod, who were former slaves, she was graduated from Scotia Seminary (now Barber-Scotia College) in 1893. After graduating from Moody Bible Institute in Chicago in 1895, she began a teaching career and until 1903, taught in a succession of small Southern schools. Bethune later received a number of degrees, including: an honorary A.M. from Wilberforce University in 1915; an honorary M.S. from South Carolina State College in 1938; an LL.D. degree from Lincoln University in Philadelphia in 1935, from Howard University in 1942, from Wiley College in 1943, and from Atlanta University in 1945; and an H.H.D. from Bennett College in Greensboro, North Carolina in 1945, from West Virginia State College in 1947, and from Rollins College in Winter Park, Florida in 1949.

In 1904, Bethune moved to the east coast of Florida where a large black population had grown up at the time of the construction of the Florida East Coast Railway. In Daytona Beach she opened the Daytona Normal and Industrial Institute for Negro Girls. Having virtually no tangible assets with which to start, she worked tirelessly to build a schoolhouse, solicit help and contributions, and enlist the goodwill of both the black and white communities.

In 1923, the school was merged with the Cookman Institute for Men, then in Jacksonville, Florida, to form Bethune-Cookman College in Daytona Beach. Bethune remained president of the college until 1942 and resumed the position in 1946-47 before retiring as president emeritus.

Bethune's efforts on behalf of education and improved racial relations brought her to national prominence. She was awarded the Spingarn Medal of the National Association for the Advancement of Colored People in 1935, and was appointed the next year as director of Negro Affairs of the National Youth Administration, a post she held until 1944. In 1937, she founded the National Council of Negro Women, of which she was president, and was advisor on minority affairs to President Franklin D. Roosevelt. She also advised the secretary of war on the selection of officer candidates for the Women's Auxiliary Corps (WAAC), established in 1942. In 1945, she went as an observer with the United States delegation to the organizational conference of the United Nations in San Francisco.

Bethune received a number of other awards, including: the Frances Drexel Award in 1937, the Thomas Jefferson Award in 1942, the Haitian Medal Honor and Merit in 1949, the Robert A. Abbott Memorial Award in 1953, the Elijah P. Lovejoy medal in 1953, and the Dorie Miller Gold Cup in 1954. She was also a contributor to numerous books and magazines.

Mary McLeod Bethune married Albertus Bethune in May 1898. The couple had one son. She died in Daytona Beach on May 18, 1955.

BLACKWOOD, IRBA CHARLES, (1878-1936) — Seventy-second state governor (D) of South Carolina, 1931-1935.

Born in Blackwood, South Carolina on November 21, 1878, the son of Charles and Louvenia (Burns) Blackwood. He attended Furman University, and Wofford College where he graduated in 1898. He studied law privately and in 1902 was admitted to the South Carolina Bar. He established a law practice in Spartanburg, meanwhile serving as a member of the South Carolina House of Representatives from 1902 to 1906. He was married to Margaret Hodges on October 4, 1915. From 1914 to 1916, Blackwood was a U.S. Revenue Agent. Following that, from 1916 to 1930, he was a solicitor for the Seventh Judicial Circuit of South Carolina. He ran for the Democratic gubernatorial nomination in 1926, but was unsuccessful. Four years later, he won both the nomination and the general election. As governor, he worked for judicial reform, recommending changes to criminal court procedure and simplification of the system for selecting petty jurors. Also during his term, the South Carolina Public Service Authority was established; Prohibition was repealed and the State took on the task of regulating liquor. In 1934, more than half of South Carolina's 80,000 textile workers went on strike, and in Honea Path, the protest became violent and seven strikers were shot and killed by deputies. After leaving office in 1935, Blackwood returned to his law practice in Spartanburg. He died in Spartanburg the following year, on February 12.

BLAIR, JAMES, (1790?-1834) — a U.S. Representative from South Carolina; born in the Waxhaw settlement, Lancaster County, S.C., about 1790; engaged in planting; sheriff of Lancaster Dis trict; elected to the Seventeenth Congress and served from March 4, 1821, to May 8, 1822, when he resigned; elected as a Jacksonian to the Twenty-first through Twenty-third Congresses and served from March 4, 1829, until his death in Washington, D.C., April 1, 1834; interment in Congressional Cemetery.

BLANCHARD, FELIX A(NTHONY), (1924-?) — United States Army Cadet and amateur football star once described as the "human blockbuster," was born in McColl, South Carolina in 1924 and spent his youth in Bishopville. His father, a physician, was known as "Doc" and Felix became known as "Little Doc." Introduced to football as a young boy, he played the game all through his school years, and because of his obvious talent, was offered numerous college scholarships after high school, finally settling on North Carolina's Chapel Hill. A "burly six-footer," Blanchard's trainer once noted that "there were several men on the varsity who got so they wouldn't try to tackle him. Once he knocked out two would-be tacklers on the same play." After Blanchard finished his freshman year in 1943, he enlisted in the United States Army. At the end of his basic training he was assigned to the department of chemical warfare, and in 1944, he was accepted into West Point.

Blanchard was immediately put on the school's football team as fullback, and because of him and several other talented players, West Point produced a team to be reckoned with. Even Colonel Earl "Red" Blaik, the head football coach known for his reticence about promoting one player over the other, said: "I certainly never saw anybody like Blanchard before...He has the weight of a fullback and the speed of a halfback." After impressing just about everybody with his football playing, several news organizations honored him as one of the country's top players, including the United Press, Associated Press, and *Sporting News*, among others.

In 1945, after being given the rank of cadet corporal, Blanchard was picked to serve as the guard of honor for the April funeral of President Franklin Roosevelt. During that year, Blanchard continued his impressive football playing. Teamed with Glenn Davis, who played halfback, the two players were dubbed the "Touchdown Twins," and they led the team to two winning seasons and two Lambert Trophies. That year, Blanchard was also honored with the Heisman Trophy, the Maxwell Trophy, and a Touchdown Club award.

Aside from football, Blanchard also showed a talent in track, which garnered him the Intercollegiate Amateur Athletic Association championship, as well as the I.C.A.A.A.A. outdoor shot-put championship.

Although Blanchard suffered an injury that slowed down his playing, he continued to help lead his team to victory during the 1946 season. According to *Current Biography*: "At the close of their football careers, the

'Touchdown Twins' had scored 537 of the 1,176 points won by Army from the beginning of the 1944 season to the end of 1946."

BLEASE, COLEMAN LIVINGSTON, (1868-1942) — Sixty-fifth state governor (D) of South Carolina, 1911-1915.

Born near Newberry, South Carolina on October 8, 1868, the son of Henry and Mary Ann (Livingston) Blease. He attended Newberry College, the University of South Carolina, and Georgetown University where he received his LL.B. degree in 1889. He was admitted to the South Carolina Bar that same year and went into private practice with his brother in Newberry. In 1890, he married Lillie Sumners.

Blease was a member of the South Carolina House of Representatives from 1890 to 1894 and again from 1899 to 1900. During that time, from 1891 to 1892, he was Speaker Pro Tempore of the House. He was a presidential elector in 1896 and 1900. From 1901 to 1902, he served as city attorney of Newberry. He was elected to the State Senate and served from 1904 to 1908, acting as President Pro Tempore from 1907 to 1908. In 1910, he was Mayor of Newberry. That same year, he ran for governor of South Carolina as a Democrat and won in an uncontested election. He was reelected in 1912. He was at odds with the Legislature during much of his administration, and as a consequence many of his vetoes were overridden. Even so, a number of state institutions were established during this time. These included the State Tuberculosis Sanitarium, the University of South Carolina Press, and the Medical College of Charleston which came under state funding. In response to complaints from the federal government about inefficiency in the South Carolina militia, Blease decided to dismiss the militia entirely. He resigned his office one week later on January 14, 1915, just five days before the end of his second term.

After leaving office Blease continued to participate in Democratic Party politics. He was a U.S. senator from South Carolina from 1925 to 1931. He was also a delegate to numerous state conventions; was a member of the State Executive Committee for eighteen years; was president of the 1926 State Convention; and served as a delegate to the Democratic National Convention of 1936. He was married to Mrs. Caroline Floyd Hoyt in 1937, his first wife having died in 1934. In 1941, he was elected to serve on the State Unemployment Commission. He died on January 19, 1942.

BONHAM, MILLEDGE LUKE, (1813-1890) — forty-fifth state governor (D) of South Carolina, 1862-1864.

He was born in Red Bank, Edgefield District, South Carolina, the son of Sophie Smith and James Bonham.

Bonham was educated at Edgefield Academy and Abbeville Academy, and subsequently attended South Carolina College, graduating in 1834. He studied law at Edgefield Court House and while there, volunteered for military service, becoming a commander of the South Carolina Brigade in the Seminole War.

Bonham began a private law practice in Edgefield, South Carolina in 1837. In 1840, he was elected to the South Carolina House of Representatives, and kept his seat until 1844.

He rejoined the military, becoming a major general of the South Carolina militia, and was appointed lieutenant colonel of the Twelfth Infantry in 1847 by President James K. Polk. He was promoted to colonel before he resigned from federal service in July 1848.

He became solicitor of the Southern Circuit of South Carolina from 1848 through 1857, when he was elected to the United States House of Representatives, serving until 1860.

In 1860, he was appointed commander-in-chief of the South Carolina troops around Charleston, but waived his rank and served under Confederate Brigadier General P.G.T. Beauregard. After an appointment as brigadier-general in the Confederate Army in April 1861, he resigned his commission in 1862, and was elected a member of the Confederate House of Representatives, keeping this seat until his election as governor of South Carolina in December of 1862.

During his administration, the tides of war began to flow against the Confederacy, and South Carolina's economy was suffering from shortages and inflation. In

1863, the Legislature renewed its prohibition against distilling, except for medicinal purposes, and attempted to increase food production by limiting the number of acres which could be planted in cotton.

South Carolina continued to contribute heavily to the war effort, Charleston's port remaining the center of Confederate blockade running. By January 1864, the State had furnished 60, 127 men to the militia. As the possibility of defeat increased, enthusiasm for the war began to turn to disillusionment, and many leading secessionists were defeated in their bids for political re-election.

When Bonham's term ended in December 1864, he rejoined the Confederate Army, was reappointed a brigadier-general of Cavalry, and served until the end of the conflict.

Bonham was again elected a member of the South Carolina House of Representatives in 1865, serving until 1867, and was a delegate of the Democratic National Convention in 1868. He then resumed his law practice, operated an insurance business, and resumed planting. He was actively involved in the South Carolina Taxpayers' Conventions in 1871 and 1874, and was appointed South Carolina Railroad Commissioner in 1878.

Bonham was married to Ann Patience Griffin in November 1845. He died at White Sulphur Springs, Virginia in August 1890, and was buried in Columbia, South Carolina.

BOWEN, CHRISTOPHER COLUMBUS, (1832-1880) — a U.S. Representative from South Carolina; born in Providence, R.I., January 5, 1832; attended the public schools; moved to Georgia in 1850; engaged in agricultural pursuits; studied law; was admitted to the bar in 1862 and commenced practice in Charleston, S.C.; during the Civil War enlisted in the Confederate Army and served throughout the war as a captain in the Coast Guard; resumed the practice of law in Charleston, S.C.; member of the Republican State convention at Charleston in May 1867; first chairman of the Republican State central committee; delegate to the State constitutional convention in November 1867; upon the readmission of South Carolina to representation tionwas elected as a Republican to the Fortieth and Fortyfirst Congresses and served from July

20, 1868, to March 3, 1871; unsuccessful candidate for reelection in 1870 to the Forty-second Congress; member of South Carolina house of representatives, 1871-1872; elected sheriff of Charleston in November 1872; died in New York City, June 23, 1880; interment in St. Laurence Cemetery, Charleston, S.C.

BOYCE, WILLIAM WATERS, (1818-1890) — a U.S. Representative from South Carolina; born in Charleston, S.C., October 24, 1818; attended South Carolina College (now the University of South Carolina) at Columbia and the University of Virginia at Charlottesville; studied law; was admitted to the bar in 1839 and practiced in Winnsboro, S.C.; member of the State house of representatives, 1846-1847; elected as a Democrat to the Thirty-third and to the three succeeding Congresses and served from March 4, 1853, until his retirement on December 21, 1860; chairman, Committee on Elections (Thirty-fifth Congress); aPPointed a delegate for South Carolina to the Confederate Provisional Congress January 4, 1861; elected as a member of the First and Second Confederate Congresses 1862-1864; moved to Washington, D.C., in 1866 and practiced law until his retirement a few years before his death; died at his country home, "Ashland," in Fairfax County, Va., February 3, 1890; interment in the Episcopal Cemetery, Winns boro, Fairfield County, S.C.

BOYD, JULIAN P(ARKS), (1903-1980) — editor of nineteen volumes of *The Papers of Thomas Jefferson*, part of a 60- volume effort considered one of the most comprehensive historical publishing projects in the United States. The son of Robert Jay and Melona (Parks) he was born November 3, 1903 in Converse, South Carolina. His father, a railroad telegrapher, came from a long line of Methodist ministers, one of whom worked closely with John Wesley, the founder of Methodism. His mother came from a family of planters and landowners who lost everything in the Civil War, but slowly earned back much of their wealth.

Boyd spent summers with his maternal grandparents, and when he dropped out of high school his freshman year he went to work for his grandfather at the Bank of Parksville. After two years he entered Baird's Preparatory School for Boys in Charlotte, North Carolina then entered Trinity College, which was renamed Duke University while he was attending. He graduated with honors in 1925, then earned his M.A. in political science. He worked as a teacher and principal at Alliance High School in Alliance, North Carolina, then did more graduate work at the University of Pennsylvania, teaching part-time. In 1927 he married Grace Wiggins Welch, and they eventually had one child.

From 1928 to 1932 Boyd worked for the Wyoming Historical and Geological Society editing the first five volumes of *The Susquehannah Company Papers* in Wilkes-Barre, Pennsylvania. These papers related the story of the migration from Connecticut to northeastern Pennsylvania, sponsored by the Susquehannah Company. This move had many ramifications for the western claims of the States after the Revolution. Boyd researched the last six volumes of this compilation, then turned the editing over to Robert J. Taylor. Boyd also wrote *Minor's Essays of Poor Robert the Scribe*, published in 1930. Afterwards went on to become director of the New York State Historical Association, a position he held until 1934, then spent the next five years as librarian of the Historical Society of Pennsylvania. In 1938 he and several others collaborated on the *Indian Treaties Printed by Benjamin Franklin*, which documented Pennsylvania's Indian policy during the mid-eighteenth century.

In 1940 Boyd was appointed librarian of Princeton University, where he was instrumental in planning the Harvey S. Firestone Memorial Library there. While in the planning stages with the library he saw the need to share information with other libraries, so he established a foundation of the cooperative committee on library building plans, which promoted the exchange of ideas and information on planning and using libraries nationwide. Boyd was also an acting consultant for the Library of Congress, and helped develop the Farmington Plan, which made at least one copy of every scholarly journal or publication printed overseas available to the U.S.

While at Princeton Boyd wrote two significant books. The first, *Anglo-American Union: Joseph Galloway's Plans to Preserve The British Empire, 1774-1788* (1941), documented and analyzed plans by conservatives to reunite the colonies with the British Empire through the Revolutionary War and afterward. His second book, *The Declaration of Independence: The Evolution of the Text as Shown in Facsimiles of Various Drafts by its Author, Thomas Jefferson* (1945), contained copies of every draft of the Declaration in Jefferson's hand, including notes by John Adams and Benjamin Franklin. Boyd went into depth analyzing the idea that the Declaration was not the work of one man but, in the words of Jefferson, "an expression of the American mind." Boyd also wrote for numerous periodicals, including one essay, "Subversive of What?" which was published in the *Atlantic Monthly* in August of 1948. The article is considered one of his best and relevant today.

Boyd had been planning a comprehensive compilation of works by Thomas Jefferson for years, starting in 1943 when he was named historian of the Thomas Jefferson Bicentennial Commission. The Commission was authorized by the Congress to put together the entire body of Jefferson's writings, and funding was provided by the New York Times Company, the Ford Foundation and the National Historical Publications Commission. The first volume was finished in 1950, and the event was celebrated by special ceremonies at the Library of Congress attended by President Harry S. Truman.

Boyd's work was praised by numerous historians, who found his work to be the most complete and accurate to date. The next fourteen volumes were issued over seven years, covering Jefferson's life from 1760-89. Boyd not only analyzed writings associated with the American Revolution, but Jefferson's time as as the minister in France, 1785 to 1789, a period which is often overlooked by other historians. The next four, released between 1958 and 1971 were equally impressive, including documentation of Jefferson's time as Secretary of State.

Boyd worked on other books as well, including *The Articles of Confederation and Perpetual Union* (1960) and *Fundamental Laws and Constitutions of New Jersey, 1664-*

1964 (1964). His most revealing work was *Number 7: Alexander Hamilton's Secret Attempts to Control American Foreign Policy* (1964). Documents in this volume prove Hamilton had secret contact with a British spy, using the code name Number 7. Hamilton then misrepresented the information he learned about England's intentions and the activities of the United States representative in London to President George Washington.

While compiling his works Boyd taught as a professor of history at Princeton University. In 1964 he was elected president of the American Historical Association, and from 1973 to 1976 he was president of the American Philosophical Society. Other affiliations include: membership on the National Portrait Gallery Commission; the committee of the American Civil Liberties Union; the board of trustees of the Institute for Advanced Study; the Henry Francis de Pont Museum; the Harry S. Truman Library Institute; the Society of American Archivists, of which he is a founding member; the Institute of Early American History and Culture; board membership with the Thomas Jefferson Memorial Foundation; the advisory committee of the Franklin D. Roosevelt Library; and the National Historical Publications Commission. He received honorary degrees from Franklin and Marshall College, Duke University, Washington and Jefferson College, Rutgers, and Yale.

Boyd died in Princeton, New Jersey, May 21, 1980.

BRATTON, JOHN, (1831-1898) — a U.S. Representative from South Carolina; born in Winnsboro, Fairfield County, S.C., March 7, 1831; attended the Academy of Mount Zion Institute in Winns boro; was graduated from South Carolina College at Columbia in 1850 and from South Carolina Medical College at Charleston in 1853; engaged in the practice of medicine in Winnsboro from 1853 to 1861; also engaged as a planter; volunteered in the Confederate Army as a private and served throughout the Civil War, attaining the rank of brigadier general; member of the State constitutional convention in 1865; served in the State senate in 1866; chairman of the South Carolina delegation in the Democratic National Convention in 1876; delegate to the Democratic National Convention in

1880; elected comptroller general of South Carolina by the legislature, to fill a vacancy, in 1881; elected to the Forty-eighth Congress to fill the vacancy caused by the death of John H. Evins and served from December 8, 1884, to March 3, 1885; was not a candidate for renomination in 1884; retired from active politics and again engaged in planting at "Farmington," near Winnsboro; died in Winnsboro, S.C., January 12, 1898; interment in the Episcopal Cemetery.

BRAWLEY, WILLIAM HUGGINS, (1841-1916) — (cousin of John James Hemphill and great-uncle of Robert Witherspoon Hemphill), a U.S. Representative from South Carolina; born in Chester, Chester County, S.C., May 13, 1841; attended the common schools, and was graduated from South Carolina College at Columbia in 1860; enlisted as a private in Company F, Sixth Regiment, South Carolina Infantry, Confederate States Army, April 11, 1861; lost an arm in the Battle of Seven Pines and was retired from service; traveled and studied in Europe in 1864 and 1865; studied law; was admitted to the bar in 1866 and commenced practice at Chester, S.C.; elected solicitor of the sixth judicial circuit of South Carolina in 1868 and served until his resignation in 1874; moved to Charleston and continued the practice of his profession; member of the State house of representatives 1882-1890; elected as a Democrat to the Fifty-second and Fifty-third Congresses and served from March 4, 1891, until February 12, 1894, when he resigned to accept a position on the bench; appointed January 18, 1894, United States district judge of the district of South Carolina and served from February 12, 1894, until his resignation June 14, 1911; lived in retirement until his death in Charleston, S.C., November 15, 1916; interment in Magnolia Cemetery.

BREVARD, JOSEPH, (1766-1821) — a U.S. Representative from South Carolina; born in Iredell, Iredell County, N.C., July 19, 1766; entered the Continental Army when still a boy; was commissioned lieutenant in the North Carolina Line in 1782 and Berved throughout the Revolutionary War; moved to Camden, S.C.; sheriff of Camden District 1789-1791; commissioner in equity October 14,

1791; studied law; was admitted to the bar in 1792 and commenced practice in Camden, S.C.; engaged in the compilation of the law reports which bear his name 1793-1815; member of South Carolina house of representatives, 1796-1799; elected judge of the State supreme court December 17, 1801, and served until December 1815, when he resigned; resumed the practice of law in Camden; elected to the Sixteenth Congress (March 4, 1819-March 3, 1821); was not a candidate for renomination in 1820; unsuc cessful candidate for Congress at a special election held in 1821; died in Camden, Kershaw County, S.C., October 11, 1821; interment in the Quaker Cemetery.

BROOKS, PRESTON SMITH, (1819-1857) — a U.S. Representative from South Carolina; born in Edgefield District, S.C., August 5, 1819; attended the common schools and was graduated from South Carolina College (now the University of South Carolina) at Columbia in 1839; studied law; was admitted to the bar in 1845 and commenced practice in Edgefleld, S.C.; member of the State house of representatives in 1844; served in the Mexican War as captain in the Palmetto Regiment of South Carolina Volunteers; elected as a Democrat to the Thirtythird and Thirty- fourth Congresses and served from March 4, 1853, until July 15, 1856, when he resigned even though the attempt to expel him for his assault upon Charles Sumner on May 22, 1856, had failed through lack of the necessary two-thirds vote; chairman, Committee on Expenditures in the Department of State (Thirty- fourth Congress); reelected to the Thirty-fourth Congress to fill the vacancy caused by his own resignation and served from August 1, 1856, until his death in Washington, D.C., January 27, 1857; had been reelected to the Thirty-fifth Congress; interment in Willow Brook Cemetery, Edgefield, S.C.

BRYSON, JOSEPH RALEIGH, (1893-1953) — a U.S. Representative from South Carolina; born in B'evard, Transylvania County, N.C., January 18, 1893; moved, with his parents, to Greenville, Greenville County, S.C., in 1900; attended the public schools; was graduated from Furman University, Greenville, S.C., in 1917 and from the law department of the University of South Carolina at Columbia in 1920; enlisted on September 28, 1915, as a private in Company A, First Infantry, South Carolina National Guard, and served until discharged on August 9, 1916; reenlisted on August 3, 1917, in the Medical Reserve Corps, being discharged as a second lieutenant of Infantry on December 12, 1918; was admitted to the bar in 1920 and commenced practice in Greenville, S.C.; member of the State house of representatives 1921-1924; served in the State senate 1929-1932; elected as a Democrat to the Seventy-sixth and to the seven succeeding Congresses, and served from January 3, 1939, until his death in the naval hospital at Bethesda, Md., March 10, 1953; interment in Woodlawn Memorial Park, Greenville, S.C.

BULL, JOHN, (1790?-1802) — a Delegate from South Carolina; born in Prince William's Parish, South Carolina, about 1740; justice of the peace of Greenville County; member of the Provincial house of commons in 1772; deputy secretary of the Province in 1772; delegate to the First and Second provincial congresses in 1775 and 1776; member of the first general assembly in 1776; served in the State house of representatives 1778-1781 and in 1784; Member of the Continental Congress 1784-1787; served in the State senate in 1798; died in South Carolina in 1802; interment in Prince William's Parish Churchyard, Beaufort County, S.C.

BURKE, AEDANUS, (1743-1802) — a U.S. Representative from South Carolina; born in Galway, Ireland, June 16, 1743; attended the theological college at St. Omer, France; visited the West Indies; immigrated to the American Colonies and settled in Charles Town (now Charleston), S.C.; served in the militia forces of South Carolina during the Revolutionary War; appointed a judge of the State circuit court in 1778 and served until the enemy overran the State; member of the South Carolina house of representntives 1779-1788; again served in the Revolutionary Army 1780-1782; when the courts were reestablished resumed his seat on the bench, and in 1785 was appointed one of three commissioners to prepare a digest of the State laws; member of the convention in

1788 called to consider ratification of the Constitution of the United States, which he opposed; elected to the First Congress (March 4, 1789-March 3, 1791); declined to be a candidate for reelection in 1790 to the Second Congress, the legislature having passed a law prohibiting a State judge from leaving the State; elected a chancellor of the courts of equity in 1799 and served until his death in Charleston, S.C., March 30, 1802; interment in the cemetery of the Chapel of Ease of St. Bartholomew's Parish, near Jacksonboro, Colleton County, S.C.

BURT, ARMISTEAD, (1802-1883) — a U.S. Representative from South Carolina; born at Clouds Creek, near Edgefield, Edgefield District, S.C., November 13, 1802; moved with his parents to Pendleton, S.C.; completed preparatory studies; studied law; was admitted to the bar in 1823 and practiced in Pendleton; moved to Abbeville, S.C., in 1828 and continued the practice of law; also engaged in agricultural pursuits; member of the South Carolina house of representatives, 1834-1835, and 1838-1841; elected as a Democrat to the Twenty-eighth and to the four succeeding Congresses (March 4, 1843-March 3, 1853); chairman, Committee on Military Affairs (Thirty-first and Thirty-second Congresses); served as Speaker pro tempore of the House of Representatives during the absence of Speaker Winthrop in 1848; was not a candidate for renomination in 1852; resumed the practice of law in Abbeville; delegate to the Democratic National Convention in 1868; died in Abbeville, S.C., October 30, 1883; interment in Episcopal Cemetery.

BUTLER, ANDREW PICKENS, (1796-1857) — (son of William Butler and uncle of Matthew Calbraith Butler), a U.S. Senator from South Carolina; born in Edgefield, S.C., November 18, 1796; attended Doctor Waddell's Academy at Willington, Abbeville County, S.C., and was graduated from South Carolina College (now the University of South Carolina) at Columbia in 1817; studied law; was admitted to the bar in 1818 and practiced in Columbia, Edgefield, Lexington, Barnwell, and Newberry; member, State house of representatives; member, State senate 1824-1833; aide on the staff of the Governor 1824; appointed judge of the session court in 1833; judge of the State court of common pleas 1835-1846; appointed and subsequently elected as a States Rights Democrat to the United States Senate to fill the vacancy caused by the resig nation of George Mc-Duffie; reelected in 1848 and again in 1854 as a Democrat and served from December 4, 1846, until his death near Edgefield, S.C., May 25, 1857; chairman, Committee on Judiciary (Thirtieth through Thirty-fifth Congress); interment in Big Creek Butler Churchyard, Edgefield, S.C.

BUTLER, MATTHEW CALBRAITH, (1836-1909) — (son of William Butler (1759-1821) and nephew of Andrew Pickens Butler), U.S. Senator from South Carolina; born near Greenville, Greenville County, S.C., March 8, 1836; attended the local academy in Edgefield, S.C., and South Carolina College at Columbia; studied law; was admitted to the bar in 1857 and commenced practice in Edgefield; elected to the State house of representatives ativesin 1860; entered the Confederate Army as captain in June 1861 and served throughout the Civil War, attaining the rank of major general; again elected to the State house of representatives in 1866; unsuccessful candidate for lieutenant governor of South Carolina in 1870; elected as a Democrat to the United States Senate in 1876; reelected in 1882 and again in 1888 and served from March 4, 1877, until March 3, 1895; unsuccessful candidate for reelection; chairman, Committee on Civil Service and Retrenchment (Fortysixth Congress), Committee on Interstate Commerce (Fiftythird Congress); resumed the practice of law in Washington, D.C.; during the Spanish-American War was appointed major general of United States Volunteers, and was one of the commissioners appointed to supervise the evacuation of Cuba by the Spanish forces in 1898; returned to Edgefield, S.C., and resumed the practice of law; died in Columbia, S.C., April 14, 1909; interment in Willow Brook Cemetery, Edgefield, S.C.

BUTLER, PIERCE MASON, (1798-1847) — thirty-first state governor (D) of South Carolina, 1836-1838.

He was born in Mount Willing, Edgefield District, South Carolina, the son of Behethland Foote Moore and

William Butler. His father served under General Lincoln in the American Revolution.

Butler was educated at the Moses Waddel's Academy in Abbeville, South Carolina. He entered the military as a second lieutenant in the United States Army in 1818, and rose to the rank of captain by the time he resigned in 1829.

After leaving his military commission, Butler joined the banking profession and became president of the State Bank of South Carolina for several years. When the Seminole War broke out, he served as a lieutenant colonel in the South Carolina militia, returning afterwards to Columbia.

Butler was elected governor of South Carolina in 1836. During his tenure, he sought to eliminate the residual bitterness remaining from the tariff and nullification controversy which had raged between 1828 and 1833, and he appointed a commission which would survey the public school system of the State and make recommendations for improvements. He also gave strong support to the proposed Louisville, Cincinnati and Charleston Railroad, which would stretch west from South Carolina into Kentucky and Ohio. He believed that the construction of the rail system would result in better commercial and political relations between the South and the West.

When his term expired, Butler was appointed United States agent to the Cherokees. After the war with Mexico broke out, he was made colonel of the Palmetto Regiment, South Carolina Volunteers, and led his men during the Battle of Cerro Gordo. At the Battle of Churubusco, he was wounded in the leg, but went on to lead his men through dangerous Mexican lines until he was fatally shot in the head, December 22, 1846. His body was returned to Edgefield District for burial.

Butler was married to Miranda Julia Duval in 1829. The couple had six children.

BUTLER, SAMPSON HALE, (1803-1848) — a U.S. Representative from South Carolina; born near Ninety Six, Edgefield District, S.C., January 3, 1803; attended the country schools and South Carolina College (now the University of South Carolina) at Columbia; studied law;

was admitted to the bar in 1825 and commenced practice in Edgefield, S.C.; moved to Barnwell, S.C., and continued the practice of law; sheriff of Barnwell County 1832-1839; member of the State house of representatives tives1832-1835; elected as a Democrat to the Twenty-sixth and Twenty-seventh Congresses and served from March 4, 1839, until September 27, 1842, when he resigned; resumed the practice of law; moved to Florida; died in Tallahassee, Fla., March 16, 1848; interment in a cemetery in that city.

BUTLER, WILLIAM, (1759-1821) — (father of William Butler (1790-1850) and Andrew Pickens Butler and grandfather of Matthew Calbraith Butler), a U.S. Representative from South Carolina; born in Prince William County, Va., December 17, 1759; attended grammar schools; moved to South Carolina; served in the Snow campaign under General Richardson in 1775 and in Gen. Andrew Williamson's expedition against the Cherokee Indians in 1776; lieutenant in Pulaski's legion, under Gen. Benjamin Lincoln, in 1779; served under Gen. Andrew Pickens at the siege of Augusta in 1780, as captain under General Henderson in 1781, and as captain of Mounted Rangers under General Pickens in 1782; member of the State convention which adopted the Federal Constitution; member of the State house of representatives in 1787-1795; sheriff of the Ninety-sixth District in 1791; elected major general of the upper division of State militia in 1796; elected as a Republican to the Seventh and to the five succeeding Congresses (March 4, 1801-March 3, 1813); was not a candidate for reelection; major general commanding the troops raised for the defense of South Carolina during the War of 1812; retired to his plantation on the Saluda River, near Mount Willing, Edgefield County, S.C., and died there November 15, 1821; interment in the farnily burial ground at Butler Methodist Church, near Saluda, Edgefield (now Saluda) County, S.C.

BUTTZ, CHARLES WILSON, (1837-1913) — a U.S. Representative from South Carolina; born in Stroudsburg, Monroe County, Pa., November 16, 1837; moved with his parents to Buttzville, ly. J., in 1839; completed academic studies; studied law in Belvidere, N.J.; entered the Union Army in 1861 as second lieutenant in the Eleventh Pennsylvania Cavalry; was promoted to first lieutenant in 1862; was wounded in 1863; resigned on ac count of impaired health in October 1863; received two brevet ranks from the President, one as captain and the other as major, both dating May 1865; was admitted to the bar in 1863 and commenced the practice of law in Norfolk, Va.; delegate to the Republican National Convention in 1864; appointed director of the Exchange Bank of Virginia in 1864; Commonwealth attorney for King William County in 1866; moved to Charleston, S.C., in 1870; solicitor of the flrst judicial circuit 1872-1880; contested as a Republican the election of Edmund W. M. Mackey to the Forty- fourth Congress, but the House decided that neither was entitled to the seat; subsequently elected to fill the vacancy caused by the decision of the House and served from November 7, 1876, to March 3, 1877; was not a candidate for renomination in 1876; moved to Fargo, N.Dak., in 1878; procured the offlcial organization of Ransom County in 1882, and established his residence in what is now known as Buttzville, N.Dak.; State's attorney 1884-1886; member of the State house of representatives 1903-1909; died in Lisbon, Ransom County, N.Dak., July 20, 1913; interment in Oakwood Cemetery.

BYRNES, JAMES FRANCIS, (1879-1972) — Eightieth state governor (D) of South Carolina, 1951-1955.

Born in Charleston on May 2, 1879, the son of James and Elizabeth (McSweeney) Byrnes. He attended school until age fourteen, when he was forced to quit due to family finances. Later however, he studied law and was admitted to the South Carolina Bar in 1903. He worked as a court reporter in the Second Circuit Court of South Carolina from 1900 to 1908. In 1906, he married Maude Busche.

Byrnes established a law practice in Aiken, South Carolina and from 1908 to 1910 was a solicitor for the Second Circuit Court. Also around this time, he became owner and editor of the Aiken *Review and Journal*. He was elected to the U.S. House of Representatives and served from 1911 to 1925. He made an unsuccessful bid for the U.S. Senate in 1924. In 1930, he was elected to the Senate and served until 1941 when he became a member of the U.S. Supreme Court. He remained on the court only until the following year. With the coming of World War II, he served as director of Economic Stabilization of the United States (1942-43) and director of the U.S. War Mobilization Board (1943- 45.) He was with President Roosevelt at the Yalta Conference in 1945.

After the war, he returned to his law practice. He served as U.S. Secretary of State from 1945 to 1947, and was present with President Truman at the Potsdam Conference. In 1946, he was a senior delegate to the U.N. General Assembly. Four years later, he ran for governor of South Carolina as a Democrat in an unopposed election and won easily. He entered office in January, 1951. During his term the U.S. Supreme Court ruled in the case of *Brown vs. Board of Education of Topeka, Kansas* that school segregation was unconstitutional. The South Carolina Legislature appropriated $75,000,000 to upgrade black schools to the level of white public schools, and instituted a three percent sales tax to provide the funds. Byrnes left office at the end of his term in January, 1955. He died on April 4, 1972.

C

CADDELL, PATRICK HAYWARD, (1950 -) — is a renowned expert in the analyzing of public opinion.

Born in Rock Hill, South Carolina on May 19, 1950, the son of Newton P. and Janie (Burns) Caddell, Patrick Caddell was graduated from Harvard University in 1972, where he majored in history and government.

Caddell's interest in polling and public opinion began very early in his life. As early as fifth grade, he conducted a poll of his classmates, predicting that Richard Nixon would carry that city in the 1960 presidential election. His fascination continued throughout high school and college. Interestingly, while in college Caddell did not specialize in courses in statistics and mathematics, the tools of the polltaking craft, stating in a New York *Times* interview that he "went to one statistics class and lasted five minutes...I discovered that whatever they were doing and I was doing had nothing in common." As a Harvard undergraduate, Caddell helped to compile some 2,000 pages of public opinion research for the successful 1970 gubernatorial campaign of John J. Gillian of Ohio. Not long after, he and two classmates, John Gorman and Daniel Porter, established their own company, Cambridge Survey Research, Inc. In the next few years, Caddell accumulated numerous clients, including senators Edmund Muskie and George McGovern during the 1972 presidential campaign. This led to work for a number of Senate and House candidates. He worked exclusively for Democrats, usually liberals.

In 1974, Caddell and his associates set up an additional corporation, Cambridge Reports, Inc., which produced major in- depth surveys of American public opinion on economic, political and social questions. Its clients included Exxon, Westinghouse Electric, Aetna Life and Casualty, Amoco and Sears.

Training his sights on the 1976 presidential election, Caddell switched his allegiance from McGovern to Jimmy Carter in 1975. He had met Carter in 1972, during a Mc-Govern campaign trip through the South. Working closely with Carter, Caddell was the only non- Georgian admitted to the intimate circle of Carter advisors. A principal advisor on campaign strategy, he again stressed the need for the candidate to win over voters who were dissatisfied with the entire American political process. He urged Carter not to conduct the traditional issue-oriented campaign since voters were becoming increasingly skeptical as to whether candidates would translate their promises on issues into effective action.

Unlike other close Carter advisors, Caddell never formally entered government service. Despite his non-governmental status, however, he had considerable political influence and was regarded as an insider at the White House during Carter's administration. He encountered criticism throughout this period for his memos to Carter and his opinions on the changing perception of the public about the office of president. Caddell also received occasional criticism for alleged conflicts of interest. One example was his work on behalf of Westinghouse Electric — to which he offered a March 1976 memorandum proposing that the corporation engage in a campaign to increase public acceptance of nuclear energy. When representatives of the Scientist Institute for Public Information learned of the memo, it canceled its contract for a poll with Caddell's firm. In his own defense, Caddell maintained that he supplied nothing more than a service to his clients, that his Cambridge reports are "purely a research project" and that his company plays "no advocacy or representative role."

In addition to serving the Carter Administration and business clients, Caddell's client list involved more than 20 political campaigns. Those included: Connecticut governor, Ella T. Grasso; Florida governor, Bob Graham; and the presidential campaign of Gary Hart. With Gerald Rafshoon he also handled publicity and marketing research for director Frances Ford Coppola's Vietnam War film, *Apocalypse Now* in 1979.

CAIN, RICHARD HARVEY, (1825-1887) — a U.S. Representative from South Carolina; born in Greenbrier County, Va., April 12, 1825; moved with his father to Gallipolis, Ohio, in 1831 and attended school; entered the ministry, and was a pastor in Brooklyn, N.Y., from 1861 to 1865; moved to South Carolina in 1865 and settled in Charleston; delegate to the constitutional convention of South Carolina in 1868; member of the State senate 1868-1872; manager of a newspaper in Charleston in 1868; elected as a Republican to the Forty-third Congress (March 4, 1873-March 3, 1875); was not a candidate for renomination in 1S74; elected to the Forty-fifth Congress (March 4, 1877-March 3, 1879); was not a candidate for renomination in 1878; appointed a bishop of the African Methodist Episcopal Church in 1880 and served until his death in Washington, D.C., January 18, 1887; interment in Graceland Cemetery.

CALDWELL, PATRICK CALHOUN, (1801-1885) — a U.S. Representative from South Carolina; born near Newberry, S.C., March 10, 1801; was graduated from South

Carolina College (now the Uni versity of South Carolina) at Columbia in 1820; studied law; was admitted to the bar in 1822 and commenced practice in South Carolina; member of the State house of representatives 1838-1839; elected as a Democrat to the Twenty-seventh Congress (March 4, 1841-March 3, 1843); unsuccessful candidate for reelection to the Twenty-eighth Congress; served in the State senate in 1848; died in South Carolina November 22, 1855.

CALHOUN, JOHN CALDWELL, (1782-1850) — Secretary of War (1817-25), Vice President (1825-31), and Secretary of State (1843-45), was born in Abbeville District, South Carolina on March 18, 1782, a descendant of a race of Calvinists.

His grandfather, James Calhoun, emigrated from Donegal, Ireland, to Pennsylvania in 1733, bringing his family with him. He first moved to Virginia, then in 1756, settled in South Carolina, establishing the "Calhoun Settlement." His son, Patrick, married Martha Caldwell, daughter of an Irish Presbyterian emigrant, and they became the parents of John C. Calhoun. John's father died while he was a child, and the boy spent his youth on his mother's farm, receiving very little schooling until he was placed under the care of his brother-in- law, Rev. Dr. Waddell, a Presbyterian clergyman, who prepared him for college.

Calhoun entered Yale College in 1802, graduating with honors. He studied law for three more years, and was admitted to the bar in South Carolina in 1807. He engaged in a law practice in Abbeville, but soon gave up his profession to devote himself to politics. He was elected to the State Legislature, served two terms, and in 1811, was elected to Congress, taking his seat at a time when war with Great Britain was imminent. He was placed on the Committee of Foreign Affairs, and wrote a report that was presented to the House, urging a declaration of war, claiming that "The law of self-preservation is never safe, except under the shield of honor."

In the same year, he married his cousin Floride, whose comfortable fortune enabled him to pursue his career with the assurance of competence, whatever misfortunes might befall him. After the war, in 1815, the country was confronted with various important questions, which gave Calhoun an opportunity to develop his original views. He urged the bank bill, organized the tariff of 1816 so favorable to his native state, and urged a system of roads and canals, although he afterward modified his views on these matters, declaring that remedies that were proper and suitable for a certain state of things were not advisable for another. In 1817, President Monroe appointed him Secretary of War, in which office he displayed great energy and ability, and won undisputed fame. He straightened out the confused affairs of the department, reduced the expenditure of the army without sacrificing its efficiency or comfort, and drew up a bill for organizing the department.

In 1824, Calhoun was elected Vice-President of the United States by a large majority, and this period of his life may be said to be the beginning of his career as a constitutional statesman. In 1837 he said, "The station, from its leisure, gave me a good opportunity to study the genius of the prominent measure of the day, called then the American system, by which I profited. He referred to Henry Clay's system, the bank, the protective tariff, the internal improvement system and general welfare rule, all flourishing at that time. In 1828, Jackson was elected President and Calhoun was reelected Vice-President.

In the early part of his career, Calhoun advocated broad and patriotic views, but in later years, he became a leader of distinctly Southern interests, though it is probable that he thought they involved the benefit of the whole country. He sided with South Carolina against the protective system, and his "Exposition," with amendments, was adopted by the legislature of that state. He hoped that President Jackson would veto the tariff bill, but as he did not do so, Calhoun moved to South Carolina in 1829, and had passed in the Legislature, the famous resolution "that any state in the Union might annul an act of the Federal government." Virginia, Georgia, and Alabama gave in their adhesion, and the dissolution of the Union seemed imminent.

Calhoun delivered an address on the relations of the states to the general government in 1831 and drew up a report for the Legislature in the same year. He also wrote an address to the people of the state at the close of that session, a letter to Governor Hamilton on state interposition in 1832, and an address to the people of the United States by the convention of South Carolina in 1832, in all of which he maintained the doctrine of state interposition, or "nullification." Calhoun's relations with the President became strained, he lost much of his popularity, and in 1831, resigned the vice-presidency. However, he was elected to the Senate soon afterward. He stood alone as the champion of his state, defending its ordinance of nullification, both political parties and the administration being opposed to him. But Calhoun had the courage of his convictions, and was indifferent to personal consequences.

In November, 1832, the President issued his proclamation, which was followed by the "Force Bill," and the following February, Calhoun made a powerful speech against it, followed by a reply from Daniel Webster, who dwelt with considerable length upon certain resolutions proposed by Calhoun. The latter brought forward his resolutions, and made a speech of great power and brilliancy, to which, however, Webster did not reply. The issue was on the first resolution: "That the people of the several states comprising these United States are united as parties to a constitutional compact, to which the people of each state acceded, as a separate and sovereign community, each binding itself by its own particular ratification; and that the union, of which the said compact is the bond is a union between the states ratifying the same."

Many of the Democrats and Whigs held that the Constitution was a compact, but denied the right of nullification by a state, and many denied the right of secession. There were some who believed in the right of secession, but not of nullification. It was claimed for the doctrine of nullification that it was a remedy within the Union, reserved to the state— a remedy for evils— to declare void an unconstitutional law, and to save the Union, not dissolve it. During President Jackson's last term, Calhoun acted with the Whig Party on the bank and tariff questions. He claimed to lead the "state-rights" men, who acted from principle, and who were not governed by party motives nor ambition. He called an extra session of Congress in 1837, in connection with the financial panic of that ear, advocated a total separation of the government from the banks, and was favorable to the constitutional treasury plan. In 1838, he made his famous speech on slavery.

He regarded slavery as a natural relation, and the abolition movement caused him great anxiety. If it proved successful, he believed that the fate of the Southern people "would be worse than that of the Aborigines," and that the fruitful fields of the South would be reduced to their primeval condition. "To destroy the existing relations," he said, "would be to destroy the prosperity of the Southern states, and to place the two races in a state of conflict, which must end in the expulsion or extirpation of one or the other." He looked on social and political equality as the necessary consequence of emancipation, but believed that such equality must forever be impossible between the races.

In 1841, Calhoun was a leader of the Democratic Party, and discussed the tariff question in a series of brilliant speeches, taking the ground that a tariff for revenue only was constitutional and proper. On August 5, 1842, the closing words of his speech on this subject were: "The great popular party is already rallied almost *en masse* around the banner which is leading the party to its final triumph. The few that still lag will soon be rallied under its ample folds. On that banner is inscribed: Free trade; low duties; no debt; separation from banks; economy; retrenchment, and strict adherence to the constitution. Victory in such a cause will be great and glorious; and long will it perpetuate the liberty and prosperity of the country."

In 1843, Calhoun was appointed Secretary of State, and during his term of office, established the rights of the United States to Oregon and Washington territories, which resulted in the Treaty of 1846. He prophetically spoke of the future triumphs of steam and electricity in a speech saying: "Providence has given us an inheritance stretching across the entire continent from ocean to ocean...our great mission as a people is to occupy this vast domain; to replenish it with an intelligent, virtuous, and industrious population, to convert the forests into cultivated fields; to drain the swamps and morasses, and cover them with rich harvests; to build up cities, towns, and villages in every direction, and to unite the whole by the most rapid intercourse between all the parts...Secure peace and time, under the guidance of a sagacious and cautious policy, 'a wise and masterly inactivity,' will speedily accomplish the whole...War can make us great; but let it never be forgotten that peace only can make us both great and free."

On retiring from the State Department, Calhoun was elected to the Senate, and did all he could to prevent the war with Mexico. During the progress of the war, the Wilmot Proviso was proposed by the Anti-Slavery Party, which declared that slavery should never be allowed in any Mexican territory acquired by treaty. This caused great agitation throughout the country, and on February 19, 1847, Calhoun expressed his views in the following resolutions: "...that the territories of the United States belong to the several states composing the Union, and are held by them as their joint and common property; that Congress, as the joint agent and representative of the states of the Union, has no right to make any law or do any act whatever, that shall directly, or by its effects, make any discrimination between the states of this Union, by which any of them shall be deprived of its full and equal right in any territory of the United States, acquired or to be acquired."

The question was not settled until 1850, when the compromise measures were passed, and Calhoun's last speech was on this subject on March 4, 1850, the speech being read for him. Henry Clay said of Calhoun: "He possessed an elevated genius of the highest order." Daniel Webster said: "He was a man of undoubted genius and of commanding talent. All the country and all the world admit that...he had the basis, the indispensable basis of all high character, and that was unspotted integrity, unimpeached honor and character. If he had aspirations, they were high and honorable and noble...I do not believe he had a selfish motive or selfish feeling." Edward Everett said: "Calhoun, Clay, Webster! I name them in alphabetical order. What other precedence can be assigned them?"

John Calhoun died in Washington, D.C. on March 31, 1850.

CALHOUN, JOSEPH, (1750-1817) — (cousin of John Caldwell Calhoun and John Ewing Colhoun), a U.S. Representative from South Carolina; born in Staunton, Augusta County, Va., October 22, 1750; moved with his father to South Carolina in 1756 and settled in Granville District, on Little River, near the present town of Abbeville; received a limited education; engaged in agricultural pursuits; served as a member of the South Carolina house of representatives in 1804 and 1805; colonel of State militia; elected as a Republican to the Tenth Congress to fill the vacancy caused by the death of Levi Casey; reelected to the Eleventh Congress and served from June 2, 1807, to March 3, 1811; declined to be a candidate for reelection in 1810 to the Twelfth Congress; resumed agricultural pursuits and engaged in milling; died in Calhoun Mills, Abbeville District (now Mount Carmel, McCormick County), April 14, 1817; interment in the family burying ground near his home.

CAMPBELL, CARROLL A. JR., (1940 -) — was the 112th governor of South Carolina who stressed education reform and economic development.

Born in Greenville, South Carolina on July 24, 1940, the son of Carroll and Anne (Williams) Campbell, Carroll A. Campbell, Jr. was educated in the Greenville public schools and was graduated from McCallie School. He was unable to attend college full-time for financial reasons. Instead, he went to work and studied when he could. He attended both the University of South Carolina and the American University in Washington, D.C. At age 19 he was working in the real estate business when he and a partner established Handy Park Company, a chain of parking facilities. In 1967, he helped found Rex Enterprises, which developed a chain of Burger King restaurants.

Campbell became interested in Republican politics in about 1960 and for many years managed campaigns, including the campaign that elected the first Republican mayor of Greenville. Campaigning for himself in 1970, he was elected to the South Carolina House of Representatives where he remained until 1974. He served as assistant minority leader during that time. Campbell ran for lieutenant governor in 1974, but lost in a close race. In

1975, he was executive assistant to Governor James B. Edwards, and in 1976, he won election to the South Carolina Senate. Two years later, he was elected to the United States Congress, where he served for eight years. While in Congress, he continued his formal education and earned an M.A. in political science. Campbell was the South Carolina campaign chairman for Ronald Reagan's presidential race in 1980 and 1984.

In 1986, Campbell ran for governor of South Carolina. During his campaign he promised to throw out the "good ol' boy" system of entrenched politicians. Stressing education, economic development and political ethics, he called for cutting insurance rates, reorganizing state government and lowering taxes. In the campaign, he seemed to be following a strategy developed in 1985 at a meeting of leading Republican governors, members of Congress and political consultants. The group, convened by Governor Lamar Alexander of Tennessee, concluded that Republicans could not win state elections by running on the "Washington agenda" of foreign policy and social issues. Although Republicans had won national elections by promising to restrain the role of the federal government, they had to recognize that people expected state government to be active and involved in solving their problems. Campbell was viewed by political analysts as a model of a new breed of Republicans emerging in the modern South.

Campbell won the election by a narrow margin of 51 percent to 49 percent, and became only the second Republican elected to that office within the century on January 14, 1987. He was the state's 112th governor. Campbell immediately extended an olive branch to the Democratically controlled legislature, calling for an era of "unparalleled opportunity for all South Carolinians." As promised in his campaign, once in office, he stressed education reform and economic development. He also announced that ensuring the well being of the state's children would be a top priority of his administration. In the area of higher education, he proposed eliminating remedial courses at four-year institutions, using the savings to finance a research program linking the state's three major universities. He has encouraged the state's universities to help in the development of new jobs. Campbell is known as a proponent of fiscal responsibility and a supporter of rights for the handicapped.

In the opinion of political observers, Campbell has been instrumental in building an effective Republican party in the state. The Republicans have done a better job of generating candidates able to win local elections in South Carolina that in other Southern states. Because of his successes, Campbell has frequently been mentioned as a rising star in national Republican politics. His name appeared on a long list of contenders for a spot as George Bush's vice presidential running mate on the 1988 ticket. Campbell's term of office expires in January 1995.

Carroll Campbell married Iris Rhodes in 1959. The couple has two sons.

CAMPBELL, JOHN, (brother of Robert Blair Campbell), a U.S. Representative from South Carolina; born near Brownsville, Marlboro County, S.C.; was graduated from South Carolina College (now the University of South Carolina) at Columbia in 1819; studied law; was admitted to the bar and commenced practice in Brownsville, S.C.; moved to Parnassus, Marlboro District, and continued the practice of law; elected as a Jacksonian to the Twenty-first Congress (March 4, 1829-March 3, 1831); elected as a Nullifier to the Twenty-fifth Congress and as a Democrat to the three succeeding Congresses (March 4, 1837-March 3, 1845); chairman, Committee on Elections (Twenty-sixth Congress), Committee on District of Columbia (Twenty-eighth Congress); died in Parnassus (now Blenheim), Marlboro County, S.C., on May 19, 1845; interment in a private cemetery near Blenheim, S.C.

CAMPBELL, ROBERT BLAIR, (brother of John Campbell of South Carolina), a U.S. Representative from South Carolina; born in Marlboro County, S.C.; educated by a private tutor; attended school in Fayetteville, N.C., and was graduated from South Carolina College (now the University of South Carolina) at Columbia in 1809; engaged in agricultural pursuits; commissioned captain in South Carolina Militia in 1814; unsuccessful candidate in 1820 for election to the Seventeenth Congress; served in the State senate 1821-1823; elected to the Eighteenth Congress (March 4, 1823-March 3, 1825); unsuccessful candidate for reelection in 1824 to the Nineteenth Congress and for election in 1826 to the Twentieth Congress and in 1830 to the Twenty-second Congress; elected to the State senate in 1830; elected as a Nullifier to the Twenty-third Congress to fill the vacancy caused by the death of Thomas B. Singleton; reelected to the Twentyfourth Congress and served from February 27, 1834, to March 3, 1837; in 1833 during the nullification movement was commissioned general of South Carolina troops; moved to Lowndes County, Ala., about 1840; member of the State house of representatives in 1840; appointed on September 28, 1842, consul at Habana, Cuba, and served until July 22, 1850; moved to San Antonio, Tex.; was appointed on March 16, 1853, a commissioner for the United States to aid in settlement of the disputed boundary line between Texas and Mexico; appointed consul at London, England, and served from August 3, 1854, to March 1861, when he was recalled; moved to Ealing, London, England, where he died July 12, 1862; interment in the crypt of Kensington Church.

CARPENTER, LEWIS CASS, (1936-1908) — a U.S. Representative from South Carolina; born in Putnam, Conn., February 20, 1836; attended the public schools; moved to New Jersey, where he taught school; appointed State inspector of Public schools in New Jersey in 1863; at an early age began writing for the press, and was connected with the New York papers for several years; went to Washington, D.C., in 1864 and was employed in the Treasury Department; studied law at Columbian (now George Washington) University; was admitted to the bar and practiced; Washington newspaper correspondent; moved to Charleston, S.C., in 1867 and became editor of the Charleston Courier; assisted in establishing the Charleston Republican in 1868; secretary to United States Senator William H. Buckingham, of Connecticut, 1868-1873; elected as a Republican to the Forty- third Congress to fill the vacancy caused by the resignation of Robert B. Elliott and served from November 3, 1874, to March 3, 1875; unsuccessful candidate for election to the Forty-fifth Congress; moved to Denver, Colo., in 1878, and thence, in 1879, to Leadville, where he edited a newspaper; appointed supervisor of the census for Colorado in 1880; appointed United States post- office inspector in 1881 and resigned in 1883; engaged in the insurance business 1883-1890; resumed the practice of law; died in Denver, Colo., March 6, 1908; interment in Fairmount Cemetery.

CARR, JOHN DICKSON, (1906-1977) — a prolific mystery novelist and the official biographer of Sir Arthur Conan Doyle. Carr was born November 30, 1906 in Uniontown, Pennsylvania. His father, Wood Nicholas, was a U.S. Congressman and later a postmaster. His mother's name was Julia. Carr started college with the hope of becoming a lawyer, but he changed his mind and went into journalism. He graduated from Haverford College in 1928, traveled to Paris to study at the Sorbonne, and began writing his first novel. Carr married Clarice Cleaves in 1931, and the couple lived in England until 1948. They eventually had three children together. Carr writing propaganda for the British Broadcasting Company in London during World War II, but otherwise spent his life in the world of mysteries.

Carr's first book, *It Walks by Night* (1930) introduced Detective Henri Bencolin. Others in the series included *Castle Skull* (1931); *The Lost Gallows* (1931); *The Corpse in the Waxworks* (1932); and *The Four False Weapons; Being the Return of Bencolin* (1937). Carr quickly distinguished himself as a lover of the macabre and a master of the "locked room" or "impossible crime" story. "If there's one thing I can't stand it's a nice *healthy* murder," Carr once said in *New Yorker* magazine. His murders were often ghastly and took place in unusual places, such as opium dens, wax museums or medieval castles. Yet he did not place an emphasis on violence, allowing the logic and deduction that lead the story plot to create the excitement. Carr is credited as the master of the locked-room mystery, in which bodies are found in rooms locked from within, or with no footprints surrounding them. Yet he did not use the common "cop-out" of many authors, revealing trap doors or secret passages at the end of the story. He gave the reader every bit of information that was needed, and still managed to deliver a surprise ending. "You don't ever have to mislead the reader," he once said. "You just state the evidence, and the reader will mislead himself." Critics accuse him of using too much plot and not enough character development, Carr is credited for introducing attractive female characters to mystery literature.

Another popular character Carr created was Dr. Gideon Fell, a portly, eccentric Oxford fellow modeled after British journalist and writer G.K. Chesterton. Novels in this series include: *Hag's Nook* (1933); *The Mad Hatter Mystery* (1933); *The Blind Barber* (1934); *The Eight of Swords* (1934); *Death-Watch* (1935); *The Three Coffins* (1935); *The Arabian Nights Murder* (1936); *To Wake the Dead* (1938); *The Crooked Hinge* (1938); *The Problem of the Green Capsule* (1939); *The Problem of the Wire Cage* (1939); *The Man Who Could Not Shudder* (1940); *The Case of the Constant Suicides* (1941); *Death Turns the Tables* (1941); *Till Death Do Us Part* (1944); *He Who Whispers* (1946); *The Sleeping Sphinx* (1947); *The Dead Man's Knock* (1948); *Below Suspicion* (1949); *In Spite of Thunder* (1960); *The House at Satan's Elbow* (1965); *Panic in Box C* (1966); and *Dark of the Moon* (1967).

Under the pseudonym Carter Dickson, Carr created another character, Sir Henry Merrivale, a buffoon with a fowl mouth and an attitude, with some similarity to Winston Churchill and Carr himself. Books based on Merrivale include: *The Plague Court Murders* (1934); *The White Priory Murders* (1934); *The Red Widow Murders* (1935); *The Unicorn Murders* (1935); *The Magic Lantern Murders* (1936); *The Third Bullet* (1937); *The Peacock Feather Murders* (1937); *Death in Five Boxes* (1938); *The Judas Window* (1938); *The Reader Warned* (1939); *And So to Murder* (1940); *Nine- And Death Makes Ten* (1940); *Seeing is Believing* (1941); *The Gilded Man* (1942); *She Died A Lady* (1943); *He Wouldn't Kill Patience* (1944); *The Curse of the Bronze Lamp* (1945); *My Late Wives* (1946); *The Skeleton in the Clock* (1948); *A Graveyard to Let* (1949); *Night at the Mocking Widow* (1950); *Behind the Crimson Blind* (1952); and *The Cavalier's Cup* (1953).

Other novels Carr has written include: *Poison in Jest* (1932); *The Burning Court* (1937); *The Emperor's Snuf-*

fbox (1942); *The Bride of Newgate* (1950); *The Devil in Velvet* (1951); *The Nine Wrong Answers* (1952); *Captain Cut-Throat* (1955); *Patrick Butler for the Defense* (1956); *Fire Burn!* (1957); Scandal at High Chimneys: A Victorian Melodrama (1959); *The Witch of the Lowtide: An Edwardian Melodrama* (1961); *The Demoniacs* (1962); *Papa La-Bas* (1968); *The Ghosts' High Noon* (1969); *Deadly Hall* (1971); and *The Hungry Goblin: A Victorian Detective Novel* (1972). Under the pseudonym Carr Dickson he wrote *The Bowstring Murders* (1933) and under the name Carter Dickson he wrote *Fatal Descent* (1939) with John Rhode and *Fear is the Same* (1956).

As well as a writer of mystery novels Carr was a fan as well. He owned one of the most extensive crime libraries in the world and collected books on witchcraft, poison and murder. Carr was an especially big fan of Sir Arthur Conan Doyle, creator of Sherlock Holmes. In 1949 Doyle's family approached him to write Doyle's official biography in collaboration with Doyle's son. Carr took the project very seriously, going through piles of family letters, Doyle's notebooks and personal papers. Critics hailed the final work, saying it showed all sides of Doyle's complex personality. He went on to edit *Arthur Conan Doyle, Great Stories* (1959) and with Adrian Conan Doyle wrote *The Exploits of Sherlock Holmes* (1954).

A craftsman with novels and short stories, Carr also wrote some of the most chilling radio broadcast mysteries. During the 1930's and 1940's he wrote for such series as "Appointment with Fear," "Suspense," "Cabin B-13," "The Silent Battle," and others. The short story "Death in the Dressing Room" was adapted as an episode of the "Murder Clinic" serial, broadcast in 1942; the book *Fire, Burn!* was adapted for radio in 1958; and *The Hollow Man* was adapted and broadcast in 1959. A collection of Carr's radio scripts is printed in *The Dead Sleep Lightly* (1983). Several of his works were made into movies as well, including "Man With a Cloak" (1951); "Dangerous Crossing" (1953); "Colonel March of Scotland Yard" (1954); and *The Emperor's Snuffbox* was filmed as "City After Midnight" in 1959. The film rights to the short story "The Gentleman from Paris" were sold.

Carr was known to be a workaholic, sitting at his typewriter for up to 18 hours a day, seven days a week. As well as writing approximately 70 novels and radio scripts he wrote short story collections including *Dr. Fell, Detective, and Other Stories* (1947); *The Third Bullet and Other Stories* (1954); *The Men Who Explained Miracles* (1963); *The Door to Doom and Other Detections* (1980); and under the name Carter Dickson *The Department of Queer Complaints* (1940). He wrote the nonfiction *The Murder of Sir Edmund Godfrey* (1936), contributed to *The Mystery Writer's Art*, edited by Francis M. Nevins, Jr., and he edited *Maiden Murders* in 1952. For his work he received two Edgar awards (1949 and 1962), was presented with the *Ellery Queen* prize twice for short stories, and was honored with the Grand Masters Award from the Mystery Writers of America in 1962.

After returning to the United States in 1948 Carr lived in Mamaroneck, New York, for a time, and eventually moved to Greenville, South Carolina, where he died February 27, 1977.

CARTER, JOHN, (1792-1850) — a U.S. Representative from South Carolina; born on the Black River, near Camden, Sumter District, S.C., September 10, 1792; was graduated from South Carolina College (now the University of South Carolina) at Colum bia in 1811; studied law; was admitted to the bar in 1814 and commenced practice in Camden, S.C.; served as commissioner in equity 1814-1820; elected to the Seventeenth Congress to fill the vacancy caused by the resignation of James Blair; reelected to the Eighteenth and Nineteenth Congresses and reelected as a Jacksonian to the Twentieth Congresses and served from December 11, 1822, to March 3, 1829; resumed the practice of law in Camden, S.C.; moved to Georgetown, D.C., in 1836, and died there June 20, 1850.

CHAMBERLAIN, DANIEL HENRY, (1835-1907) — fifty-first state governor (R) of South Carolina, 1874-1876.

He was born in West Brookfield, Massachussetts, the son of Achsah Forbes and Eli Chamberlain.

Chamberlian was educated in public schools, afterwards attending Amherst Academy, Phillips Academy, and Worcester High School. He graduated from Yale University in 1862, and entered Harvard Law School, but withdrew in November 1863 to enter the military.

He was commissioned a second lieutenant of the Fifth Massachusetts Regiment in 1863, and was promoted to captain in December 1865. From 1852 to 1858, he also taught school intermittently.

Chamberlain moved to South Carolina in 1866 and became a cotton planter. He was elected Attorney General of South Carolina in 1868, and remained in this office until 1872. He was also a member of the South Carolina Constitutional Convention in 1868, and maintained a law practice in Columbia from 1872 to 1874.

After a nomination from the Republican State Convention, Chamberlain was elected governor of South Carolina on November 3, 1874. He immediately instituted several reform measures, including reducing public expenditures, revising assessment laws, and curbing the power of several State boards. He refused, often against the wishes of Republican leaders, to commission corrupt public officials.

Chamberlain was renominated by the Republicans in 1876; the Democratic nominee was Wade Hampton. After a very bitter campaign, Chamberlain was apparently elected by a vote of 86,216 to Hampton's 83,071, and was inaugurated on December 7th. The Democrats, however, challenged the election results and established a rival government; they inaugurated Hampton on December 14.

Both governors claimed authority until April 1877, when President Rutherford B. Hayes withdrew federal troops from South Carolina as part of the Compromise of 1877. Without the support of the troops, Chamberlain was forced leave office.

Chamberlain afterwards practiced law in New York. In 1883, he accepted a professorship of Constitutional Law at Cornell University. He retired to West Brookfield in 1897, and traveled to Europe before settling in Charlotteville, Virginia.

Chamberlain was married to Alice Ingersoll in December 1867. The couple had one son. He died in Charlotteville, Virginia in April 1907.

CHAPPELL, JOHN JOEL, (1782-1871) — a U.S. Representative from South Carolina, born on Little River, near Columbia, Fairfield District, S.C., where the family was on a visit, January 19, 1782; as an infant was taken by his parents to their home on the Congaree River, Richland District, S.C.; attended the common schools and was graduated from the law department of South Carolina College (now the University of South Carolina) at Columbia; was admitted to the bar in 1805 and commenced practice in Columbia, Richland County, S.C.; appointed adjutant of the Thirty-third South Carolina Regiment in 1805 and elected captain and then colonel of the same regiment in 1808; member of the State house of repre sentatives 1808-1812; appointed trustee of South Carolina College in 1809; served in the War of 1812; elected as a Republican to the Thirteenth and Fourteenth Congresses (March 4, 1813-March 3, 1817); chairman, Committee on Pensions and Revolutionary Claims (Thirteenth and Fourteenth Congresses); resumed the practice of law until 1837; director of the Columbia branch of the State Bank of South Carolina 1830-1858; moved to Lowndes County, Ala., and became a cotton planter; died in Lowndes County, Ala., May 23, 1871; interment in First Baptist Church Cemetery, Columbia, S.C.

CHESNUT, JAMES, JR., (1815-1885) — a U.S. Senator from South Carolina; born near Camden, S.C., January 18, 1815; was graduated from the law department of the College of New Jersey (now Princeton University) in 1837; was admitted to the bar the same year and commenced practice in Camden, S.C.; member, State house of representatives 1842-1854; delegate to the southern convention at Nashville in 1850; served in the State senate 1854-1858; elected as a Democrat to the United States Senate to fill the vacancy caused by the death of Josiah J. Evans and served from December 3, 1858, until November 10, 1860, when he withdrew; expelled from the Senate in 1861 for support of the rebellion; delegate to the Confederate Provisional Congress in 1861; during the Civil War served as colonel in the Confederate Army; appointed brigadier general in 1864; resumed the practice of law in Camden, Kershaw County, S.C., and died there on February 1, 1885; interment in Knights Hill Cemetery, near Camden, S.C.

CHEVES, LANGDON, (1776-1857) — a U.S. Representative from South Carolina; born September 17, 1776, in Bulltown Fort, near Rocky River, Ninety-sixth District (now Abbeville County), S.C., where the settlers had taken refuge from the onslaught of the Cherokee Indians; received his early education at his home and Andrew Weed's School near Abbeville, S.C.; joined his father in Charleston, S.C., in 1786 and continued his schooling in that city; studied law; was admitted to the bar October 14, 1797, and commenced practice in Charleston; city alderman in 1802; member of the State house of representatives 1802-1804 and 1806-1808; elected attorney general of the State in 1808; elected as a Republican to the Eleventh Congress to fill the vacancy caused by the resignation of Robert Marion, having previously been elected to the Twelfth Congress; reelected to the Thirteenth Congress, and served from December 31, 1810, to March 3, 1815; succeeded Henry Clay as Speaker of the House of Representatives during the second session of the Thirteenth Congress; chairman, Committee on Ways and Means (Twelfth Congress), Committee on the Naval Establishment (Twelfth Congress); declined to be a candidate for reelection in 1814 to the Fourteenth Congress and also the position of Secretary of the Treasury tendered by President Madison; resumed the practice of law; elected associate justice of law and appeal in December 1816; resigned in 1819; declined to accept an appointment as Associate Justice of the Supreme Court of the United States; elected president of the Bank of the United States March 6, 1819, and held this office until 1822, when pointment as Associate Justice of the Supreme Court of the United States; elected president of the Bank of the United States March 6, 1819, and held this office until 1822, when he resigned; chief commissioner of claims under the treaty of Ghent; resided in Philadelphia and

Washington 1819-1826 and in Lancaster, Pa., 1826-1829; returned to South Carolina in 1829; engaged extensively in the cultivation of rice in South Carolina and Georgia; tendered an appointment by the Governor of South Carolina to the United States Senate to fill the vacancy caused by the death of John C. Calhoun, but declined; delegate to the Southern convention at Nashville, Tenn., in 1850 and to the State convention at Columbia, S.C., in 1852; died in Columbia, S.C., June 26, 1857; interment in Magnolia Cemetery, Charleston, S.C.

CLARK, MARK WAYNE, (1896-1984) — was a United States lieutenant general who was one of the top five commanders in World War I.

Born on May 1, 1896 at Madison Barracks in New York, Mark Wayne Clark was graduated from West Point Military Academy in 1917 and the following year was sent to France, where he took part in allied actions in the Vosges Mountains, at St. Mihiel, and on the Meuse-Argonne front. Promoted to captain in 1919, he returned to the United States and for 20 years served at a succession of posts and attended the Command and General Staff School. He was a student and an instructor at the Army War College.

In May of 1942, Clark, then a major general, was named chief of staff of the army ground forces and two months later assumed command of all United States ground forces in Europe. After overseeing the organization of combat training in England, he was assigned to the planning phase of the North African campaign. In negotiations highlighted by a dramatic secret trip to North Africa by submarine, he secured the cooperation of the Free French forces in North Africa, a delicate diplomatic task, and served in the campaign itself as deputy to General Dwight D. Eisenhower.

In 1943, as a lieutenant general, he was appointed to command the U.S. 5th Army in the invasion of Italy. The Italian campaign involved some of the hardest fighting of the war, with bitter German resistance maintained all the way from the Salerno beachheads through Cassino and Anzio to Rome (taken in June 1944), and north to the Apennines. In December of 1944, Clark became commander of the 15th Army Group; the following spring he was promoted to general and in June, after the surrender of Germany, he was appointed high commissioners and commander of United States forces in occupied Austria. In 1947, he returned to the United States, commanded the 6th Army and then the Army Field Forces, and in 1952 succeeded General Matthew Ridgeway as supreme commander of the United Nations forces in the Korean War, retaining the post through the long and difficult period of negotiations at the end of the fighting. Clark signed the armistice for the United Nations in July of 1953. Later that year, he retired from the army. From 1954 until 1966, he was president of The Citadel.

Clark published two volumes of war memoirs, *Calculated Risk* in 1950 and *From the Danube to the Yalu* in 1954.

Clark received the Distinguished Service Medal in 1942, the Distinguished Service Cross for Heroism in 1945 and Italy's Grand Cross of Order of Merit in 1975.

He died in Charleston, South Carolina on April 17, 1984.

CLOWNEY, WILLIAM KENNEDY, (1797-1851) — a U.S. Representative from South Carolina; born in Union County, S.C., March 21, 1797; attended private schools and an academy; was graduated from South Carolina College at Columbia in 1818; taught in the public schools of Unionville and in the University of South Carolina; member of the State house of representatives tives1830-1831; studied law; was admitted to the bar and began practice in Union; commissioner in equity of South Carolina 1830-1833; elected as a Nullifier to the Twentythird Congress (March 4, 1833-March 3, 1835); elected as a Nullifier to the Twenty- fifth Congress (March 4, 1837-March 3, 1839); chairman, Committee on Expenditures in the Department of War (Twenty-fifth Congress); member of the State senate in 1840; Lieutenant Governor of South Carolina; died in Union, Union County, S.C., March 12, 1851; interment in Fairforest Cemetery, Union County, S.C.

COHEN, OCTAVUS ROY, (1891-1959) — a civil engineer, lawyer, journalist, and author of mystery novels. Cohen was born June 26, 1891 in Charleston, South Carolina to parents Octavus and Rebecca (Ottolengui). He attended the Porter Military Academy, graduating in the class of 1908, then he earned his B.A. from Clemson College three years later.

Cohen's first position was as a civil engineer for the Tennessee Coal, Iron and Railroad Company. He stayed for one year, then started writing for newspapers, including the Birmingham *Ledger* in Alabama, the Charleston *News and Courier* in South Carolina, plus the Bayonne *Times* and the Newark *Morning Star*, both in New Jersey. At the same time he studied law, and was admitted to the South Carolina bar in 1913. He practiced for two years, then devoted himself to writing full-time.

In October of 1914 Cohen married Inez Lopez, and they eventually had one son together. His first book, *The Other Woman* was written with J.U. Giesy, and published in 1917. It was followed by *The Crimson Alibi* (1919); *Polished Ebony* (1919); *Gray Dusk* (1920); *Come Seven* (1920); *Six Seconds of Darkness* (1921); *Highley Colored* (1921); *Midnight* (1922); and *Assorted Chocolates* (1922). Cohen began contributing short stories to the *Saturday Evening Post* in 1918, a practice he continued throughout his career.

In 1923 Cohen introduced one of his most popular characters, Jim Hanvey, in the book *Jim Hanvey, Detective*. Hanvey also appeared in *The May Day Mystery* (1929) and *The Backstage Mystery* (1930). Cohen continued to write about other detectives as well, in books such as *Dark Days and Black Nights* (1923); *Sunclouds* (1924); *Bigger and Blacker* (1925); *The Iron Chalice* (1925); *Black and Blue* (1926); *The Outer Gate* (1927); *Detours* (1927); *The Other Tomorrow* (1927); and *The Light Shines Through* (1928).

In 1928 Cohen introduced another popular detective, Florian Slappey, a comedic character whose adventures take him from his home in Alabama to New York and Europe. Slappey was featured in the books *Florian Slappey Goes Abroad* (1928) and *Florian Slappey* (1938). Cohen's other books include: *Sprint Tide* (1928); *The Val-*

ley of Olympus (1929); *Epic Peters, Pullman Porter* (1930); *Lilies of the Alley* (1931); *Cameos* (1931); *Star of the Earth* (1932); *Carbon Copies* (1933); *The Townsend Murder Mystery* (1933); *Scarlet Woman* (1934); *Transient Lady* (1934); *Scrambled Yeggs* (1934); *Black to Nature* (1935); *With the Benefit of Clergy* (1935); *Child of Evil* (1936); *I Love You Again* (1937); *East of Broadway* (1938); *Strange Honeymoon* (1939); *Romance in Crimson* (1940); *Kid Tinsel* (1941); *Lady In Armor* (1941); *Masquerade in Miami* (1942); *Sound of Revelry* (1943); *Romance in the First Degree* (1943); *Danger in Paradise* (1944); *Love Has No Alibi* (1945); *Dangerous Lady* (1946); *Don't Ever Love Me* (1947); *My Love Wears Black; More Beautiful Than Murder* (1948); *A Bullet for My Love* (1950); *The Corpse That Walked* (1951); *Lost Lady* (1952); *Borrasca* (1953); and *Love Can Be Dangerous* (1955).

Cohen also wrote several plays including *The Crimson Alibi*, written in 1919 with George Broadhurst; *The Scourge* (1920); *Come Seven* (1920); *Shadows* (1920); *Every Saturday Night* (1921); and *Alias, Mrs. Wallace* (1928). He contributed to motion pictures and television programs, including the "Amos 'n' Andy" radio series from 1945 to 1946. He earned a Literature Degree from Birminghan- Southern College in 1927, and was a lieutenant in the United States Navel Reserve from 1930 to 1940. He died January 6, 1959.

COKER, DAVID ROBERT, (1870-1938) — agriculturist and merchant, was born in Hartsville, South Carolina on November 20, 1870, son of James Lide and Susan Armstrong Coker. He received a grammar and high school education in Society Hill and Hartsville, South Carolina and graduated with an A.B. degree from the University of South Carolina in 1891. In January of the following year, he went to work for J.L. Coker & Co., general merchants in Hartsville. This firm had been founded by his father and grandfather in 1865 and following the completion in 1889 of the Hartsville Railroad, which his father helped construct, it grew rapidly until it became the largest department store in Eastern South Carolina.

Because of ill health, he had to relinquish his connection with the firm temporarily in 1897. He then became interested in scientific plant breeding and in 1902, organized Coker's Pedigreed Seed Co., of which he was president until his death. Through this enterprise, he exercised an important influence on the improvement of agriculture in South Carolina and the Southeast generally. His achievements included the originating of new varieties of cotton, a highly productive type of wheat, new varieties of corn, a new yam-type potato, smut and cold- resisting oats, a superior type of cigarette tobacco and other crop improvements. One of the notable results of these contributions was a marked improvement in the field, quality and length of staple of the cotton crop in the Southeast and the Mississippi Valley.

Coker's enthusiasm for this work was due in part to his interest in agriculture as a science and in still greater part to his desire to help the southern farmer. In addition to the breeding work in its strictest sense, he devoted much time and effort in solving many general farm problems, such as the effect of fodder pulling on the yield and quality of corn, spacing and fertilizer experiments with both corn and cotton, and proper seeding rates for small grains. He also devoted much money and effort to finding out the cheapest and most effective method of weevil control. Besides these direct contributions, he continually tried to teach the southern farmer how to make life more prosperous and happy by growing basic food and feed crops in addition to the main money crop, by beautifying his home and its surroundings.

The fame of his work spread, and his experiment station was visited every year not only by thousands of farmers but also by scores of government officials of various nations. Following his father's death in 1918, he became president of J.L. Coker & Co., assuming management of it in association with Joseph James Lawton. He was also a partner in the Coker Cotton Co.; vice- president of the Sonoco Products Co. and the Hartsville Oil Mill, and a director of the Federal Reserve Bank of Richmond, Virginia.

From 1897 to 1899, Coker was mayor of Hartsville. In the First World War, he served as federal food administrator of South Carolina, chairman of the South Carolina State Council of Defense and a member of the National Agricultural Advisory Commission on behalf of which he visited Europe in 1918. In 1932, he was delegate-at-large to the Democratic National Convention. The following year, he became a member of the Industrial Advisory Committee of the National Recovery Administration. He was also a member of the Business Advisory and Planning Council organized by the U.S. Department of Commerce, and a member of the South Carolina Land Assessment Committee. He was a trustee of the Charleston Museum, the University of South Carolina, and Coker College at Hartsville, which had been founded by his father in 1908.

He was awarded the University of South Carolina McMaster medal in 1916 and the American Legion distinguished service medal in 1928. The honorary degree of D.Sc. was conferred on him by Duke University in 1930 and that of LL.D. was awarded him by the University of North Carolina in 1932, College of Charleston in 1935 and Clemson College in 1937. Coker was a member of the American Genetics Society, Phi Beta Kappa and Chi Xi.

Personally, he was a genial, likeable, hospitable man, of cultivated, scholarly tastes. He loved music and all the varied manifestations of beauty in nature. He was married twice: the first time to Jessie Ruth Richardson, with whom he had five children. His second wife was Margaret May Roper, with whom he had three more children.

David Coker died in Hartsville, South Carolina on November 28, 1938.

COLCOCK, WILLIAM FERGUSON, (1804-1889) — a U.S. Representative from South Carolina; born in Beaufort, S.C., November 5, 1804; attended Hulburt's School, Charleston, S.C., and was graduated from South Carolina College (now the University of South Carolina) at Columbia in 1823; studied law; was admitted to the bar in 1825 and commenced practice in Coosawhatchie, Jasper County, S.C.; also engaged in planting; member of the State house of representatives 1830-1847; elected as a Democrat to the Thirty-first and Thirty-second Congresses (March 4, 1849- March 3, 1853); a Regent of the Smithsonian Institution 1850- 1853; collector of the port of Charleston 1853-1865, serving first under the United States Government and subsequently under the Confederate States Government; delegate to the Democratic National Convention at Charleston in 1860; resumed the practice of law; died in McPhersonville, Hampton County, S.C., on June 13, 1889; interment in Stoney Creek Cemetery, Beaufort County, S.C.

COLHOUN, JOHN EWING, (1749-1802) — (cousin of John Caldwell Calhoun and Joseph Calhoun), a U.S. Senator from South Carolina; born in Staunton, Augusta County, Va., around 1749; attended the common schools and was graduated from the College of New Jersey (now Princeton University) in 1774; member, State house of representatives 1778-1800; studied law; was admitted to the bar in 1783 and commenced practice in Charleston, S.C.; farmer; elected a member of the privy council and also a commissioner of confiscated estates in 1785; member, State senate 1801; member of the committee which was instructed to report a modification of the judiciary system of the United States; elected as a Republican to the United States Senate and served from March 4, 1801, until his death in Pendleton, S.C., October 26, 1802; interment in the family cemetery, Old Pendleton District, now Pickens County, South Carolina.

COOPER, ROBERT ARCHER, (1874-1953) — Sixty-eighth state governor (D) of South Carolina, 1919-1922.

Born in Laurens County, South Carolina on June 12, 1874, the son of Henry and Elizabeth (Jones) Cooper. He studied law at the Polytechnic Institute in San German, Puerto Rico, and was admitted to the South Carolina Bar in 1898. He started a law practice in Laurens, South Carolina, and was magistrate in that town from 1899 to 1900. In 1899, he married Mamie Machen. She died in 1914, and three years later he married Dorcas Calmes. He was the father of two children.

Cooper was a member of the State House of Representatives from 1900 to 1904. In 1905, 1908 and 1912, he was elected solicitor for the Eighth Judicial District of South Carolina. Also during this time, he served as a trustee for Anderson College, and Furman University. He ran for governor in 1918 on the Democratic ticket, and won in an unopposed general election. He was reelected in 1920, again without opposition. Accomplishments during his terms included increases to teachers' salaries; imposition of a seven month school term and a compulsory school attendance law; funding for road construction and increased public health services; legislation which limited working hours in textile mills to fifty-five hours a week or ten hours a day; and stricter enforcement of tax laws.

Cooper resigned the governorship in 1922 to take a position of the Federal Farm Loan Board. He remained there until 1927. From 1929 to 1932, he served as assistant to the chairman of the Executive Committee of the Democratic National Committee. He was the U.S. District Judge for Puerto Rico from 1934 to 1947. Cooper died on August 7, 1953.

COOPER, THOMAS, (1759 - 1840) — scientist and author, second president of South Carolina College, was born in London, England on October 22, 1759. He studied chemistry, law and medicine at Oxford University.

Thomas Cooper was active in politics and joined a Democratic Club in Manchester, of which the inventor James Watt was a member. He was well-known for his outspoken political commentary. For example, because of his writings in response to Burke's *Reflections on the Revolution in France*, he was threatened with prosecution. He later moved to France and was considered on intimate terms with the leaders of the French Revolution. His legal problems continued after he moved to the United States and settled in Northumberland, Pennsylvania, where his father-in-law, Joseph Priestly — the philosopher and scientist — lived. Cooper published an attack upon the administration of John Adams in the Reading *Weekly Advertiser* and, in 1800, he was tried under the alien and sedition acts. He was fined $400 and served six months in prison. In 1825, he petitioned for a restitution of this fine on the grounds that the acts were unconstitutional, but did not receive the settlement, with interest, until a few years before his death.

Cooper held several positions of public office, including land commissioner and common please court judge. He also served as professor at Dickinson College, the University of Pennsylvania, the University of Virginia, and South Carolina College. He was appointed president of South Carolina College in 1821. He was known for his enthusiastic and often controversial opinions. He was an ardent supporter of public access to education and was considered to be a man ahead of his time.

After leaving the presidency at South Carolina College in 1834, again under the pressure of controversy, he dedicated his remaining years to the editing and publishing of the statutes of the state by appointment of the legislature. Five volumes were published. It has been said that Cooper's influence upon South Carolina legislation rivals that of Thomas Jefferson in Virginia.

CORLEY, MANUEL SIMEON, (1823-1902) — a U.S. Representative from South Carolina; born in Lexington County, S.C., February 10, 1823; was a student in Lexington Academy four years; engaged in business in 1838; opposed the first attempt at secession of South Carolina in 1852, when an effort was made to expel him from the State; editor of the South Carolina Temperance Standard in 1855 and 1856; entered the Confederate Army in 1863; captured by Union troops at Petersburg, Va., April 2, 1865; took the oath of allegiance June 5, 1865; delegate to the constitutional convention of South Carolina in 1867; upon the readmission of South Carolina to representation tationwas elected as a Republican to the Fortieth Congress and served from July 25, 1868, to March 3, 1869; special agent of the United States Treasury in 1869; commissioner of agricultural statistics of South Carolina in 1870; treasurer of Lexington County in 1874; died in Lexington, S.C., November 20, 1902; interment in St. Stephen's Lutheran Cemetery.

COTHRAN, JAMES SPROULL, (1852-1897) — a U.S. Representative from South Carolina; born near Abbeville, Abbeville County, S.C., August 8, 1830; attended the country schools; was graduated from the University of Georgia at Athens in 1852; studied law; was admitted to the bar in 1853 and commenced practice in Abbeville, S.C.; entered the Confederate service as a private at the beginning of the Civil War and was with his company at the surrender of the Army of Northern Virginia at Appomattox, having attained the rank of captain; re sumed the practice of law in Abbeville; elected solicitor of the eighth judicial circuit in 1876 and 1880; appointed to the judgeship of that circuit to fill a vacancy caused by the death of Judge Thomson in 1881; elected by the legislature to the same office the following winter, and reelected in 1885; elected as a Democrat to the Fiftieth and Fifty-first Congresses (March 4, 1887-March 3, 1891); was not a candidate for renomination in 1890; again resumed the practice of law in Abbeville and Greenville, S.C.; died in a sanitarium in New York City, December 5, 1897; interment in Upper Long Cane Cemetery, Abbeville, S.C.

CRAIG, ELISABETH MAY ADAMS, (1888-1975) — journalist, was born in Coosaw Mines, South Carolina on December 19, 1888, the daughter of Alexander and Elizabeth Craig. Her father was an English immigrant who worked in the local phosphate mines. Her mother died giving birth to her twin sisters when she was four years old. Following this tragedy her father allowed her to be adopted by Frances and William Weymouth, who owned the mines where he worked.

The little girl took up reading the family library and soon was an eager student. When she was 12 her second family moved to Washington D.C. where she completed high school, and embarked upon a writing career. Determined to develop many skills, she also enrolled in George Washington University's Nursing School. This independent course of action led to a split with the Weymouths, but did not deter her direction. In 1909 she married Donald Craig, a newspaper columnist with the Washington bureau of the *New York Herald.*

The new couple soon had two children and a housekeeper/nursemaid, which allowed Ms. Craig to continue her writing career. That career included various feature articles on woman's rights, a subject that deeply interested her. Following her husband's serious injury in a 1923 automobile accident, she began to help him with his column *On the Inside in Washington*. This effort proved successful, and in 1931 she began her own column in the Gannett newspaper chain. By the late 1930's she had achieved prestige and influence in journalism, and become a close friend of Eleanor Roosevelt.

Women's rights in her chosen field remained on her agenda, and she became the president of the Woman's National Press Club in 1943. She managed to overcome the discrimination against women war correspondents, and in 1944 toured the front lines in France. At the end of the war, Ms. Craig became a popular panelist on the *Meet the Press* radio and T.V. program. Her fame opened many new doors to her, and she traveled extensively around the world as a correspondent. To her went the honor of being the first woman correspondent to live on a combat ship at sea, take part in the Berlin airlift, and attend the truce talks in Korea. She retired in 1965, and lived with her daughter until 1970. Craig died on July 15, 1975 in Silver Spring, Maryland.

CROFT, THEODORE GAILLARD, (1874-1920) — (son of George William Croft), a U.S. Representative from South Carolina; born in Aiken, Aiken County, S.C., November 26, 1874; attended the common schools; was graduated from Bethel Military Academy, War renton, Va., in 1895 and from the law department of the University of South Carolina at Columbia in 1897; was admitted to the bar the same year and commenced practice in Aiken, S.C.; elected as a Democrat to the Fifty-eighth Congress to fill the vacancy caused by the death of his father, George W. Croft, and served from May 17, 1904, to March 3, 1905; was not a candidate for renomination in 1904; resumed the practice of law in Aiken, S.C.; member of the State house of representatives in 1907 and 1908; served in the State senate 1909-1912; enlisted in the U.S. Army October 29, 1918; was assigned to duty as a private in the Field Artillery Central Officers' Training School, Camp Zachary Taylor, and served until December 5, 1918, when he was honorably discharged; resumed the practice of law; died in Aiken, S.C., March 23, 1920; interment in St. Thaddeus' Episcopal Churchyard.

D

DANIEL, CHARLES EZRA, (1895-1964) — a U.S. Senator from South Carolina; born in Elberton, Elbert County, Ga., November 11, 1895; moved with his family to Anderson, S.C., in 1898 and attended the public schools; student at The Citadel, Charleston, S.C., 1916-1918; during the First World War served as a lieutenant in the Infantry 1917-1919; businessman; interests in construction, banking, building supplies, telecommunications, insurance, and airlines; life trustee of Clemson College and member of the board of South Carolina Foundation of Independent Colleges; appointed as a Democrat to the United States Senate to fill the vacancy caused by the death of Burnet R. Maybank and served from September 6, 1954, until his resignation December 23, 1954; was not a candidate for election to fill the vacancy; resumed management of his business interests; died in Greenville, S.C., September 13, 1964; interment in Springwood Cemetery.

DANIELS, JONATHAN WORTH, (1902-1981) — a journalist, government official and revealing author. The son of Josephus Daniels and Addie Worth (Bagley), Daniels was born April 26, 1902 in Raleigh, North Carolina. He was named after his great- grandfather, a former governor. His father was the editor of the family-owned Raleigh *News and Observer*, and when he was appointed Secretary of the Navy under President Wilson the family moved to Washington D.C. Daniels remembered growing up in Raleigh most, and accompanying his father on his many travels by train. "I had an acute sense then, never equaled since, of seeing the world," he said later.

Daniels went to college at the University of North Carolina at Chapel Hill, receiving his B.A. in 1921 and his M.A. a year later. He attended the Columbia University Law School for one year, and even though he was admitted to the North Carolina Bar, he never practiced. He married Elizabeth Bridgers of Raleigh September 5, 1923 and settled down in Raleigh. His first steady job was as a reporter for the Louisville *Times*. Later he worked for his father at the *News and Observer* and in 1925 he was assigned to be a correspondent in Washington, where he stayed for three years. After he returned home he covered local news and wrote a novel at night. His wife died in 1929, and his novel, about the angels of heaven and hell, *Clash of Angels* (1930), did not sell well. Daniels did receive the Guggenheim Fellowship for his book, however, and he took the money and traveled throughout Europe with his daughter.

Daniels returned in 1930, and started writing for *Fortune* magazine. In 1932 he married Lucy Billing Cathcart and they became co-associate editors of the *News and Observer*. In 1933 Daniels' father was made Ambassador of Mexico and Daniels took over the editorship of the paper. Daniels was a liberal and strong New Dealer who found that an editor's work is never done. "I used to think that by the time I became editor father would have everything settled and there wouldn't be anything left for me." He fought local power companies to allow the PWA to install more power plants, and he campaigned to close tobacco warehouses when the market was glutted and prices were low. He continued writing for other periodicals as well, such as the *Saturday Evening Post*, *Collier's*, *Atlantic Monthly*, and *Harper's*, and for two years he wrote a regular column for *The Nation*.

Then in 1937 Daniels took a leave of absence and started traveling through the South, talking to people from all walks of life. Starting conversations and getting to know people was not difficult for Daniels, as friends said the only prerequisite for entering into conversation with him is to be born human. He covered approximately 3,000 miles exploring cotton fields and industrial centers, talking to hillbillies and aristocrats. The result was his book *A Southerner Discovers the South* (1938), hailed as one of the best books on the modern south. Daniels tried to recreate the same feeling in his book *A Southerner Discovers New England* (1940), when he traveled from Maine through Connecticut. Critics were a little tougher on this effort, however, saying it was too superficial.

For his next work Daniels focused on home, and he documented the story of his own state, from its beginnings to the present day, and charted its place in the scheme of U.S. history. *Tar Heels: A Portrait of North Carolina* received favorable reviews from the critics, and was well-read. While working on this book Daniels continued to travel around the country lecturing and writing. He became especially interested in defense centers, and because of his interest was asked to serve as assistant director of the Office of Civilian Defense in charge of civilian mobilization. He turned the editor's position at the paper back over to his father, and moved to Washington.

Daniels served in that position for one year, then was asked to be administrative assistant and press secretary for President Franklin D. Roosevelt. In 1946 he wrote the book *Frontier on the Potomac*, then he returned to the paper as executive editor in 1947. In 1948 Daniels took over as editor again, a position which he held until 1969. From 1949 to 1952 Daniels was very active in the Democratic National Committee, promoting the campaigns of Harry S. Truman in 1948 and Adlai Stevenson in 1952. He was the U.S. Representative on the United Nations Subcommission on Prevention of Discrimination and Protection of Minorities from 1947 to 1953, and was a member of the Federal Hospital Council of the U.S. Public Health Service from 1950 to 1953.

Daniels continued writing as well, mostly historical books. In 1954 *The End of Innocence* was published, a book that revealed, seemingly in passing, the affair between President Roosevelt and Lucy Page Mercer. In 1966 Daniels detailed the affair even more in his book *The Time Between Wars*. Other books by Daniels include *The Man of Independence* (1950); *The Forest Is the Future* (1957); *Prince of Carpetbaggers* (1958); *Mosby: Gray Ghost of the Confederacy* (1959); *Stonewall Jackson* (1959); *Robert E. Lee* (1960); *October Recollections* (1961); *The Devil's Backbone: The Story of the Natchez Trace* (1962); *They Will Be Heard* (1964); *Washington Quadrille: The Dance Beside the Documents* (1967); *Ordeal of Ambition* (1970); and *The Randolphs of Virginia* (1972). Daniels had three more daughters in his second marriage, and died November 6, 1981, on Hilton Head Island in South Carolina.

DARGAN, GEORGE WILLIAM, (1841-1898) — (great-grandson of Lemuel Benton), a U.S. Representative from South Carolina; born at "Sleepy Hollow," near Darlington, Darlington County, S.C, May 11, 1841; attended the schools of his native county and the South Carolina Military Academy; served in the Confederate Army throughout the Civil War; studied law; was ad mitted to the bar in 1872 and practiced in Darlington, S.C.; elected to the State house of representatives in 1877; solicitor of the fourth judicial circuit of South Carolina in 1880; elected as a Democrat to the Forty-eighth and to the three succeeding Congresses (March 4, 1883-March 3, 1891); was not a candidate for renomination in 1890; resumed the practice of law; died in Darlington, S.C., June 29, 1898; interment in First Baptist Churchyard.

DAVIS, MENDEL JACKSON, (1942-   ) — a U.S. Representative from South Carolina; born in North Charleston, Charleston County, S.C., October 23, 1942; attended the North Charleston public schools; B.S., College of Charleston, 1966; J.D., University of South Carolina School of Law, 1970; admitted to the South Carolina bar in 1970 and commenced practice in North Charleston; district assistant to Congressman L. Mendel Rivers for ten years; elected as a Democrat, by special election, April 27, 1971, to the Ninety-second Congress to fill the vacancy caused by the death of L. Mendel Rivers; reelected to the four succeeding Congresses and served from April 27, 1971, to January 3, 1981; was not a candidate for reelection in 1980 to the Ninety-eighth Congress; resumed the practice of law; is a resident of North Charleston, S.C.

DE BOW, JAMES DUNWOODY BROWNSON, (1820-1867) — an editor and statistician who started his career on less than a shoestring, becoming one of the most successful publishers in the South.

The son of Garret De Bow, a once successful merchant from New Jersey, De Bow was born July 10, 1820. Little is known about De Bow's mother, and he was orphaned when he was still young. He used his inheritance to enter a mercantile house, then saved to attend the Cokesbury Institute. He later entered the College of Charleston, working and studying around the clock to sustain himself and graduate in 1843 at the head of his class. He started studied law for a year, still living hand to mouth, until he was admitted to the bar. His hard work did not pay off, however, as he was a poor speaker and his emancipated appearance was a strike against him in courtroom situations.

De Bow did find some success however, writing philosophical and political essays for the *Southern Quarterly Review*. Soon he was named editor, and in July of 1845 he wrote his most famous article, "Oregon and the Oregon Question." In it he debated the claims of France, England and the United States for land in the northwest, and the article stimulated debate as far away as the French Chamber of Deputies. That same year De Bow participated at the Memphis Convention, where discussion centered on internal improvements in the South and financial expectations from the federal government. These two events inspired De Bow to start a magazine devoted to economic and social development in the South, the first of its kind.

He moved his operation to New Orleans, considered the commercial capital of the South, and in January 1846 published the first issue of the *Commercial Review of the South and Southwest* with little more than a wing and a prayer. The lack of supporters and subscribers caused a suspension of the *Review* in August, but entrepreneur Maunsel White saw promise in De Bow and the publication, loaning him the money to continue the magazine. De Bow and an assistant worked night and day on the magazine, sleeping in the office and spending less than ten cents a day on food. This time his hard work and determination was rewarded, as within two years the magazine had the largest circulation of any periodical in the south. De Bow paid his debts, moved into a better office and was able to eat steak and pork chops for the first time in his life.

The magazine became popularly known as *De Bow's Review*, which became extremely influential, and played an important role in the onset of the Civil War. At first De Bow vowed not to become involved in the issues that were dividing the North and the South. He gradually changed his mind on those issues however, and became more outspoken with his partisan beliefs. He felt that protective tariffs were necessary, and while he supported Southern industry he wanted to see agriculture remain a predominant force in Southern economics. He also believed that, "the negro was created essentially to be a slave, and finds his highest development and destiny in that condition." He supported the construction of a transcontinental railroad through the South, direct trade between the South and Europe, and a canal through Central America.

Along with the journal De Bow had an interest in education. When the University of Louisiana was established in 1848 he pushed for the inclusion of economic and commercial classes in the curriculum. The University did him one better and appointed him chairman of the department, but much to his disappointment no students enrolled in the program. He was also asked to lead the new Louisiana Bureau of Statistics, where he developed a questionnaire and presented the results to the Louisiana legislature. However, the legislature failed to act on any of his recommendations. De Bow was also one of the founders of the Louisiana Historical Society, which was unsuccessful until it merged with the Academy of Sciences.

De Bow did find greater success with his appointment as the superintendent of the United States Census. He issued the census of 1850, and in 1854 the results were published. De Bow also made suggestions for improving the census in the future, such as appointing a permanent superintendent and staff. In 1855 he left the government position, and he continued to publish the *Review* as well as lecture and write for the Encyclopedia Britannica. He married Caroline Poe in 1854, then in 1860 he married Martha E. Johns, with whom he had three children.

During the Civil War publication of the *Review* was suspended and De Bow was appointed chief agent for the purchase and sale of cotton for the Confederates. After the war he revived the paper in the hope of healing some of the social and political wounds of the war. He also served as the president of the Tennessee Pacific Railroad Company, reviving his dream of a transcontinental railroad in the South, but the project never got off the ground. After visiting the bedside of his dying brother, B.F. De Bow in Elizabeth, New Jersey, De Bow contracted pleurisy and died February 27, 1867. The *Review* continued to be published until 1880.

DE LARGE, ROBERT CARLOS, (1842-1874) — a U.S. Representative from South Carolina; born in Aiken, S.C., March 15, 1842; received such an education as was then attainable and was graduated from Wood High School; engaged in agricultural pursuits; delegate to the State constitutional convention in 1868; member of the State house of representatives 1868-1870; was one of the State commissioners of the sinking fund; elected State land commissioner in 1870 and served until elected to Congress; presented credentials as a Republican Memberelect to the Forty- second Congress and served from March 4, 1871, until January 24, 1873, when the seat was declared vacant, the election having been contested by Christopher C. Bowen; local magistrate until his death in Charleston, S.C., February 14, 1874; interment in Brown Fellowship Graveyard.

DE SAUSSURE, WILLIAM FORD, (1792-1870) — a U.S. Senator from South Carolina; born in Charleston, S.C., February 22, 1792; was graduated from Harvard University in 1810; studied law; was admitted to the bar and practiced in Charleston and Columbia, S.C.; member, State house of representatives 1846; judge of the chancery court 1847; appointed and subsequently lyelected as a Democrat to the United States Senate to fill the vacancy caused by the resignation of R. Barnwell Rhett and served from May 10, 1852, to March 3, 1853; resumed the practice of law in Columbia; trustee of South Carolina College (now the University of South Carolina) at Columbia for many years; died in Columbia, Richland County, S.C., March 13, 1870; interment in Presbyterian Churchyard.

DE SOTO, HERNANDO, (1500-1542) — an early Spanish explorer and soldier who discovered the Mississippi River and during his quest for gold was one of the first Europeans to travel through South Carolina.

De Soto's hunger for respect and wealth probably started early, as he was born to a noble family with little money. Pedrarias Davila, the governor of Panama, took on the patronage of the family, and paid for De Soto's education at the University of Salamanca. De Soto married Davila's daughter, Isabel, thus becoming a brother-in-law to another explorer, Vasco Nunez de Balboa. The young man accompanied Davila to Central America in 1532, serving as captain on his ship. De Soto was to serve Francisco Pizarro and Diego Almagro in the conquest of Peru once he arrived. He developed a respect for the Incas, and they admired his horsemanship and abilities with a weapon. The respect ended when De Soto lead the attack on the Incas, although he did later criticize his leader for unnecessary massacres. A feud developed between De Soto, Almagro and Pizarro over possession of the city of Cuzco, so De Soto left Peru, leaving behind his mistress, Princess Curicuillar, and their daughter. He returned to Spain a wealthy man, carrying with him a huge load of Inca gold.

De Soto charmed royalty, and they were impressed with his past feats along with his relatively humane attitude toward the indigenous people he conquered. He obtained a contract from Charles V in 1537 to take Florida and he was made governor of Cuba. With an army of 1,000 Spaniards and Portuguese men De Soto set up base in Cuba, which was operated by his wife, and he set forth for Florida with 500 of his men, landing in 1539. De Soto's method of conquering land was to capture the chiefs he visited and forced them to provide food and a guide for the territory. He marched his army north through Florida and entered what is now Georgia, North and South Carolina, Tennessee, Alabama, Mississippi, Arkansas, Oklahoma and Texas. Some of his men may also have gone through parts of Missouri and Louisiana. His men were anxious to set up colonies, but De Soto was determined to find gold, although all he discovered was rich soil and copper. They spent their first winter in Florida, and sent a detachment to Cuba for more supplies, to be delivered the next year.

The second year De Soto and his men traveled north again reaching the Savannah at Cofitachequi, an Indian village, below Silver Bluff. An unnamed queen presented them with freshwater pearls, but De Soto continued on his search for gold. Again they wandered through North Carolina, Georgia, Tennessee and Alabama. It was in Mauvila, between the Alabama and Tombigbee rivers that De Soto and his men were met by a surprise attack by the Indians, killing many of their soldiers and horses. Mortified, De Soto decided not to meet with the party that was to bring them supplies in Florida, but decided instead to winter in Mississippi.

Throughout the winter the explorers were continually attacked by the Indians, and in April 1541 they decided to trudge through the swamps of the delta and leave Mississippi. It was then that they discovered the great Mississippi River, and still not completely discouraged, decided to travel it, again in search of fortune. For a year the men traveled the river and its tributaries through Tennessee, Arkansas, Oklahoma and possibly Missouri. They spent another winter in Arkansas, then decided to take the river through Louisiana, hoping to find Florida. The lack of good vessels and unfriendly Indians made the river nearly impossible to cross, then De Soto became ill and died. His successor, Luis de Moscoso decided to sink the body in the Mississippi, so the Indians would not know their leader was dead. Moscoso then took the approximately 300 survivors of the expedition through Louisiana and part of Texas, before finally arriving in Cuba in 1543.

DERRICK, BUTLER CARSON, JR., (1936-   ) — a U.S. Representative from South Carolina; born in Springfield, Hampden County, Mass., September 30, 1936; attended the public schools in Mayesville, S.C., and Florence, S.C.; attended University of South Carolina, 1954-1958; LL.B., University of Georgia Law School, 1965; admitted to the South Carolina bar in 1965 and commenced practice in Edgefield; served in the South Carolina house of representatives, 1969-1974; delegate to South Carolina State Democratic conventions, 1972, 1974; delegate to Democratic National Convention, 1974; elected as a Democrat to the Ninety- fourth and to each succeeding Congresses; deputy majority whip; member;

Task Force on Rural Elderly; Task Force on Social Security and Women; a resident of Edgefield, S.C.

DIBBLE, SAMUEL, (1837-1913) — a U.S. Representative from South Carolina; born in Charleston, S.C., September 16, 1837; pursued an academic course in Bethel, Conn., and Charleston, S.C.; attended the College of Charleston for two years, and was graduated from Wofford College, Spartnnburg, S.C., in 1856; engaged in teaching 1856-1858; studied law; was admitted to the bar in 1859 and commenced practice in Orangeburg, S.C.; served in the Confederate Army throughout the Civil War; resumed the practice of law in Orangeburg, S.C.; also edited the Orangeburg News; member of the State house of representatives in 1877 and 1878; trustee of the University of South Carolina at Columbia in 1878; member of the Board of School Commissioners of Orangeburg County; delegate to the Democratic National Convention in 1880; presented credentials as a Democratic Member-elect to the Forty-seventh Congress to fill a vacancy thought to exist by reason of the death (pending a contest) of Michael P. O'Connor, and served from June 9, 1881, to May 31, 1882, when the seat was awarded to Edmund W.M. Mackey under the original election; elected to the Forty-eighth and to the three succeeding Congresses (March 4, 1883-March 3, 1891); chairman, Committee on Public Buildings and Grounds (Fortyninth and Fiftieth Congresses); declined to be a candidate for reelection in 1890; engaged in banking and other business interests in Orangeburg, Orangeburg County, S.C.; died near Baltimore, Md., September 16, 1913; interment in Sunny Side Cemetery, Orangeburg, S.C.

DOMINICK, FREDERICK HASKELL, (1877-1960) — a U.S. Representative from South Carolina; born in Peak, Newberry County, S.C., February 20, 1877; attended the public schools of Columbia, Newberry (S.C.) College, South Carolina College at Columbia, and the law school of the University of Virginia at Charlottesville; was admitted to the bar in 1898 and commenced practice in Newberry, S.C.; member of the State house of repre sentatives 1901-1902; chairman of the Democratic county committee

1906-1914; assistant attorney general of South Carolina 1913- 1916; delegate to the Democratic National Conventions in 1920 and 1924; elected as a Democrat to the Sixty-fifth and to the seven succeeding Congresses (March 4, 1917-March 3, 1933); unsuccessful candidate for renomination in 1932; one of the managers appointed by the House of Representatives in 1926 to conduct the impeachment proceedings against George W. English, judge of the United States District Court for the Eastern District of Illinois; during the Second World War served as assistant to the Attorney General, Department of Justice, Washington, D.C.; practiced law in Newberry, S.C., until his death there March 11, 1960; interment in Rosemont Cemetery.

DORN, WILLIAM JENNINGS BRYAN, (1916-   ) — a U.S. Representative from South Carolina; born near Greenwood, Greenwood County, S.C., April 14, 1916; attended the public schools; engaged in agricultural pursuits; served in the State house of representatives ativesin 1939 and 1940; member of the State senate in 1941 and 1942; enlisted as a private in the Army Air Forces and served from June 20, 1942, until discharged as a corporal on October 12, 1945, nineteen months of which were in the European Theater; elected as a Democrat to the Eightieth Congress (January 3, 1947-January 3, 1949); was not a candidate for renomination in 1948, but was an unsuccessful candidate for the Democratic nomination for United States Senator; resumed agricultural pursuits; elected to the Eightysecond Congress; reelected to the eleven succeeding Congresses and served from January 3, 1951, until his resignation December 31, 1974; chairman, Committee on Veterans' Affairs (Ninety-third Congress); was not a candidate for reelection in 1974 to the Ninety-fourth Congress; was an unsuccessful candidate for Governor; chairman, South Carolina Democratic party, 1980-1984; is a resident of Greenwood, S.C.

DRAYTON, JOHN, (1767-1822) — thirteenth and seventeenth state governor (D-R) of South Carolina, 1800-1802 and 1808-1810.

He was born in Charleston, the son of William Henry and Dorothy Drayton.

Drayton attended school in Charleston until the age of ten, when he accompanied his father, who had been elected a delegate to Congress, to Little York, Pennsylvania. After receiving his education there, he went to grammar school in Princeton, New Jersey. In August 1779, he was admitted to the College of New Jersey (Princeton), but his father's death soon after forced him to return to South Carolina.

In 1783, Drayton entered school in Charleston, afterward studying law in the office of General Charles Cotesworth Pinckney, a friend and former schoolmate of his father. At the age of twenty-one, he was admitted to the South Carolina Bar, and practiced until 1794 when he retired from practice to engage in rice planting.

His introduction to public life began when he was elected a warden of Charleston in 1789. He was elected one of thirty members who represented Charleston in the convention at Columbia. He was appointed and held the office of member of the State House of Representatives for many years. He was also elected to the State Senate.

In 1798, Drayton was appointed lieutenant-governor of South Carolina by the Legislature. Upon the death of Edward Rutledge in January 1800, Drayton assumed the duties of governor of the State. In December of that year, he was elected governor of South Carolina and served a two-year term. During his administration, he recommended establishing a college in Columbia; an act passed by the Legislature in December 1801 established the South Carolina College. Because of his services to this institution, Drayton was conferred the degree of LL.D.

Also during his administration, country courts were abolished, and district courts established in their place, and construction on the Santee Canal was completed. After his gubernatorial term, Drayton was elected State senator, an office he held until December 1810, when he was again elected governor of the State. At the close of his second term, he declined re-election to the Legislature. He was appointed by Madison in 1821 as Judge of the district of South Carolina and continued in this office until his death.

Drayton authored several works, including *Letters Written During a Tour Through the Northern and Eastern States*, (1794); *A View of South Carolina*, (1802); and *Memoirs of the American Revolution*, (1821).

Drayton was married in October 1794 to Hester Rose, with whom he had seven children. He died in Charleston in November 1822.

DRAYTON, WILLIAM, (1776-1846) — a U.S. Representative from South Carolina; born in St. Augustine, Fla., December 30, 1776; attended preparatory schools in England; returned to the United States in 1790 and settled in Charleston, S.C.; studied law; was admitted to the bar December 12, 1797, and commenced practice in Charleston; member of the State house of repre sentatives 1806-1808; entered the United States Army as lieutenant colonel of the Tenth Infantry March 12, 1812; became colonel of the Eighteenth Infantry July 25, 1812; inspector general August 1, 1814, and served throughout the War of 1812; resumed the practice of law in Charleston; recorder of Charleston 1819-1824; elected to the Nineteenth Congress to fill the vacancy caused by the resignation of Joel R. Poinsett; reelected as a Jacksonian to the Twentieth, Twenty-first, and Twenty-second Congresses and served from May 17, 1825, to March 3, 1833; chairman, Committee on Military Affairs (Twentieth through Twenty-second Congresses); declined the appointment of Secretary of War in the Cabinet of President Jackson and also as Minister to England; opposed nullification in 1830; moved to Philadelphia, Pa., in August 1833; president of the Bank of the United States in 1840 and 1841; died in Philadelphia, Pa., May 24, 1846; interment in Laurel Hill Cemetery.

DRAYTON, WILLIAM HENRY, (1792-1779) — a Delegate from South Carolina; born at Drayton Hall, on Ashley River, S.C., in September 1742; pursued classical studies; attended Westminister School and Balliol College, Oxford, England; returned to South Carolina in 1764; studied law and was admitted to the bar; visited England again in 1770 and was appointed by King George III privy councilor for the Province of South Carolina; while on his way home was appointed assistant judge, but took such an active part in the pre-Revolutionary movement that he was deprived of both positions; president of the council of safety in 1775, and in 1776 was chief justice; Member of the Continental Congress in 1778 and served until his death in Philadelphia, Pa., on September 3, 1779; interment in Christ Church Cemetery.

E

EARLE, ELIAS, (1762-1823) — uncle of Samuel Earle and John Baylis Earle and great-grandfather of John Laurens Manning Irby and Joseph Haynsworth Earle), a U.S. Representative from South Carolina; born in Frederick County, Va., June 19, 1762; at tended private school; moved to Greenville County, S.C., in September 1787; was one of the earliest ironmasters of the South, and prospected and negotiated in the iron region of Georgia; member of South Carolina house of representatives, 1794-1797; member of the State senate in 1800; elected as a Republican to the Ninth Congress (March 4, 1805-March 3, 1807); elected to the Twelfth and Thirteenth Congresses (March 4, 1811-March 3, 1815); again elected to the Fifteenth and Sixteenth Congresses (March 4, 1817-March 3, 1821); died in Centerville, S.C., May 19, 1823; interment in Old Earle Cemetery, Buncombe Road, Greenville, S.C.

EARLE, JOHN BAYLIS, (1766-1863) — (nephew of Elias Earle and cousin of Samuel Earle), a U.S. Representative from South Carolina; born on the North Carolina side of the North Pacolet River, near Landrum, Spartanburg County, S.C., October 23, 1766; moved to South Carolina; completed preparatory studies; served as a drummer boy and soldier during the Revolutionary War; engaged in agricultural pursuits; elected as a Republican to the Eighth Congress (March 4, 1803-March 3, 1805); declined to be a candidate for reelection in 1804; resumed agricultural pursuits; adjutant and inspector general of South Carolina for sixteen years; served throughout the

War of 1812; member of the nullification convention of 1832 - and 1833; died in Anderson County, S.C., February 3, 1863; interment in the cemetery on his plantation, "Silver Glade," in Anderson County, S.C.

EARLE, JOSEPH HAYNSWORTH, (1847-1897) — (great-grandson of Elias Earle, cousin of Johm Laurens Manning Irby, and nephew of William Lowndes Yancey), a U.S. Senator from South Carolina; born in Greenville, Greenville County, S.C., April 30, 1847; attended private schools in Sumter, S.C.; at the outbreak of the Civil War enlisted in the Confederate Army; graduated from Furman University, Greenville, S.C., in 1867; taught school for two years; studied law; was admitted to the bar in 1870 and commenced practice in Anderson, S.C.; returned to Sumter, S.C., in 1875 and continued the practice of law; also interested in the logging business and in agricultural pursuits; member, State house of representatives 1878-1882; member, State senate 1882-1886; attorney general of South Carolina 1886-1890; declined the nomination for Governor in 1888; unsuccessful candidate for Governor in 1890; returned to Greenville in 1892; elected circuit judge in 1894; elected as a Democrat to the United States Senate and served from March 4, 1897, until his death in Greenville, S.C., May 20, 1897; interment in Christ Churchyard.

EARLE, RALPH, (1751-1801) — was a renowned painter of Revolutionary War battle scenes.

Born in Shrewsbury, Massachusetts on May 11, 1751, the son of Ralph and Phebe (Whittemore) Earle, Ralph Earle did not attend college.

Earle taught himself to paint and became an itinerant portrait artist. He traveled throughout Massachusetts and Connecticut and made his living on commissions. Strongly influenced by the work of John Singleton Copley, he developed a style that gained him a reputation as a popular portrait artist.

Earle lived in New Haven, Connecticut for a time in 1774. However, the next year he was in Lexington, Massachusetts painting scenes of the Revolutionary battle there. Earle returned to New Haven in 1776. In 1778, his loyalist sympathies forced him to flee to England, where he studied with Benjamin West and was elected as a member of the Royal Academy. While there, he painted the portraits of many prominent individuals, including members of the royal family. He returned to the United States in 1785 and for the remaining years of his life continued to travel about New England, making a living painting the portraits of well-known individuals and becoming one of the most accomplished portrait artists of the time.

Among his most famous paintings are: "The Battle of Lexington", "The Battle of North Bridge, Concord", "A View of the South Part of Lexington" and "Niagara Falls".

Earle was married twice: first to Sarah Gates in 1774 and then to Anne Whitesides. He had four children. Ralph Earle died on August 16, 1801 in Bolton, Connecticut.

EARLE, SAMUEL, (1760-1833) — (nephew of Elias Earle and cousin of Johm Baylis Earle), a U.S. Representative from South Carolina; born in Frederick County, Va., November 28, 1760; moved to South Carolina in 1774; participated in the Revolutionary War, enteri4g the service as an ensign in 1777 and leaving as captain of a company of rangers in 1782; member of the State house of representatives 1784-1788; delegate to the State convention that ratified the Federal Constitution May 12, 1788; delegate to the State constitutional convention in 1790; elected as a Republican to the Fourth Congress (March 4, 1795-March 3, 1797); died in Pendleton District, S.C., November 24, 1833; interment in Beaverdam Cemetery, Oconee County, S.C.

EDWARDS, JAMES BURROWS, (1927-   ) — Eighty-sixty state governor (R) of South Carolina, 1975-1979.

Born in Hawthorne, Florida on June 24, 1927, the son of O. Morton and Bertie (Hieronymus) Edwards. He attended the College of Charleston, the University of Louisville and the University of Pennsylvania where he studied dentistry. He was a resident at Henry Ford Hospital in Detroit from 1958 to 1960. From 1944 to 1947, he was in the U.S. Maritime Service, and from 1955 to 1957, he served in the U.S. Naval Reserve. He was married in 1951 to Ann Norris Darlington. They have two children.

Edwards moved to Charleston and began a dental practice in 1960. He was a consultant for the U.S. Public Health Service in 1964. In 1966, he became vice-president of the East Cooper Private School Corporation in Mount Pleasant, South Carolina. Two years later, he was named clinical associate in oral surgery at the Medical University of South Carolina.

He was also active in politics during this time. From 1964 to 1969, he was chairman of the South Carolina Republican Committee in Charleston County. He was a delegate to the Republican National Convention in 1968; a member of the Steering Committee of the Charleston County Republican Committee, 1969 to 1972; and a member of the Steering Committee of the South Carolina Republican Committee, 1969 to 1970. He ran for the U.S. House of Representatives in 1971, but was unsuccessful. In 1972, however, he was elected to the State Senate. Two years later he ran for governor and won, becoming the first Republican elected in South Carolina in almost a century. His victory was attributed in part to poor organization and infighting within the Democratic Party.

Edwards entered office on January 21, 1975. During his administration, new oil sites were discovered offshore, and the U.S. Marine base at Paris Island was investigated. Also, the Legislature passed a bill requiring malpractice insurance for doctors. A proponent of nuclear energy, Edwards established the South Carolina Energy Research Institute to study the energy problem, and he urged the reopening of the nuclear reprocessing plant in Barnwell, which had been closed as part of President Carter's nuclear nonproliferation policy. He also alienated many of the State's blacks when he ran a campaign to cut down on allegedly wasteful practices within the Welfare Department. Ineligible constitutionally to seek a second term, Edwards returned to his dental practice in 1979. In 1981, President Reagan named him Secretary of the Department of Energy. He remained at that post until 1982, when he became president of the Medical University of South Carolina.

ELLERBE, JAMES EDWIN, (1867-1917) — a U.S. Representative from South Carolina; born in Sellers, Marion County, S.C., January 12, 1867; attended Pine Hill Academy and the University of South Carolina at Columbia; was graduated from Wofford College, Spartanburg, S.C., in 1887; engaged in agricultural pursuits; member of the State house of representatives 1894-1896; delegate to the State constitutional convention in 1895; elected as a Democrat to the Fifty-ninth and to the three succeeding Congresses (March 4, 1905-March 3, 1913); unsuccessful candidate for renomination in 1912; resumed his agricultural pursuits; died in Asheville, N.C., October 24, 1917; interment in the family burial ground near Sellers, S.C.

ELLERBE, WILLIAM H., (1862-1899) — sixty-first state governor (D) of South Carolina, 1897-1899.

He was born in Marion, South Carolina, the son of Sarah Elizabeth Haselden and William Shackelford Ellerbe.

Ellerbe was educated at Pine Hill Academy in Marion. He attended Wofford College in Spartanburg, South Carolina, and Vanderbilt University in Nashville, Tennessee, but withdrew before graduating due to poor health. He became a planter and businessman, and established a home near Marion.

Ellerbe was elected comptroller general of South Carolina in 1890, and again in 1892. He was defeated in a bid for governor of the State in 1894.

The first statewide primary election was held in 1896. County primaries were to select delegates to a state nominating convention, but the Democratic Executive Committee, now replaced, refused to sanction the new system. After it was agreed that a primary voter must pledge to abide by the results, and that black party members must have ten whites swear that they had voted Democratic from 1876, the Executive Committee withdrew its objection.

Ellerbee was elected governor of South Carolina in November 1896. While he was in office, the counties of Bamberg, Cherokee, Dorchester, and Greenwood were organized, and all railroads operating in South Carolina were required to provide separate coaches for whites and

85

blacks. The State also raised two regiments, an independent battalion of infantry, and a unit of naval reserves, to serve in the Spanish-American War.

Ellerbe was elected to a second term in November 1898. He died in June 1899, while he was still in office. He was married in June 1887 to Henrietta Rogers, with whom he had six children.

ELLIOTT, ROBERT BROWN, (1842-1884) — a U.S. Representative from South Carolina; born in Boston, Mass., August 11, 1842; attended High Holborn Academy, London, England, in 1853, and was graduated from Eton College, England, in 1859; studied law; was admitted to the bar and practiced in Columbia, S.C.; member of the State constitutional convention in 1868; member of the State house of representatives from July 6, 1868, to October 23, 1870; assistant adjutant general of South Carolina 1869-1871; elected as a Republican to the Forty-second and Forty- third Congresses and served from March 4, 1871, until his resignation, effective November 1, 1874; again a member of the State house of representatives 1874-1876, and served as speaker; unsuccessful candidate for election as attorney general of South Carolina in 1876; moved to New Orleans, La., in 1881 and practiced law until his death there on August 9, 1884; interment in St. Louis Cemetery.

ELLIOTT, WILLIAM, (1838-1907) — a U.S. Representative from South Carolina; born in Beaufort, Beaufort County, S.C., September 3, 1838; attended Beaufort College and Harvard University; studied law at the University of Virginia at Charlottesville, and was admitted to the bar in Charleston, S.C., in 1861; upon the outbreak of the Civil War entered the Confederate Army as a Leutenant and served throughout the war attaining the rank of lieutenant colonel; at the close of the war commenced the practice of law in Beaufort, S.C.; member of the State house of representatives in 1866; intendant of Beaufort in 1866; delegate to the Democratic National Convention in 1876; unsuccessful Democratic candidate for election in 1884 to the Forty-ninth Congress; elected as a Democrat to the Fiftieth Congress (March 4, 1887-March 3, 1889);

presented credentials as a Member-elect to the Fifty-first Congress and served from March 4, 1889, until September 23, 1890, when he was succeeded by Thomas E. Miller, who contested the election; elected to the Fifty-second Congress (March 4, 1891-March 3, 1893); was not a candidate for renomination in 1892; presented credentials as a Memberelect to the Fifty-fourth Congress and served from March 4, 1895, until June 4, 1896, when he was succeeded by George w. Murray, who contested the election; elected to the Fiftyflfth, Fifty-sixth, and FiFty-seventh Congresses (March 4, 1897-March 3, 1903); was not a candidate for renomination in 1902, but was an unsuccessful candidate for election- to the United States Senate; appointed by President Theodore Roosevelt in 1906 as commissioner of the United States to mark the graves of Confederate dead in the North and served in this capacity until his death in Beaufort, S.C., on December 7, 1907; interment in St. Helena Churchyard.

ELMORE, FRANKLIN HARPER, (1799-1850) — a U.S. Representative and a Senator from South Carolina; born in Laurens District, S.C., October 15, 1799; was graduated from the South Carolina College at Columbia in 1819; studied law; was admitted to the bar in 1821 and commenced practice in Walterboro, S.C.; solicitor for the southern circuit 1822-1836; colonel on the staff of the Governor 1824-1826; elected as a State Rights Democrat to the Twenty-fourth Congress to fill the vacancy caused by the resignation of James H. Hammond; reelected to the Twenty- fifth Congress and served from December 10, 1836, to March 3, 1839; president of the Bank of the State of South Carolina 1839- 1850; declined appointment by President James Polk as Minister to Great Britain; appointed as a Democrat to the United States Senate to fdl the vacancy caused by the death of John C. Calhoun and served from April 11, 1850, until his death in Washington, D.C., May 29, 1850; interment in First Presbyterian Churchyard, Columbia, S.C.

ERVIN, JAMES, (1778-1841) — a U.S. Representative from South Carolina; born in Williamsburg District, S.C., October 17, 1778; was graduated from Rhode Island College (now Brown University), Providence, R.I., in 1797; studied law; was admitted to the bar in 1800 and commenced practice in Peedee, S.C.; member of the State house of representatives 1800-1804; solicitor of the northern judicial circuit 1804-1816; trustee of South Carolina College 1809-1817; again a member of the State house of representatives in 1810 and 1811; elected as a Republican to the Fifteenth Congress and reelected to the Sixteenth Congress (March 4, 1817-March 3, 1821); declined to be a candidate for renomination in 1820; engaged in agricultural pursuits; member of the State senate 1826-1829; served as a delegate to the State convention in 1832; died in Darlington, S.C., July 7, 1841; interment at his home.

EVANS, DAVID REID, (1769-1843) — a U.S. Representative from South Carolina; born in Westminster, England, February 20, 1769; immigrated to the United States in 1784 with his father, who Settled in South Carolina; attended Mount Zion College; studied law; was admitted to the bar in 1796 and commenced practice in Winnsboro; member of the State house of repre sentatives 1802-1805; solicitor of the middle judicial circuit 1804-1811; elected as a Republican to the Thirteenth Congress (March 4, 1813-March 3, 1815); declined to be a candidate for reelection and returned to his plantation; member of the State senate 1818-1826; first president of the Fairfield Bible Society; died in Winnsboro, Fairfield County, S.C., March 8, 1843; interment at a private residence in Winnsboro.

EVANS, JOHN GARY, (1863-1942) — sixtieth state governor (D) of South Carolina, 1894-1897.

Born in Cokesbury, South Carolina on October 15, 1863, the son of General Nathaniel and Ann Victoria (Gary) Evans. He attended Cokesbury Conference School, and Union College in Schenectady, New York. From 1894 to 1897 he was a trustee of South Carolina College. He read law and was admitted to the South Carolina Bar in 1886. In 1897, he married Emily Mansfield Plume. They had one daughter.

Evans served as the director of the Bank of Commerce in Spartanburg. From 1888 to 1892 he was a member of the State House of Representatives, and between 1892 and 1894, he served in the South Carolina Senate. He was elected Governor in 1894 on the Democratic ticket. During his term he presided over the South Carolina Constitutional Convention of 1895, helping to frame a constitution which prohibited interracial marriages, legalized school segregation, and virtually disenfranchised most black voters. The new constitution also made each county liable to pay $2000 to heirs of victims of lynchings that took place within the county's borders, and limited the incumbency of South Carolina governors to two years and a total of two terms.

Evans left office in 1897 and served as Major and Inspector General in the First Division, Seventh Army Corps during the Spanish-American War. He was later on the staff of Major General William Ludlow in Havana, Cuba, and he took part in establishing civil government in Havana when the war ended. Evans was a delegate to the Democratic National Conventions of 1896, 1900, 1912 and 1916. He was a member of the Democratic National Committee from 1918 to 1930. He died on June 27, 1942.

EVANS, JOSIAH JAMES, (1786-1858) — a U.S. Senator from South Carolina; born in Marlboro District, S.C., November 27, 1786; graduated from South Carolina College at Columbia in 1808; studied law; was admitted to the bar and began practice in Marlboro District in 1811; member, State house of representatives 1812-1813; moved to Darlington District in 1816; member, State house of representatives; State solicitor for the northern district of South Carolina 1816-1829; judge of the circuit court 1829-1835; judge of the State supreme court 1829-1852; elected as a Democrat to the United States Senate and served from March 4, 1853, until his death in Washington, D.C., May 6, 1858; chairman, Committee to Audit and Control the Contingent Expense Thirty- third through Thirtyfifth Congresses), Committee on Revolutionary Claims (Thirty-fourth and Thirty-fifth Congresses); interment in a private cemetery at his ancestral home at Society Hill, Dar lington County, S.C.

EVELEIGH, NICHOLAS, (1748?-1791) — a Delegate from South Carolina; born in Charleston, S.C., about 1748; moved with his parents to Bristol, England, about 1755; was educated in England; returned to Charleston, S.C., in 1774; during the Revolutionary War was appointed captain in the Second South Carolina Regiment (Continentals) June 17, 1775; engaged in the battle with the British fleet and forces at Fort Moultrie on June 28, 1776; was promoted to colonel and appointed deputy adjutant general for South Carolina and Georgia on April 3, 1778; resigned August 24, 1778; engaged in agricultural pursuits; member of the State house of representatives in 1781; Member of the Continental Congress in 1781 and 1782; member of the State legislative council in 1783; appointed First Comptroller of the United States Treasury on September 11, 1789, and served until his death in Philadelphia, Pa., April 16, 1791; interment probably in Philadelphia.

EVINS, JOHN HAMILTON, (1830-1884) — a U.S. Representative from South Carolina; born in Spartanburg District, S.C., July 18, 1830; attended the common schools and was graduated from South Carolina College at Columbia in 1853; studied law; was admitted to the bar in 1856 and commenced practice in Spartanburg, S.C.; entered the Confederate Army as a lieutenant and served until the close of the Civil War, attaining the rank of lieutenant colonel; resumed the practice of law in Spartanburg; member of the State house of representatives, 1862- 1864; delegate to the Democratic National Convention in 1876; elected as a Democrat to the Forty-fifth and to the three succeeding Congresses and served from March 4, 1877, until his death in Spartanburg, S.C., October 20, 1884; chairman, Committee on Territories (Forty-eighth Congress); interment in Magnolia Street Cemetery.

F

FARROW, SAMUEL, (1759-1824) — a U.S. Representative from South Carolina; born in Virginia in 1759; moved to South Carolina with his father's family, who settled in Spartanburg District in 1765; served in the Revolutionary War; studied law; was admitted to the bar in 1793 and commenced practice in Spartanburg, s.c.; also engaged in agricultural pursuits near Cross Anchor; Lieutenant Governor of South Carolina 1810-1812; elected as a Republican to the Thirteenth Congress (March 4, 1813-March 3, 1815); was not a candidate for renomination in 1814; resumed the practice of law; also engaged in agricultural pursuits; member of the State house of representatives 1816-1819 and 1822-1823; died in Columbia, S.C., November 18, 1824; interment in the family burial ground on his plantation, near the battlefield of Musgrove Mill, Spartanburg County, S.C.

FELDER, JOHN MYERS, (1782-1851) — a U.S. Representative from South Carolina; born in Orangeburg District, S.C., July 7, 1782; was graduated from Yale College in 1804; studied law in the Litchfield (Conn.) Law School; was admitted to the bar in 1808 and commenced practice in Orangeburg, S.C.; major of drafted militia in the War of 1812; elected a trustee of South Carolina College in 1812; member of the State house of representatives 1812-1816 and 1822-1824; served in the State senate 1816-1820; elected as a Jacksonian to the Twentysecond Congress and as a Nullifier to the Twenty-third Congress (March 4, 1831-March 3, 1835); declined to be a candidate for renomination in 1834; engaged extensively in agricultural pursuits and in the lumber business; member of the State senate from 1840 until his death in Union Point, Ga., September 1, 1851; interment in the family burial ground on his former plantation, " "Midway," near Orangeburg, S.C.

FINLEY, DAVID EDWARD, (1861-1917) — a U.S. Representative from South Carolina; born in Trenton, Phillips County, Ark., February 28, 1861; attended the public schools of Rock Hill and Ebenezer, S.C., and was graduated from the law department of South Carolina College (now the University of South Carolina) at Columbia in 1885; was admitted to the bar in 1886 and commenced practice in York, S.C.; member of the State house of representatives 1890-1891; served in the State senate 1892-1896; trustee of the University of South Carolina 1890-1896; elected as a Democrat to the Fifty-sixth and to the eight succeeding Congresses and served from March 4, 1899, until his death; had been reelected to the Sixty-fifth Congress; died in Charlotte, N.C., on January 26, 1917; interment in Rose Hill Cemetery, York, S.C.

FLOYD, CARLISLE (SESSIONS, JR.), (1926-) — composer and teacher, was born on June 11, 1926 in Latta, South Carolina. Floyd's musical talent was apparent by the time he had reached the age of ten when he began playing the piano without having taken any lessons. He attended Converse College on a scholarship he won when he was sixteen. He continued his education at Syracuse University, earning a Bachelor of Music degree in 1946, and the following year, accepted a teaching position at Florida State University. In 1949, while on a leave of absence, he returned to Syracuse University and got his Master of Music degree, after which, he became a piano instructor at the School of Music of Florida State University.

Floyd has written several operas, including: *Slow Dusk, Fugitives, Susannah, Wuthering Heights,* and *The Passion of Jonathan Wade. Susannah,* perhaps his most popular score and libretto, was presented at the New York City Opera Company in 1956, and was a hit with both the public and the critics. One of the latter exclaimed that it was a "hit show in the American operatic repertory if there ever was one," and the production garnered the New York Music Critics Circle Award. Critic Ronald Eyer wrote in his *Tempo* piece that it was "vitally, emotionally alive...a straightforward, unadorned story of malice, hypocrisy and tragedy of almost scriptural simplicity of language and characterization."

His next opera, *Wuthering Heights*, which had been commissioned by the Santa Fe, New Mexico Opera Association, got mixed reviews at first, but after some revisions were done, the new production was described as "a wholly successful and deeply moving opera— one of the best from an American composer." A production of this opera was performed by the Boston Lyric Opera in 1993.

Floyd is married to Margery Kay Reeder.

FRAZIER, JOE, (1944-) — prizefighter who became heavyweight boxing champion of the world. Frazier was born 12th in a family of 13 children in Beaufort, South Carolina on January 17, 1944. His parents, Rubin and Dolly, were farmers. Frazier was especially close to his father, who lost his left arm in a shotgun accident before Frazier was born. He called the young boy his "left-hand man" for his helpfulness. At the age of nine Frazier was winning neighborhood fights, and practiced punching an old flour sack filled with sand. His father would tell him, "When you grow up, you're going to be the second Joe Louis," and the boy was determined to make that dream come true.

Expelled from school for fighting in the ninth grade, Frazier began working in construction. At fifteen he married Florence Smith, and they had a son one year later. Frazier left town suddenly after beating up a white man who had insulted him with a racial slur. He traveled to Philadelphia and found a job at a slaughterhouse, then sent for his wife and child. They eventually had four more daughters.

After work Frazier would train at the Police Athletic League, where he was discovered by Yancy "Yank" Durham, who became his trainer, mentor, and inspiration. The two worked together and Frazier lost 45 pounds, bringing him down to a competition weight of 195. He won Golden Gloves titles in 1963 and 1964, then became first alternate on the Olympic team. As luck would have it, the first choice broke his hand, and Frazier was able to compete in Tokyo. He broke his left thumb in the semifinals, but he kept it secret and fought with one hand, bringing home the only Olympic boxing gold.

With a broken hand Frazier was unable to box professionally or return to work. The Olympic gold medalist found a job as a janitor, which he worked until the next spring, when he could train again. On August 16, 1965 he made his professional boxing debut, knocking out Elwood Goss in one minute and 42 seconds. After three more knockout fights Durham organized a group of 40 Philadelphia investors to buy shares in Cloverlay, Inc. which sponsored Frazier's career. He sold 80 shares at $250 each, and within 19 months there were 270 stockholders in for $3,600 each, a figure which soon doubled. In 1966 Frazier had his first fight with a rated opponent, Oscar Bonavena of Argentina in Madison Square Garden. Frazier was knocked down twice in the second round, but by the fourth round he turned the fight around and won by a decision.

By the end of 1967 Frazier had 19 straight wins under his belt, all but two won by knockouts. 'Smokin' Joe' Frazier was not what was known as a finesse fighter, but many experts agree he had much more skill than he was given credit for. He boxed out of a crouch, which was disconcerting to most fighters, who were used to seeing competitors at eye level. He would duck and weave with his head down, delivering a deadly left-hook and a strong right too. That year Muhammad Ali was stripped of his heavyweight championship title, and his boxing license was suspended because he refused to enter the draft for religious reasons. The World Boxing Association held a tournament and Jimmy Ellis won the title, while Frazier fought Buster Mathis for the New York State Athletic Commission, and was recognized as heavyweight champion for New York, Massachusetts, Illinois and Maine. Afterward he won four other bouts, and the Boxing Writers Association named him Fighter of the Year 1969. To clear up confusion, Frazier finally fought Jimmy Ellis, February 16, 1970. Ellis went down twice in the fourth round, and a technical knockout was called in the fifth. Frazier was finally declared the Heavyweight Boxing Champion of the World.

There was still one fight to be won. In the fall of 1970, a federal court ruled that it was "arbitrary and unreasonable" to deny Muhammad Ali his license to fight. Frazier and Ali finally met in the ring at Madison Square Garden March 8, 1971. It was one of the most publicized fights ever, dubbed the "Fight of the Century." The event brought in over a million dollars in ticket sales, and almost 17 million dollars in closed circuit fees for those who wanted to watch it on television. The two fighters waged a verbal battle in the press long before the event, and they were ready to go at it in the ring. Frazier stayed low and pummeled Ali around the waist and stomach, while Ali pounded Frazier in the face and head. Through a unanimous decision by the judges Frazier won the fight after fifteen rounds, but he had to be hospitalized due to injuries. Ali himself stayed in bed for weeks, unable to tolerate anything heavier on his bruised body than a light sheet.

Frazier held the title for three years, some say resting too comfortably on his laurels. In one of the most surprising upsets in boxing history, George Foreman knocked out Frazier in the second round in January of 1973. Frazier felt he could do better, but the re-match gave the same results. Some say Frazier was past his prime, too involved in other interests, or maybe he had lost his will after trainer Durham died. Whatever the reason, Frazier retired in 1976.

While fighting Frazier was singer and manager for his rock- blues bands The Knockouts and Joe Frazier's Review. He also owns Joe Frazier's Gymnasium and Joe Frazier and Sons Limousine Service, plus manages his son's fighting career.

FULMER, HAMPTON PITTS, (1875-1944) — (husband of Willa L. Fulmer), a U.S. Representative from South Carolina; born near Springfield, Orangeburg County, S.C., June 23, 1875; attended the public schools and was graduated from Massey's Business College, Columbus, Ga., in 1897; engaged in agricultural and mercantile pursuits in Norway, S.C.; also engaged in banking; member of the State house of representatives 1917-1920; elected as a Democrat to the Sixty-seventh and to the eleven succeeding Congresses and served from March 4, 1921, until his death; chairman, Committee on Agriculture (Seventy-sixth through Seventy-eighth Congresses); had been nominated for reelection to the Seventy-ninth Congress; died in Washington, D.C., October 19, 1944; interment in Memorial Park Cemetery, Orangeburg, S.C.

FULMER, WILLA LYBRAND, (1844-1968) — (wife of Hampton P. Fulmer), a U.S. Representative from South Carolina; born in Wagener, Aiken County, S.C., February 3, 1884; attended the Wagener, (S.C.) public schools and Greenville (S.C.) Female College; elected as a Democrat to the Seventy-eighth Congress to fill the vacancy caused by the death of her husband, Hampton P. Fulmer, and served from November 7, 1944, to January 3, 1945; was not a candidate for election to the Seventy-ninth Congress; engaged in agricultural pursuits until her retirement; died May 13, 1968, aboard a ship en route to Europe; interment in Memorial Park Cemetery, S.C.

FURMAN, RICHARD, (1755-1825) — one of the most influential Baptist ministers in American history.

The son of Wood and Rachel (Brodhead) Furman, he was born October 9, 1755 in Esopus, New York, while his father was in South Carolina looking for a new home for his family. Eventually the infant, his mother, and his older sister joined his father and brother near Charleston, where Wood worked as a surveyor, and eventually local magistrate and judge of probate. Young Furman was educated by his father at home. In 1770 the family moved to the High Hills of Santee, where he became a member of the Baptist church and starting preaching almost immediately. He was ordained at age nineteen and soon married Elizabeth Haynesworth, whose brother married Furman's sister.

As rumors of a Revolution grew stronger, Furman marched with his brother to Charleston to serve, but the Governor requested that the young preacher return home, because he was such an influential leader there. During the war a reward was offered by the British Army to the person to kill Furman, so he hid in North Carolina and Virginia until the revolution was over. Before he turned thirty he was considered a leader in the Baptist church not only in South Carolina, but the entire South. He accepted a new post in Charleston in 1787, the same year his wife, Elizabeth, died. In 1789 he married Dorothea Maria Burn.

Furman was an influential member of the 1790 convention, which wrote the South Carolina constitution. He became a Federalist and favored strong central authority, not only in government but in church politics as well. In 1785 he presented a plan for the Charleston Baptist Association, recommending that the Charleston Association act as the uniting group for the Baptists of South Carolina. His ideas were challenged by conservatives in the church who were suspicious of change and feared giving away their control, but eventually the Baptist State Convention was organized in in 1821, and Furman was elected president.

Furman's greatest achievement was his work in education. He taught future ministers in his home for many years, and felt that there was a strong need for an institution for teaching young pastors. He went to the stronger churches to raise money for such a project, throwing his full support behind a proposal that Baptists in Georgia and South Carolina build a college together. He died a year before the college was built in Edgefield. Eventually it was named Furman University, and moved to Greenville.

In 1814 Furman was elected president of the Baptist Triennial Convention, which supported efforts in foreign missionary work. In 1817 he was elected to that position again, and in his address he emphasized the importance of ministerial education. This speech is considered the catalyst that lead to the establishment of Columbian College (later George Washington University). Furman died in Charleston August 25, 1825.

G

GADSDEN, CHRISTOPHER, (1723-1805) — a Delegate from South Carolina; born in Charleston, S.C., February 16, 1723; attended schools in England; employed in a commercial house in Philadelphia, Pa., 1742-1745;

delegate to the Stamp Act Congress that met in New York in 1765; Member of the First Continental Congress in Philadelphia, Pa., 1774-1776; served as an officer in the Continental Army 1776-1783, and participated in the defense of Charleston in 1780; entered the service as colonel and subsequently attained the rank of brigadier general; was a framer of the State constitution in 1778; Lieutenant Governor 1778-1780; elected Governor of South Carolina in 1781, but declined; died in Charleston, S.C., September 15, 1805; interment in St. Philip's Churchyard.

GARDEN, ALEXANDER, (1731-1791) — Scottish-born doctor and naturalist from whom the gardenia gets its name.

Born in Aberdeenshire, Scotland in 1731, Garden graduated from Marischall College in Aberdeen with a medical degree in 1753. He decided to practice medicine in America, and settled in Charleston, South Carolina. He established a large medical practice, and on the side traveled the countryside identifying unique plants and animals.

In 1755 Garden joined an expedition in Cherokee country, reporting his plant and mineral finds to scientists in England. European scientists showed little respect for Garden's efforts, and rarely acknowledged or published his work. He eventually made friends with British naturalist John Ellis, who opened many doors for Garden. Garden sent numerous specimens of plant and animal life across the Atlantic, including salamanders unique to eastern American swamps, the Congo snake, and the mud eel. He also helped send electric eels for the first time. Garden was instrumental in clessifying many American plants and discovered the vermifugal properties of pink-root. After years of hard work he was finally acknowledged by the Europeans, who elected him to the Royal Society of Upsala in 1763, and in 1773 allowed him to become a fellow of the Royal Society of London.

A steadfast Loyalist, Garden was strongly against the Revolution, and disapproved of his son's participation in it. Because of his beleifs Garden was banished from the country, yet he was able to leave his land to his son. He moved to London in 1783 and traveled throughout Europe. He was elected vice- president of the Royal Society of London, a position in which he served until his death April 15, 1791. John Ellis later named the gardenia for the late doctor.

GARDEN, ALEXANDER, (1757-1829) — a revolutionary soldier and author defied his family to dedicate himself to the American Revolution.

The son of Scottish naturalist Dr. Alexander Garden and Elizabeth Peronneau, he was born in Charleston, South Carolina December 4, 1757. Garden attended the Westminster School in London from 1771 to 1775, then the University of Glasgow, graduating in 1779. While still in school he begged his father to allow him to come home and become involved in the revolutionary war, but his father, a Loyalist, forbid it. In 1780 he returned to South Carolina and enlisted, seeing active service until 1782. Charleston was evacuated in December of 1782, and although he never forgave his son for his participation in the revolution, Garden's father left over 1500 acres of land in trust to him before leaving, which saved the land from being confiscated.

In 1784 Garden married Mary Anna Gibbes and became a farmer. They adopted his wife's nephew, who was his only heir. In 1784 Garden was elected to the Assembly for one term, and then he traveled around much of the country. He was a popular writer and speaker, in demand for his eulogies and orations. His two most popular books were *Anecdotes of the Revolutionary War in America* (1822) and *Anecdotes of the American Revolution...Second Series* (1828). Both were written to inspire patriotism in young people. Garden died February 24, 1829.

GARY, FRANK BOYD, (1860-1922) — a U.S. Senator from South Carolina; born in Cokesbury, Abbeville County, S.C., March 9, 1860; attended the Cokesbury Conference School and Union College, Schenectady, N.Y.; studied law; was admitted to the bar and commenced practice in Abbeville, S.C., in 1881; member, State house of representatives 1890-1900, serving as speaker 1895-1900; delegate to the State constitutional convention in 1895;

member, State house of representatives 1906; elected as a Democrat to the United States Senate to fill the vacancy caused by the death of Asbury C. Latimer and served from March 6, 1908, to March 3, 1909; was not a candidate for reelection in 1908; member, State house of representatives tives1910; elected judge of the eighth judicial circuit in 1912 and served until his death in Charleston, S.C., December 7, 1922; interment in Long Cane Cemetery, Abbeville, S.C.

GASQUE, ALLARD HENRY, (1873-1938) — (husband of Elizabeth Hawley Gasque), a U.S. Representative from South Carolina; born on Friendfield plantation, near Hyman, Marion (now Florence) County, S.C., March 8, 1873; attended the public schools; worked on a farm and taught in the country schools for several years; was graduated from the University of South Carolina at Columbia in 1901; principal of Waverly Graded School, Columbia, S.C., in 1901 and 1902; elected superintendent of education of Florence County in 1902 and served by reelection until 1923; president of the county superintendents' association of the State in 1911 and 1912 and of the State teachers' association in 1914 and 1915; member of the Democratic State executive committee 1912-1920; chairman of the Democratic county committee 1919-1923; elected as a Democrat to the Sixty-eighth and to the seven succeeding Congresses and served from March 4, 1923, until his death in Washington, D.C., on June 17, 1938; chairman, Committee on Pensions (Seventy-second through Seventy- fifth Congresses); interment in Mount Hope Cemetery, Florence, S.C.

GASQUE, ELIZABETH HAWLEY, (1896-   ) — (now Mrs. A.J. Van Exem) (wife of Allard Henry Gasque), a U.S. Representative from South Carolina; born Elizabeth Mills Hawley on February 26, 1896, near Blythewood, on Rice Creek Plantation, Richland County, S.C.; attended private schools, South Carolina Coeducational Institute in Edgefield, and graduated from Greenville Female College in 1907; moved to Florence, S.C., in 1908; elected as a Democrat to the Seventy-fifth Congress to fill the vacancy caused by the death of her husband, Allard H. Gasque, and served from September 13, 1938, to January 3, 1939; was not a candidate for election to the Seventy-sixth Congress; active in dramatics; author and lecturer; is a resident of Cedar Tree Plantation, Ridgeway, S.C.

GEDDES, JOHN, (1777-1828) — twenty-second state governor (D-R) of South Carolina, 1818-1820.

He was born in Charleston, South Carolina, the son of Henry Geddes. His father emigrated from Ireland in 1773 and settled in Charleston, where he became a merchant.

Geddes graduated from the College of Charleston in 1795, studied law, and was admitted to the South Carolina Bar in 1797. He served in the State militia, was a major of cavalry in 1808, and was further appointed a major general.

His public career began with an election into the House of Representatives in 1808; he served through 1814, and was Speaker of the House for his last four years of service. In 1816, he was elected a member of the South Carolina Senate, and kept this position for two years.

Geddes was elected governor of South Carolina in 1818. When he first came into office, the tariff issue was of great importance in the State. In 1820, a problem arose concerning the protectionist policy of the United States Congress, and a mass meeting was held in Charleston in September of that year in protest of the policy.

The slavery issue also was becoming more volatile. In 1820, Congress declared the African slave trade an act of piracy, and provided the death penalty for any American citizens participating in the importation of slaves. However, in the same year, the question of slavery expansion appeared less critical after the acceptance of the Missouri Compromise, which permitted slavery in parts of the Louisiana Territory.

Geddes served as governor until the close of his term in 1820. Afterward, he became Intendant of Charleston, holding that office in 1824 and 1825.

Geddes was married in 1798 to Harriet Chalmers. He married a second time, to Ann Chalmers, in 1805. He died in Charleston in March 1828, and was buried in the Scotch Presbyterian Churchyard.

GERVAIS, JOHN LEWIS, (1741-1798) — a Delegate from South Carolina; born of Huguenot parents in Hanover, Germany, circa 1741; attended schools and colleges in Hanover; immigrated to England and later to the United States, arriving in Charles ton, S.C., on June 27, 1764; merchant, planter, and landowner; delegate to the provincial convention and Provincial Congress in 1775 and 1776; member of the council of safety in 1775, 1776, and 1781; appointed by Congress deputy postmaster general for South Carolina in 1778; served in the Revolutionary War, in organizing the Army and in the defense of Charleston in 1780; member of the State senate in 1781 and 1782 and served as president; Member of the Continental Congress in 1782 and 1783; commissioner of public accounts for South Carolina in 1794 and 1795; died in Charleston, S.C., August 18, 1798; interment in St. Philip's Churchyard.

GETTYS, THOMAS SMITHWICK, (1912-   ) — a U.S. Representative from South Carolina; born in Rock Hill, York County, S.C. June 19, 1912; educated in the Rock Hill public schools; attended Clemson College; Erskine College, A.B., 1933; graduate work at Duke University and Winthrop College; served with the Navy in the Pacific Theater, 1942-1946; taught and coached at Rock Hill High School, 1933-1935; principal at Central School, 1935-1941; secretary to Congressman James P. Richards, 1942-1951; postmaster, Rock Hill, 1951-1954; studied law; was admitted to the South Carolina bar in 1953 and practices law in State and Federal courts, 1954 to present; past member and chairman of the board of trustees of Rock Hill School District Three, 1953-1960; elected as a Democrat to the Eighty-eighth Congress, November 3, 1964, in a special election to fill the vacancy caused by the resignation of Robert W. Hemphill and at the same time elected to the Eighty-ninth Congress; reelected to the four succeeding Congresses and served from November 3, 1964, until his resignation December 31, 1974; was not a candidate for reelection in 1974 to the Ninety-fourth Congress; is a resident of Rock Hill, S.C.

GIBSON, ALTHEA, (1927-) athlete, was born August 25, 1927 in Silver, South Carolina, the daughter of Daniel and Annie B. (Washington). The family moved to New York City, where she soon developed a proficiency at paddle tennis. By 1942 she switched to tennis, and the following year won the New York State Negro Girls' championship. This led to a national championship in the same division in 1945 and 1946, then starting in 1947 she held the national Negro women's title for ten consecutive years. Gibson moved in 1949 to study at Florida A&M University on an athletic scholarship. While there her outstanding tennis ability led to her acceptance for competition at the National grass court championship at Forest Hills, Long Island. Gibson lost this trial, but became the first black American to compete in the All- England championships at Wimbledon in June of 1951.

After earning her B.S. in 1953 Gibson was appointed athletic instructor at Lincoln University in Jefferson City, Missouri. Over the next several years an uneven record led to her reduction in placement by the United States Lawn Tennis Association. Then suddenly during a goodwill tour in 1956 the 29 year-old player gained her stride, and burst on women's tennis like a meteorite. She won major victories in Britain, France, and India, and crowned that year by winning the doubles final at Wimbledon. Further wins followed and in 1957 she beat Darlene Hard to win the All-England women's singles at Wimbledon, the premier victory in tennis. Gibson came home to a ticker-tape parade in New York, then took the U.S. women's singles championship at Forest Hills.

In 1958 she won singles and doubles at Wimbledon again, plus saw victory at Forest Hills for a second time. Gibson appeared in the movie, *The Horse Soldiers* and wrote her autobiography, *I Always Wanted to Be Somebody.* She turned pro in 1959, toured with the Harlem Globetrotters and was also community relations representative for Ward Baking Company. In 1963 she started golfing professionally, with limited success. She was appointed to the New York State Recreation Council in 1964, was a staff member for the Essex County Parks Commissioner in New Jersey in 1970 and recreation supervisor 1970-71. She was Director of Tennis Programs and professional for Valley View Racquet Club in Northvale, New Jersey in 1972, athletic commissioner for the state of New Jersey starting in 1975, and recreation manager for the City of East Orange, New Jersey in 1980.

In recognition for her achievements in sports Gibson was named to the Lawn Tennis Hall of Fame and Museum in 1971, the Black Athletes Hall of Fame in 1974, the South Carolina Hall of Fame in 1983, and the Florida Hall of Fame in 1984.

GILDERSLEEVE, BASIL LANNEAU, (1831-1924) — a classical linguist and educator, he was considered one of America's foremost classical scholars.

Born October 23, 1831 in Charleston, South Carolina, Gildersleeve was a child prodigy. The only education he received was from his father, Rev. Benjamin Gildersleeve, yet it is reported he read the Bible from cover to cover by age five, and as a young boy was translating Latin and reading the New Testament in Greek. At the age of fourteen he received one year of formal schooling, then entered the College of Charleston. He spent one year at Jefferson College, Pennsylvania, then eventually graduated from Princeton at age 18. He taught the classics at a school in Richmond, meticulously translating all of his lectures into Greek for no other purpose than practice. He also read English, French, German, Italian and Spanish literature in his spare time.

In the summer of 1850 Gildersleeve traveled to Europe and studied in Berlin, Bonn and Gottingen. In 1853 he earned his PH.D. from Gottingen, then came home to continue his studies, write some papers, and tutor private students. Eventually he accepted a position at the University of Virginia, teaching Greek and Latin. He enlisted in the Confederate Calvary, and served during his summer breaks. He was wounded in 1864, and was haunted by memories of the war for the rest of his life. In 1866 he married Eliza Fisher Colston and they had a son and a daughter, both especially intelligent.

Gildersleeve published his first book in 1867, *Latin Grammar* (revised in 1872 and 1894). In 1875 he finished additional volumes, including the *Latin Primer*, *Latin Reader*, and *Latin Exercise-Book* along with an annotated edition of the satires of *Persius*. In 1876 he was asked to help develop curriculum for the new Johns Hopkins University, where he stayed as a Professor of Greek from 1876 to 1915. He was considered to be an unforgiving teacher, treating each mistake a "crime," but he was still loved by his students. In 1877 he published *Justin Martyr*, and in 1885 he wrote *Pindar, Olympian and Pythian Odes*, considered a landmark in the study of Pindar. In 1890 *Essays and Studies* was printed, considered brilliant yet appealing to a general audience.

In 1880 Gildersleeve founded the *American Journal of Philology*, which he edited for the next forty years. The *Journal* was a clearinghouse for American scholars, and it was a showcase for Gildersleeve's talent and skill.

In 1900 Gildersleeve finished he most long-awaited work, *Syntax of Classical Greek*, Part I. This was a part of his life work of grammar and translation. Part II was published in 1911, and the rest of the work remained unpublished until his death. On his 70th birthday he published *Studies on Honor of Basil L. Gildersleeve* (1902) a 511-page volume including contributions by former pupils. He was given many awards and honors for his works, including being twice elected to the presidency of the American Philological Association (1878 and 1909). After 60 years of teaching he retired from Johns Hopkins then he died in Baltimore January 9, 1924.

GILLESPIE, JOHN BIRKS "DIZZY", (1917-1993) — was a jazz musician who developed the bebop style of music.

Born on October 21, 1917 in Cheraw, South Carolina, the son of John and Lottie Gillespie, his father was a brick layer but also the director of a local band. There were several instruments in the house and the young boy learned to play piano, drums and trombone. By the time he was 14 years old, he had picked up the trumpet and won a full scholarship to Laurinberg Technical Institute to study both the trumpet and the piano. During this time his mother, now widowed, moved to Philadelphia. Just before his graduation in 1935, he left the school and traveled north with his trumpet.

Arriving in Philadelphia as "a real country boy", the young musician soon had a job playing in the band of Frank Fairfax. Members of the band began to call him "Dizzy" in honor of his eccentric mannerisms, such as breaking into dance on stage. A two-year stint with the Teddy Hill orchestra followed and included his first recordings. When the Hill orchestra disbanded in 1939, Gillespie quickly joined the Cab Calloway band. The next year he began his after-work experimentation with the likes of Charlie Parker and Thelonious Monk on a new style of jazz. While trying to explain the rhythm to a struggling musician, he coined the phrase "be-bop, be-bop." This new type of music was a complex and difficult mode characterized by the use of the flatted fifth, intricate chromaticism and dizzylingly fast chord progressions.

During the war, Gillespie played with such stellar talents as Benny Carter, Earl Hines and Duke Ellington. His attempts to play the new jazz led to controversy, but also to a growing fame in the jazz world. Following the war, "be-bop" became a fad, and Gillespie toured Europe to wildly enthusiastic audiences. Over the next decade his fame grew and his techniques worked their way into progressive jazz.

Gillespie toured extensively for the United States State Department in 1956 as part of an international exchange program. For the remainder of the decade and into the 1960s, Gillespie toured tirelessly, pursuing his goal as establishing jazz as a "concert music, a form of art." To that end, he brought his various groups to such bastions of serious art as the Museum of Modern Art, Lincoln Center for the Performing Arts, and Carnegie Hall, all in New York City. This phase of Gillespie's career was marked by a turning away from pure bebop toward a further integration of Brazilian and Afro-Cuban influences.

Although Gillespie's music was by this time widely accepted, his bands continued to face obstacles, particularly racial ones. One incident occurred in 1960, when Tulane University in New Orleans canceled a scheduled Gillespie concert because of a Louisiana state ordinance that banned racially mixed groups from performing — Gillespie's pianist at the time, Lalo Schifrin, was white. To put a stop to such discrimination, Gillespie became involved in an effort, backed by Norman Granz, among others, to include in the contracts of jazz musicians non-segregation clauses that applied to both the band and their audiences. Gillespie's interest in civil rights led him, in 1963, to declare his candidacy for the office of president of the United States. Gillespie ran a write-in campaign on a platform that included the elimination of federal income tax, the dissolution of the FBI and the deportation of the archsegregationalist George Wallace, then governor of Alabama, to Vietnam. He also stated he would appoint Max Roach, Charles Mingus, Louis Armstrong, Duke Ellington and other jazz musicians to cabinet posts. Gillespie never got on the ballot, but he did garner a respectable number of write-in votes.

In the 1960s, the popularity of bebop began to decline as younger music lovers turned to "free jazz" and rock. While many of his fellow veteran musicians languished, Gillespie continued to flourish. By the middle of the decade there appeared to be a bebop renaissance, with musicians like Gillespie finding themselves once again in the spotlight. Gillespie's career flourished throughout his life. Well into his 70s he maintained a full touring schedule.

Gillespie received a number of awards, including the Handel Award (New York City's highest cultural honor) for his work at the Newport Jazz Festival, a Grammy Lifetime Achievement Award and a James Smithson Bicentennial Medal from the Smithsonian Institution, among many others. His recording output has been extensive and includes the well-known albums, *Afro* and *Dizzy Gillespie, World Statesman*.

Dizzy Gillespie married Lorraine Willis in 1940. He died in Engelwood, New Jersey on January 6, 1993.

GIST, WILLIAM H., (1809-1874) — forty-third state governor (D) of South Carolina, 1858-1860.

He was born in Charleston, South Carolina, the son of Francis F. Gist.

Gist attended South Carolina College, but withdrew in his senior year, in 1827, and studied law. He was subsequently admitted to the South Carolina Bar, and began a successful law practice in the Charleston area.

From 1840 to 1844, Gist was a member of the South Carolina House of Representatives. He was then elected to the State Senate, keeping his seat from 1844 through 1856. In 1848, he was elected lieutenant governor by the the legislature, but failed to qualify and remained in the Senate.

Gist was elected governor of South Carolina in 1858. As a strong supporter of secession, he made a series of speeches to the legislature which predicted South Carolina's withdrawal from the Union. In October 1860, he sent letters to all the cotton states except Texas, stating that South Carolina would probably secede, and asking for their cooperation. In the same month, he called the legislature into extra session to select presidential electors, and expressed that some action might be necessary for the protection and safety of the State. When the legislature met in November 1860, Gist recommended that it remain in session until the outcome of the presidential election: He proposed that in the event Lincoln was elected, a convention be called and militia strengthened.

After Lincoln's election, the Secession Convention was called to meet on December 17, 1860. Gist left the gubernatorial office the same day the convention convened, and was a signer of the Ordinance of Secession on December 20. Later, he was appointed by his successor, Governor Francis W. Pickens, to the Executive Council, which virtually superceded the State's regular government. Gist was married first, to Louisa Bowen in May 1828, and second, to Mary Rice in October 1832. He died at Rose Hill, his plantation in South Carolina, in September 1874.

GOLDSTEIN, JOSEPH L(EONARD), (1940-) — physician, scientist, educator, was born in Sumter, South Carolina on April 18, 1940. He attended Washington and Lee University in Lexington, Virginia earning a B.S. degree in chemistry, *summa cum laude*, in 1962. He continued his studies at Southwestern Medical School of the University of Texas Health Science Center, receiving an M.D. degree in 1966, then did his residency at Massachusetts General Hospital.

While at the latter facility, he met another resident, Michael Brown, with whom he would work closely in future years. Both men wanted to be involved in medical research, and after they finished their residency, they went to work at the National Institutes of Health in Maryland. Goldstein worked directly under Marshall W. Nirenberg in the laboratory of biochemical genetics, and also took care of the patients of Donald S. Fredrickson who was head of the National Heart Institute. At the time, Fredrickson was researching hypercholesterolemia, a genetic disease which causes exceedingly high levels of cholesterol in blood, a condition that Goldstein was very interested in.

In 1972 Goldstein left the National Institutes of Health and moved to Seattle to work with genetic expert Arno G. Motulsky at the University of Washington School of Medicine. Goldstein was overseer of a breakthrough study concerning hereditary hyperlipidemias, which is a disease of high blood-fat levels. Later in 1972, Goldstein was chosen to head the first medical genetics department at the University of Texas Health Science Center, where he could do extensive research on what causes familial hypercholesterolemia. It was at that facility that he also reconnected with his research partner, Dr. Michael Brown, who was on staff there.

Together, Goldstein and Brown, who were so inseparable as a team that their colleagues called them "Brownstein" in jest, discovered "the existence of the cells of 'receptor' molecules that function to bind LDL's and bring them inside the cell," according to one source. The real importance of the discovery had to do with the receptor cells' connection with cholesterol and blood-fat. Genetic expert Arno G. Motulsky remarked in a *Science* article: "In a series of brilliant studies since 1974, each step in the pathway of cholesterol through the cells was meticulously defined." Writer Joanne Silberner enthusiastically noted in a *Science News* article that "Finding the LDL receptor was the initial step in a cascade of research."

Beginning in 1977, Goldstein became Paul J. Thomas professor of medicine at the University of Texas Health Science Center, and was also chairman of the department of molecular genetics. In 1985, he was named regental professor. In 1983, he was given a non-resident fellowship at The Salk Institute.

Along with co-authoring *The Metabolic Basis of Inherited Disease*, 5th edition, in 1983, Goldstein served on the editorial board of several journals, including: *Journal of Biological Chemistry*, 1981-85; *Cell*, 1983; *Journal of Clinical Investigation*, 1977-82; *Annual Review of Genetics*, 1980-85; *Arteriosclerosis*, 1981-87; and *Science*, 1985.

Along with a large number of awards and honors for their work, Goldstein and Brown received the prestigious Nobel Prize in Physiology or Medicine in 1985. The citation noted that the two researchers had "revolutionized our knowledge about the regulation of cholesterol metabolism and the treatment of diseases caused by abnormally elevated cholesterol levels in the blood." Asked to describe in simple terms what their research meant, Goldstein said: "We discovered a molecule, called a receptor, on the surface of cells that controls the blood cholesterol level." Their pioneering work opened the floodgates of research into other receptor-related areas, including those connected with myasthenia gravis, diabetes, and pernicious anemia. The new research was given the name "receptorology."

GORRIE, JOHN, (1803-1885) — probably the inventer of the first ice producing machine.

Born in Charleston, South Carolina in October of 1803, Gorrie became a physician after graduating from the College of Physicians and Surgeons in New York City in 1833. He moved to Apalachicola, Florida, to open his practice, where he married Caroline (Myrick) Beeman in May of 1838. He became active in community politics serving as postmaster from 1834 to 1838, as city treasurer and a councilor from 1835 to 1837, and as mayor from 1837 to 1839.

As a prominent physician Gorrie began experimenting with new procedures to bring down high fevers in his patients. His ideal was to create a hospital room that could maintain a constant low temperature. Using the common expansion method and ordinary air as the coolant, he succeeded, quite possibly as early as 1842. Gorrie became so infatuated with the project that he gave up his medical practice in 1845 and concentrated solely on developing machinery for making ice. In 1851 he received what could possibly have been the first U.S. patent for a refrigerating device. He spent years looking for financial backing for his project, hoping to build a large, commercial ice plant. He never found the financial aid he needed for his dream, and he died discouraged in June of 1855 in Apalachicola. His invention was displayed in a special exhibition in London in the summer of 1862 and Gorrie was later chosen as one of Florida's two representatives to be portrayed in sculpture for Statuary Hall in Washington D.C.

GOSS, JAMES HAMILTON, (1820-1886) — a U.S. Representative from South Carolina; born in Union, Union County, S.C., August 9, 1820; attended the common schools and the Union Male Academy; engaged in mercantile pursuits; served with the South Carolina Militia during the Civil War; delegate to the State constitutional convention in 1867; upon the readmission of the State of South Carolina to representation was elected as a Republican to the Fortieth Congress and served from July 18, 1868, to March 3, 1869; was not a candidate for renomination in 1868; member of the board of commissioners of Union County 1871- 1874; appointed postmaster of Union August 12, 1875, and served until September 23, 1884; died in Union, S.C., October 31, 1886; interment in the Presbyterian Cemetery.

GOURDIN, THEODORE, (1764-1826) — a U.S. Representative from South Carolina; born near Kingstree, Williamsburg County, S.C., March 20, 1764; was educated in Charleston, S.C., and in Europe; engaged in planting; elected as a Republican to the Thir teenth Congress (March 4, 1813-March 3, 1815); resumed agricultural pursuits; died in Pineville, S.C., January 17, 1826; interment in Episcopal Cemetery, St. Stephen, S.C.

GOVAN, ANDREW ROBISON, (1794-1841) — a U.S. Representative from Youth Carolina; born in Orange Parish, Orangeburg District, S.C., January 13, 1794; pursued classical studies at a private school in Willington, S.C., and was graduated from South Carolina College at

Columbia in 1813; member of the State house of representatives 1820-1821; elected to the Seventeenth Congress to fill the vacancy caused by the death of James Overstreet; reelected to the Eighteenth and Nine-teenth Congresses and served from December 4, 1822, to March 3, 1827; moved to Mississippi in 1828 and devoted the remainder of his life to planting; died in Marshall County, Miss., June 27, 1841; interment in the family cemetery on the estate, "Snowdown" plantation, Marshall County, Miss.

GRAYSON, WILLIAM JOHN, (1788-1863) — a U.S. Representative from South Carolina; born in Beaufort, S.C., November 2, 1788; pursued classical studies, and was graduated from South Carolina College at Columbia in 1809; studied law; was admitted to the bar in 1822 and commenced practice in Beaufort, S.C.; member of the State house of representatives, 1813-1815 and 1822-1825; served in the State senate 1826-1831; elected commissioner in equity for Beaufort District in 1831 and resigned from the senate; elected as a Nullifier to the Twenty-third and Twenty-fourth Congresses (March 4, 1833- March 3, 1837); collector of customs at Charleston from August 9, 1841, to March 19, 1853; retired to his plantation; was a frequent contributor to the Southern Quarterly Review; died in Newberry, S.C., on October 4, 1863; interment in Magnolia Cemetery, Charleston, S.C.

GREGG, WILLIAM, (1800-1867) — was a pioneer industrialist who is considered the father of southern cotton manufacturing.

Born on February 2, 1800 near Carmichaels in Monongalia County (now West Virginia), William Gregg was apprenticed to a watchmaking uncle with whom he also operated a small cotton factory during the War of 1812. By 1824, when he was 24 years old, he had completed his training and begun his own watchmaking business in Columbia, South Carolina. Within 10 years, ill health forced his retirement but he had managed to amass a small fortune and was free to follow his growing interest in manufacturing.

Gregg acquired an interest in a small cotton factory and was able to turn it into a profitable business. In 1838, he moved to Charleston and began to develop his ideas on the need for industrialization in the one-crop "Cotton Kingdom." As a result of a tour of manufacturing areas in New England and the middle states, he published, in 1844, a series of articles on industrialization in the *Charleston Courier*. These articles appeared as a pamphlet, titled *Essays on Domestic Industry*, the following year. The effect was immediate. In 1846, after obtaining with great difficulty the first limited liability charter granted by the South Carolina legislature, Gregg began erecting a factory and a town for workers near Aiken. The enterprise included housing, educational, health and recreational facilities for the tenants. The factory was opened two years later and was highly successful. Landless whites, who had no place in the predominantly agricultural economy, eagerly took up factory work and Graniteville quickly grew to a population of 900. With this as an example, similar communities were built throughout the South. In 1856 and 1857, Gregg served in the state House of Representatives, but apart from that interruption, devoted himself to his mill and his mill work.

Although he was pro-industry and in favor of protective tariffs, in 1860 Gregg supported secession at the South Carolina convention. In *Debow's Review* he published an article urging southerners to prepare for war. During the Civil War, he was able to maintain the factory's production, however, in 1867 a flood seriously damaged the factory. His efforts to repair the plant led to his death.

Gregg's success stemmed from the fact that unlike the few others in the antebellum South who advocated industrial development, Gregg practiced what he preached. He did not leave supervision to others, but gave every phase of construction and operation his personal attention. In demonstrating the advantages of a varied economy — manufacture, agriculture and internal commerce — he was undoubtably influenced by Henry C. Carey of Philadelphia, who was a supporter of widespread American economic development. However, his support for the institution of slavery, in contrast to Carey, was his downfall. After striving to imitate the diversified economy of the

North, and to discourage hostility to that section, he ended by approving of secession and produced war materials for the Confederacy. In proof of his error, widespread industrial progress in the South waited upon military and political defeat, and did not commence until the 1880s.

William Gregg married Marina Jones in 18229. He died on September 13, 1867 in Graniteville, South Carolina.

GRIFFIN, JOHN KING, (1789-1841) — a U.S. Representative from South Carolina; born near Clinton, Laurens County, S.C., August 13, 1789; pursued an academic course; engaged as a planter; served in the State house of representatives 1816-1819; member of the State senate 1820-1824 and again in 1828; elected as a Nullifier to the Twenty-second through Twentyfifth Congresses and as a Democrat to the Twenty-sixth Congress (March 4, 1831-March 3, 1841); died near Clinton, S.C., August 1, 1841; interment in Little River Church Cemetery.

GRIMKE, ANGELINE E., (1805-1879) — abolitionist who met with other reformers in New Jersey, was born in Charleston, South Carolina, the daughter of Judge John F. Grimke and his wife, who owned a number of slaves. She was educated at home. Following her older sister Sarah's disgust with the slave-owning society, she joined the Quakers in Charleston, but failed to get any of her other family members to stop keeping slaves. When their parents died in 1826, Sarah and Angelina freed all the slaves. Angelina then joined her sister in "voluntary exile" from the South, becoming a member of the Philadelphia Society of Friends in 1831. She wrote an abolitionist article for the *Liberator* journal in 1835, which made her prominent in anti-slavery circles. Her "Appeal to Christian Women of the South" was published in London in 1836 and widely distributed by American Quakers. The American Anti-Slavery Society in New York invited her to lecture to men and women in private houses. The Grimkes also actively pursued equal rights for women with their articles "Letters to Catherine Beecher," and "Letters on the Equality of the Sexes and the Condition of Women," both published in 1838. That same year, Angelina married abolitionist Theodore Weld, a Presbyterian, which caused her ouster from the Society of friends. The Welds and Sarah Grimke then moved to New Jersey, in Raritan Bay Union at Belleville. There they founded a communal group with a school where anti-slavery proponents could develop their ideas. Angelina had three children which she reared there. After 1865 , she moved to Hyde Park, Massachusetts to teach in the Lewis Progressive School. She died there after many years of advocating women's rights and abolition.

GRIMKE, SARAH MOORE, (1792-1873) — social reformer, fighting for the rights of blacks and women. Born November 26, 1792 in Charleston, South Carolina, Grimke's name is closely associated with her younger sister's, Angelina Emily. The two were raised in a wealthy, aristocratic family, but were dissatisfied with the debutante lifestyle and the structure of the Episcopalian Church. They questioned the institution of slavery, and Grimke was especially disappointed when she was not allowed to study law because she was a woman. While on a trip to Philadelphia when she was 27 Grimke was introduced to the Society of Friends, or the Quaker church, which supported the abolition of slavery. She studied many religions, and decided a year later to move north and join the church, encouraging her sister to do the same.

The two became dissatisfied again however, as the Philadelphia Friends seemed to be strict in their lifestyles of modesty, economy and charity, yet wavered on the dedication to the cause of Abolition. The sisters wanted to do more to serve humanity. The younger took the first step by writing an encouraging letter to William Lloyd Garrison, which was published in the *Liberator*. Grimke disapproved of more active participation at first, but eventually she joined her sister in speaking and writing. Grimke wrote the pamphlet *Epistle to the Clergy of the Southern States* in 1827, encouraging clergy to become more involved in the Abolition movement on a moral basis.

At about this time their father passed away, and the two asked for the slaves as their portion of the estate, which they promptly freed. Of that decision Grimke said, "As I left my native state on account of slavery, deserted the home of my fathers to escape the sound of the driver's lash and the shrieks of the tortured victims, I would gladly bury in oblivion the recollections of those scenes with which I have been familiar. But it may not, can not be; they come over my memory like gory spectres, and implore me with resistless power in the name of humanity, for the sake of the slave-holder as well as the slave, to bear witness to the horrors of the southern prison-house."

The two began speaking for larger and larger audiences, and were generally received with great enthusiasm. Yet some were not comfortable with women as speakers and leaders in a movement. The General Association of Congregational Ministers of Massachusetts wrote a pastoral letter condemning female preachers and reformers. Because of this letter the two felt it was important to become more involved in the woman's rights movement. They felt that the issues of slavery and woman's rights were closely connected, serving to oppress women both black and white, especially in the South. In her pamphlet *Letter on the Equality of the Sexes and the Condition of Woman* (1838) Grimke wrote that the pages of history were "wet with woman's tears" and the dominion over women in the name of protection was unrighteous, and that women should "plant themselves, side by side, on the platform of human rights, with man, to whom they were designed to be companions, equals and helpers in every good word and work." Eventually the two won many abolitionists over to the cause of women's rights.

In 1838 Grimke joined her sister and her new husband, Abolitionist Theodore Dwight Weld, in the operation of a school in Belleville, New Jersey. Later the three moved to Hyde Park, Massachusetts, where the sisters remained involved in woman's rights and Abolition. In 1867 Grimke translated Lamartine's Joan of Arc to English. She died December 23, 1873.

GUERARD, BENJAMIN, (1740-1789) — fifth state governor of South Carolina, 1783-1785.

He was born in South Carolina. His grandfather, John Guerard, was a French Huguenot of noble extraction who immigrated to London in 1865, after the repeal of the

Edict of Nantes. The family subsequently settled in Charleston. His father was married to the daughter of Chief Justice Charles Hill, and Guerard developed an interest in law from this association.

Guerard earned a commission to practice law at the South Carolina Bar in January 1761. At the outbreak of the American Revolution, he identified himself with the patriots and rose to a position of prominence among their ranks. When the British overtook Charleston, he was captured, taken prisoner, and moved to Philadelphia. Many of his fellow captives there were destitute, and he generously offered to come to their aid; he possessed extensive property, and asked to pledge it as security for a sum to be exclusively appropriated for their care. Although he failed in this undertaking, his conduct paved the way for his subsequent success in a public career.

Guerard was chosen a member of the Privy Council under Governor Mathews and, along with Edward Rutledge, acted as commissioner to negotiate an agreement with the British which would prevent plunder when they evacuated Charleston.

He was elected governor of the State of South Carolina in February 1883, continuing in office until the end of his term in 1785. During his administration, Charlestown became incorporated under its present name of Charleston. The town of Stateburg was also founded by Gen. Sumter during his appointment, and cotton was first cultivated in the State for export on a limited scale.

Guerard was married in November 1766 to Sarah Middleton. He was married a second time to the granddaughter of Benjamin Godin. He died in Charleston, South Carolina in January 1789.

H

HAGOOD, JOHNSON, (1829-1898) — fifty-fifth state governor (D) of South Carolina, 1880-1882.

He was born in Barnwell, South Carolina, the son of Indina Allen and James O. Hagood.

Hagood attended Richmond Academy in Augusta, Georgia, and graduated from The Citadel in Charleston, South Carolina in 1847. After studying law under Judge Edmond Bellinger, he was admitted to the South Carolina Bar in 1850.

Hagood was appointed adjutant-general of the South Carolina Militia in 1851. He was afterward appointed commissioner in equity for Barnwell District, and kept this position until he resigned in 1861 at the outbreak of the Civil War.

Hagood was given the rank of colonel of the First South Carolina Regiment, and was promoted to brigadier-general in 1862. His command surrendered with Johnston in Greensboro, North Carolina.

After the war, Hagood resumed supervision of his planting interests. He was an unsuccessful candidate for the United States Congress in 1888. He was a member of the Taxpayers' Convention in 1871 and 1874, and was named vice president of the Democratic State Convention in 1876. In 1876, he was appointed the comptroller-general of South Carolina, and kept this office through 1880.

Hagood was elected governor of South Carolina in November 1880. During his term, he worked to give the State a business- like administration, and to stimulate the State's economy. Also during his tenure, Hagood worked to end formal dueling among State politicians, and succeeded in passage of a law in 1881 which disqualified for public office any person who acted as a principal or second in a duel.

After his term ended, Hagood chose not to run for re-election. Returning to his plantation near Barnwell, he subsequently was elected president of the Agricultural and Mechanical Society, president of the board of visitors of the South Carolina Military Academy, and served two terms as the chairman of the State Board of Agriculture.

Hagood was married to Eloise B. Butler in November 1856. He died in Barnwell, South Carolina in January 1898.

HAMILTON, JAMES, JR., (1786-1857) — twenty-eighth state governor (D) of South Carolina, 1830-1832.

He was born in Charleston, South Carolina, the son of Elizabeth Heyward and James Hamilton.

Hamilton received his early education in Newport, Rhode Island, and his formal schooling in Dedham, Massachusetts. He studied law in Charleston, and was admitted to the State Bar in 1810. He volunteered for military duty during the War of 1812, and became First Lieutenant of Rifles in June 1812. After a transfer to the Eighteenth Infantry in August 1812, he became a regimental adjutant and was promoted to captain in 1813, then to major in 1814.

At the war's end, he formed a law partnership with James Louis Petigru. In 1822, he became Intendant of Charleston and a member of the United States House of Representatives, holding this position through 1829.

Hamilton was elected governor of South Carolina in 1830. A staunch supporter of the doctrine of nullification throughout the State, he challenged the federal Tariff Act of 1832. In October 1832, a special session of the Legislature, the Nullification Convention of 1832, was called. Hamilton was its president, and the Ordinance of Nullification passed, which declared the federal tariffs of 1826 and 1832 null and void within the State after February 1833.

His term ended in December 1832, but Hamilton was quickly given the rank of brigadier-general and placed in command of the State's troops. He raised a force of 27,000 men; however, he was opposed to a civil war, and supported the compromise which settled the tariff issue.

Hamilton left public life for a time, and operated five rice and two cotton plantations, organized the Bank of Charleston, and served as a director of the Louisville, Cincinnati and Charleston Railroad. He was made a perpetual citizen of the Republic of Texas in 1835, held a seat in the South Carolina Senate in 1836, and was appointed the Diplomatic Agent of the Republic of Texas to France, Great Britain, Belgium, and the Netherlands in 1839. In 1855, he moved to Texas, where he held a large land grant.

Hamilton died on November 15, 1857, when the steamship *Opelousas*, on which he was a passenger, collided with the ship, *Galveston*, and sank in the Gulf of Mexico.

HAMILTON, PAUL, (1762-1816) — fifteenth state governor (D-R) of South Carolina, 1804-1806.

He was born in St. Paul's Parish, South Carolina, the son of Rebecca and Archibald Hamilton.

Hamilton attended local schools until the age of sixteen, when he was forced to withdraw because of financial considerations.

He served in the South Carolina militia during the American Revolution, and fought as a guerilla during the latter part of the war. Hamilton became a rice and indigo planter at the war's end, and was also a tax collector for St. Paul's Parish in 1785 and 1786. He was a Justice of the Peace in 1786.

Hamilton's public life began in 1787 when he was elected to the South Carolina House of Representatives, and was a member of the State Convention which ratified the United States Constitution in 1789. He was elected to the South Carolina Senate in 1794, and again in 1798.

In December 1804, he was elected governor of South Carolina. During his administration, the question of importation of slaves once again became a major issue. When the U.S. Congress proposed a tax on imported slaves, the State Legislature threatened to repeal its restriction on the importation of male slaves over fifteen years of age, and the congressional action was dropped. During Hamilton's gubernatorial term, there was an attempt to reapportion the Legislature in the State, but the plan was defeated by the House of Representatives.

After his term as governor, Hamilton served as Secretary of the Navy under President James Madison from 1809 to 1812. Difficulties with Great Britain were in serious condition at the time, and war was declared by the U.S. on June 18, 1812. Authority was given for the construction of four naval ships, six frigates, and six sloops of war. In August 1812, the naval ship *Constitution* captured the British ship *Guerriere*. In October of that year, a British frigate surrendered to the American sloop of war *Wasp*, and in the same month, the frigate

United States captured the British *Macedonia*. Hamilton resigned his position in December 1812.

Hamilton was married to Mary Wilkinson in October 1782. He died in Beaufort, South Carolina in June 1816.

HAMLIN, TALBOT FAULKNER, (1889-1956) — was a Columbia University professor and architect.

Born in New York City on June 16, 1889, the son of Alfred Dwight Foster and Minnie Florence (Marston) Hamlin, Talbot Hamlin received an A.B. degree from Amherst College in 1910 and a B. Arch. from Columbia University School of Architecture in 1914. He also received an honorary D. Sc. from Dickinson College in 1952.

Hamlin gained notoriety as an architect, as a teacher in Columbia University's School of Architecture, and as the author of many books and articles. Throughout his life, he made clear his philosophy that buildings exist primarily for people and not as an expression of any particular style or dogma. He said that "today's buildings should be modern because people are modern."

Hamlin's long career began in 1914, when he went to work as a draftsman for the firm of Murphy & Dana in New York. In 1920, he was made a partner and the firm became Murphy, McGill & Hamlin. Among its clients was Ginling College in Nanking, China, which took him overseas in a supervisory capacity in 1922. Other construction with which Hamlin was concerned were buildings of the College of New Rochelle in New Rochelle, New York. In 1925, the name of his firm became McGill & Hamlin.

In 1930, he went into business for himself, but the Depression was a bad time for architects. Fortunately, many years before this, in 1916, Hamlin had started his career at the Columbia School of Architecture as a lecturer in extension courses. In later years, 1935 until 1945, he was also librarian of the Avery Library in the School of Architecture and of the Fine Arts Library. He made full professor in 1947.

Hamlin's writing career began in 1916 when he published the first of the many critical books on architecture for which he is known. This work was *The Enjoyment of Architecture*, of which Claude Bragdon wrote in *Dial* in

January of 1917, "His book is full of the fine enthusiasm of youth without the rawness of youth...but the great defect of Hamlin's attitude is his incorrigible optimism." This optimism was not so great, however, that it prevented Hamlin from writing books and magazine articles in which he was sometimes very critical of American architectural fads.

In 1926, Hamlin published *The American Spirit in Architecture*; in 1939 he published *Some European Architectural Libraries* and in 1940 he published, *Architecture Through the Ages*, which was heralded by *Books* as "the most comprehensive, authoritative and interesting one-volume history of architecture in English."

Other books by Hamlin include: *Greek Revival Architecture in America*, 1944; a rewritten *The Enjoyment of Architecture*, with a new title of *Architecture, An Art for All Men*, 1947; and *We Took to Cruising*, written with his third wife, Jessica, in 1951. He edited a four-volume work, *Forms and Functions of Twentieth Century Architecture*, which was published in 1954. Hamlin's biography of Benjamin Henry Latrobe won him the Pulitzer Prize in 1956.

When Hamlin retired from Columbia University in 1954, becoming a professor emeritus, the New York *Times* reported him as saying "New York architecture is dead, killed by high land cost and a striving for the last tenth of one percent of rent. Manhattan is getting to be one vast slum with oases of luxury apartments for the wealthy." He proposed that a new development plan for New York and surrounding areas be studied, with more attention given to providing parks in outlying boroughs and more action be taken on limited-dividend slum clearance housing projects in Manhattan by savings banks and insurance companies.

The architect contributed to the fourth edition of the *Encyclopedia Britannica* and the *Dictionary of American Biography*. He was a fellow of the American Institute of Architects, an honorary associate of the New York Historical Society, and for many years was on the architectural committee of the Museum of Modern Art in New York City. He also served on the architects' advisory committee of the Federal Public Housing Authority. He was a member of Phi Beta Kappa.

Talbot Hamlin was married three times. He married Hilda B, Edwards on September 11, 1916. They had three children. This marriage ended in divorce and on November 17, 1926, he married Sarah H.J. Simpson. She died in 1930. His third wife was Jessica V. Walters, to whom he was married on June 10, 1931. He died on October 7, 1956.

HAMMOND, JAMES HENRY, (1807-1864) — a U.S. Representative and a Senator from South Carolina; born in Newberry District, S.C., November 15, 1807; graduated from the South Carolina College (now the University of South Carolina) at Columbia in 1825; taught school and wrote for a newspaper; studied law, was admitted to the bar in 1828 and practiced in Columbia; established a newspaper to support nullification; planter; elected as a Nullifier to the Twenty-fourth Congress in 1834 and served from March 4, 1835, until February 20, 1836, when he resigned because of ill health; spent two years in Europe; returned to South Carolina and engaged in agricultural pursuits; Governor of South Carolina 1842-1844; elected as a Democrat to the United States Senate in 1857 to fill the vacancy caused by the resignation of Andrew P. Butler and served from December 7, 1857, to November 11, 1860, when he retired; died at "Redcliffe," Beach Island, S.C., November 13, 1864.

HAMPTON, WADE, (1752-1835) — (grandfather of Wade Hampton (1818-1902), a U.S. Representative from South Carolina; born in Virginia in 1752; received a thorough education; engaged in agricultural pursuits; moved to South Carolina; served in the Revolutionary War as lieutenant colonel of the regiment of light dragoons in General Sumter's brigade of State troops; served in the state assembly, 1779-1786 and 1791; elected as a Republican to the Fourth Congress (March 4, 1795-March 3, 1797); unsuccessful candidate for reelection; elected to the Eighth Congress (March 4, 1803-March 3, 1805); unsuccessful candidate for reelection; colonel in the United States Army in 1808; appointed brigadier general in February 1809 and major general March 2, 1813; served in the War of 1812 until April 6, 1814, when he resigned;

died in Columbia, S.C., on February 4, 1835; interment in Trinity Churchyard, Columbia, S.C.

HAMPTON, WADE, (1818-1902) — fifty-second state governor (R) of South Carolina, 1876-1879.

He was born in Charleston, South Carolina, the son of Ann Fitzsimmons and Colonel Wade Hampton.

Hampton received his education at Columbia Academy, earned an A.B. degree at South Carolina College in 1836, and studied law.

During the Civil War, he raised and commanded "Hampton's Legion," was promoted to major general in August 1863, and commanded the Cavalry of the Army of North Virginia.

He was elected to the South Carolina House of Representatives in 1852, serving until 1858, when he was elected to the South Carolina Senate. He kept his Senate seat until 1861, when he was appointed a trustee of South Carolina College.

Hampton organized the "Red Shirts" in South Carolina to oppose the reconstruction policies of the Radical Republicans, carpetbaggers, and "scalawags." As the Democratic nominee for governorship in 1876, Hampton appeared to have lost the election. The results were dubious, however, since the State Canvassing Board had rejected all votes cast in Edgefield and Laurens counties. When the State Supreme Court ordered votes counted from the two counties, the final count was in Hampton's favor, 92,261 to Chamberlain's 91,127.

Chamberlain refused to leave office, however; Hampton did not take control of the executive office until April 1877, when federal troops were withdrawn from South Carolina by President Rutherford B. Hayes as part of the Compromise of 1877.

Hampton's election symbolized the end of Reconstruction in the State. He immediately ordered the new Legislature, now controlled by the Democrats, into special session, and began work on the State's usury law and the public debt.

Hampton was elected to a second gubernatorial term in February 1879, but resigned from office because of a serious wound received in a hunting accident. He was later elected to the United States Senate, serving from 1879 through 1891. In 1893, he was appointed United States Railroad Commissioner; he held this post until 1897.

Hampton was married to Margaret Preston in 1838, and was married a second time, to Mary Singleton Duffie, in 1851. He died in Columbia, South Carolina in April 1902.

HARE, BUTLER BLACK, (1875-1967) — (father of James Butler Hare), a U.S. Representative from South Carolina; born on a farm in Edgefield (now Saluda) County, near Leesville, S.C., November 25, 1875; attended the public schools; was graduated from Newberry (S.C.) College in 1899; taught in the public schools 1900-1903; secretary to Representative George W. Croft in 1904 and to his successor, Representative Theodore G. Croft, in 1905; professor of history and economics in Leesville (S.C.) College 1906-1908; special agent in the woman and child labor investigation conducted by the United States Bureau of Labor in 1908 and 1909; was graduated from George Washington University, Washington, D.C., in 1910, and from its law department in 1913; was admitted to the bar in 1913 and and commenced practice in Saluda, S.C., in 1915; worked for the United States Department of Agriculture 1911-1924; engaged in agricultural pursuits; resumed the practice of law in Saluda, S.C., in 1924 and 1925; elected as a Democrat to the Sixty-ninth and to the three succeeding Congresses (March 4, 1925-March 3, 1933); chairman, Committee on Insular Affairs (Seventy-second Congress); was not a candidate for renomination in 1933; resumed his former pursuits; elected to the Seventy-sixth and to the three succeeding Congresses (January 3, 1939-January 3, 1947); unsuccessful candidate for renomination in 1946; resumed the practice of law and his agricultural pursuits; died in Saluda, S.C., December 30, 1967; interment in Travis Park Cemetery.

HARE, JAMES BUTLER, (1918-1966) — (son of Butler Black Hare), a U.S. Representative from South Carolina; born in Saluda, S.C., September 4, 1918; attended the public schools; was graduated from Newberry College in

1939; postgraduate work at Erskine College, Due West, S.C., in 1941; enlisted in the United States Navy in August 1940 and released to inactiYe duty in the Naval Reserve as a lieutenant commander in January 1946 with thirty-two months in the Pacific Theater; was graduated from the law school of the University of South Carolina in 1947; was admitted to the bar the same year and commenced the practice of law in Saluda, S.C.; member of the board of trustees of the University of South Carolina; elected as a Democrat to the Eighty-first Congress (January 3, 1949-January 3, 1951); unsuccessful candidate for renomination in 1950; recalled to active duty in the United States Navy January 1, 1950, and served as law specialist until released to inactive duty as a commander in May 1952; resumed the practice of law in Saluda, S.C.; died in Columbia, S.C., July 16, 1966; interment in Travis Park Cemetery, Saluda, S.C.

HARLEY, JOSEPH EMILE, (1880-1942) — Seventy-fifth state governor (D) of South Carolina, 1941-1942.

Born in Williston, South Carolina on September 14, 1880, the son of Lunsford and Mary (Hummel) Harley. He received his education at South Carolina Co-Educational Institute and the University of South Carolina. During the Spanish-American War, he was a sergeant in the First South Carolina Volunteers. He was later captain of the South Carolina National Guard, eventually rising to the rank of colonel and serving on the staff of Governor Thomas G. McLeod. He was married to Sarah Richardson and had three children.

For several years, Harley had a private law practice in Barnwell. In 1905, he became a member of the State House of Representatives. He served until 1906, and again from 1927 to 1930. In 1908, 1920, and 1938 he was a delegate to the Democratic National Convention. Meanwhile, from 1912 to 1922, he was Mayor of Barnwell. The South Carolina Supreme Court appointed him in 1924 as a special judge. In 1934, he became Lieutenant Governor of South Carolina. He remained at that post until November, 1941 when Governor Maybank resigned to take a seat in the U.S. Senate. Harley succeeded to the governorship but served only four months.

His short time in office was mainly concerned with putting the state on a wartime footing as the country entered World War II. He died in office on February 27, 1942.

HARPER, ROBERT GOODLOE, (1765-1825) — a U.S. Representative from South Carolina and a U.S. Senator from Maryland; born near Fredericksburg, Va., in January 1765; moved with his parents to Granville, N.C., about 1769; received his early education at home and later attended grammar school; joined a volunteer corps of Cavalry when only fifteen years of age and served in the Revolutionary Army; made a surveying tour through Kentucky and Tennessee in 1783; graduated from the College of New Jersey (now Princeton University) in 1785; studied law in Charleston, S.C., teaching school at the same time; was admitted to the bar in 1786 and commenced practice in Ninety-Sixth District, S.C.; moved to Charleston, S.C., in 1789; member, State house of representatives 1790-1795; elected from South Carolina to the Third Congress to fill the vacancy caused by the death of Alexander Gillon; reelected to the Fourth, Fifth, and Sixth Congresses and served from February 1795 to March 1801; unsuccessful candidate for reelection in 1800 to the Seventh Congress; chairman, Committee on Ways and Means (Fifth and Sixth Congresses); one of the managers appointed by the House of Representatives in 1798 to conduct the impeachment proceedings against William Blount, a U.S. Senator from Tennessee; moved to Baltimore, Md., and engaged in the practice of law; served in the War of 1812, attaining the rank of major general; assisted in organizing the Baltimore Exchange Co. in 1815 and was a member of The Board of Directors; member, State senate of Maryland; elected from Maryland to the United States Senate for the term beginning March 4, 1815, and served from January 1816 until December 1816, when he resigned; unsuccessful Federalist candidate for vice president in 1816; traveled extensively in Europe in 1819 and 1820; took a prominent part in the ceremonies on the occasion of Lafayette's visit to Baltimore in 1824; died in Baltimore, Md., January 14, 1825; interment in the family burial ground on his estate, "Oakland"; reinterment in Greenmount Cemetery, Baltimore, Md.

HARPER, WILLIAM, (1790-1847) — a U.S. Senator from South Carolina; born on the island of Antigua, West Indies, January 17, 1790; immigrated to the United States with his parents, who settled in Charleston, and later in Columbia, S.C., in the 1790s; attended the common schools, Mount Bethel Academy, and Jefferson Monticello Seminary; graduated from South Carolina College (now the University of South Carolina) at Columbia in 1808; studied medicine for a time in Charleston and later studied law; was admitted to the bar in 1813 and commenced the practice of law in Columbia; trustee of South Carolina College in 1813; member, State house of representatives tives1816-1817; moved to Missouri in 1818; chancellor of the State of Missouri 1819-1823; member of the State constitutional convention in 1821; returned to Columbia, S.C., in 1823; reporter of the State supreme court 1823-1825; appointed as a Jacksonian to the United States Senate to fill the vacancy caused by the death of John Gaillard and served from March 8 to November 29, 1826, when a successor was elected; practiced law in Charleston; member, State house of representatives 1827-1828, serving as speaker; chancellor of the State of South Carolina 1828-1830; returned to Columbia, S.C.; appointed judge of the court of appeals 1830-1835; member of the State convention in 1832 and 1833 (known as the Nullification Convention); again chancellor of the State from 1835 until his death in Fairfield District, S.C., October 10, 1847; interment in Means Family Burial Ground, Fairfield County, S.C.

HARRELSON, KENNETH SMITH, (1941 -) — was a Cleveland Indians baseball player known for his nonconformist demeanor.

Born on September 4, 1941 in Woodruff, South Carolina, Ken Harrelson was an accomplished athlete by the time he was graduated from high school. He rejected many offers of basketball scholarships and opted to go into professional baseball directly from high school in 1959. Of the six major league teams that wanted him, the Brooklyn Dodgers (now the Los Angeles Dodgers) and the Kansas City Athletics (now the Oakland Athletics) made him the best offers. He signed with the Athletics for $27,000, a bonus to be paid out over three years.

Harrelson's first assignment in the Kansas City farm system was to Olean, New York, where he played outfield. Throughout the next few years he played for teams in Sanford, Florida; Visalia, California; Binghamton, New York; Portland, Oregon; and Dallas, Texas.

As a starting first baseman for the Athletics in 1965, Harrelson batted .238 and led the team in home runs (23) and RBI's (66). The Kansas City playing field, with its distant, high right field, was unfavorable to right-handed power hitters like Harrelson, and coach Al Vincent taught Harrelson to shorten his swing and to settle, when expedient, for short hits. Under the tutelage of Alvin Dark, who became manager of the Athletics after 1965 season, he improved his concentration and general attitude. "Baseball...wasn't just a job to me anymore," Harrelson told John Devaney of *Sport* in October of 1968.

In June of 1966, Harrelson was traded to the Washington Senators. With Washington, Harrelson batted .237 in 1966 and .203 in the first two months of the 1967 season. After he was traded back to Kansas City in June of 1967, his batting average rose to .305 and his final season tallies were a .273 average, nine homers and 40 RBI's. After turbulent Athletics owner Charles O. Finley fired manager Alvin Dark, in August of 1967, Harrelson told reporters that Finley's actions had been "bad for baseball." When Harrelson refused to retract his statement, Finley unconditionally released him from his contract.

The dismissal turned out to be a blessing for Harrelson. At Kansas City, Finley was paying him only $12,500 a year and Harrelson, who tended to underestimate his financial worth, was $20,000 in debt. As soon as his availability was announced, other clubs approached him with more money. He accepted the offer of the Boston Red Sox of a $73,000 bonus and at least $25,000 a year, which was later raised to $50,000. Harrelson played 23 games with Boston at the end of the 1967 season, driving in 14 runs as the Red Sox took the American League pennant. In 1968, he led the league in RBI's (109) and finished second in homers (35). He had a batting average of . 280.

Just as important, he became a celebrated public personality. Harrelson fan clubs sprang up throughout New England and spectators at sell-out games in Fenway Park shouted "Hawk (his nickname) Baby, we love you." He became a common figure on television, as a featured guest and endorser of commercial products, and even became the subject of a rock song, "Don't Walk the Hawk."

At the beginning of the 1969 season, Boston needed desperately to strengthen its pitching and catching staff, and the front office decided to make Harrelson the key figure in a multi-player deal designed to bring pitcher Sonny Seibert and other players from the Cleveland Indians. When the deal was announced on April 19, 1969, Harrelson "retired" from baseball in protest. However, after a four-hour meeting with Bowie Kuhn, the commissioner of baseball, and Gabe Paul, general manager of the Indians — who offered him more money than he had been making with the Red Sox — Harrelson relented.

Upset over leaving Boston, he slumped badly in batting. He finished the season with a tally of 30 home runs and 92 RBI's. His batting average was .221 and his fielding average was .985. During the 1970 season, he was sidelined with a leg injury.

After a bad start in the 1971 season, Harrelson retired from baseball at the age of 29. He then took up professional golf, but dropped out of the Professional Golfers' Association qualifying tournament when he made 24 over par.

Ken Harrelson married Betty Pacifici in 1959.

HARVEY, WILSON GODFREY, (1866-1932) — Sixty-ninth state governor (D) of South Carolina, 1922-23.

Born in Charleston on September 8, 1866, the son of Wilson and Cornelia (Elbridge) Harvey. He attended Charleston High School until age sixteen, then went to work as a clerk for the Charleston *New Courier.* Within five years, he had become manager of the *World and Budget* newspaper in Charleston. He was named state manager for Bradstreet Company (later Dun and Bradstreet, Inc.) in 1892. In 1894, he married Mary Franklin. They had three children.

Harvey continued his way up the ladders of business, helping to organize and becoming cashier for the Enterprise Bank of Charleston in 1894. Ten years later, he was president of the Enterprise Bank. In addition, he became interested in politics and in 1903 was elected to the Charleston Board of Aldermen. He served until 1911. In 1910, he was Mayor Pro Tempore of Charleston; from 1916 to 1920 he served as chairman of the Sanitary and Drainage Commission of Charleston County. He was president of the South Carolina Bankers' Association in 1911; president of the Charleston Chamber of Commerce from 1912 to 1914; and president of the Charleston Clearing House Association from 1913 to 1914. His first wife, Mary, having died in 1911, he remarried to Margaret Waring on June 24, 1914.

Harvey was elected Lieutenant Governor of South Carolina and served from 1921 to 1922. When Governor Cooper resigned in the latter year, Harvey succeeded him in office. As governor, he sought to establish higher standards within the state school system, and promoted the construction of concrete highways. He served only eight months, to complete Governor Cooper's remaining term, and left office on January 16, 1923. In the years that followed, he worked in Greenville as an agent for the Carolina Life Insurance Company, and later in Columbia as state manager for that same company. In January, 1932 he moved to Tampa, Florida, as the Florida state manager of the Carolina Life Insurance Company. He died there on October 7, 1932.

HAYNE, ARTHUR PERONNEAU, (1788 or 1790-1867) — (brother of Robert Young Hayne), a U.S. Senator from South Carolina; born in Charleston, S.C., March 12, 1788 or 1790; pursued classical studies; engaged in business; served in the War of 1812 as first lieutenant, major, and inspector general; brevetted lieutenant colonel for gallant conduct at New Orleans; studied law; was admitted to the bar and practiced; served in the Florida War as commander of the Tennessee Volunteers and retired in 1820; member, State house of representatives; United States naval agent in the Mediterranean for five years; declined the Belgian mission; appointed to the United States Senate to fill the vacancy caused by the death of Josiah J. Evans and served from May 11, 1858, to December 2, 1858; was not a candidate to succeed himself; died in Charleston, S.C., January 7, 1867; interment in St. Michael's Churchyard.

HAYNE, ROBERT YOUNG, (1791-1839) — twenty-ninth state governor (D) of South Carolina, 1832-1834.

He was born in St. Paul's Parish, Colleton District, South Carolina, the son of Elizabeth Peronneau and William Hayne.

Hayne received his education in private schools, and studied law in the office of Langdon Cheves. He was admitted to the South Carolina Bar in 1812. After enlisting in the military as a lieutenant in the Charleston Cadet Infantry, Third South Carolina Regiment in the War of 1812, he went on to become a captain of the Charleston Cadet Riflemen, and a quartermaster general of South Carolina in 1814.

He was elected to the South Carolina House of Representatives in 1814, serving until 1818, when he became its Speaker. In December of the same year, he was appointed Attorney General of South Carolina, filling this office until 1822, when he was chosen a member of the United States Senate. He remained in this capacity until 1832, when he resigned his seat.

Hayne was elected governor of South Carolina in December 1832. During his tenure, the nullification conflict was foremost in the minds of South Carolina citizens. Hayne was president of the South Carolina Nullification Convention which met in that year, and he continued to defend the Nullification Ordinance, which provided that an individual state could declare an act of Congress unconstitutional, making it null and void within its boundaries.

When President Andrew Jackson issued his "Proclamation to the People of South Carolina," Hayne called for the State to furnish 10,000 troops to repel a potential federal invasion. However, he sought to avoid a civil war, and when Clay's compromise act was passed by Congress, which sought to adjust revenue and lower import duties on certain articles of necessity and convenience, he concurred.

The representatives of South Carolina called a convention to repeal the Ordinance of Nullification, and Hayne presided over its deliberations. Once the crisis was past, he urged moderation, and did much to mitigate factional strife within the State.

After his gubernatorial term ended, Hayne served as mayor of Charleston from 1835 to 1837. He also developed an interest in the construction of a railroad linking South Carolina and the Ohio Valley and, in 1836, served as president of the Knoxville, Kentucky Convention, which promoted such a railway. In the same year, he became president of the Louisville, Cincinnati and Charleston Railroad Company, but the Panic of 1837 and the subsequent depression made the raising of construction funds an impossible task.

Hayne was married to Frances Henrietta Pinckney. After her death, he married a second time to Rebecca Mott Alston. He died in September 1839 while attending a railroad convention in Asheville, North Carolina, and was buried in St. Michael's Churchyard in Charleston.

HAYNSWORTH, CLEMENT FURMAN, (1886 - 1953) — lawyer, was born in Greenville, South Carolina on April 16, 1886, the son of Harry John and Annie (Furman) Haynsworth. Clement F. Haynsworth attended the local Greenville schools. He received a B.A. from Furman University in 1904 and an A.B. from Harvard in 1906 (LL.B. 1909). After being admitted to the South Carolina bar, he began his law practice in Greenville as a member of Haynsworth & Haynsworth, in association with his father. He specialized in corporation law and his clients included the J.P. Stephens Company, Union Bleachery, South Carolina National Bank and 69 insurance companies.

For many years Haynsworth was chairman of the Greenville Democratic Executive Committee and from 1912 until 1914, he was a member of the South Carolina state legislature. He was a trustee of Greenville Woman's College for a number of years, prior to its consolidation with Furman University in 1936. He was also a member of the board of governors of Greenville General Hospital during 1916-26; chairman of the board of trustees of the Burgess Charities, Greenville, from 1941 to 1953; and president of the Greenville Community Chest in 1932 as well as a member of many other community organizations.

During the early part of World War I, he served as a member of the Greenville Home Guard, later enlisting in the U.S. Army Infantry, although the Armistice was signed before he was called to active duty.

Haynsworth was married and had three sons and one daughter.

HENEGAN, B(ARNABAS) K(ELET), (1798-1855) — thirty-third state governor (D/acting) of South Carolina, 1840.

He was born in Marlboro County, South Carolina, the son of Darby and Drusilla Henegan.

Henegan received a medical education. Prior to his election to the South Carolina Senate in 1834, he was a trustee of South Carolina College, and was South Carolina Commissioner of Public Buildings. In 1838, immediately following his service in the State Senate, he was elected lieutenant-governor of South Carolina.

Upon the death of Governor Patrick Noble in April 1840, Henegan was confirmed as governor of South Carolina. During his administration, the Charleston banks recovered sufficiently from the Panic of 1837 to resume specie payments, in July 1840. Also, efforts of reconciliation between "Nullifiers" and "Unionists" were so successful that in December 1840, John C. Richardson, a Unionist, was elected governor.

After Henegan left office, he served as South Carolina's Secretary of State from 1846 to 1850.

Henegan was married to Mary Savage Gibson in April 1831. He married a second time, to Ann Maria Wickham Ellerbee. He died in January 1855 in Marion, South Carolina.

HENRY, EDWARD LAMSON, (1841-1919) — was an artist who chiefly painted genre and interiors. His work was considered to be of greater historic than artistic merit.

Born in Charleston, South Carolina on January 12, 1841, the son of Frederick and Elizabeth (Fairbanks) Henry, Edward Henry received his academic education in New York City. He began his art education at the Pennsylvania Academy of Fine Arts in Philadelphia and continued it in Paris under Suisse, Gleyre and Courbet. He returned to America in 1864.

Henry's major interest was in the history and customs of the United States, especially during the first half of the 19th century. He painted chiefly genre pictures and interiors representing American colonial life and historical pieces. He painted compositions which were accurate to the most minute detail. Owing in part to this attention to detail, his work was considered to be of greater historic than artistic merit. In his desire to include as many people as possible in his representation of notable occasions, he frequently crowded his canvases. Primarily an illustrator in oils, he found an appreciative audience in those individuals who prefer pictures that tell a story.

Some of Henry's noted works were: "The Reception in Lafayette", "Off for the Races" and "Leaving at Early Morning in a Northeaster." His "Railway Station — New England" was sold in 1876 for $530.

In 1867, he was made an associate of the National Academy of Design and in 1869 became a member. He exhibited his pictures at the large national fairs in New Orleans, Chicago, Buffalo and Charleston, and received a medal or honorable mention at each. In addition, he received an honorable mention at the Paris Exposition of 1889.

Edward Henry married Frances Livingston Wells in June 1875. He died in Ellenville, New York on May 9, 1919.

HEYWARD, DUNCAN CLINCH, (1864-1943) — Sixty-third state governor (D) of South Carolina, 1903-1907.

Born in Richland County, South Carolina on June 24, 1864, the son of Edward Barnwell and Catherine (Clinch) Heyward. His parents died when he was six years old. He attended Cheltenham Academy in Pennsylvania, then went on to Washington and Lee University in Virginia from 1882 to 1885. He was married the following year to Mary Elizabeth Campbell. They had four children.

Heyward served a captain in the cavalry based in Colleton County. In subsequent years, he worked in business and as a rice planter. He was president of Standard Warehouse Company; president of Columbia Savings Bank and Trust Company; and special agent of the Group Division of the Protective Life Insurance Company. He was elected Governor of South Carolina in 1902, running as a Democrat with no opposition. Developments during his administration included passage of the Brice Act, which enabled counties to vote out the liquor dispensary system if they desired. Heyward was vocal about the lack of gubernatorial power, declaring in 1905 that the "governor is practically powerless where the details of the enforcement of law are concerned." He was elected to a second term in 1904 in an unopposed election.

Since the constitution limited the governor from serving more than two terms, Heyward left office in 1907. In 1913, he was appointed Collector of Federal Internal Revenue Taxes for South Carolina. He was the author of the book, *Seed of Madagascar* (1937). Heyward died on January 23, 1943 in Columbia.

HEYWARD, EDWIN DUBOSE, (1885-1940) — author and playwright, was born in Charleston, South Carolina on August 31, 1885, the son of Edwin and Jane Heyward. Coming from a poor family, he began to help support them at the age of nine by selling newspapers. The young man worked a variety of jobs in Charleston until he contracted a mild case of polio in 1903. The disease forced him to rest and he spent the next three years reading voraciously. Upon recovery he set up an insurance firm until a relapse forced him to journey west for health.

Returning to Charleston in 1920 he met and collaborated with writer Hervey Allen, and they subsequently published *Carolina Chansons* in 1922. This book of verse received wide attention and led to many requests for lectures and readings. While giving a reading in New Hampshire in 1922 he met his future wife, and began to consider a career devoted to writing. They bought a farm in the North Carolina Mountains, and in 1924 he published another work *Skylines and Horizons*. His next work, *Porgy*, was published in 1925 and received immediate critical acclaim. His wife did a dramatization, and after revision they published the play. *Porgy* was produced by the Theatre Guild in New York in 1927 and ran for over 350 performances before going on tour throughout the country.

Heyward continued his work and in 1926 produced a novel *Angel*; a story, *Mamba's Daughters*, in 1929; a book of poetry *Jasbo Brown and selected poems* in 1931; and another novel *Peter Ashley* in 1932. In 1935 the Theater Guild produced an opera based on *Porgy*. Renamed *Porgy and Bess*, the music was composed by George Gershwin with the libretto written by Heyward and Ira Gershwin. Critics acclaimed the arrival of a modern American classic, a judgment upheld by the next generation. Heyward continued this success in 1939 when *Mamba's Daughters* was adapted as a play on Broadway. Ethel Waters had the chief role, which marked the first time a black woman had appeared on Broadway in a leading role. Heyward continued his work until his death in Tyron, North Carolina on June 16, 1940.

HEYWARD, THOMAS, JR., (1746-1809) — a Delegate from South Carolina; born on his father's plantation; settled in that part of St. Helena's Parish which later became St. Luke's Parish, South Carolina, July 28, 1746; pursued academic studies; studied law in the Middle Temple at London; returned to South Carolina in 1771; was admitted to the bar and established himself in the practice of law; member of the Commons House of Assembly of South Carolina in 1772; delegate to the provincial convention in 1774; member of the council of safety in 1775 and 1776; member of the general assembly 1776-1778; Member of the Continental Congress 1776-1778; signer of the Declaration of Independence; member of the State constitutional committee in 1776; served in the State house of representatives 1778-1780 and 1782-1790; served in the Revolutionary War as captain; taken prisoner at the capture of Charlestown May 12, 1780, and was a prisoner at St. Augustine one year; judge of the circuit court 1779-1789; founder and first president of the Agricultural

Society of South Carolina in 1785; engaged in agricultural pursuits; member of the State constitutional convention in 1790; died on his plantation, "White Hall," in St. Luke's Parish, South Carolina, March 6, 1809; interment in the family burial ground on his father's plantation, "Old House," near Ridgeland, S.C.

HIGBE, WALTER KIRBY, (1915-1985) — was a professional baseball player, major league scout and author.

Born on April 8, 1915 in Columbia, South Carolina, Walter Kirby Higbe finished the seventh grade in school. In 1932, he signed with a Pittsburgh organization for a $500 bonus and a $300 a month pay check. He played for a Tulsa team in the Texas League. He played semipro baseball briefly then, in 1933, landed with a Muskogee team in the Western League. He spent the next few years with Atlanta and Birmingham in the Southern League, Portsmouth and Columbia in the Piedmont League and with Moline in the Illinois League.

Higbe pitched for five major league teams during a 12-year career that began with the Chicago Cubs in 1937. He enjoyed his best years with the Brooklyn Dodgers, a team he helped lead to the National League pennant in 1941 by winning 22 games while losing only nine. Higbe's .648 winning percentage as a Dodger ranked among the best in that team's history. He was eventually traded by Brooklyn because he refused to be on the same team with black player Jackie Robinson.

A member of the South Carolina Athletic Hall of FAme, Higbe also pitched for the Philadelphia Phillies, the Pittsburgh Pirates, and the New York Giants. He appeared in the 1946 All- Star game. Higbe won 118 of 219 decisions before retiring and becoming a major league scout.

In later years, Higbe worked for the post office, then for a chemical company. After writing several bad checks during a period of unemployment, Higbe was jailed for 40 days. He again ran afoul of the law when he smuggled sleeping pills into jail and was given a three-year suspended sentence, with three years probation.

In 1967, he wrote *The High Hard One* with Martin Quigley.

Walter Kirby Higbe died on May 6, 1985.

HINES, JOHN ELBRIDGE, (1910-?) — Protestant Episcopal bishop, was born on October 3, 1910 in Seneca, South Carolina. He attended the University of the South in Tennessee, earning a B.A. degree in 1930. He next studied at the Virginia Theological Seminary, receiving a Bachelor of Divinity degree in 1934.

Ordained as a deacon of the Episcopal Church in 1933, Hines became a priest the following year. During 1934-35, Hines served as curate of the Church of St. Michael and St. George, located in St. Louis. His next assignment was as rector of the Trinity Episcopal Church in Hannibal, Missouri. He moved to Augusta, Georgia in 1937 where he served as rector of St. Paul's Episcopal Church until 1941. After the start of World War II, Hines was named rector of Houston's Christ Episcopal Church, and in 1945, he was elected to serve as bishop coadjutor of the Diocese of Texas, a post in which he was assistant to the diocesan bishop. In 1955, Hines was chosen to be the diocesan bishop of Texas, the fourth person to hold that position. During his tenure, Hines became known for his liberal stance, and was often outspoken against such ultra-conservative groups as the John Birch Society. Two years later, Hines was elected to the national council of the Episcopal Church, and served on several important committees.

In the fall of 1964, the House of Bishops and the House of Delegates elected Hines as the twenty-second Presiding Bishop of the Episcopal Church, making him the youngest person to hold that position in the history of the church. His inaugural ceremony was held in January of 1965, in the church he would be presiding from, the National Cathedral in Washington, D.C. In his speech that day, he gave his thoughts on the responsibility of the church, which he said was "caught up today in the throes of a worldwide convulsion, the basic ferment of which is the thrust for freedom and dignity and hope on the part of the little people of the world. The church as an agent of God's reconciling love cannot survive this revolution as an observer."

In his position, Hines was overseer of the executive council, consisting of forty-two members. In addition, he was responsible for the entire Episcopal Church organization in the United States, which by 1968, included 104 dioceses (some of which were overseas), 11,000 clergy, over 7,000 parishes and missions, fourteen seminaries, eleven colleges, and over 100 secondary schools.

In keeping with his liberal views, he was pleased that after the Selma march, St. Paul's Episcopal Church in Selma, Alabama became the first Protestant church to allow blacks to attend services in March of 1965. He remarked: "This action...should aid men of good will to minister to the scarred human relations of the community and to encourage forces of order and reconciliation to effect a just peace." He was also a staunch supporter of women being admitted to the minstry.

In addition to issues concerning the church itself, Hines brought his religious community into issues that concerned the nation, co-chairing a 1966 national inter-religious conference on peace, the first of its kind. The conference included leaders from many different religions such as Unitarian, Roman Catholic, Reformed Jewish, Methodist, and Greek Orthodox. Their main objective was to persuade President Lyndon B. Johnson to try and enforce a cease-fire in Vietnam, which would include an immediate halt to all bombing raids. At subsequent interfaith conferences, Hines supported the protest against the continued escalation of the Vietnam War.

When the Episcopal Church held its sixty-second general convention, the attending delegates, in supporting the more liberal views of its leader, voted for a number of important reforms. *Current Biography* listed them as such: "Laymen were granted permission to administer the chalice; a greatly simplified liturgy of the Lord's Supper was authorized for trial use; women were allowed to attend future sessions of the general convention; heresy trials were made more difficult to institute; and the functions of the Presiding Bishop were more formally defined."

For his compassion and vision, Hines, in 1965, was given the Human Relations award of the Southwest advisory board of the Anti-Defamation League of B'nai

B'rith. He is married to Helen Orwig, and the couple have five children.

HITCHCOCK, THOMAS, JR., (1900-1944) — considered the greatest American polo player ever, and possibly the greatest polo player in the world. He was also a heroic fighter pilot in World War I and died while serving in World War II.

Born February 11, 1900 in Aiken, South Carolina, Tommy Hitchcock grew up in a home where polo was a priority. His father was rated a 10-goal player, the highest possible handicap in polo, and he was also a great steeplechase trainer. His mother was considered an authority on polo, and organized the first American female polo team. Hitchcock started riding horses at age three, and played polo competitively at 13. At the age of 16 he joined the Meadow Brook Club team, which at the time was the leading team in the country.

Hitchcock dropped out after his first year with the club however, and tried to join the army aviation corps. He was rejected because of his age, so he sailed to France where he joined the French aviation service. He was assigned to the famous French Lafayette Escadrille and engaged in ten skirmishes, bringing down two German planes. In 1918 he was shot down behind enemy lines, suffering a bullet wound in the right thigh and a hand injury. The King of Spain negotiated for his release, but after six weeks in the hospital Hitchcock saw his chance to make a daring escape. While being transferred to a concentration camp he stole a map and money from a sleeping guard's pocket. He jumped from a moving train and traveled by foot over 100 miles in 10 days to the Swiss border. After his adventure he returned to his squadron, and later transferred to the U.S. Army, where he served until the end of the war. He was decorated with the Croix de Guerre with two palms for his service.

At home Hitchcock returned to his position on the Meadow Brook team, and started school at Harvard. He studied for one year at Brasenose College in England, then graduated from Harvard in 1922, embarking on a career in banking. He also started his polo career in earnest. In his first year on the American team he earned

10-goal handicap status, a ranking he maintained for 17 of the 18 years he played. He was known for both his technical skills and his reckless daring, which was attributed to his bravery as a fighter pilot. His strategy, anticipation, and strokes were considered superb. As captain he helped the American team win 10 straight matches against the British between 1921 and 1939, including five Westchester Cup victories. He competed with the National Open Champions in 1923, 1927, 1935, and 1936 and with the winners of the Monty Waterburg Memorial Cup in 1928, 1932, 1935, and 1939. He also lead the U.S. team against Argentina for the Copa de las Americas in 1928.

Besides his skill, Hitchcock's other contribution to the sport was his campaign to make polo accessible to all people, not just the blue-blooded upper-class it was associated with. He fought to allow two "cowboys" from Texas, Rube Williams and Cecil Smith, to compete on the American team against Britain. There was a great outcry from traditional polo fans, but the addition of the stylish western riders attracted so much extra publicity that by the end of the series more than 40,000 people had come out to watch competition.

Yet despite his love for polo, Hitchcock was not ashamed of his love for aviation. He once said, "Polo is exciting, but you can't compare it to flying in wartime. That's the best sport in the world. People call duck-shooting sport. It's not real sport unless the duck can shoot back at you — that's what flying is during war."

When rumors of war broke out again in the late 1930's, Hitchcock was anxious to get back in the game. He was one of the youngest fighter pilots in World War I, and now he was ready to fly again as one of the oldest. He officially retired from international polo competition after the 1939 Westchester Club match. In 1942 he was commissioned as a lieutenant colonel in the Army Air Corps and sent to England as an air attache. At the age of 44 he was placed in command of a P-51 Mustang fighter group within the ninth Air Support Command. His daring career ended when his plane crashed during a routine training flight in Salisbury, England April 19, 1944.

HOGE, SOLOMON LAFAYETTE, (1836-1909) — a U.S. Representative from South Carolina; born in Pickreltown, Logan County, Ohio, July 11, 1836; attended Bellefontaine (Ohio) public schools and Northwood College, Northwood, Ohio (now Geneva College, Beaver Falls, Pa.); received a classical education and was graduated from the Cincinnati Law School in 1859; was ad mitted to the bar in 1859 and commenced practice in Belle fontaine, Ohio; entered the Union Army in 1861 as first lieutenant in the Ohio Volunteer Infantry and was subsequently promoted to the rank of captain; moved to Columbia, S.C. in 1868; associate justice of the State supreme court 1868-1870; successfully contested as a Republican the election of J.P. Reed to the Forty-first Congress and served from April 8, 1869, to March 3, 1871; comptroller general of South Carolina in 1874 and 1875; elected to the Forty-fourth Congress (March 4, 1875-March 3, 1877); was not a candidate for renomination in 1876; moved to Kenton, Ohio, in September 1877 and practiced law until 1882; president of the First National Bank of Kenton; died in Battle Creek, Mich., February 23, 1909; interment in Grove Cemetery, Kenton, Ohio.

HOLLAND, KENNETH LAMAR, (1934-) — a U.S. Representative from South Carolina; born in Hickory, Catawba County, N.C., November 24, 1934; attended the public schools of Gaffney, S.C.; A.B., University of South Carolina, Columbia, 1960; LL.B., University of South Carolina Law School, Columbia, 1963; admitted to the South Carolina bar in 1963 and commenced practice in Camden; served in the South Carolina National Guard, 1952-1959; chairman, South Carolina State Board of Municipal Canvassers, 1971-1973; delegate, South Carolina State Democratic conventions, 1968-1972; delegate, Democratic National Convention, 1968; member, South Carolina Highway Commission, 1972-1975; elected as a Democrat to the Ninety-fourth and to the three succeeding Congresses (January 3, 1975-January 3, 1983); was not a candidate for reelection in 1982 to the Ninety-eighth Congress; is a resident of Gaffney, S.C.

HOLLINGS, ERNEST FREDERICK, (1922-) — governor and U.S. Senator, born in Charleston, South Carolina, January 1, 1922. The son of Adolph and Wilhelmine (Meyer), his family owned a prosperous paper mill which went bankrupt during the 1930s. Hollings continued attending high school in Charleston, then enrolled in The Citadel, a military college. He graduated in 1942 with a B.A. and joined the Army, spending the next three years serving in North Africa and Europe.

Hollings was discharged a captain in 1945 after earning seven campaign stars. He married Martha Patricia Salley in 1946 and they eventually had four children together. He enrolled in the University of South Carolina to study law, and was admitted to the bar in 1947. In 1948 Hollings ran for and won a seat in the South Carolina House of Representatives. He served as Speaker Pro Tempore of the House from 1950 to 1954 and on Hoover's Commission on Intelligence Activities from 1954 to 1955, along with the Federal Commission on Organization of the Executive Branch. In 1955 he was elected Lieutenant Governor, remaining in that post for four years.

In 1959 Hollings was elected governor of South Carolina, running unopposed. The Civil Rights movement was gaining momentum at this time, and even though he was opposed to it, Hollings integrated South Carolina schools and other public areas to avoid the difficulties experienced by other Southern states. Hollings also put together a new economic development program for South Carolina, which included raising teacher salaries, implementing new educational programs, balancing the state budget, and creating a new tax structure that favored industry. He toured the country seeking new industry for his state and served on the Regional Advisory Council on Nuclear Energy during the Southern Governors' Conference. On the national level he served on the Federal Advisory Commission on Intergovernmental Relations. Hollings left the office of Governor in 1963, and went into private law practice.

In the presidential elections of 1960 Hollings was one of the few Southern political leaders to support John F. Kennedy, and he helped insure the nomination of southerner Lyndon Johnson as Kennedy's running mate. In

1962 Hollings unsuccessfully ran for the U.S. Senate, then he tried again in 1966 when there was an opening due to a death in the office. After extremely vigorous campaigning Hollings was elected, and went to Washington. Once in the capital he compiled a conservative voting record, including voting for cuts in federal spending. He won re-election in 1968 with a comfortable margin, and gradually evolved toward the political center. He served on Budget, Commerce, and Appropriations Committees as well as the Senate Democratic Policy Committee. In 1970 he wrote the book, *The Case Against Hunger: A Demand for National Policy*.

In 1971 Hollings married Rita Liddy. During the 1970's he urged increased defense spending, but voted with liberals on such issues as tax relief for low income taxpayers, federal support for day care centers, and marine mammal protection. Along with budget and commerce committees he served on the Select Committee on Intelligence, the National Ocean Policy Study Committee, the Defense Committee, Legislative Affairs, Labor, Health and Human Services, Education, and subcommittees on energy and water development.

Hollings steadfastly opposed Reaganomics when it arrived in Washington in 1981. He liked the increased defense spending, but thought the large tax cuts would lead to enormous deficits. Senator Hollings has received many honors over the course of his career, including awards for his contributions to environmental legislation and wildlife protection.

HOLMES, ISAAC EDWARD, (1796-1867) — a U.S. Representative from South Carolina; born in Charleston, S.C., April 6, 1796; attended the common schools, received private tuition, and was graduated from Yale College in 1815; studied law; was admitted to the bar in 1818 and commenced practice in Charleston; member of the city council; served in the State house of representatives 1826-1829 and 1832-1833; elected as a Democrat to the Twenty-sixth and to the five succeeding Congresses (March 4, 1839-March 3, 1851); chairman, Committee on Commerce (Twenty- eighth Congress), Committee on Naval Affairs (Twenty-ninth Congress); practiced law in San Francisco,

Calif., 1851-1854, when he returned to Charleston, s.c.; again resided in San Francisco 1857-1861; returned to South Carolina in 1861 and was appointed a commissioner of the State to confer with the Federal Government; died in Charleston, S.C., February 24, 1867; interment in Circular Churchyard.

HUGER, BENJAMIN, (1768-1823) — a U.S. Representative from South Carolina; born at or near Charleston, S.C., in 1768; pursued an academic course; engaged in the cultivation of rice on the Waccamaw River; member of the State house of representatives tives1796-1798; elected as a Federalist to the Sixth, Sev-i enth, and Eighth Congresses (March 4, 1799-March 3, 1805); again a member of the State house of representatives 1806- ' 1813; elected to the Fourteenth Congress (March 4, 1815- March 3, 1817); member of the State senate 1818-1823 and served as president 1819-1822; died on his estate on Waccamaw River, near Georgetown, S.C., July 7, 1823; interment in All Saints' Churchyard.

HUGER, DANIEL ELLIOTT, (1779-1854) — (son of Daniel Huger), a U.S. Senator from South Carolina; born on Limerick plantation, near Charleston, S.C., June 28, 1779; pursued classical studies in Charleston; graduated from the College of New Jersey (later Princeton University) in 1798; studied law; was admitted to the bar in 1799 and began practice in Charleston, S.C.; member, State house of representatives 1804-1819; brigadier general of State troops in 1814; judge of the circuit court 1819-1830; member, State senate 1830-1832, 1838-1842; opposition member of the State nullification convention in 1832; elected as a State Rights Democrat to the United States Senate to fill the vacancy caused by the resignation of John C. Calhoun and served from March 4, 1843, to March 3, 1845, when he resigned; delegate to the state-rights convention in 1852, where he urged moderation; died on Sullivans Island, 1854; interment in Magnolia Cemetery.

HUNTER, JOHN, (1732 or 1760) — a U.S. Representative and a U.S. Senator from South Carolina; born in

HUNTER, JOHN, (1732 or 1760) — a U.S. Representative and a U.S. Senator from South Carolina; born in South Carolina in either 1732 or 1760; completed preparatory studies; engaged in agricultural pursuits near Newberry, S.C.; member, State house of representatives 1786-1792; Federalist presidential elector in 1792; elected to the Third Congress (March 4, 1793-March 3, 1795); elected as a Republican to the United States Senate to fill the vacancy caused by the resignation of Pierce Butler and served from December 8, 1796, to November 26, 1798, when he resigned; resumed agricultural pursuits on his plantation; died in 1802; interment in the family plot in the Presbyterian Church Cemetery, at Little River, S.C.

HUNTER-GAULT, CHARLAYNE, (1942-) — a television and print journalist with a single-minded determination that allowed her to receive her education and move forward in the world of journalism.

Hunter-Gault decided at the age of 12 to become a journalist, and follow in the footsteps of her idol, comic-strip character Brenda Starr. Real life was a lot harder for her than it was for an animated charactor, but Hunter-Gault was determined not to be deterred. She was the oldest of three children of Charles S.H. Hunter, a Methodist chaplin in the United States Army. She was born in Due West, South Carolina, where the family lived until 1954, when they moved to Atlanta, Georgia. Hunter-Gault's father was called overseas for much of her childhood, so she was raised mostly by her mother, who worked as a secretary, and her grandmother. She credits her grandmother, who continued to read and grow even though she never graduated grammar school, for helping to build her character. "She used to read three newspapers a day," said Hunter-Gault in an article in the Washington Review. "She was innately curious about the world. She was intrepid and strong. But she was also very gentle, and I think I owe a lot of my character to her." Her grandmother not only read a lot but she traveled often too, and took Hunter- Gault with her.

When she was 16 years-old Hunter-Gault converted to Roman Catholicism, a decision that shocked her strongly Protestant family. In high school she fought with her guidance counselor as well, who encouraged her to go into education and attend a black college, rather than follow her dream into journalism. She graduated high school with honors, and was determined to attend the only college in Georgia with a journalism school, the all- white University of Georgia. She applied in 1959, a year when the Civil Rights Movement was beginning to grow in numbers and strength. Martin Luther King Jr. was working with the Southern Christian Leadership Conference and other activists had just formed the Student Nonviolent Coordinating Committee. "It was just the spirit and the atmosphere of the times that you broke barriers," she said to Dial magazine. "I did not set out with a global aim. There was something to be done— and it turned out to have monumental consequences, but it was my effort to secure for myself the type of education I needed.

With the help of prominent Atlanta civil rights activists, Hunter-Gault, along with Hamilton Holmes, a friend from high school, went to federal court to request an integration order. The court fought over the issue for two years, and in the meantime Hunter-Gault attended Wayne State University in Detroit, Michigan. Finally, in January 1961 she and Holmes became the first black students to enter the University of Georgia. Even though this was a monumental win in the courts, the media attention over the issue came as a shock to her. "At the time, I wasn't happy with the celebrity that followed because I felt that, but for the color of my skin, getting accepted to college was a fairly routine exercise," she said later.

She did learn some important lessons about journalism, however, just by watching the reporters. "I saw how different journalists worked and how I was treated as a story," Hunter- Gault said later. "There were journalists who were sensitive and I wanted to be like them. On the other hand, there was one reporter who pulled a mob together so that he could film them— he missed the riot."

Another lesson she quickly learned was that getting into college was the first battle, and staying in and fighting 175 years of University of Georgia tradition was another. During her second night on campus students gathered outside her window, chanting and throwing rocks. One brick came through her dorm-room window. The police arrived and used tear gas to disperse the crowd. After the riot Hunter-Gault and Holmes were expelled for their safety, but their lawyers protested and they were admitted to classes the next day.

Despite the continued harassment, threats, and vandalism, Hunter-Gault continued toward her degree. The editors of the campus newspaper did not exactly welcome her on staff, so she worked on weekends for the Atlanta Inquirer, which was established by college students from around the state angry with the coverage of the civil rights movement by the mainstream media. She secretly married Walter Stovell, a white student, while attending college. The marriage produced one daughter, but ended in divorce.

Hunter-Gault finally graduated with a B.A. in journalism in 1963. She started as a secretary for the New Yorker, working up to a staff writer. She left in 1967 to accept the Russell Sage Fellowship to study social science at Washington University in St. Louis, Missouri. She edited articles for the Trans-Action magazine, and took the assignment of covering the Poor People's Campaign in Washington D.C. As a result of that assignment she joined the staff of WRC-TV in Washington as investigative reporter and anchorwoman.

In 1968 she moved on again, to work as a reporter for the New York Times, covering black issues. She earned a reputation as a tough but sensitive reporter, with an eye for detail. In 1970 she shared the New York Times Publishers' Awards with reporter Joseph Lelyveld for the story of a 12 year-old heroin addict. She later won two additional Publishers' Awards, one for "writing under deadline pressure" when Mayor Abraham Beame's nominated of Paul Gibson Jr. as New York City's first black deputy mayor in 1974. The other was for "outstanding performance on a beat," which included her front-page stories on black crime and the renaming of Harlem's Muslim Mosque for Malcolm X. She also received the National Urban Coalition Award for Distinguished Urban Reporting, and the Lincoln University Unity Award for an article on teenage unemployment.

Hunter-Gualt stayed at the Times for nine years, despite an occasional disagreement with the editorial board. At one point she went head-to-head with her bosses, who insisted on continuing to use the word "Negro" as a matter of editorial style, rather than "black," which was approved by civil rights leaders. Hunter-Gault wrote a long, forceful, yet convincing memorandum, which swayed the editorial board's opinion on the matter.

In 1971 she married Ronald Gualt, a vice-president for the First Boston Corporation, specializing in public finance. They have one son together.

In 1978 Hunter-Gualt took the opportunity to audition as the third correspondent on the MacNeil/Lehrer Report. The new PBS program was designed to provide more in-depth coverage of the news than other television programs, and Hunter-Gault saw it as a chance to expand her range of reporting. She was hired for the position, and when MacNeil/Lehrer expanded to one hour, she was named the show's national correspondent. True to her prediction, Hunter-Gault was able to interview all kinds of people, from comedians, to Prime Ministers, to the Pope. In 1983 she was the first correspondent allowed into Grenada after the multinational invasion, and she won a National News and Documentary Emmy for her reports which focused on the effect the invasion had on the people. She also won an Emmy for her 1985 profile of a young man who contracted cancer from Agent Orange, which was used on the orders of his own father. She has covered national issues with a great deal of sensitivity, such as health care for the poor and high infant mortality among black teenagers. Her most honored piece was a five-part series on Apartheid, which won the 1986 George Foster Peabody Award, among others.

Hunter-Gualt has contributed to numerous other publications as well, such as Vogue, Ms., Life, Saturday Review, Coronet, the New Leader and Change. She often speaks on college campuses throughout the United States. She serves on numerous boards including the Committee to Protect Journalists, the Center for Communication and the Foundation for Child Development. She has been honored by the Newswomen's Club of New York Front Page Award, the Good Housekeeping Broadcast Personality of the Year Award, the American Women in Radio and Television Award, the Atlanta Women in Communications Award for Excellence in Journalism, two awards from the Corporation for Public Broadcasting for excellence in local programming, and the Woman of Achievement Award from the New York chapter of the American Society of University Women.

HUTSON, RICHARD, (1748-1795) — a Delegate from South Carolina; born in Prince William parish, South Carolina, July 9, 1748; pursued classical studies and was graduated from Princeton College in 1765; studied law; was admitted to the bar and practiced in Charleston, S.C.; member of the State house of representatives 1776-1779, 1781, 1782, 1785, and 1788; Member of the Continental Congress in 1778 and 1779 and signed the Articles of Confederation; captured at the fall of Charleston and was confined as a prisoner at St. Augustine, Fla., in 1780 and 1781; member of the Legislative Council of South Carolina 1780-1782; Lieutenant Governor in 1782 and 1783; first intendant of Charleston in 1783 and 1784; chancellor of the court of chancery of South Carolina 1784-1791; member of the State constitutional convention in 1788 which adopted the Federal Constitution; senior judge of the chancery court 1791-1795; died in Charleston, S.C., April 12, 1795; interment in the Perrineau family vault in Independent Congregational Church Cemetery.

I

IRBY, JOHN LAURENS MANNING, (1854-1900) — (great- grandson of Elias Earle and cousin of Joseph Haynsworth Earle), a U.S. Senator from South Carolina; born in Laurens, Laurens County, S.C., September 10, 1854; attended Laurensville Male Academy, Laurens, S.C., Princeton College, Princeton, N.J., in 1870-1871, and the University of Virginia at Charlottesville 1871-1873; studied law; was admitted to the bar in 1875, com menced practice at Cheraw, Chesterfield County, S.C., returned to

Laurens; appointed lieutenant colonel of the South Carolina Militia 1877; intendant of Laurens 1877; member, State house of representatives 1886-1892, serving as speaker in 1890; elected as a Democrat to the United States Senate and served from March 4, 1891, to March 3, 1897; was not a candidate for reelection; chairman, Committee on Transportation Routes to the Seaboard (Fifty-third Congress); subsequently an unsuccessful candidate for election to the United States Senate in 1897 to fill the vacancy caused by the death of his cousin Joseph H. Earle; delegate to the State constitutional convention in 1895; resumed the practice of law and also engaged in agricultural pursuits; died in Laurens, S.C., on December 9, 1900; interment in the City Cemetery.

IZARD, RALPH, (1741-1804) — a Delegate and a U.S. Senator from South Carolina; born at "The Elms," near Charleston, S.C., January 23, in 1741 or 1742; pursued classical studies in England; returned to America briefly in 1764, but went abroad to reside, taking up his residence in London in 1771; moved to Paris, France, in 1776; appointed commissioner to the Court of Tuscany by the Continental Congress in 1776, but was recalled in 1779; returned to America in 1780; pledged his large estate in South Carolina for the payment of war ships to be used in the Revolutionary War; Member of the Continental Congress in 1782 and 1783; elected to the United States Senate and served from March 4, 1789, to March 3, 1795; served as President pro tempore of the Senate during the Third Congress; one of the founders of the College of Charleston; retired from public life to the care of his estates; died near Charleston, May 30, 1804; interment in the churchyard of St. James Goose Creek Episcopal Church, near Charleston, S.C.

IZLAR, JAMES FERDINAND, (1832-1912) — a U.S. Representative from South Carolina; born near Orangeburg, Orangeburg County, S.C., November 25, 1832; attended the common schools; was graduated from Emory College, Oxford, Ga., in 1855; studied law; was admitted to the bar in 1858 and commenced practice in South Carolina; served as an officer in the Confederate Army during the Civil War; resumed the practice of law in Orangeburg, S.C.; member of the State senate 1880-1890; elected by the general assembly judge of the first judicial circuit in 1889; delegate to the Democratic National Convention in 1884; elected as a Democrat to the Fifty-third Congress to fill the vacancy caused by the resignation of William H. Brawley and served from April 12, 1894, to March 3, 1895; was not a candidate for renomination in 1894; again , engaged in the practice of law in Orangeburg until 1907, when he retired; died in Orangeburg, S.C., May 26, 1912; interment in the Episcopal Cemetery.

J

JACKSON, ANDREW, (1767-1845) — seventh President of the United States, was born in the district on the border between North and South Carolina, known as the Waxhaw Settlement, March 15, 1767. He was of Irish ancestry, many generations of his family having lived in or near the town of Carrick Fergus, on the North coast of Ireland. From that section, his father, Andrew Jackson, migrated to America in 1765. He came of a family who had been engaged in the prevailing trade ofthe North of Ireland-- that of linen--and Andrew Jackson's wife, the future President's mother, Elizabeth Hutchinson and her family, were all linen weavers.

The family located on what might be considered, in its relation to the birthplace of the Andrew Jackson under consideration--as disputed territory. That is to say, for many years the argument has been kept up and well-sustained on both sides, whether President Andrew Jackson was born in North or South Carolina. It was finally settled by the historical and biographical authorities that what was known as the Waxhaw Settlement, which was first supposed to be wholly in South Carolina, was, after many years, found to lie on both sides of the boundary line between the two states, and that portion of it in which the Jacksons lived was actually in North Carolina. Nevertheless, General Jackson twice announced himself as a native of South Carolina, once in a letter written in 1830, and again in the proclamation addressed to the South Carolina Nullifiers in 1832. This last might reasonably be considered an excusable political aberration, because Parton, after thorough research, determined that at the time of his birth, the place where he was born was within the limits of North Carolina.

Shortly after the birth of Andrew, his mother moved across the border into South Carolina, and that fact, and because his infancy and youth were passed there, probably had a great deal to do with his own impressions as to his birthplace; where all was a wilderness it would indeed be difficult to be absolutely certain on a queston of this kind. The means for obtaining intellectual instruction in the wild country where Andrew was born were few and inadequate. The "field" schools of the colonies in those days were only appropriate to the country in which they were placed. The schooling was of the simplest, and mostly conducted by itinerant teachers, who might possibly have come from the old country under a cloud, with a good university education, or have been simply grounded, as was more frequently the case, in the merest rudiments of instruction, and of this have only conveyed a very limited degree of what was considered education. In truth, the learning of Andrew Jackson amounted to no more than reading, writing and arithmetic.

His mother appears to have had ambition for him, and decided that he should obtain better instruction than was practicable in her neighborhood. So long as she lived, he was sent to schools kept by clergymen, where most of his instruction included the classics and a certain limited preparation for collge, with an eye to the ministry as a conclusion; but Andrew never attended college, and never had the slightest inclination toward the theological profession. He appears to have been an impetuous, lively, reckless boy, and possessed only a slight inclination toward book knowledge, to which very little was added as he grew older; and as a man he might be fairly counted as comparatively uneducated in relation to his position.

His natural character, however, combined qualities which were of the greatest importance and value to himself, and, as it proved, to his country. He possessed physical and moral courage to an unusual degree, and his willpower, while not descending to obstinacy, was a most positive force--as those who had occasion to come into contact with it in later years could surely testify. But while, as a matter of fact, he was never able to write his own language correctly, he was a born fighter, and in that capacity, made his mark at an early age.

His mother died in 1781, and for the following two years, Andrew succeeded in obtaining employment as a school teacher in the Waxhaw district, and after the proclamation of peace between Great Britain and the colonies, he decided to study law, and entered the office of Mr. Spruce McCay in Salisbury, North Carolina. Here he studied very little, amusing himself in cock- fighting, horseracing, card-playing, and generally in sowing his wild oats, of which he was master of an unusual crop. At the age of twenty, he is described as standing six feet and an inch in his stockings, very slender, with a long, thin face, a high narrow forehead, a mass of sandy hair, and deep blue eyes. His education up to that period included splendid marksmanship, while he was also an accomplished horseman. His temper was irritable and he was easily forced into seemingly ungovernable rage, yet he had a strength of character and common sense which prevented him from flying into a really dangerous passion.

In 1788, Jackson went by wagon train to Nashville, Tennessee, where he began to practice law, and in the next three or four years, he had all the business he wanted. It was during 1790-91, that the remarkable romance which resulted in Jackson's marriage began. His wife was Rachel Donelson, a North Carolinian by birth, daughter of Colonel John Donelson, who was a well-to-do surveyor, and who had migrated from Virginia, to the vicinity of Nashville, ten years before. During those ten years, Rachel married Captain Lewis Robards. She was a bright, active woman, full of vivacity, a fine rider and dancer, and disposed to enjoy company, while her husband seems to have been jealous and tyrannical to an unreasonable degree. At first the couple lived with Rachel's mother-in-law, who took in boarders, as was common in the Southwest at that time. After a while, her husband began to complain regarding his wife and her relations with persons boarding in the house, and eventually sent her home to the residence of her mother in Tennessee.

Andrew Jackson boarded at her mother's house, and the result of this accidental acquaintance was to bring about still further disturbance between Mrs. Robards and her husband, the latter having become reconciled to his wife and settled in the neighborhood.

According to history current at the time, nothing could properly have been said against his character in this unfortunate affair. He was curiously romantic in his chivalrous regard for the sex and his elevated impressions concerning women. Notwithstanding this fact, and that the relations of Jackson with Mrs. Robards were well-recognized as correct in every way, her jealous husband applied for a divorce, the application including an accusation against Jackson. The suit was undertaken in Kentucky, and as the distances were greater in those days, and false impressions more easily conveyed and less easily contradicted, there resulted the fact that Jackson was given to understand that a divorce had actually been granted, and under the circumstances, while experiencing a deep and sincere affection for Mrs. Robards, he felt also a duty in regard to her, and accordingly, in 1791, went to Natchez, where he married her. Two years later, Capt. Robards went into court and demonstrated easily enough the existence of the facts which he required for the purpose of procuring his divorce, and obtained it. On hearing of this, Jackson procured a new license and had the marriage ceremony performed over again.

Jackson made his first advent into political life as a member of a convention called in the Territory of Tennessee for the purpose of making a constitution, in preparation to applying for admission as a state. The movement resulted in the success of the application, and the new state being entitled to only one member in the House of Representatives, Andrew Jackson was elected in 1796 to serve the people in the national legislature, and heard President Washington in person deliver his last message to Congress. In the meantime, as a thoughtful and far-seeing man, Jackson had begun to formulate his opinions with regard to great public questions. The result of this was to throw him in opposition to the Federalists, and particularly to arouse his condemnation of the policy of Alexander Hamilton. Already, too, began in his mind the objections which afterward became so important a factor in national history--objections to the theory and practice of a National Bank. His frontier nature revolted against anything like extraordinary expenditures in carrying on the government, and he is noted as having objected violently to an appropriation of money with which to furnish the newly erected presidential mansion in Washington. Perhaps the strongest motive with him at this time was his hatred of England, and he was even anxious to see the British throne overturned by Napoleon.

From the House of Representatives, Jackson went, in 1797, to the U.S. Senate, and it was said of him by Jefferson, who presided over that body, that he had seen Jackson get up in a passion to speak, and so choke up with rage that he could not speak a word. He felt himself out of place in the Senate, whose dignity and slowness seemed to him tedious and ridiculous. Returning to Tennessee, he was chosen by the Legislature to a seat on the bench of the Supreme Court of the state, the salary being $600 a year. He held this position until 1804, when he resigned, in order to settle up his private affairs.

As was the case at that period with many of his ablest and best supporters, Jackson was desperately in debt, and immediately on leaving his judicial position, he sold his house and personal estate at Hunter's Hill, as it was called, and some 25,000 acres of land in other parts of the state, an act which enabled him to pay off all his debts; whereupon he took his slaves and moved to the places ever after known as The Hermitage, where he once more lived in a house of logs until his new mansion was comnpleted, the location being about eleven miles from Nashville, Tennessee. He now formed a partnership with John Coffee, and ran his plantations and sold his produce with great success, showing a good head for business, and thriving in every direction. His slaves were always treated considerately and everything about his plantation was systematic and well-arranged.

Toward his inferiors, Jackson was always kind, courteous, and gentle: with his social equals, on the contrary, he was apt to be arrogant, dictatorial, and even quarrelsome. Already, in 1795, after some words with an opposing counsel while he was practicing law, he had fought a duel, and in 1796 he was near to shooting at sight the celebrated John Sevier, Governor of Tennessee, on account of some disagreement in regard to the circumstances of Jackson's marriage, always a sore point with him. Ten years later he fought his duel with Charles Dickinson, in which Dickinson was killed and Jackson received a wound, from whose effects he never recovered.

Old Tom Benton said of Jackson: "Retired from the U.S. Senate, and from the supreme judicial bench of the state, this future warrior and president was living upon his farm on the banks of the Cumberland when the War of 1812 broke out. He was a major-general in the Tennessee militia, the only place he would continue to hold. His friends believed he had military genius." But in the meantime Burr's attempted treason had brought the Machiavellian conspirator into communication with Jackson, though without result so far as involving the latter in Burr's mysterious expedition was concerned. One incident, however, of this acquaintance was that Jackson became opposed to Jefferson, and made a speech in Richmond attacking him, which also brought him into conflict with Madison. Yet when Madison was President and the War of 1812 broke out, Jackson gathered together more than 2,000 men, and offered their services and his own to the government.

The earliest operations of the United States in this war had proved unsuccessful, Hull's failure in Canada had caused the Americans to fear the direction of the British forces against the forts of the Gulf of Mexico and the Governor of Tennessee was requested to send troops for the reinforcement of General Wilkinson, who was in command at New Orleans. This brought into service General Jackson and his volunteers, and on January 7, 1813, he started down the river for New Orleans; but through some irregularity, on his arrival at Natchez, Jackson received orders from Wilkinson to halt, as no preparations had been made for his troops at New Orleans. This amounted practically to an order to disband 500 miles from home, without pay, means of transport or commissariat or hospital stores; but Jackson, determined to permit no such outrage as this, and, though in disobedience of orders, marched his troops back to their own state, reaching Nashville May 22, 1813; and his conduct on this occasion was afterward approved by the government, which eventually paid the expenses of the movement.

It was during this trip from Natchez that Jackson obtained the name of "Old Hickory," which was an outgrowth of a remark by some soldier that he was tough, followed by the assertion that he was "tough as hickory," this being reduced to "hickory," and finally, as mark of affection, the whole being included in the phrase "Old Hickory." The war with England had brought about Indian encroachments, the result, practically, of the western progress of white settlers constantly driving the natives before them. Tecumseh had planned to organize the tribes of the entire country between Florida and the lakes in a determined effort to push back the white man to the coast. Tecumseh's own work was among the Cherokees, Creeks and Seminoles. In the meantime, General Harrison had overwhelmingly defeated Tecumseh's brother at Tippecanoe, and broken the plan at that point, but 1812-13 proved to be Tecumseh's years, and the movement was started by an outbreak in Alabama, August 30, 1813, known as the "Massacre of Fort Mimms."

This outrage aroused Tennessee, and General Jackson, as commander-in-chief within that state, issued a call for volunteers in his position. Within a month he had sent Colonel Coffee, with 500 cavalry, to Huntsville, Alabama, and followed him shortly after with reinforcements, fighting on November 8th, the Battle of Talladega, in which the Indians were driven back, leaving 290 dead on the field. Jackson pushed forward, having now about 1,000 troops raiding the Indians wherever he could find them. This continued until the latter part of March, when the Creeks made their final stand at a bend of the Tallapoosa River, about fifty-five miles from Fort Strother, having about 900 warriors. Here Jackson completely crushed them with his army of 2,000 men, only a few escaping, 557 dead Creeks being found on the battlefield.

This wiped out the Indian movement in Florida, and Jackson immediately started for New Orleans, which he found protected by only 2,000 men, with the immortal schooner *Caroline* and the ship *Louisiana* lying at anchor in the river, without men. In the meantime, the army of Pensacola, under General Coffee was approaching, and volunteers from Tennessee, under General Carroll, were moving toward him, so that he had two or three thousand troops in hand, 4,000 more on the way, six gunboats, two armed vessels, and the forts garrisoned by a few regulars. With this small force, mostly inexperienced volunteers, he had to contend with a fleet of fifty ships, carrying 1,000 guns, and a land force of 20,000 veterans. On the afternoon of December 23, 1814, with the British encamped nine miles below the city, Jackson sent the little *Caroline* against them, and a broadside of her small armament dealt great destruction among the British soldiers. Jackson's land force followed up this movement and produced a considerable impression on the enemy.

That night he began his celebrated fortification of New Orleans. Meanwhile the British made their preparations for reducing the city, and on January 1, 1815, they began to bombard the American works, which consisted of earth and cotton bales, but the American batteries proved to be too strong for them, and after some severe firing, the British retired, and made a movement to turn the American line. Just before dawn, on Sunday January 8th, General Pakenham gave the signal for assault, and the American fire was so fierce that in twenty-five minutes, thousands of British veterans were repulsed and entirely routed. In two houars, every British gun was silenced, and its defenders driven to the rear. On the British side there were 700 killed, 1,400 wounded, and 500 prisoners, while Jackson's loss was eight killed and thirteen wounded. It was a great victory, and the news of it, as it spread through the country, raised General Jackson to the position of a hero. Resolutions of thanks and praise to him were passed by the legislatures of nearly all the states of the Union, while the thanks of Congress were given him by a unanimous vote, and a gold medal ordered to be struck and presented to him as a testimonial of his splendid achievement. This battle ended the war, which had really been closed by the treaty of peace made at Ghent,

December 24, 1814, news of which did not reach Washington until February 14, 1815.

On April 6th, Jackson returned to Tennessee, and settled down for a summer's rest at the "Hermitage." So great was the enthusiasm aroused by Jackson's military success that he was now freely mentioned as a possible candidate for the Presidency, to succeed President Madison, who at that time, was closing his second term. However, in November of 1817, he was again called into the field to repress a revolt of the Seminole Indians in Florida. Jackson's actions through this conflict were imperious and dictatorial. The Indian trouble was complicated wth the Spanish authority in Florida, and, as a matter of fact, Jackson invaded the dominion of a king who was at peace with the United States, seized a fortress of his province, and expelled its garrison, all of which placed the U.S. government in a delicate situation. However, John Quincy Adams, Secretary of State, supported Jackson in his action, being opposed by Henry Clay, who was severe in his comment and criticism. Out of this course, on the part of Clay, began the persistent feud which existed between the two men.

Jackson was, however, sustained by the committee of the whole. Spain ceded Florida to the United States, and President Monroe appointed Jackson its first governor. Finding his powers as governor more strictly limited than suited his views, Jackson only held the office for a few weeks, and in November, 1821, returned to "The Hermitage." On July 20, 1822, Jackson was nominated by the Tennessee Legislature for the Presidency. The following year, he was again elected to the U.S. Senate, where he was known as a high tariff man, but taking little part in debate. His feeling with regard to his nomination for the Presidency may be judged from a statement made by Bishop Paine, who at that time called at "The Hermitage" and spoke to the general in regard to it. The latter said: "I have been looking forward to a release from public office and its cares, thinking I would then attend in earnest to my religious affairs, and I dread the excitement likely to spring up if my friends persist. I do not covet more honors; my country has honored me enough, and I prefer quiet; but having said that no one should seek the office, nor any patriot reject it when called to it, I can only say I could not refuse it if tendered."

The election in November, 1824, showed 99 electoral votes for Jackson; 84 for Adams; 41 for Crawford, and 37 for Clay. None of the candidates having a majority, the election was thrown into the House of Representatives, where a President must be chosen from the three highest names on the list, thus throwing out Clay altogether; the election resulted in Adams becoming President, he having obtained the support of Clay. The charge was made, and it was believed by many that this was the result of a corrupt bargain between Adams and Clay, and this belief brought about the duel between the latter and John Randolph of Roanoke. In the course of a debate on the subject of an international congress of American republics, Randolph denounced the administration, alluding to Adams and Clay as a "combination of the Puritan and blackleg." Clay challenged Randolph, and a bloodless duel was fought April 8, 1826. Jackson and his friends felt the defeat seriously, although with no real grounds for it, and Jackson could never be made to change his opinion that Clay was in some way responsible. The nomination of Jackson was such a departure from established precedent as to carry defeat in its trail. Up to that period, the Presidents of the United States had been men distinguished for everything which Jackson lacked. Highly educated, rendered courtly and diplomatic by their associations, they were the exact opposites to the "field" school formed Jackson, with his after-plantation and rough battlefield and campaign experiences--but none of this mattered in the end.

His defeat caused a state of feeling which, being backed by Martin Van Buren with his powerful influence, resulted in the determination, on the part of those who had been beaten to nominate and elect Jackson in 1828, and this was precisely what was done. At the election that year, Jackson received 178 votes in the electoral college, being 47 more than was necessary. Before he had entered office, however, on December 22, 1828, he met with the misfortune of losing his beloved wife. She died very suddenly, and the anguish of the old general at this unexpected bereavement is described as most intense. He sat in a chair by her dead body, with his face bowed and his head in his hands, weeping. To friends who called to console him, he said: "What are the world and its honors to me since she is taken from me?" He never was quite the same man afterward. His spirit was subdued, and it is said that his old-time exclamation, "By the Eternal!" very rarely passed his lips after the death of Mrs. Jackson.

Jackson's first administration was most noted, perhaps, for the establishment of the system "To the victors belong the spoils." This principle he carried out practically, and during the year 1829, his removals from office wre greater than had ever been known before, and they were acknowledged to be removals because of opposition to him, while the concurrent appointments were made from among those who had aided his election. Jackson's next important administrative act was brought about by his contest with the Bank of the United States, which was flourishing at that time, with a capital of $35,000,000; $6,000,000 or $7,000,000 on deposit of public money, and $6,000,000 more of private deposits. Its circulation was $12,000,000; its discounts more than $40,000,000 a year, and its annual profits were over $3,000,000. The central bank was in Philadelphia, and it had twenty-five branches located in the principal cities of the Union. Every state in the Union was represented among its stockholders.

In his first message, Jackson attacked the principle upon which the Bank of the United States existed. In the first session of the twenty-second Congress, the question of rechartering the bank came up, and a bill to that effect was passed. The President vetoed it. His reason was, in a word, "Monopoly." It was impossible to pass the bill over his veto, and the bank as a government institution, came to an end on March 4, 1836. It continued business as a private bank for six years, when it later failed, ruining thousands.

It was during Jackson's first administration that the expression "kitchen cabinet" came into use. It was brought into existence by the fact that Jackson, who, excepting Martin Van Buren, had no prominent or well-known men in his cabinet, made clerks of his secretaries, while using as confidential advisers, a few intimate friends: Amos Kendall, Duff Green, Isaac Hill and others, who became known as the "kitchen cabinet." They were all machine politicians, two of them being editors of partisan newspapers, and the men who were doubtlessly responsible for many of the political evils that existed in the governmental system of the United States after that time. Of all the Presidents of the United States, except Jefferson and Lincoln, Jackson may be considered to have exerted the most important impression on the politics, and thus on the history of the country.

In 1832, Jackson was reelected to the Presidency by a still larger majority in the electoral college than before. The year 1832 was important on account of the nullification action of South Carolina, headed by John C. Calhoun, the point being the avowed determination on the part of that state to disobey the Tariff Law of 1828 and the amendment to the same of 1832, and the announcement on the part of the state that if the government of the United States should attempt to enforce the Tariff Law, South Carolina would no longer consider itself a member of the Federal Union. Jackson was equal to the occasion. He issued a proclamation which electrified the country and scared South Carolina from its threatened plans of nullification. In fact, the President resolved that with the first overt act, John C. Calhoun would find himself a prisoner of state, charged with high treason.

When General Jackson lay on his deathbed, he was asked by Dr. Edgar what he would have done if Calhoun and the other nullifiers had kept on. "Hung them, sir, high as Haman. They should have been a terror to traitors to all time, and posterity would have pronounced it the best act of my life." In 1833, Mr. Clay quieted the nullification excitement by his celebrated "Compromise Bill" for the regulation of the tariff, which the president reluctantly signed. Jackson retired from the Presidency at the age of seventy with shattered health. Jackson's methods in his foreign policy were not unlike those just described in regard to home quarrels. An instance occurred in 1833, when France defaulted on a payment of money arranged by treaty stipulation. The draft was presented to the French minister of finance, and payment was refused on the plea that the proper appropriation had not been made by the chambers. In his next message to Congress, Jackson recommended the passage of a law authorizing the capture of French vessels enough to make up the amount due. The French govenrment was naturally infuriated, and war was threatened unless the President would apologize; whereupon the British government recommended to France a more amicable attitude, with the result that the claim was paid without further delay.

Jackson died at his home, "The Hermitage," June 8, 1845, and was buried in a corner of the garden of that property, eighty yards from the dwelling, where his remains were afterward, in company with those of his wife, covered by a massive monument of Tennessee limestone.

JACKSON, JESSE (LOUIS), (1941-) — reverend, and longtime civil rights activist, was born on October 8, 1941 in Greenville, South Carolina. Heavily involved in sports throughout his high school years, he was awarded a football scholarship to the University of Illinois. After being informed that blacks were basically relegated to being linemen instead of quarterbacks, Jackson only stayed at Illinois one year before transferring to the all-black North Carolina Agricultural and Technical State College. There, he not only fulfilled his wish to be a football quarterback, but also served as student body president. It was also during that time that Jackson became politically active, not only on campus, but in the town of Greensboro, targeting various businesses known to refuse service to blacks, with sit-ins and picket lines, activities which made him a public figure throughout the state.

Jackson received his B.A. degree in 1964, after which, he worked a short time for Governor Terry Stanford of North Carolina. He then moved to Chicago after receiving a scholarship from the Chicago Theological Seminary. With only one more semester to go after two-and-a-half years of study, he left for Atlanta, Georgia to work full-time for the Southern Christian Leadership Conference, which was headed by charismatic leader, Dr. Martin Luther King Jr.

In 1966, at the request of Dr. King, Jackson went to Chicago to head Operation Breadbasket. During his tenure, Jackson used picketing and boycotts as a way to secure several jobs for blacks in companies within their own neighborhoods. One of the most notable of the organization's various protests was against A&P supermarkets, which lasted for sixteen weeks. The end result, was that A&P "eventually signed an agreement to hire 268 more blacks, including store managers and warehouse supervisors, and agreed to stock some twenty-five brands of black-manufactured goods." In August of 1967, Jackson was named national director of Operation Breadbasket.

On April 4, 1968, Jackson was standing on the porch of a hotel room in Memphis, along with Martin Luther King, Jr., when the latter was assassinated. Although it was assumed that Jackson might be named to succeed the fallen leader as the president of the SCLC, the position went to Reverend Ralph Abernathy.

Jackson, who became a reverend himself after being ordained in June of 1968, stayed with the SCLC for another three-and-a-half years, then at the end of 1971, organized Operation PUSH, which had its headquarters in Chicago. Continuing in the same vein as Operation Breadbasket, the intent of the new organization was to "push for a greater share of economic and political power for poor people in America in the spirit of Dr. Martin Luther King Jr."

Jackson strove to gain national attention for his new organization by traveling throughout the country, giving numerous speeches during which the crowds would join him in chanting: "I am somebody. I may be poor, but I am somebody. I may be on welfare, but I am somebody. Nobody can save us, for us, but us." Knowing it was especially important to reach children with his message, he created PUSH-Excel (PUSH for Excellence) in 1976. With help from the Ford Foundation who gave him a $200,000 grant, Jackson visited numerous urban classrooms and stressed to the students the importance of having pride in themselves, explaining that the way to attain it was through education. In order to give them some encouragement, he persuaded them to sign pledges saying that they would give up television and radio for two hours a night in order to study.

In November of 1983, Jackson announced his candidacy for the Presidency. Outlining his platform, Jackson promised support for the "poor and dispossessed of this nation," saying he would create a "rainbow coalition" of groups who are "rejected and...despised" and "left naked before the Lord in the wintertime." Although Jackson's campaign had no money for television and radio ads, and was somewhat disorganized, his steadfast determination to speak for the disenfranchised, coupled with his articulate flair for the dramatic, got him several magazine covers and front page stories.

The high point of his campaign was his being able to persuade Syrian president Hafez al-assad to release United States Navy pilot Lieutenant Robert O. Goodman Jr., who was being held captive after his plane had been shot down by Syrian soldiers in December of 1983. Unfortunately a few months later, the campaign hit a low point when Jackson was quoted in the *Washington Post* by black reporter Milton Coleman as having referred to Jews as "Hymies," and New York City as "Hymietown," the remarks having been overheard in a private conversation. Embarrassed by the gaffe, Jackson later apologized to a synagogue congregation, saying, "It was not in the spirit of meanness, but an off-color remark having no bearing on religion or politics."

Although Jackson was able to reestablish support, enough for him to be a contender all the way up through several primaries, he, along with Senator Gary Hart, eventually lost to Walter Mondale. Speaking before the 1984 Democratic National Convention, Jackson spoke passionately about the mistakes he'd made, saying: "If in my low moments in word, deed, or attitude, through some error of temper, taste, or tone, I have caused anyone discomfort, created pain, or revived someone's fears, that was not my truest self...I am not a perfect servant, I am a public servant, doing my best against the odds. As I develop and serve, be patient. God is not finished with me yet."

In April of 1986, Jackson founded a new organization, the National Rainbow Coalition. He continued to remain politically active and fervently supported a bill making the birthday of Dr. Martin Luther King Jr. a national holiday.

He was an unsuccessful candidate for president in 1988 and declined to run in 1992.

On January 23, 1993 Jackson went on a two-day visit to Haiti as an unofficial U.S. envoy to tell the Haitian military that it faced the choice of cooperating in the restoration to power of exiled President Aristide, or of resisting, and facing the possibility of international or U.S. force.

Jackson is married to Jacqueline Lavinia Brown and the couple have five children.

JEFFRIES, RICHARD MANNING, (1889-1964) — Seventy-sixth state governor (D) of South Carolina, 1942-1943.

Born in Union County (now Cherokee County), South Carolina on February 27, 1889, the son of John and Mary Jeffries. He studied law at the University of South Carolina and was admitted to the South Carolina Bar in 1912. Soon after, he started a private law practice in Walterboro. He was married to Annie Keith Savage in 1911.

Jeffries was Superintendent of Jasper County in 1912. He also served on the South Carolina Democratic Executive Committee that same year. From 1913 to 1927, he was the Master in Equity and Probate Judge for Colleton County. He was elected to the State Senate and was a member from 1926 to 1958, serving as President Pro Tempore of the Senate from 1941 to 1942. Always active in Democratic politics, he was a delegate to the Democratic State Convention for more than thirty years, and he attended the Democratic National Convention in 1924, 1928, 1932, 1936, 1940, 1944, 1956, and 1960.

In 1941, when Governor Maybank resigned his office, Lieutenant Governor Joseph Harley took over as governor. When he died after just four months in office, the governorship devolved upon Jeffries who was President Pro Tempore of the State Senate. He entered office on March 2, 1942 just as the state had begun to organize its World War II effort, which included major shifts in the economy, and legislation to allow South Carolina citizens serving in the military to vote by absentee ballot. In 1942, German submarines mined the harbor in Charleston. Jeffries left office in January, 1943 when the newly elected, Olin Johnston, was inaugurated.

After leaving the governorship, Jeffries returned to the State House of Representatives. He continued to work for the war effort as chairman of the South Carolina War Fund from 1943 to 1946, and director of the National War Fund from 1944 to 1945. He was general manager of the South Carolina Public Service Authority from 1944 to 1964. In addition, he served on the South Carolina Tax Study Commission and the Democratic National Platform Committee. He died on April 20, 1964.

JENRETTE, JOHN WILSON, JR., (1936-   ) — a U.S. Representative from South Carolina; born in Conway, Horry County, S.C., May 19, 1936; attended public schools; B.A., Methodist Men's (now Wofford) College, Wofford, S.C.; LL.B., University of South Carolina Law School, Columbia, 1962; admitted to the South Carolina bar in 1962 and commenced practice in North Myrtle Beach; served as North Myrtle Beach city judge, 1962-1965; city attorney, 1965-1969; served in the South Carolina house of representatives, 1964-1972; unsuccessful candidate for election in 1972 to the Ninety-third Congress; delegate, Democratic National Conventions, 1974, 1976; elected as a Democrat to the Ninety-fourth, Ninety-fifth and Ninety-sixth Congresses and served from November 5, 1975, Until his resignation, December 10, 1980; president of an advertising and public relations firm in Florence and Myrtle Beach, S.C.; is a resident of North Myrtle Beach, S.C.

JETER, THOMAS BOTHWELL, (1827-1883) — fifty-fourth state governor (D) of South Carolina, 1880.

He was born in Union County, South Carolina, the son of Elizabeth Gaulman and John C. Jeter.

Jeter was graduated from South Carolina College in 1846, studied law, and was admitted to the South Carolina Bar in 1848. He became a partner in a law firm with Andrew Wallance Thomson and practiced in Union, South Carolina until 1868.

Jeter was elected to the South Carolina House of Representatives in 1856. He served in the South Carolina Senate from 1872 to 1882, and was president pro tempore of this body from 1876 to 1882.

In February 1879, upon Governor Wade Hampton's resignation from office, Lieutenant Governor William D. Simpson became chief executive of the State. As president pro tempore of the South Carolina Senate, Jeter was next in line of succession, and became the lieutenant governor of the State. Simpson's resignation in September 1880 moved Jeter into the governorship of South Carolina. He held the office only three months, however, before Johnson Hagood's inauguration in November 1880.

After leaving the State's gubernatorial office, Jeter served as a member of the South Carolina Railroad Commission from 1882 until his death in May 1883. He was married to Ann Henderson Thompason in February 1857.

JOHNSON, DAVID, (1782-1855) — thirty-seventh state governor (D) of South Carolina, 1846-1848.

He was born in Louisa County, Virginia, the son of Elizabeth Dabney and Christopher Johnson.

Johnson was educated at the Hurlburt School and at South Carolina College. He studied law under Judge Abraham Nott, was admitted to the South Carolina Bar, and became a partner of Nott in a private law firm.

Johnson's public life began as a South Carolina Commissioner and a member of the South Carolina House of Representatves in 1812. From 1812 until 1815, he was a solicitor of the Middle Circuit, Union District, South Carolina, and was a circuit judge from 1815 through 1824. Johnson became a judge of the South Carolina Court of Appeals in 1824, remaining in this office until 1835, when he became Chancellor of South Carolina.

Johnson was elected governor of South Carolina in December 1846. A major issue during his administration was the Wilmot Proviso, which was an attempt to prevent, by congressional action, the extension of slavery into any territory acquired by the United States from Mexico. This conflict led to demands from secessionists who were calling for the State to leave the Union. John C. Calhoun, United States Senator from South Carolina, firmly defended the Southern contention that the federal government had no right to interfere with slavery, and that non-slaveholding states should cease efforts to disturb the South's "peculiar institution."

Johnson organized and dispached the Palmetto Regiment under Colonel Pierce Mason Butler for service in the Mexican War.

He was married to Barbara Herndon, with whom he had five sons and two daughters. He died in January 1855 in Limestone Springs, South Carolina.

JOHNSON, JOSEPH TRAVIS, (1858-1919) — a U.S. Representative from South Carolina; born in Brewerton, Laurens County, S.C., February 28, 1858; attended the common schools and was graduated from Erskine College, Due West, S.C., in 1879; taught school for several years; studied law; was admitted to the bar in 1883; practiced law in Laurens and later in Spartanburg; elected as a Democrat to the Fifty-seventh and to the seven succeeding Congresses and served from March 4, 1901, until April 19, 1915, when he resigned; Federal judge of the western district of South Carolina from 1915 until his death in Spartanburg, S.C., May 8, 1919; interment in Oakwood Cemetery.

JOHNSON, WILLIAM, (1771-1834) — was an early justice of the Supreme Court.

Born in Charleston, South Carolina on December 27, 1771, the son of William and Sarah Nightingale Johnson, William Johnson was graduated from Princeton University in 1790. After reading law with Charles Cotesworth Pinckney, he was admitted to the bar in 1793.

Departing politically from his Federalist mentor, he aligned himself with the new Jeffersonian Republican (Democratic Republican) Party and was elected three times to the South Carolina House of Representatives between 1794 and 1798. He served as speaker during his last term. In December of 1798, he was elected to the state's highest court where he remained until his appointment to the United States Supreme Court by President Thomas Jefferson, who hoped to counter the control of the court by Chief Justice John Marshall, a Federalist. Johnson's 30 years on the court were marked by a protracted struggle with Marshall, who, in trying to make the court the acknowledged spokesman of the law and the Constitution, not only wrote the opinions in important cases but also sought the unanimous support of his colleagues for them. After 1811, although only two Federalists remained on the seven-man bench, Marshall continued to dominate the court's decisions in most major cases, Nevertheless, Johnson managed to create a tradition of dissent, partly at Jefferson's insistence. Johnson wrote to Jefferson in 1822 that, despite the many difficulties, he had finally managed to prevail upon the justices "to adopt the course they now pursue which is to appoint someone to deliver the opinion of the majority, and leave it to the discretion of the rest to record their opinions or not *ad libitum.*"

After Marshall's opinions, those of Johnson were the most numerous in the early years of the court, and his emphasis on the government's power to control economic affairs anticipated later developments. As was then the custom, Johnson continued to hold circuit court in Charleston while serving on the Supreme Court. His judicial independence was shown in decisions in which he declared illegal several federal and state measures. Although he was deeply concerned for individual rights, his impetuous manner nevertheless often involved him in controversy.

Johnson moved from South Carolina to Pennsylvania in 1833, partly because of his opposition to nullification.

William Johnson married Sarah Bennett on March 20, 1794. He died following surgery in Brooklyn, New York on August 4, 1834.

JOHNSTON, OLIN DEWITH TALMADGE, (1896-1965) — Seventy- third and seventy-seventh state governor (D) South Carolina, 1935-39 and 1943-45.

Born near Honea Path, South Carolina on November 18, 1896, the son of Edward and Leila (Webb) Johnston. He served as a sergeant in the U.S. Army during World War I. On his return, he attended Wofford College (A.B.), and the University of South Carolina (M.A. and LL.B.) After graduation in 1924, he was admitted to the South Carolina Bar and he established a law practice in Spartanburg. In 1923, he married Gladys Atkinson. They had three children.

Johnston moved to Columbia and became a partner in the legal firm, Johnston and Williams. He was elected to the State House of Representatives and served from 1923 to 1924 and from 1927 to 1930. From 1934 to 1940 and again between 1944 and 1948, he was a member of the Democratic National Committee. He won the state governorship in 1934 in an unopposed general election. During his term, he ordered the National Guard to occupy the offices of the State Highway Department because of alleged violations which proved to be unfounded. Also, during this time, the South Carolina Public Welfare Act and Alcoholic Beverage Control bill were both passed into law.

Since he was constitutionally ineligible to succeed himself in office, Johnston left the governorship in 1939. After a time had elapsed however, he ran again, and in 1942, was elected to a second term in office. His second administration was concerned with World War II and with keeping South Carolina on a wartime status. He resigned the governorship in 1945 to take a seat in the U.S. Senate, where he served for the next twenty years. He died on April 18, 1965.

JOHNSTONE, GEORGE, (1846-1921) — a U.S. Representative from South Carolina; born in Newberry, S.C., April 18, 1846; attended the common schools; entered the State Military Academy, from which he enlisted in the Confederate Army as a member of the battalion of State cadets and served until the close of the Civil War; attended the University of Edinburgh, Scotland, 1866-1869; returned to the United States; studied law; was admitted to the bar in 1871 and commenced practice in Newberry, S.C.; declined a nomination to the State house of representatives in 1874; member of the State house of representatives 1877-1884; declined to be a candidate for reelection; member of the commission that revised the tax laws and suggested amendments to the State constitution in 1881; member of the State executive committee of the Democratic Party 1880-1884; elected as a Democrat to the Fifty- second Congress (March 4, 1891-March 3, 1893); unsuccessful candidate for renomination in 1892; resumed the practice of law in Newberry, S.C.; member of the

State constitutional convention in 1895; died in Newberry, S.C., March 8, 1921; interment in Johnstone Cemetery.

JUST, ERNEST EVERETT, (1883-1941) — born in Charleston, South Carolina in 1883 Just made significant contributions to the world of biological science, but he eventually left the United States because stigma of racism followed him even into the laboratory.

The oldest of three children by Charles Frazier and Mary (Mathews) Just, Ernest Just grew up in a religious family that emphasized education as the way to improve the status of the black race. His father died when he was four, and his mother open a school for black children, where Just attended. At the age of eleven he started segregated public school in Orangeburg, South Carolina. He applied for admission to the Kimball Union Academy in Meriden, New Hampshire, after reading about the institution in a magazine. In 1900 he was accepted, and he made his way north working on a ship. He completed the academy's four-year course in three years, and won a scholarship to Dartmouth College in Hanover, New Hampshire. He specialized in zoology there, was elected Phi Beta Kappa, and received his A.B. degree magna cum laude in 1907. He was accepted on the faculty at Howard University in Washington D.C., where he started as an instructor. In 1912 he married Ethel Highwarden of Columbus, Ohio, a fellow teacher at Howard, and they had three children together.

While beginning his graduate work, Just trained at the Marine Laboratory in Woods Hole, Massachusetts. He returned there every summer for the next 20 years, studying the fertilization and early development of eggs. He received funding for his work from the National Research Council. Back at Howard Just was named full professor and head of the department of zoology in 1912. He also served for eight years as professor of physiology in the medical school. In 1915 he was the first recipient of the Spingarn Medal from the National Association for the Advancement of Colored People, in recognition of his research and his effective efforts to improve the quality of medical training at Howard. He took a leave of absence from Howard in 1915 so he could complete his graduate study at the University of Chicago and receive is Ph.D., magna cum laude.

During his years of research Just developed new cytological and embryological techniques which he used to study the fertilization and physiology of the eggs of marine organisms. He examined the process of cell division, the mechanism of water transfer in living cells, and artificial parthenogenesis. He used ultraviolet rays to change the number of chromosomes in the reproductive cell, and studied the changes in the development of the egg. Just's most famous theory was that the ectoplasm (cortex) of an animal egg cell is the prime factor in the initiation of development (fertilization), and through its interplay with cytoplasm is a causative factor in differentiation and in the building up of nuclear material. According to his theory, both the differentiation and the action of the gene is heredity result from an interplay of the ectoplasm and the nucleus with the cytoplasm. He was a pioneer in the investigations of the biochemical constitution and function of the cell surface, and membranes in general.

Just published a number of papers and was deeply respected by the scientists of his day. He was a fellow of the American Association for the Advancement of Science, vice-president of the American Society of Zoologists (1930), and a member of a number of other scientific organizations. He collaborated on the book General Cytology (1924) and served as an editor for Physiological Zoology, the Biological Bulletin, Protoplasma (Berlin) and the Journal of Morphology. However, despite his many titles, as a black Just did not receive the respect given to white researchers of his caliber. He was never invited to a post at an American university or research institute, where he could have a permanent laboratory and facilities. He was very sensitive to the treatment he received, both personally and professionally, but found the climate in Europe to be entirely different. There he was warmly welcomed and given a great deal of respect, and being fluent in French and German he felt at home. Finally in the early 1930's Just gave up teaching altogether and moved to Europe, working at the Kaiser Wilhelm Institute in Berlin and at laboratories in Italy, France and Russia. He published two books while there, Biology of the Cell Surface (1939) and Basic Methods for Experiments on Eggs of Marine Animals (1939). Just finally returned to the United States in 1941, where he died of cancer in Washington D.C.

K

KALB, JOHANN, (1721-1780) — was a French soldier who fought in the Carolina campaigns.

Born in Huttendorf, Bavaria on June 29, 1721, the son of Johan Leonhard and Margarethe Seitz (Putz) Kalb, Johann Kalb was originally a peasant, but by the time he was 22 and serving as a lieutenant in a French infantry regiment, he was calling himself Jean de Kalb. He later gained the name of Baron de Kalb.

Unremittingly ambitious for glory, he served with distinction as a major in the Seven Years' War. He went to America on a secret mission for the French government in 1768, remained there for four months and returned to France when his dispatches were intercepted. However he retained a desire to fight in the New World. Kalb got his wish in 1777, when promised by Silas Deane to receive a major general's commission, he arrived in America with his young friend, the Marquis de Lafayette. Kalb was disappointed, however, when Lafayette received the commission and Kalb was left without a command. When he returned to France late that year, Kalb was made major general and was assigned to serve under Lafayette.

Kalb spent the winter of 1777-78 with General George Washington at Valley Forge and was with the Continental Army until 1780, although he had no opportunity to distinguish himself. In April of that year he was ordered to South Carolina, where he served under General Horatio Gates in the Carolina Campaign. Gates wanted, against Kalb's advice, to attack the British after Charleston had fallen to General Sir Henry Clinton. The troops encountered Lord Cornwallis' army near Camden, South Carolina on August 16, 1780. Gates troops fled the enemy three times and, when his position was seen to be hopeless, led his few remaining men forward in a last desperate attack. Kalb fought heroically during the battle, but was wounded in the attack and died three days later.

Johann Kalb married Anna Van Robais on April 10, 1764. He died on August 19, 1780 in Camden, South Carolina.

KEITT, LAURENCE MASSILLON, (1824-1864) — a U.S. Representative from South Carolina; born in Orangeburg District, S.C., October 4, 1824; pursued classical studies and was graduated from South Carolina College (now the University of South Carolina) at Columbia in 1843; studied law; was admitted to the bar in 1845 and commenced practice in Orangeburg; member of the state house of representatives, 1848-1853; elected as a Democrat to the Thirty-third and Thirty-fourth Congresses and served from March 4, 1853, to July 16, 1856, when he resigned after the Thirty-fourth Congress censured him on July 15, 1856, for his role in the assault made upon Senator Charles Sumner on May 22, 1856; again elected to the Thirty-fourth Congress to fill the vacancy caused by his own resignation; reelected to the Thirty- fifth and Thirty-sixth Congresses and served from August 6, 1856, until his retirement in December 1860; chairman, Committee on Public Buildings and Grounds (Thirty-fifth Congress); delegate to the secession convention of South Carolina; member of the Provisional Congress of the Confederacy in Montgomery, Ala., in February 1861 and in Richmond, Va., in July 1861; raised the Twentieth South Carolina Regiment of Volunteers and was commissioned its colonel on January 11, 1862; subsequently promoted to the rank of brigadier general; wounded in the Battle of Cold Harbor, near Richmond, Va., and died as a result of his wounds the following day, June 4, 1864; interment in the family cemetery, near St. Matthews, S.C.

KELLOGG, CLARA LOUISE, (1842-1916) — was an opera singer whose adaption of Marguerite in *Faust* was considered the definitive portrayal of the role.

Born in Sumterville, South Carolina on July 12, 1842, the daughter of George and Jane Elizabeth (Crosby) Kellogg, Clara Kellogg received her education at the Ashland Seminary in Catskill. She studied singing in New York City and from French and Italian masters.

After a concert tour in which she sang selections from the part of Linda in Donizetti's *Linda di Chamounix*, Kellogg made her New York debut in 1861 as Gilda in Verdi's *Rigoletto* at the Academy of Music. She then sang in *Sonnambula* in Boston before Civil War conditions ended the season. In 1863, she appeared in Gounod's *Faust* as Marguerite. After its first New York presentation at the Academy of Music on November 25, 1863, *Faust* became one of the major productions offered by operatic companies during the next three decades. Kellogg's adaption of the heroine was considered to be the definitive portrayal of the role.

In 1867, Kellogg made her London debut in the role of Marguerite. From 1868 until 1873, she toured the United States in Italian opera and concert productions. She also appeared in London as Linda. In 1873, she organized an English opera company and was said to have done more for the American musical art than had been done before. Her organization was considered the best that had been heard in the English opera. She provided employment to a large number of young singers who, beginning their careers with her chorus, soon advanced to higher places in the musical world.

During the winter season of 1874-75 she sang no less than 125 nights. Thereafter she divided her time between Europe and America. She sang in London, in the Italian opera in Vienna, and in St. Petersburg. Her repertory included more than 40 roles. Kellogg published her autobiography, *Memoirs of an American Prima Donna* in 1913.

As a singer, Kellogg was equally at home both in dramatic and in lyric roles. Her voice was a pure, sweet soprano of extraordinary range. In the course of her long and successful career, she established a reputation for her readiness to respond to charitable appeals, especially in connection with musical objects, and for her generosity in encouraging and financing struggling aspirants to musical fame. For some 20 years, Kellogg maintained the best traditions of Italian and French operatic singing in the

United States, and by means of her artistic gifts and popularity as a native prima donna, advanced the cause of opera sung in English.

Clara Kellogg married Carl Strakosch, her impresario, in 1887. She died on May 13, 1916.

KERSHAW, JOHN, (1765-1829) — a U.S. Representative from South Carolina; born in Camden, Kershaw County, S.C., September 12, 1765; attended Rushworth School and Oxford College, England; studied law; was admitted to the bar and commenced practice in Camden, S.C.; engaged in planting and wheat milling; tobacco inspector in 1789; member of the constitutional convention in 1790; judge of the county court of Kershaw when first established in 1791; member of the State house of representatives in 1792- 1794 and 1800-1801; mayor of Camden in 1798, 1801, 1811, and 1822; justice of quorum from Kershaw County in 1806; captain of the First South Carolina Light Dragoons; elected as a Republican to the Thirteenth Congress (March 4, 1813-March 3, 1815); chairman, Committee on Accounts (Thirteenth Congress); unsuccessful candidate for reelection in 1814 to the Fourteenth Congress; engaged in the settling of his father's estates and planting; died in Camden, S.C., August 4, 1829; interment in the Kershaw family burial ground.

KEYSERLING, LEON H., (1908-1987) — United States Government official, economist, lawyer, was born in Charleston, South Carolina on January 22, 1908. He attended Columbia University, earning an A.B. degree in 1928. He continued his education at Harvard University, receiving his LL.B. degree in 1931, then did his graduate studies back at Columbia between 1931 and 1933.

Columbia University was also where he began teaching economics during 1932-33. In the latter year he moved to Washington, D.C., becoming a staff attorney involved with the Agricultural Adjustment Act. He described himself during that time as one of "the glittering flight of bright young men" who wanted to work in Government service under President Franklin D. Roosevelt.

Later in 1933, Keyserling became secretary and legislative assistant to U. S. Senator Robert F. Wagner, a post he held until 1937. Concurrently, he also worked for the United States Senate Committee on Banking and Currency from 1935 to 1937. During 1937-38, he was general counsel for the U.S. Housing Authority, serving as deputy administrator and general counsel from 1938 to 1942; during 1941-42, he served as acting administrator. In the latter year, Keyserling became general counsel of the National Housing Agency, staying in that position until 1946. Between 1946 and 1949, he was vice-chairman on the President's Council of Economic Advisors, serving as chairman between 1949 and 1953. Beginning in 1953, Keyserling more or less freelanced as an attorney and consulting economist to several different government agencies, as well as foreign governments, private companies, and individuals. That same year he also founded the Congress on Economic Progress.

In 1944, Keyserling won the Pabst Post-War Employment Award for his essay entitled "The American Economic Goal: A Practical Start Toward Post-War Full Employment," in which he wrote: "Full employment in a free society is not just jobs. Hitler provided jobs— while he lasted. Full employment in a democracy means supplying the kind of jobs that add most to meeting a people's physical needs— plus the kind of leisure that adds most to their cultural advancement." "The achievement of full employment," he continued, "is predominantly a task for the system of American enterprise...working in a democratic environment which encourages collective bargaining by all groups and discourages restrictive monopolies by any."

Books that Keyserling has written include: *The Federal Budget and the General Welfare*, 1959; *Inflation: Cause and Cure*, 1959; *Key Policies for Full Employment*, 1960; *The Peace Investment Corporation*, 1961; *Poverty and Deprivation in the U.S.*, 1962; *Taxes and the Public Interest*, 1963; *Two Top Priority Programs to Reduce Unemployment*, 1963; *The Prevalent Monetary Policy and Its Consequences*, 1964; *Progress on Poverty: The U.S. at the Crossroads*, 1964; *The Role of Wages in a Great Society*, 1966; *A Freedom Budget for All Americans*, 1966; *More Growth Without Inflation or More Inflation Without*

Growth?, 1970; and *Full Employment Without Inflation*, 1975; among several others.

While working as a consultant to members of the House of Representatives and the Senate, Keyserling, according to *Contemporary Authors*, was "a major participant in studies related to and the actual drafting of legislation. These pieces of legislation include the National Industrial Recovery Act, public works and relief acts, the Social Security Act, the Employment Act of 1946, and the Housing Act of 1949."

Keyserling was married to Mary Dublin. He died on August 9, 1987.

KILLIAN, JAMES R(HYNE), JR., (1904-1988) — educator, government official, was born on July 24, 1904 in Blacksburg, South Carolina, and raised in Concord, North Carolina. He attended Trinity College (later Duke University) for one year. Deciding to pursue an engineering career, Killian enrolled at the Massachusetts Institute of Technology, earning a B.S. degree in 1926. After his graduation, Killian garnered a position as assistant managing editor of the scientific journal, *Technology Review*, eventually becoming managing editor, then editor.

In 1939 Killian was asked to take a position as executive assistant to Dr. Karl T. Compton, president of M.I.T. Killian moved up to executive vice-president in 1943, became vice- president in 1945, and three years later, was named president of that school. *Current Biography* noted that during Killian's tenure as president, he "promoted the expansion of M.I.T., with its ties to private business, radiation research, radar, computation, and missile guidance systems, and the whole range of weapons technology. His administration was also marked by a greater emphasis on the humanities and social sciences in the education of scientists and engineers."

Killian's expertise was also put to good use in government service, beginning when President Harry S. Truman asked him to be a member of his Communications Policy Board, a post Killian served in during 1950-51. From 1950 to 1952, he served on Truman's Advisory Commission on Management, and during those years, became a member of the Science Advisory Committee of the Office of Defense Mobilization.

President Dwight D. Eisenhower, after learning that the Russians had sent the first artificial earth satellite into space, also asked for Killian's help in 1957, naming him special assistant for science and technology, a position in which Killian was to review, update, and streamline the U.S.'s various military programs. When his appointment was announced, *Business Week* wrote admiringly: "Perhpas Killian's finest attribute for his job is his ability to understand scientists. His thirty years at M.I.T. have taught him how to mold into a productive group hundreds of brilliant specialists, all of whom were apt to be going in different directions at once. Because he understands these people, where each is going, and what is the relationship of each project to the whole, he is genuinely respected. This means that scientists now have somebody at the top they can turn to who will be receptive to their ideas."

In addition to several published speeches, Killian has written such books as: (with Harold E. Edgerton) *Flash! Seeing the Unseen by Ultra High-Speed Photography*, 1939; *Sputnik, Scientists and Eisenhower*, 1977; and (with Harold E. Edgerton) *Moments of Vision*, 1979.

Along with numerous honorary degrees, Killian was given the President's Certificate of Merit in 1948, the Army Department's Certificate of Appreciation in 1953, the Public Welfare Medal of the National Academy of Sciences, and the Exceptional Civilian Service Award, the latter two in 1957.

Killian remained president of M.I.T. until 1959 when he was named corporation chairman, a post he held until 1971. From 1971 to 1979 he served as honorary chairman. Between 1965 and 1967, as chairman of the Carnegie Commission on Educational Television, Killian was in charge of the development of a government- supported public television network. He also served as chairman of the Corporation for Public Broadcasting during 1973-74.

Killian was married to Elizabeth Parks and the couple had two children. He died on January 29, 1988.

KINLOCH, FRANCIS, (1755-1826) — a Delegate from South Carolina; born in Charleston, S.C., March 7, 1755; educated by private tutors; went to England in 1768 and entered Eton College, from which institution he graduated in 1774; studied law at Lincoln's Inn, London, which he entered in 1774 and was admitted to the bar in that city; studied in Paris and Geneva 1774-1777; returned to the United States and served as volunteer, lieutenant, and captain in the Revolutionary War 1778-1781; served in the State house of representatives in 1779 and 1786- 1788; Member of the Continental Congress in 1780; was an extensive rice planter at "Kensington," Georgetown District, S.C.; delegate to the State convention which ratified the Federal Constitution May 23, 1788; elected warden of the city of Charleston and justice of the peace and quorum in 1789; member of the State legislative council in 1789 and of the State constitutional convention in 1790; died in Charleston, S.C., February 8, 1826; interment in St. Michael's Church Cemetery.

KIRKLAND, (JOSEPH) LANE, (1922-?) — labor union official, was born in Camden, South Carolina on March 12, 1922. He attended Newberry College for a year, then joined the United States Merchant Marines, serving on the *S.S. Liberator.* After studying at their academy, he graduated in 1942. With the country in the midst of World War II, he was assigned to various merchant ships that were carrying war equipment and supplies. After earning his master's license, he signed up with the International Organization of Masters, Mates and Pilots.

After the war ended, Kirkland moved to Washington, D.C. and while attending night school at Georgetown University's School of Foreign Service, he supported himself with a job at the United States Navy Hydrographic Office where he drafted nautical charts. Kirkland earned his B.S. degree in 1948, and soon after, became a staff researcher with the American Federation of Labor. Having a talent for writing, Kirkland was soon penning speeches for Alben Barkley, the running mate of President Harry S. Truman, and later on, also did the same for Adlai Stevenson when the latter ran for President in 1952 and 1956. Kirkland moved up from staff researcher at the AFL to assistant director of the Social Security department. In 1958 he went to work for the International Union of Operating Engineers as director of research and education. In 1960 Kirkland returned to the AFL (which by this time had merged with the CIO), at the request of the organization's president, George Meany, who asked Kirkland to work as his executive assistant, a post he held for nine years. "As the federation's chief troubleshooter," says *Current Biography*, Kirkland "mediated jurisdictional disputes between warring member unions, resolved maritime problems, and worked behind the scenes to settle a crippling mass transit strike in New York City in 1966." His main method of settling disputes involved trying to achieve "accommodation" between management and labor.

Somewhat of a liberal, Kirkland was passionate about civil rights and used his position to fight racial discrimination both within the union, and in the social arena, which included the areas of education, voting, and housing. He was also outspoken about his support for the "war on poverty" welfare programs initiated by President Lyndon Johnson.

In May of 1969 Kirkland was voted in to the position of secretary-treasurer of the AFL-CIO, making him one step away from the presidency. During his tenure, he publicly disagreed with President Richard M. Nixon who wanted to stop much needed wage increases for workers by creating wage and price controls, a decision that Kirkland called "a flagrant injustice." His outspoken rebellion earned him a place on Nixon's infamous "enemies list."

On Labor Day in 1975, which was the twentieth anniversary of the AFL-CIO merger, Kirkland gave an interview to the New York *Times* about the goals of that organization, saying: "Our interests relate to the best interests of working people. We have no visionary world, no utopia, that we're working toward, but we do have building blocks, and to the extent that we can develop it, we're trying to get the blocks in place...We're interested in a more humane society in which everybody has his chance."

When AFL-CIO president George Meany stepped down in 1979, Kirkland was chosen to replace him. During his tenure as president, Kirkland continued to fight discrimination against women and other minority groups who were often ignored for recruitment into the union, and also spoke out against industry, noting that they seemed to be determined to destroy unionism by waging what he termed a "class war."

Kirkland has been married twice: to Edith Draper Hollyday, with whom he had five children, and to his current wife, Irena Neumann.

KITT, EARTHA, (1928-   ) — singer, was born in the town of North, South Carolina on January 26, 1928, the daughter of William and Anna Kitt. Her father was a sharecropper who died two years after her birth, and although her mother struggled on, she too died when Eartha was six. Eartha and her sister only escaped utter poverty when her aunt who lived in New York sent for them. The little girl soon demonstrated singing and dancing talent and won various prizes at public school. At 16 an audition with Katherine Dunham resulted in a dance scholarship. Eartha's natural ability with language and singing skills soon landed her a solo role in Ms. Dunham's touring troupe. She toured the United States, Mexico, and South America, and in 1948 traveled to Europe. In Paris she left the troupe and quickly became a hit singing in clubs along the left bank.

Ms. Kitt's aunt died in 1951 and she returned to New York for the funeral. When she returned to Paris Orson Wells gave her the role of Helen of Troy in *Faust*, a performance which led to rave reviews by the critics. This role led to two films, and a successful night club engagement in New York. During the 1950's film roles, night club engagements, and record deals kept the singer busy and prosperous. She scored a major hit on Broadway in the 1952 *New Faces*, and another success as Mehitabel the Cat in *Shinbone Alley* in 1957. The actress received international notoriety in 1968 when she interrupted Lady Bird Johnson at a White House lunch to denounce the Vietnam War. Ms. Kitt has a daughter and lives in London.

L

LAURENS, HENRY, (1724-1792) — was a political leader who was a member of the United States Constitutional Convention in 1787.

Born in Charleston, South Carolina on March 6, 1724, the son of Jean Samuel and Esther (Grasset) Laurens, Henry Laurens received his education in the colonies and then spent three years, until the death of his father in 1747, as a clerk in England. Returning to Charleston to settle the estate, he remained there and became active as an importer-exporter. His business thrived and he became one of the wealthiest men in Charleston.

As his interest in business lessened, Laurens became more active politically. He served in the state assembly from 1757 until 1764 and 1765 until 1774. In the growing disputes between England and the American colonies, he sided with the colonies. He was vocal in his opposition to British aggression and had frequent contests with crown judges, especially in respect to their decisions in marine law and the courts of admiralty. His great legal ability was demonstrated in the pamphlets he published against these measures.

Retiring from business, Laurens went to England in 1771 to oversee the education of his sons. While in London he was one of 38 Americans who signed a petition in 1774 to dissuade parliament from passing the Boston Port Bill.

In 1775 he returned to Charleston and served on the Council of Safety and, after helping to draft a state constitution, became the state vice president in 1776. In January of the following year he was a delegate to the Continental Congress and in November succeeded John Hancock to become the second president of the Congress. Laurens resigned the presidency in December 1778 in the controversy over the actions of United States representative Silas Deane in France.

Laurens remained in Congress until November 1779, when he undertook a mission to the Netherlands to gain financial support for the colonies. His departure was delayed until August 1780, and he was captured by the British off Newfoundland and imprisoned in the Tower of London despite his diplomatic immunity. In addition, the discovery among his papers of the outline of a treaty between the United States and the Netherlands led to a British declaration of war against the Dutch. Laurens remained confined for more than a year (October 1780 until December 1781) and was finally exchanged for General Charles Cornwallis in April 1782.

Laurens was the subject of considerable criticism after his release for sending what were felt to be submissive petitions to the British authorities during his imprisonment, but his diplomatic status was confirmed by Congress in September 1782 and in November he joined John Adams, Benjamin Franklin and John Jay at the peace conference that produced the Treaty of Paris in 1783. Laurens returned to the United States late in 1784 and retired to his plantation near Charleston the next year. Laurens was a member of the United States Constitutional Convention in 1787.

Laurens married Eleanor Ball on July 6, 1750. The couple had 12 children. He died on December 8, 1792 in Charleston.

LEGARE, GEORGE SWINTON, (1869-1913) — a U.S. Representative from South Carolina; born in Rockville, Charleston County, S.C., November 11, 1869; moved to Charleston in boyhood; was graduated from Porter Academy, Charleston, S.C., in 1889 and attended the law department of the University of South Carolina at Columbia for two years; was graduated from Georgetown University Law School, Washington, D.C., in 1893; was admitted to the bar the same year and commenced practice in Charleston, S.C.; corporation counsel 1898-1903; elected as a Democrat to the Fifty-eighth and to the four succeeding Congresses and served from March 4, 1903, until his death, before the close of the Sixty-second Congress; had been reelected to the Sixty-third Congress; died in Charleston, S.C., January 31, 1913; interment in Magnolia Cemetery.

LEGARE, HUGH SWINTON, (1797-1843) — a U.S. Representative from South Carolina; born in Chaleston, S.C., January 2, 1797; attended Charleston College and the school of Rev. Moses Waddell at Abbeville; was graduated from the College of South Carolina (now University of South Carolina) at Columbia in 1814; studied law 1814-1817; pursued further studies in Paris and Edinburgh in 1818 and 1819; admitted to the bar in 1822 and commenced practice in Charleston, S.C.; member of the State house of representatives 1820-1821 and 1824-1830; one of the founders and editor of the Southern Review 1828- 1832; attorney general of South Carolina 1830-1832; Charge d'Affaires to Brussels 1832- 1836; elected as a Democrat to the Twenty-fifth Congress (March 4, 1837-March 3, 1839); unsuccessful candidate for reelection; resumed the practice of law in Charleston; Attorney General of the United States in the Cabinet of President Tyler from September 13, 1841, until his death; also filled the office of Secretary of State ad interim from May 8, 1843, up to the time of his death, in Boston, Mass., June 20, 1843; interment in Mount Auburn Cemetery, Cambridge, Mass.; reinterment in Magnolia Cem etery, Charleston, S.C.

LEVER, ASBURY FRANCIS, (1875-1940) — a U.S. Representative from South Carolina; born near Springhill, Lexington County, S.C., January 5, 1875; attended the country schools; was graduated from Newberry (S.C.) College in 1895; taught school for two years; private secretary to Representative J. William Stokes 1897-1901; was graduated from the law department of Georgetown University, Washington, D.C., in 1899; was admitted to the bar in South Carolina the same year but did not practice; delegate to the Democratic State conventions in 1896 and 1900; member of the State house of representatives in 1901; elected as a Democrat to the Fifty-seventh Congress to fill the vacancy caused by the death of J. William Stokes; reelected to the Fifty-eighth and to the eight succeeding Congresses and served from November 5, 1901, until August 1, 1919, when he resigned to become a member of the Federal Farm Loan Board, in which capacity he served until 1922; chairman, Committee on Education

(Sixty-second Congress), Committee on Agriculture (Sixty-third through Sixty-fifth Congresses); member of the boards of trustees of Clemson (S.c.) College and Newberry (S.C.) College; elected president of the First Carolinas Joint Stock Land Bank at Columbia, S.C., in 1922; field representative of Federal Farm Board; director of the public relations administration of the Farm Credit Administration until his death on April 28, 1940, at "Seven Oaks," near Charleston, S.C.; interment in College Hill Cemetery, on campus of Clemson Agricultural College, Clemson, S.C.

LIEBER, FRANCIS, (1800-1872) — a political scientist and writer who, though controversial, chronicled the American economic and political thought during in the mid-to-late 1800's better than any other writer.

Born in Berlin, March 18, 1800, Lieber paid dearly for receiving his early education from Friedrich Ludwig Jahn. Jahn's schools were considered training grounds for radicals, and Lieber was persecuted either by association, or because he had been taught to speak freely about his ideas there. Jahn was also, coincidentally, considered a founder of modern gymnastics.

Upon entering adulthood, Lieber at first wanted to be a doctor, and he started college with that aim. Yet he also dreamed of being the man to assassinate Napoleon, so he left college to join the Prussian Army, fighting in Ligny, Waterloo and the Battle of Namur, where he was severely injured. He went back to school in 1819 but he was arrested in Berlin because of his association with Jahn. He went on to Jena, where he earned his Ph.D. in mathematics, which he hoped to teach. However, he was persecuted as a member of a student's society so he moved on to Halle, where he was closely watched by the government.

Prohibited from teaching Lieber took part in the Greek revolution, then left for Rome where he worked as a tutor for the son of a Prussian Ambassador. While there he wrote a book about his travels in Greece, called The German Anacharsis (1823). With assurance from the king that he would not be arrested, Lieber returned to Berlin in 1823 to study mathematics again. Despite those promises he was arrested in 1824 in a government sweep of "liberal conspirators," then he fled to England in 1826. He worked there for a year teaching and writing, then moved to the United States, where he was appointed the head of a new gymnasium and swimming school in Boston. In 1928 he published A Popular Essay on Subjects of Penal Law, which is considered a good example of mid-century liberal thought. In 1829 he married Matilda Oppenheimer. He soon gained fame as the founder and editor of the new Encyclopedia Americana (1829-1833), which was similar to the German Conversations Lexicon. The 13-volume set was intended to fill the informational gap between newspapers and massive, expensive encyclopedias. He also translated a French work on the revolution of July, 1830, and the life of Kasper Hauser.

Successful now, Lieber received a commission from the trustees of the Girard College to form a plan of education for their newly established institution. He lived in Philadelphia until 1835, when he was offered a position as professor of history and political economy at South Carolina College. He wrote dozens of books and essays including translations and autobiographical accounts. Two of his best-known works, Manual of Political Ethics (two volumes, 1838-39), and On Civil Liberty and Self-Government (two volumes, 1853) were highly praised. These were the first philosophical and theoretical attempts to analyze the new government in America since the nation was founded. Lieber praised the limited government and the checks and balances system, but warned of the need to limit "democratic absolutism" through the operation of judicial review. Not without controversy, some of his other works, like the ancient history text Great Events Described by Distinguished Historians, Chroniclers, and Other Writers (1840) earned him the label of hack.

Judging from his numerous writings, Lieber was an economic liberal and social conservative. He opposed the communitarians, the socialists and those who attacked private property. He labored diligently for prison reform, urged the immigration restriction of nonwhites, ridiculed woman's suffrage, criticized prohibitionists and rejected pacifism. Some thought he was a brilliant, other thought he was the most egotistical man in the United States.

Although he was finally able to teach and write in the United States as he pleased, Lieber was unhappy in the South because he opposed states' rights and secessionist ideas. In 1851 he began to warn Southerners against the idea of secession. He was also growing to strongly dislike slavery, but he stayed relatively quiet on the issue while living in Charleston. For nearly 30 years he tried to obtain a university post in the North, and finally in 1855, after failing to win the presidency of South Carolina College, he resigned and moved to New York City, where he taught history and political economy at Columbia College. His advice, though sometimes controversial, was often sought by the leaders of the United States government. He wrote two books on the war, one Guerrilla Parties Considered with Reference to the Laws and Usages of War (1862) was written at the request of General Halleck and was later often quoted during the Franco- German War. A Code for the Government of Armies (1863) was the first code of military law and procedure in the world. President Lincoln ordered that it be used by his armies, and it was used by many European armies later. Lieber was also one of the founders of the "Loyal Publication Society," which published more than 100 pro-union pamphlets. The war did break up his own family though, as two of his sons enlisted in the Union Army, and one fought as a Confederate.

In 1865 Lieber starting teaching at Columbia Law School, and was appointed superintendent of the Washington bureau that oversaw the collection, arrangement and preservation of the records of the Confederate government. In 1870 he was chosen by the United States and Mexico as final arbitrator in important disputes between the two countries. He revisited Europe twice after moving to America, and wrote numerous essays on European government. He died October 2, 1872, in New York City.

LITTLEJOHN, ROBERT MCGOWAN, (1890-1982) — major general of the United States Army, and government official, was born on October 23, 1890 in Jonesville, South Carolina. He attended Clemson Agricultural College in South Carolina for a year, then became a cadet at the United States Military Academy at West Point in 1908. Graduating in 1912 at the rank of second lieutenant, he was assigned to the Eighth Cavalry, who were stationed in the Philippines. Returning to the United States in 1915, he was stationed at Fort Bliss, Texas where he eventually became part of the Seventeenth Cavalry. At the beginning of World War I, Littlejohn, who by that time was a captain, returned to West Point as an instructor, then in 1918, was sent to Camp Wadsworth in New York. Toward the end of the war, Littlejohn served in Europe, returning to the United States several months after peace had been declared.

Littlejohn spent the year after the war stationed in Raleigh, North Carolina, then in 1920, began the assignment that he would basically hold until the end of World War II— being responsible for army supply— or the "procurement, storage, and issue" of food, supplies, and clothing. Now at the rank of major, Littlejohn attended Chicago's Quartermaster Corps Subsistence School for six months, becoming a director there immediately after graduating in 1921, and then served as the school's assistant commandant from 1922 to 1925.

During 1925-26, Littlejohn studied at the Command and General Staff School in Fort Leavenworth, Kansas, and was an instructor there between 1926 and 1929. During 1929-30, he once again attended classes, this time at the Army War College in Washington, D.C., then served from 1930 to 1935 with the War Department General Staff where he was assigned to the Operation and Training Branch.

From 1935 to 1938, Littlejohn was post quartermaster at West Point, and during 1938-39, served as assistant to the quartermaster in the Philippines. While in Manila, he later became quartermaster and superintendent of the Army Transport Service. As the war was heating up in Europe, Littlejohn returned to Washington, D.C. and was assigned to the Office of the Quartermaster General, where he was overseer of the clothing and equipment division. A few months after the attack on Pearl Harbor, he went to Britain with the title of Chief Quartermaster for the European Theater of Operations. In the midst of the Allied invasion of North Africa, Littlejohn was widely admired for his ability to organize what was "seemingly insurmountable problems of supply" in that situation. When he received the Distinguished Service Medal, he was lauded for his "marked aggressiveness" and "superior quality of leadership."

According to one source, Littlejohn was "providing subsistence, clothing and equipment for over seven million persons." In ˉa letter to *Stars and Stripes*, Littlejohn pointed out proudly: "This office...has three teams in the field whose duty it is to investigate, report upon and recommend corrective action..." When he later received an Oak Leaf Cluster, the citation read: "He not only maintained anticipated requirements, but he exceeded them and established a new record for Quartermaster service."

In 1946, after retiring at the rank of major general, Littlejohn was appointed head of the War Assets Administration by President Harry S. Truman. There was a large amount of controversy surrounding the WAA by the time Littlejohn took over, with corruption the main concern, especially with the selling of supplies that were scarce. *Time* reported that "Washington politicos were most impressed by Littlejohn's courage in taking on the thankless job." According to *Current Biography*, Littlejohn "reorganized entire departments, changed rules, increased the WAA enforcement staff to clean up admitted 'widespread irregularities, favoritism and criminal misconduct...' By various means, disposal operations were speeded up; commercially non-flyable aircraft, for example, were sold on a mass basis for scrap and salvage." Known for his no-nonsense honesty, he noted during his task: "It will be my policy to hide nothing. Every successful businessman does make mistakes, admits them, profits by them, does not repeat them." Littlejohn finished the massive disposal of surplus war material by 1948.

The major general was married to Mary Lambert. He died on May 6, 1982.

LOGAN, WILLIAM TURNER, (1874-1941) — a U.S. Representative from South Carolina; born in" Summerville, Dorchester County, S.C., June 21, 1874; attended the public schools, and was graduated from the College of Charleston, South Carolina, in 1895; studied law at the University of Virginia, Charlottesville, Va.; was admitted to the bar in 1895 and commenced practice in Charleston, S.C.; member of the State house of representatives 1901-1904; corporation counsel of Charleston 1914-1918; chairman of the Democratic executive committee of Charleston County 1916-1918; chairman of the city Democratic executive committee 1918-1922 and reelected in 1922; elected as a Democrat to the Sixty-seventh and Sixty-eighth Congresses (March 4, 1921-March 3, 1925); unsuccessful candidate for renomination in 1924; continued the practice of his profession in Charleston, S.C., until his death in that city on September 15, 1941; interment in Magnolia Cemetery.

LONGSTREET, JAMES, (1821-1904) — soldier, was born in Edgefield District, South Carolina, on January 8, 1821. His family moved to Alabama in 1831, and he was appointed from that state to the West Point Military Academy, where he was graduated in 1842, and assigned to the 4th infantry. He was at Jefferson Barracks, Missouri in 1842-44; on frontier duty at Natchitoches, Louisiana in 1844-45; in Texas, 1845-46; and in Mexico at the battles of Palo Alto, Resaca de la Palma, Monterey, Vera Cruz, Cerro Gordo, San Antonio, Churubusco and Molino del Rey. For gallant conduct in the two latter engagements, he was brevetted captain and major, and had already been made first lieutenant, February 23, 1847. At the storming of Chapultepec, September 8, 1847, he was severely wounded. He was chief commissary of the department of Texas, 1849-51, was commissoned captain in December, 1852, and major and paymaster in July, 1858.

In 1861 he resigned to join the Confederate Army, of which he was immediately appointed brigadier-general, and won distinction in the first Battle of Bull Run, where he prevented a large force of Federal troops from supporting McDowell's flank attack. On May 5, 1862, he made a brave stand at Williamsburg where he was attacked by Heintrolman, Hooker and Kearny, and held his ground until Hancock arrived to reenforce his opponents when he was driven back.

At the second Battle of Bull Run he commanded the 1st corps of the army of northern Virginia at Gettysburg, and tried to dissuade Lee from ordering the disastrous charge on the third day. When Lee retreated to Virginia, General Longstreet, with five brigades, was transferred to the army of Tennessee under Bragg, and at Chickamanga, held the left wing of the Confederate forces. He rejoined Lee early in 1864, and was so prominent in the battle of the Wilderness that he was wounded by the fire of his own troops who were devoted to him. General Longstreet took up his residence in New Orleans after the war and established the commercial house of Longstreet, Owens & Co. He was appointed surveyor of the port of New Orleans by President Grant, and was afterward supervisor of internal revenue in Louisiana, and postmaster at New Orleans; in 1880 he was sent as U.S. Minister to Turkey by President Hayes, and under Garfield he was U.S. marshall for the district of Georgia. He died in 1904.

LOWNDES, RAWLINS, (1721-1800) — second president and state governor of South Carolina, 1778-1779.

He was born in St. Kitts, British West Indies, the son of Ruth Rawlins and Charles and Lowndes. His parents settled in Charleston, South Carolina in 1730, where Lowdes received most of his early education.

At the age of fourteen, he began reading law with Provost- Marshall Robert Hall. In 1742, he was appointed provost-marshall to succeed Hall, who had died two years earlier. He kept this office until 1752, when he began to practice law in Charleston.

Soon after beginning his practice, Lowndes was elected a member of the South Carolina Legislature. He subsequently became the Speaker of the House, and Justice of the quorum.

Early in 1766, Lowndes was appointed associate judge by the crown, and delivered the opinion of the court majority, which favored the legality of public proceedings without the employment of stamped paper; he also refused to enforce its use in his court. He authored the resolution passed in the South Carolina assembly to erect a statue of

William Pitt in Charleston, to acknowledge the services Pitt rendered the colonies by sustaining their constitutional rights, and especially in causing the repeal of the Stamp Act.

Although Lowndes opposed aggressive measures, when the American Revolution began, he joined the patriotic party. He was elected a member of the Provincial Congress of South Carolina, and was elected to the Committee of Safety appointed in 1775. He was a member of the Committee of Eleven which drafted a constitution for the province in 1776. The Provincial Congress of South Carolina passed a declaration of independence of the British crown on March 26, 1776, and Lowndes became a member of the legislative council created by the new constitution.

In February 1778, he was elected to succeed John Rutledge as president of the State. He remained in this office until 1779, when he declined election as governor.

He subsequently became a member of the South Carolina Senate and, upon the Declaration of Peace in 1783, was elected to the Assembly and served until the seat of government was removed from Charleston to Columbia in 1790. He strenuously opposed the United States Constitution when it was submitted to the State for adoption in 1790; his chief objections were the restrictions on slavery, the clause giving Congress the power to regulate commerce, and the centralization of power in the Federal government. It was his contention that these provisions would give a dangerous superiority to the North, and would be fatal to the liberties of the states by reducing them to the condition of mere corporations.

Lowndes was married in 1748 to Amarinthia Elliott. In 1751, he married a second time to Mary Cartwright and, in 1780, married a third time to Sarah Jones. Two of his sons, one from his second marriage and one from his third, also became statesmen in South Carolina. Lowndes died in August, 1800, at his home in Charleston.

LYNCH, THOMAS, (1727-1776) — (father of Thomas Lynch, Jr.), a Delegate from South Carolina; born in St. James Parish, Berkeley County, S.C., in 1727; attended the common schools; en gaged in planting, with extensive rice plantations on the Santee River and elsewhere; served in the commons house of assembly 1751-1757, 1761-1763, 1765, 1768, and 1772; delegate to the Colonial Congress in 1765; member of the general committee 1769- 1774; delegate to the First and Second Provincial Congresses in 1775 and 1776; member of the first State general assembly in 1776; Member of the Continental Congress in 1774-1776, but was unable to sign the Declaration of Independence because of illness; died in Annapolis, Anne Arundel County, Md., in December 1776 while en route to his home; interment in St. Anne's Churchyard, Annapolis, Md.

LYNCH, THOMAS, JR., (1749-1779) — (son of Thomas Lynch (1727-1776), a Delegate from South Carolina; born in Prince George's Parish, Winyah, S.C., August 5, 1749; educated at Eton and Cambridge, England, and studied law at the Middle Temple in London, 1764-1772; returned to America in 1772; became a planter on the North Santee River; member of the First and Second Provincial Congresses of South Carolina 1774-1776; member of the constitutional committee in 1776; member of the State general assembly in 1776; served as a captain in the First South Carolina Regiment, subsequently of the Continental Line, in the Revolutionary War from June 1775 until his election as a Delegate to the Continental Congress on February 1, 1776, and served in 1776; signer of the Declaration of Independence; did not seek reelection to the Continental Congress owing to ill health; embarked on an ocean voyage to France in 1779 and was lost at sea in that year.

M

MACKEY, EDMUND WILLIAM MCGREGOR, (1846-1884) — a U.S. Representative from South Carolina; born in Charleston, S.C., March 8, 1846; pursued classical studies; appointed assistant assessor of internal revenue in South Carolina September 8, 1865; delegate to the State constitutional convention in 1867; studied law; was admitted to the bar in 1868 and practiced; sheriff of Charleston County, 1868-1872; elected an alderman of the city of Charleston in 1868, 1873, and 1875; editor and proprietor of the Charleston Republican 1871 and 1872; member of the State house of representatives in 1873; presented credentials as an Independent Republican Memberelect to the Forty-fourth Congress and served from March 4, 1875, to July 19, 1876, when the seat was declared vacant; again a member of the State house of representatives in 1877 and served as speaker; delegate to the Republican National Convention in 1872 and 1880; assistant United States attorney for South Carolina 1878-1881; unsuccessfully contested as a Republican the election of Michael P. O'Connor to the Forty-sixth Congress; successfully contested the election of Michael P. O'Connor to the Forty-seventh Congress, succeeding Samuel Dibble, who presented credentials as a Member-elect to fill the vacancy thought to exist upon the death of Mr. O'Connor, which occurred while the contest was pending; reelected to the Forty-eighth Congress and served from May 31, 1882, until his death in Washington, D.C., on January 27, 1884; interment in Glenwood Cemetery.

MAGRATH, ANDREW GORDON, (1813-1893) — forty-sixth state governor (D) of South Carolina, 1864-1865.

He was born in Charleston, South Carolina, the son of Maria Gordon and John Magrath.

Magrath's early education was privately tutored. He graduated from South Carolina College in 1831, attended Harvard University Law School, and was admitted to the South Carolina Bar in 1835.

After setting up a private practice in Charleston, Magrath was elected to the South Carolina House of Representatives in 1840, and again in 1856. He was elected a State delegate-at- large to the Democratic National Convention in 1856, but was appointed United States judge for South Carolina by President Franklin Pierce before the convention took place.

Magrath was a member of the South Carolina Secession Convention in 1860, and was South Carolina Secretary of State during the administration of Governor Francis W.

Pickens. He served as Confederate States Judge for South Carolina until 1864.

Macrath was elected governor of South Carolina in December 1864, his term taking place during the final days of the Confederate States. He was inaugurated in Columbia, when federal troops were beseiging the city. In January and February of 1865, federal troops under William T. Sherman crossed the State in their "march to the sea," and by February 17, both Charleston and Columbia were occupied by Northern forces.

When the Confederacy fell in April 1865, Magrath was arrested by order of the United States Government and, with other prominent Confederates, was imprisoned in Fort Pulaski. After seven months, he was released in December 1865. Magrath was the last of South Carolina's governors to be elected by the State Legislature under the Constitution of 1700.

Magrath then resumed his law practice, maintaining it until his death in Charleston, South Carolina, in April 1893. He was married twice, first to Emma C. Mikell in March 1843, with whom he had nine children, and second, to Mary E. Cord in 1865.

MANN, EDWARD COKE, (1880-1931) — a U.S. Representative from South Carolina; born in Lowndesville, Abbeville County, S.C., November 21, 1880; attended the common schools and was graduated from The Citadel, Charleston, S.C., in 1901; taught school one year and was connected with a tobacco company for four years; was graduated from the law department of the University of South Carolina at Columbia in 1906 and commenced practice in St. Matthews, Calhoun County, S.C.; solicitor of the first circuit of South Carolina 1916-1919; elected as a Democrat to the Sixty- sixth Congress to fill the vacancy caused by the resignation of Asbury Francis Lever and served from October 7, 1919, to March 3, 1921; unsuccessful for renomination in 1920; practiced law in Orangeburg, S.C.; appointed master in equity for Orangeburg County in November 1923; reappointed in November 1927 and served until his death; was accidentally killed November 11, 1931, near Rowesville, S.C., while on a hunting trip; interment in Sunnyside Cemetery, Orangeburg, S.C.

MANN, JAMES ROBERT, (1920-   ) — a U.S. Representative from South Carolina; born in Greenville, Greenville County, S.C., April 27, 1920; attended the public schools of Greenville; The Citadel, B.A., 1941; University of South Carolina Law School, LL.B., 1947; editor, South Carolina Law Review, 1947; entered United States Army as second lieutenant, July 1941, and was separated March 1946 as lieutenant colonel; colonel in United States Army Reserve; member, South Carolina house of representatives, 1949-1952; was admitted to the bar in 1947 and commenced practice in Greenville, S.C.; appointed solicitor, Thirteenth Judicial Circuit of South Carolina, and elected in 1954 and reelected in 1958; secretary, Greenville County Planning Commission, 1963-1967; trustee, Greenville Hospital System, 1966-1968; commander, State of South Carolina, Veterans of Foreign Wars, 1951-1952; elected as a Democrat to the Ninety-first and to the four succeeding Congresses (January 3, 1969-January 3, 1979); was not a candidate for reelection in 1978 to the Ninety-sixth Congress; resumed the practice of law; is a resident of Green ville, S.C.

MANNING, JOHN LAURENCE, (1816-1889) — fortieth state governor (D) of South Carolina, 1852-1854.

He was born in Hickory Hill, Clarendon County, South Carolina, the son of Elizabeth Peyer Richardson and Richard Irvine Manning. His father was governor of South Carolina from 1824 to 1826.

Manning's early education was tutored by Rev. John White Chanler. He later attended Hatfield Academy in Camden, South Carolina and, in 1833, entered Princeton, but left the university in his senior year at his father's death. In 1836, he graduated from South Carolina College.

Manning's political career began with an election to the South Carolina House of Representatives in 1842. He remained in this office until 1846, when he became a member of the South Carolina Senate, serving through

1852. He was also a president elector in 1848, 1856, and 1884.

Manning was elected governor of South Carolina in December 1852. During his term, the United States Congress passed the Kansas-Nebraska Act, which repealed the Missouri Compromise of 1820, and the expansion of slavery into the territories again became an issue. During his tenure, Manning promoted the expansion of education, and established scholarships in the South Carolina College.

After his term ended, Manning remained active in State politics. He was offered the post of United States Minister to Russia by President James Buchanan, but declined the position. He was a member of the South Carolina Secession Convention, 1860- 1862; a signer of the Ordinance of Secession; a member of the South Carolina Senate, 1861-1865; and a member of the State House of Representatives, 1865-1867. He was elected to the United States Senate in 1865 but, with other Southern senators, was not allowed to take his seat. He was elected to the State Senate again in 1877, serving until 1878.

Manning was married to Susan Frances Hampton in April 1838, and to Sallie Bland Clark in April 1848. He died in Camden, South Carolina in October 1889.

MANNING, RICHARD IRVINE, (1789-1836) — twenty-fifth state governor (D-R) of South Carolina, 1824-1826.

He was born in Clarendon County, South Carolina, the son of Susannah Richardson and Laurence Manning. His father served in the American Revolution in the corps of Lighthorse Harry Lee. His maternal grandfather, Gen. Richard Richardson, also served in the patriot army.

Manning received his education and graduated from South Carolina College in 1811. When the War of 1812 broke out, he served in the militia as a captain. Afterwards, he became a planter. His career in public life began with an election to the House of Representatives in 1820. After a two-year term, he was elected to the South Carolina Senate and held the office from 1822 to 1824.

Manning was elected governor of South Carolina in December 1824. During his administration, the South

Carolina Legislature, at the urging of William Smith, formally committed itself to the doctrine of nullification. Nonetheless, Manning strongly maintained his opposition to this extreme theory of states' rights.

At the close of his tenure as governor, he remained active in both state and national politics. He was a Union Party candidate for election to the United States Congress in 1826, but was defeated. In 1830, he lost re-election as State governor. He remained a leader in opposition to the nullification movement, and was a Union Party delegate to the South Carolina Convention of 1832, where he voted against the Nullification Ordinance, and was vice president of the Union Convention held in Columbia in 1832.

After the death of James Blair in April 1834, Manning won his seat in the United States House of Representatives, and was subsequently re-elected for a full term in 1834.

Manning was married to Elizabeth Peyer Richardson, sister of James B. Richardson, who was governor of the State, 1802-1804. The couple had five sons and four daughters. He died in May 1836, and was buried in Trinity Churchyard in Columbia, South Carolina.

MANNING, RICHARD IRVINE, III, (1859-1931) — Sixty- seventh state governor (D) of South Carolina, 1915-1919.

Born on Holmesley Plantation in what is now Sumter County, South Carolina, on August 15, 1859, the son of Richard and Elizabeth (Sinkler) Manning. He received his education at Kenmore University High School in Amherst, Virginia and the University of Virginia. He was captain of the Red Shirts in 1876, and an adjutant and captain in the Volunteer State Troops in 1878. In 1881, he married Lelia Bernard Meredith. They had six sons.

In the years that followed, Manning made a name for himself in business, banking, and cotton farming. He was president of the American Products Export and Import Corporation; president of the Bank of Maysville, South Carolina; president of the National Bank of Sumter, South Carolina; president of the Cotton Warehouse Company; president of the South Carolina Land and Settlement Association; director of Sumter Telephone Company; director of the Telephone Manufacturing Company; director of Palmetto Fire Insurance Company; director of Magneto Manufacturing Company; and chairman of the board of the Peoples' State Bank of South Carolina. In addition, he served as a trustee for Clemson College and the University of South Carolina.

Manning became interested in politics and attended every Democratic state convention from 1884. In 1892 he was elected to the South Carolina House of Representatives, and served until 1896. Two years later, he entered the State Senate where he remained until 1906, acting as President Pro Tempore in 1905. In 1914, he ran for governor as a Democrat and was unopposed in the general election. He was reelected in 1916. His administration saw the creation of the State Highway Department and the State Board of Charities and Corrections. With the coming of World War I, nearly 62,000 South Carolinians joined the armed forces, and a number of army camps were set up around the state. Manning left office in 1919 at the end of his second term and moved to Charleston. Later that year, he served on the U.S. Peace Committee. He died on September 11, 1931.

MARION, FRANCIS, (1732-1795) — soldier, was born at Winyah, near Georgetown, South Carolina in 1732. His Huguenot grandfather, Benjamin Marion, left France in 1690, and his was one of the seventy or eighty exiled families which settled on the banks of the Santee River in South Carolina. Benjamin's son, Gabriel married Esther Cardes, and the pair had six children. Francis Marion was the last-born child, and the influence of ancestry in the determination of his character is discernible in his subsequent life. Physically he was diminutive and had a weak constitution to a remarkable degree. By the time he was twelve, however, his constitution had undergone a change and his health had become good.

Tiring of rural life, he longed for the ocean, and when sixteen years old, embarked in a small vessel bound for the West Indies. The ship foundered at sea, sinking so suddenly that its crew, six in number, had barely time to escape in the lifeboat, and were without food or water. Two of them later died from starvation. On the seventh day after the foundering, the four survivors were picked up by a passing vessel, and were eventually brought back to their homes. After his return, Marion resumed the humble occupation of a tiller of the soil, the family resources being very moderate.

Before he was twenty-five years old his father died, and in 1758 he was planting with his mother and his brother Gabriel, near Freison's Lock, on the Santee Canal. In 1759, they separated, with Gabriel moving to Belle Island, South Carolina and Francis settling at Pond Bluff in the parish of St. John. The year in which he took up residence at Pond Bluff, the colony of South Carolina was on the eve of an Indian war, and James's *Life of Marion* asserts that he went that year to the appointed rendezvous to engage in a campaign against the Cherokees, which had been ordered by Governor Lyttleton.

Before the month of May, 1760, another camp for the invasion of the Cherokee territory was established, and it is believed that at this time Marion was again a volunteer. Certainly in 1761, when Colonel James Grant of the Royal Scots Highland regiment, with 1,200 South Carolinians under Colonel Middleton, commanded in the Cherokee campaign, Marion served as lieutenant under Captain William Moultrie. In a sharp battle with the Indians in June at Etchoee, the command of the advance guard of thirty men was entrusted to Marion, and while marching at the foot of a hill, twenty one of the thirty were brought down by the fire of the Indians. The result of the engagement which ensued, however, was the utter breaking of the spirit of the Indians. Fourteen towns in the middle Indian settlement, as well as Etchoee, were reduced to ashes. Cornfields were ravaged and the country depleted of power to afford any subsistence to the tribe. Marion revolted from the severity of this treatment, and his comment in respect to it is worth noting: "To me it appeared a shocking sight. When we are gone the Indian children will return and ask their mothers: 'Who did this?' 'The white people, the Christians,' will be the reply."

For fifteen years at least, from this time, nothing is known of Marion except that he was quietly engaged in rural and domestic occupations. He was fond of angling and of hunting, while his firmness, his even temper and recognized bravery, secured for him the esteem and confidence of the community. In 1775 he was returned to the Provincial Congress of South Carolina as a member from St. John. This body distinguished itself by committing the people of the province to the American Revolution, adopting the Bill of Rights, as declared by the Continental Congress. Under the immediate suggestion and by direct participation of this legislative body, moreover, overt acts of treason were committed. The public armory in Charleston was broken open at night, and arms were removed. Powder was taken from the public magazines, and chests containing tea, on which duty had been imposed by the English Parliament, were tumbled into the Cooper River.

When this Congress, after adjourning for a short time, met on the first of June, it also passed, although not without considerable opposition, the "Act for Association," which had been recommended to all the colonies by the Continental Congress, and on the fourth day of its session, resolved to raise 1,500 infantry soldiers, and 450 cavalry. June 14th, a million of money was voted, and a council of safety was then elected, vested with the executive power of the province. Marion was chosen a captain in the 2nd infantry regiment of these troops, his commission dating June 21, 1775, the day preceding the adjournment of the Congress. With his friend, Captain Peter Horry, he quickly filled up, from the neighborhoods of Georgetown, Black River, and the Great Pedee, the ranks of two companies, consisting of fifty men each.

He first drew sword against the British, September 14, 1775, when he participated in the occupation of Fort Johnson, on James Island, in Charleston Harbor, but a few hours after it had been abandoned by the royalist forces. He was next placed in command of the military fort at Dorchester, at the head of navigation on the Ashley River, twenty miles from Charleston, to which place the public stores were in great part transferred. Later on he was dispatched to Fort Johnson, whose defenses he completed. Promoted to be major, he engaged so diligently in the work of drilling his regiment the 2nd, that he was styled its "architect." June 20, 1776, in an engagement with the British fleet, Marion, whose regiment was then stationed at the partly finished Fort Sullivan, bore an important part, contributing largely to a patriot victory which gave to the southern states a three years' respite from any serious attack by the enemy. Fort Sullivan was from that day known as Fort Moultrie, and Marion was subsequently placed in command there.

When General Lincoln and the French Count d'Estaing made their ill-starred attempt in September, 1779, against Savannah, Georgia, then held by British troops, Marion participated, being second in command of his regiment. After this, Lincoln withdrew his troops to Sheldon, South Carolina to drill the militia of the neighborhood. When the city of Charleston was taken by the English, May, 1770, Marion, who had just before marched into the city from Dorchester, was, fortunately, at his home in the country, suffering from a broken ankle. When the British, after occupying Charleston, began to raid the surrounding country, under Tarleton, Marion, already conspicuous by his military service, was compelled to take refuge in the forest, and in his disabled condition, he was driven from house to house, from tree to thicket, and from thicket to swamp.

As soon as he could mount his horse, he collected a few friends and set out for North Carolina to meet Baron de Kalb, who was drawing toward South Carolina at the head of a Continental force, sent from Virginia by General Washington for the relief of Charleston. On their journey, although in difficult straits, Marion was in fine spirits, and in answer to the complaints of his companion, Peter Horry, that their "happy days were all gone," he declared: "On the contrary, they are yet to come. The victory is still due. The enemy, it is true, have all the trumps, and if they had but spirit to play a generous game, they would certainly ruin us, but they have no idea of that game. They will treat the people cruelly, and that one thing will ruin them and save the country."

Reaching De Kalb, Marion found that he had been superseded in his command by General Gates, who did not comprehend Marion's capacities nor the value of his services. Governor Rutledge, of Carolina, who was in Gate's camp, exerted himself on Marion's behalf, but only succeeded in bringing about an interview between them in which Marion counseled the adoption of a scheme which was rejected by Gates, but afterward carried out by General Greene; namely, the moving of his army into the heart of South Carolina, thereby giving an opportunity for the patriots to rally, and forcing the British to concentrate their scattered forces and circumscribe their influence.

As a consequence of neglecting this advice, Gates came to grief at Camden, South Carolina, August 16th, at the hands of Lord Cornwallis, in the most disastrous defeat ever suffered by an American army. But before this, and while Marion was in Gates' camp, a messenger had reached him from the Whigs of Williamsburg, South Carolina, then newly risen in arms, summoning him to become their leader. Governor Rutledge issued this commission to Marion, and he left at once to recruit what afterward proved to be the famous "Marion's Brigade." Following Gates' defeat and the rout of Sumter's troop which occurred two days after it, this brigade was the only American force worth naming in South Carolina. Most of these troopers were men of Irish parentage, with all the Celt's bitter feeling against the Anglo-Saxon.

Four captains were chosen for as many companies before Marion's arrival; McCottry, Morrison, James, and McCauley, and they also had some skirmishing with the British troops. From the time of his reaching them, Marion, under the commission of the South Carolina governor, was known as "The General." "He came to us," says one of their number who served under him at the age of fifteen, "rather below the middle stature, lean and swarthy. His body was well set, his knees and ankles badly formed, and he still limped on one leg. He was forty-eight years of age, with frame capable of enduring fatigue and every privation. He was dressed in a close, round-bodied crimson jacket, of a coarse texture, and wore a leather cap, a part of the uniform of the 2nd regiment, with a silver crescent in front, bearing the words 'Liberty or Death.'"

He found in his command extremely deficient in all materials of service, and his first efforts to supply their deficiencies began in sacking the sawmills. The saws were wrought and hammered by rude blacksmiths into some resemblance to sabres, and two days from the day he took command, he advanced on a large body of Tories commanded by a Major Gainey at Briton's Neck, surprised them, killed their captain and several privates, dispersed their party without the loss of a man, and with only two wounded. In twenty-four hours after this, he was again in motion after a Tory captain, Barfield. But the latter was forewarned, and awaited Marion in a strong position, at which time the Americans resorted to strategy. Putting a select party of men in ambush, Marion retreated with another, and thus deceiving his opponent from his "coigne of vantage," Barfield followed, as it was hoped he would, and was badly defeated in the fight that ensued.

These two achievements gave Marion all the hold he required on his troops, and also that *eclat* in the region, which apprised the inhabitants that a man with an efficient force was at work among them. While ignorant of Gates' defeat by Cornwallis on the preceding day, he sent out Peter Horry with four companies to break up communications with Charleston and if possible, to procure gunpowder, flints and bullets. He himself marched to the upper Santee. As he did so, he heard of Gates' disaster, but did not apprise his troops of it. On the other hand, at Nelson's Ferry, he immediately surprised a strong British guard with a large body of pioneers taken from Gates, killed and took as prisoners twenty-two British regulars and two Tories, and retook 150 Continentals of the Maryland line who were being taken to Charleston from the rout of Gates' forces: this with a loss of one killed and one slightly wounded.

And so he continued, aided decisively by the cruel policy adopted by the British military authorities, until Lieutenant Colonel Tarleton wrote: "Mr. Marion, by his zeal and abilities, showed himself capable of ther trust committed to his charge." He collected his adherents at the shortest notice, and after making excursions into the friendly districts, or threatening the communicatons, to avoid pursuit he disbanded his followers. The alarm occasioned by these insurrections frequently delayed supplies on their way to the army; and a late report of Marion's strength delayed the junction of the recruits who had arrived from New York to the corps in the country.

Cornwallis wrote to Tarleton: "I most sincerely hope that you will get at Mr. Marion."

Orders were given to Tarleton and to Major Wemyss, a Tory officer, to make Marion retreat, and for a little time, he withdrew to North Carolina, with the excesses of Wemyss, as he ravaged the counry in pursuit, more and more inflaming the patriot population. Marion soon returned by a forced march, and finding a large body of Tories at Black Mongo, fifteen miles from Georgetown, although his force was very much inferior in number, fell on them and destroyed them. His next encounter was with a Tory colonel, Tynes, whose sharp defeat supplied Marion with arms and ammunition, which he greatly needed.

In view of his successes, the British redoubled their endeavors to scatter and to prevent the reassembling of his forces, and also to apprehend their leader. Tarleton sought him this time by descending the river Wateree. At once Marion essayed Tarleton's capture, but was too late to seize him, and the British leader rejoined his own troops. Marion fell back, upon Tarleton's advance, after the latter had come up with his command. Then Tarleton pursued him for twenty-five miles until he found his path blocked by a wide and deep swamp, through which his eye could see no beaten road, and when, as is supposed, he could have reached his opponent in three hours, he turned the head of his column and called out, "Come, my boys, let us go back! We will soon find (Sumter), but as for this damned swampfox, the devil himself could not catch him."

The two American soldiers were ever after known by their followers by these names. When Tarleton desisted from his pursuit of Marion, he undertook that of Sumter, but was severely handled by that officer. The Battle of King's Mountain, on October 17, 1780, in western North Carolina, with the unbroken successes of Marion, so revived colonial courage and spirit in South Carolina, that the forces of Marion received decided increase. But the unstable character of such an increase is not to be lost sight of. Marion's men, with families to provide for, came and went as they listed, their commander making such stipulatons with them for their return as he and they could agree on. In his hands, however, although he was at times sadly hampered, this material became effective for his peculiar warfare, although it is difficult to see how, in the hands of some commanders, it could have been made available for any purpose.

His next attempt was made against Georgetown, South Carolina, but was unsuccessful, and in it Marion suffered the personal loss of his nephew, Gabriel, who, being taken by the British, was put to death as soon as his name was known. The Americans immediately retired to Swan Island and established there, at the confluence of Lynch's Creek and the Pedee, what became known far and wide as "Marion's Camp." It was in substance an island, in a swamp abounding in livestock and provisions, and elevated tracts and dense cane-brakes, and some spots on which Marion's invalids and convalescents spent their time in cultivating corn. Marion secured all the boats of the neighborhood and fortified his position as necessity required, and from there sent out his scouting parties in all directions. He put the surrounding country under martial law, while he was himself secure in his fastness, sallied out on occasion to harass the British and Tories, struck his blows at them, and was back in his safe retreat almost before they could determine from where he had come, or realize that he had come at all.

Secrecy of action was a prime source of his strength. He did not entrust his plans to his most confidential officer; although he consulted them, they only learned his decision from his deeds. He left no track behind him if he could avoid it, and was often vainly hunted for by his own detachments. His favorite time for moving was with the setting sun. His living was of the plainest— he and his men were clothed in homespun apparel, slept in open air and without blankets. His first requisition from subordinates was good information. He also maintained rigid discipline. Such a life gave way to confidence between general and officers (by whom he was admirably supported) and men, and resulted in the production of a partisan force such as has seldom been seen.

A story, illustrative of the poverty of the partisan commissariat, is well known; it is to the effect that a young British officer was led blindfolded by a scouting party into the center of Marion's camp, and having transacted his business with him, was invited to stop for dinner, which consisted entirely of roasted potatoes served on pieces of bark. "But surely, general, this cannot be your ordinary fare!" "Indeed, sir it is," replied the general, "and we are fortunate on this occasion, entertaining company, to have more than our usual allowance."

When General Nathanael Greene took command of the remnants of Gates' army at Charlotte, North Carolina, December, 1781, he put himself into communication with Marion, and received from him prompt and full intelligence of the British movements and resources. A second attempt against Georgetown, South Carolina, made by Marion, January 13, 1781, after the junction of Colonel Henry Lee's forces with his own, was only partially successful, the surprise being incomplete, although the Americans secured the person of the British commandant. When Lee was recalled by Greene, Marion struck at British and Tory ports on the Pedee River, and then organized four companies of cavalry, a proceeding prompted, in part, by the scarcity of ammunition; the result of his movements was the entire breaking up of the line of communications between Charleston, South Carolina and the main army of the British under Cornwallis. This brought pursuit on Marion by Colonels' Watson and Doyle of the British army from Fort Watson, which commanded the approaches of the British Lord Rawdon, near Camden, South Carolina. It was during this pursuit that Marion gave way, for the only time of which there is any record, to despondency, saying one day to Horry, "Go to my field officers and know from them if, in the event of my being compelled to retire to the mountains, they will follow my fortunes, and with me carry on the war until the enemy is forced out of the country. Go and bring me their answer without delay." They immediately pledged themselves to this, and Marion declared: "I am satisfied; one of these parties shall feel us."

Quickly, on April 23rd, he invested and took Fort Watson. Rawdon was compelled to evacuate Camden, and fall back to Monk's Corner. Marion was at this time incessant to activity, and contributed essentially to the aid of Greene on his advance from North into South Carolina. In a short time, nothing was wanting but the fall of the

the enemy's interior chain of military posts to complete the recovery of the whole country within thirty miles of the sea by the Americans. Marion, in conjunction with Leland Eaton, at once attacked the British Fort Motte, on the Congaree, the principal depot of the British expeditions from Charleston to Camden, which quickly surrendered. While dining, after the capitulation, Marion was told that Lee's men were hanging Tory prisoners. Hurrying from the table and seizing his sword, he ran to the gallows in time to save one poor man, and with a blaze of indignation in his face, threatened to kill the first man who made any further attempt in such proceedings.

Pursuing his cooperation with Greene, Marion, in company with Sumter, now held Rawdon in check while Greene proceeded to take over the post of Ninety-Six; and as a diversion, Marion made a third and this time successful endeavor to capture Georgetown. He effected a junction with General Greene prior to the battle of Eutaw Springs, September 8, 1781, and commanded the right of the first line in that memorable action, his brigade fighting, as General Greene declared, "with a coolness and stubbornness which would have graced the veterans of the great King of Prussia." The next day, Marion and Lee together pursued the British on their retreat. On the 9th of October, he received the thanks of Congress for "his wise, decided, and gallant conduct, in defending the liberties of his country, and particularly for his prudent and intrepid attack on a body of British troops on the 31st of August; and for the distinguished part he took in the battle of the 8th of September."

With the exception of desultory fighting, this closes the record of Marion's military service. Further details of his course, which continued until the end of the war are given in the *Life*, by W.G. Simms. In January, 1782, the South Carolina Legislature met at Jacksonboro', a little village on the Edisto, a short distance from Charleston, and Marion was in its Senate. Retiring to his plantation in St. John, at the end of the war, he found it ravaged. Ten slaves returned to him when he was ready to begin farming, but everything else was to be purchased, and he was penniless. Hopes of half-pay held out to the hero were never realized.

He was again returned to the State Senate and was conspicuous in urging leniency toward the Tories, also in condemning the confiscation act passed by the Legislature in 1782. At the dinner table of Governor Matthews, while the conflict was at its highest, he was called on for a toast, and promptly said, "Gentlemen, here's damnation to the Confiscation Act." The South Carolina Senate voted him its thanks, and a gold medal for his patriotism, and in 1784, he was appointed to the command of Fort Johnson in Charleston Harbor, at an annual salary of $500. That same year, he married Mary Videau, of Huguenot stock. He spent his last years at his home at Pond Bluff in South Carolina. He was a member, in 1790, of the convention for framing the constitution of South Carolina. In 1794, he resigned his commission in the state militia. He died at Pond Bluff, February 27, 1795, his last words being: "Thank God, I can lay my hand on my heart and say, that since I came to man's estate, I have never done, intentionally, wrong to any."

MARION, ROBERT, (1766-1811) — a U.S. Representative from South Carolina; born 1766 in Berkeley District, S.C.; pursued an academic course, and was graduated from the University of the State of Pennsylvania (now the University of Pennsylvania) at Philadelphia in 1784; owned and managed plantation at Belle Isle, S.C.; justice of quorum, St. Stephen's Parish; justice of the peace, Charleston, S.C.; served in the State house of representatives, 1790-1796, and in the State senate, 1802-1805; elected as a Republican to the Ninth, Tenth, and Eleventh Congresses and served from March 4, 1805, until his resignation on December 4, 1810; died on his plantation in St. Stephen's Parish, March 22, 1811.

MARTIN, WILLIAM DICKINSON, (1789-1883) — a U.S. Representative from South Carolina; born in Martintown, Edgefield District, S.C., October 20, 1789; pursued an academic course; studied law at Edgefield and attended the Litchfield Law School; was admitted to the bar in 1811 and commenced practice in Edge field, S.C., the same year; moved to Coosawhatchie, Beaufort County, in 1813; member of the State house of representatives tivesfor St. Luke's Parish 1816-1817; clerk of the State senate 1818-1826; elected as a Jacksonian to the Twentieth and Twenty-first Congresses (March 4, 1827-March 3, 1831); judge of the circuit courts of law and appeal 1831-1833; moved to Columbia, S.C., where he resided until his death in Charleston, S.C., November 17, 1833; interment in the churchyard cemetery of St. Michael's Church.

MARTY, MARTIN, (1834 - 1896), noted Roman Catholic bishop, was born in Schevyz, Switzerland on January 12, 1834. Martin Marty studied theology at the Benedictine Abbey of Einsiedlen and in September of 1856 was ordained into the Benedictine order. In 1860 he was sent to America to join a colony of monks from Einsiedlen, who had founded the Benedictine settlement of St. Meiurad in Indiana in 1854. He soon became a leader in the community, and when a priory was established there in 1865, Dom. Marty was made its first superior. Under his administration, the population of the priory grew and mission work increased. In 1870 Pope Pius converted St. Meiurad into an abbey and Marty was made mitred abbot. The corner-stone of the abbey was laid on May 22, 1872. Abbot Marty presided for several years and perfected the institution under his care. He extended its missions, erected churches, and fostered education in connection with the Catholic church. Yet, in spite of the energy and zeal with which he devoted himself to his duties, he had always fostered a wish to labor among the Native Americans. After obtaining permission from his superiors, he set off on a mission to Dakota, where he found the work so promising and so full of interest for him, that he resigned as abbot and remained to work as a father among the Native American tribes.

In 1879 the territory of Dakota was formed into a vicariate- apostolic and Marty was consecrated as bishop. Under his administration, the Catholic church made such progress in the vicariate that after four years it contained 90 churches and 50 priests, with seven Native American missions attended by his clergy.

In 1889 the diocese of Sioux Falls, which comprised the state of South Dakota, was established and Marty was appointed its first bishop. Because of his devotion to his work and his great achievements, he became known as "The Angel of the West." His health, however, began to decline and he resigned his office. In 1894 he took over the less strenuous post at the diocese of St. Cloud, Minnesota and remained there until his death in 1896.

MATHEWES, JOHN, (1744-1802) — fourth state governor of South Carolina, 1782-1783.

He was born and raised in South Carolina. Mathewes studied law and became a barrister in England in 1764, then returned to South Carolina. In 1772, he was elected to the Commons House of Assembly, and became an active member of the Revolution Party in the State. In June 1774, he was appointed a member of the "general committee" of ninety-nine, which had primary control of governmental power of South Carolina between June 1774 and June 1775.

Mathewes was elected to the First Provincial Congress of South Carolina which met in January 1775, and also the Second Continental Congress, which met in November 1775. When the latter Congress declared South Carolina free and independent of Great Britain on March 26, 1776, an independent government was set up; Mathewes was elected one of three assistant judges of the Court of General Sessions and Common Pleas. He was elected a member of the House of Representatives established under the new Constitution in October 1776, and when the House met the following December, was chosen Speaker of the House.

In November 1778, he was re-elected, and was also chosen by the Legislature, in February 1779, one of five delegates to the Continental Congress. After a re-election to Congress in 1780, and after the defeat of Gates in South Carolina that year, it was proposed to purchase peace and independence by sacrificing the Carolinas and Georgia. Mathewes vehemently opposed the suggestion, and it was defeated before ever taking shape in Congress.

Mathewes was elected governor of South Carolina in January 1782, remaining in this office until February 1783. While undertaking his gubernatorial duties, he became involved in a controversy with General Greene, which centered around the deplorable conditions of the American soldiers at the end of the war. The Southern army, which depended solely on South Carolina for its support, had exhausted the resources of the province and, being unable to obtain further supplies, proceeded to collect food by force. The inhabitants resisted the troops, and the soldiers nearly mutanied, which would have left the State defenseless. Mathewes' intervention averted a potential disaster if the State had been unable to protect itself.

During Mathewes' term, the Assembly proceeded to reestablish all the branches of civil government, and laws were passed for the confiscation of the estates of Tories, and for banishing those who were active friends of the British. These stringent enactments were afterward modified or repealed by the terms of the British evacuation of Charleston which took place on December 14, 1782.

Upon fulfilling his duties as governor, Mathewes was elected to the Privy Council; he filled this position until his resignation in May 1784. He was elected one of three judges to the Court of Chancery by the Legislature in March 1784, and was appointed one of three judges of the Court of Equity upon the reorganization of the judiciary system of South Carolina in February 1791, remaining in this position until his resignation in November 1797.

Mathewes died in October 1802.

MAYBANK, BURNET RHETT, (1899-1954) — Seventyforth state governor (D) of South Carolina, 1939-1941.

Born in Charleston on March 7, 1899, the son of Joseph and Harriet (Rhett) Maybank. He attended Porter Military Academy and the College of Charleston. During World War I, he served in the South Carolina Naval Militia and the U.S. Naval Reserve. He married Elizabeth de Rossett in 1923. They had three children.

From 1920 to 1938, Maybank worked in the cotton export business. He was an alderman in Charleston from 1927 to 1931, and for a short time, in 1930, served as Mayor Pro Tempore for the city. Elected in his own right, he was Mayor of Charleston from 1931 to 1938. During that time, he also was a member of the South Carolina

State Advisory Board of the Federal Administration of Public Works, and chairman of the South Carolina Public Service Authority. He ran as a Democrat for governor in 1938, and won in an uncontested election. During his term, construction began on the Santee-Cooper dams and power stations; President Roosevelt made Fort Jackson a permanent army post; and the palmetto was selected as the state tree. Maybank resigned his office in 1941 to take a seat in the U.S. Senate. His wife, Elizabeth died in 1947, and he remarried a year later to Mary Randolph Piezer. He was a member of the American Battle Monuments Commission from 1947 to 1954. Maybank continued to serve in the U.S. Senate up until the time of his death, on September 1, 1954.

MAYRANT, WILIIAM, (?-?) — a U.S. Representative from South Carolina; born in that State; elected as a Republican to the Fourteenth Congress and served from March 4, 1815, until October 21, 1816, when he resigned; unsuccessful candidate for reelection; member of South Carolina house of representatives,tives 1818-1821.

MCCORKLE, PAUL GRIER, (1863-1934) — a U.S. Representative from South Carolina; born in Yorkville (now York), York County, S.C., December 19, 1863; attended the public schools of his native city and Kings Mountain Military School, York, S.C.; employed as a clerk in York, S.C.; cotton buyer and grader in Lancaster, S.C., and then in Chester, S.C.; returned to York, s.c., and engaged in business as a cotton broker and export classifier; elected as a Democrat- to the Sixty-fourth Congress to fill the vacancy caused by the death of David E. Finley and served from February 24, 1917, to March 3, 1917; was not a candidate for renomination in 1916; engaged in the cotton brokerage business in York, S.C.; coroner of York County, S.C., from 1920 until his death in Knoxville, Tenn., on June 2, 1934; interment in Rose Hill Cemetery, York, S.C.

MCCREARY, JOHN, (1761-1833) — a U.S. Representative from South Carolina; born near Fishing Creek, about eighteen miles from Chester, S.C., in 1761; received his schooling from private tutors; became a surveyor; also engaged in agricultural pursuits; served in the Revolutionary War; member of the State house of representatives, 1794-1799 and 1802; sheriff of Chester District (now Chester County); elected to the Sixteenth Con gress (March 4, 1819-March 3, 1821); resumed agricultural pursuits and surveying; died on his plantation in South Carolina November 4, 1833; interment in the Richardson Church Cemetery, Chester County, S.C.

MCDUFFIE, GEORGE, (1790-1851) — thirtieth state governor (D) of South Carolina, 1834-1836.

He was born in Columbia County, Georgia, the son of Jane and John McDuffie. His parents immigrated from Scotland soon after the American Revolution, and settled near Augusta, Georgia.

McDuffie received his early education in public schools, and also held a job as a clerk in the village store. In 1810, he studied at Moses Waddel's School in Willington, South Carolina. He entered South Carolina College as a junior in 1811, and graduated with honors in 1813. After studying law, he was admitted to the South Carolina Bar in 1814, and opened a private law practice in Pendleton, South Carolina. In 1815, he moved to Edgefield, South Carolina and became a partner of Eldred Simkins.

In 1818, McDuffie was elected to the South Carolina House of Representatives. After a two-year term, in 1821, he became a member of the United States House of Representatives, and kept this office until 1834.

In Congress, McDuffie advocated changing the Constitution in order to establish uniformity in selecting representatives, and also in the system of choosing presidential electors. He opposed congressional appropriations for internal improvements, argued against the proposed Panama Congress, and was strongly in favor of nullification. He was a delegate in the 1832 South Carolina Nullification Convention.

McDuffie was elected governor of South Carolina in 1834, and served a two-year term. Several laws concerning abolition were enacted during his administration. These acts provided that any free black who returned to

South Carolina after being expelled should be sold as a slave, prohibited the importation of any slave who had been north of Washington, D.C., and required local officials to imprison any free blacks aboard ship during the stay of a vessel in a South Carolina port. In addition, severe penalties were imposed against any person who helped slaves to avoid the State's laws.

After the expiration of his term, McDuffie served as a United States District Judge and a member of the United State Senate from 1842-1846. While holding this office, he took a leading part in passing the sub-treasury bill, in the annexation of Texas, and in passing the tariff of 1846.

McDuffie had been involved in two duels during his life, and suffered a permanent injury to his spine. He resigned from public life in 1846 due to poor health resulting from his injury.

McDuffie was married to Mary Rebecca Singleton in 1829. He died in March 1851 at Cherry Hill, Sumter District, South Carolina.

MCLEOD, THOMAS GORDON, (1868-1932) — Seventieth state governor (D) of South Carolina, 1923-1927.

Born in Lynchburg, South Carolina on December 17, 1868, the son of William and Amanda (Rogers) McLeod. He attended Wofford College and the University of Virginia where he studied law. He was admitted to the South Carolina Bar in 1896. He then taught for two years. In 1902, he married Elizabeth Alford. They had one child.

In 1903, McLeod started a law practice in Bishopville. He also served as a trustee to Winthrop College, Emory University, and Columbia College. He was elected to the South Carolina House of Representatives and served from 1900 to 1902, and then in the Senate from 1902 to 1906. In 1904 and 1924, he was a delegate to the Democratic National Convention. He served as Lieutenant Governor of South Carolina from 1907 to 1911. He was State legal advisor for a time, and served on occasion as a special judge. In 1912, he was president of the Democratic State Convention. Running as a Democrat in an unopposed general election, McLeod won the governorship in 1922. He was reelected in 1924. He entered office at a time when South Carolina was in an agricultural depression.

As governor, he worked for tax reform and called a tax convention in 1925 which formed a "Committee of Seventeen" to make recommendations to the Legislature on specific tax reforms. He also supported education, and worked to establish a more systematic state administration. During the last year of his second term the State Constitution was amended to allow a four year term for governors, but make them ineligible to succeed themselves in office. McLeod left office in 1927 and went to Nashville, Tennessee as the district manager of the Life and Casualty Insurance Company. He later became president of the Bishopville Telephone Company, and director of the Bishopville National Bank. He died on December 11, 1932.

MCMILLAN, CLARA GOODING, (1894-1976) — (wife of Thomas S. McMillan), a U.S. Representative from South Carolina; born in Brunson, Hampton County, S.C., August 17, 1894; attended the public schools, Confederate Home College, Charleston, S.C., and Flora MacDonald College, Red Springs, N.C.; elected as a Democrat to the Seventy-sixth Congress by special election, November 7, 1939, to fill the vacancy caused by the death of her husband, Thomas S. McMillan, and served from November 7, 1939, to January 3, 1941; was not a candidate for reelection in 1940 to the Seventy-seventh Congress; served in National Youth Administration, then the Office of Government Reports, Office of War Information, 1941; appointed information liaison officer for the Department of State, Washington, D.C., on January 1, 1946, and served until July 31, 1957; resided in Barnwell, S.C., where she died November 8, 1976; interment in Magnolia Cemetery, Charleston, S.C.

MCMILLAN, JOHN LANNEAU, (1898-1979) — a U.S. Representative from South Carolina; born on a farm near Mullins, Marion County, S.C., April 12, 1898; educated Mullins High School, University of North Carolina, and South Carolina, also University of South Carolina Law School and National Law School, Washington, D.C.; selected to represent United States Congress at the Interparliamentary Union in London in 1960, and in Tokyo in 1961; elected as a Democrat to the Seventy-sixth and to the sixteen succeeding Congresses (January 3, 1939- January 3, 1973); chairman, Committee on District of Columbia (Seventy-ninth, Eighty-first, Eighty-second and Eightyfourth through Ninety- second Congresses); unsuccessful candidate for renomination in 1972 to the Ninety-third Congress; resided in Florence, S.C., where he died September 3, 1979; interment in the McMillan family cemetery, Mullins, S.C.

MCMILLAN, THOMAS SANDERS, (1888-1939) — (husband of Clara Gooding McMillan), a U.S. Representative from South Carolina; born near Ulmers, Allendale County, S.C., November 27, 1888; attended the common schools near Ulmers and was graduated from Orangeburg (S.C.) Collegiate Institute in 1907; taught school at Perry, Aiken County, S.C., in 1907 and 1908; graduated from the University of South Carolina at Columbia in 1912; completed the law course at the same university in 1913; was admitted to the bar in 1913 and commenced the practice of law in Charleston, S.C.; also interested in agricultural pursuits; member of the State house of representatives 1917-1924, serving as speaker pro tempore in 1921 and 1922 and as speaker in 1923 and 1924; was not a candidate for renomination in 1924; elected as a Democrat to the Sixtyninth and to the seven succeeding Congresses and served from March 4, 1925, until his death; member of the execu tive committee of the Interparliamentary Union 1937- 1939, serving as delegate to the convention held in Oslo, Norway, in 1939; died in Charleston, S.C., September 29, 1939; interment in Magnolia Cemetery.

MCNAIR, ROBERT EVANDER, (1923-) — governor, was born in Cades, South Carolina on December 14, 1923, the son of Daniel Evander and Claudia (Crawford). During World War II he served in the U.S. Naval Reserve. He graduated from the University of South Carolina in 1948 with an LL.B. degree and was admitted to the bar that same year. In 1944 he married Josephine Robinson and they eventually had four children.

Following graduation, McNair moved to Allendale, South Carolina and began a private law practice there. He was also active in business, and served as president of Investors Heritage Life Insurance; director of the Southern Railway System, Georgia- Pacific Corporation; director of AIRCO Incorporated; and director of R.L. Ryan Company. He was elected to the South Carolina House of Representatives and served from 1951 to 1962, from 1962 to 1965 he was Lieutenant Governor of South Carolina. When Governor Russell resigned in April of the latter year, McNair took over as governor. In the 1966 election he ran for the office on the Democratic ticket and won in an uncontested race.

McNair had special interest in education, serving on the Southern Regional Education Board 1967 and 1968 and the Education Commission of the States in 1968 and 1969.

Civil Rights continued to be a major issue during this time. As governor, McNair saw graduation of the first black student from Clemson College and the election of four blacks to the State Legislature. Yet along with these successes, three black students were killed during a riot at South Carolina College in Orangeburg, and actions were begun in the courts to force compliance with desegregation laws. In other developments, approval was given to begin a hydroelectric project on the Cooper River. McNair served as chairman of the Southern Regional Educational Board; vice-chairman of the Committee of Southern Governors' Conference; and vice-chairman of the Democratic National Committee. He left the governorship in January 1971 and became a senior partner in the law firm of McNair, Konduros and Corley. In 1978 he became a Charter member of the National Advisory Council for the University of South Carolina, and founding member of the South Carolina Educational Television Endowment Fund. He is currently a member of the board of directors for the NCNB Corporation, the Georgia-Pacific Corporation, and the Norfolk Southern Corporation & RL Bryan Company. He is also a member of the advisory board for the Duke Comprehensive Cancer Center. He has received honorary degrees from the University of South Carolina; Lander College; Presbyterian College; Furman University;

the College of Charleston; and Warner Pacific College in Oregon.

MCQUEEN, JOHN, (1804-1867) — a U.S. Representative from South Carolina; born in Queensdale, near the town of Maxton, Robeson County, N.C., February 9, 1804; completed preparatory studies under private tutors and was graduated from the Uni versity of North Carolina at Chapel Hill; studied law; was admitted to the bar in 1828 and commenced practice in Bennettsville, S.C.; served in the State militia 1833-1837; unsuccessful candidate for election in 1844 to the Twentyninth Congress; elected as a Democrat to the Thirtieth and Thirty-first Congresses to fill the vacancies caused by the death of Alexander D. Sims; reelected to the Thirty-second and to the four succeeding Congresses, and served from February 12, 1849, until his retirement on December 21, 1860; Representative from South Carolina in the First Confederate Congress; died at Society Hill, S.C., August 30, 1867; interment in Episcopal Cemetery, Society Hill, S.C.

MCSWAIN, JOHN JACKSON, (1875-1936) — a U.S. Representative from South Carolina; born on a farm near Cross Hill, Laurens County, S.C., May 1, 1875; attended the public schools; was graduated from Wofford College Fitting School in 1893 and from the University of South Carolina at Columbia in 1897; taught school in Marlboro, Abbeville, and Anderson Counties; studied law; was admitted to the bar in 1901 and commenced practice in Greenville, S.C.; referee in bankruptcy 1912-1917; entered the officers' training camp at Fort Oglethorpe, Ga., May 12, 1917, and served in the First World War as captain of Company A, One Hundred and Fifty-fourth Infantry, until March 6, 1919, when he was honorably discharged; resumed the practice of law in Greenville, S.C.; elected as a Democrat to the Sixty-seventh and to the seven succeeding Congresses and served from March 4, 1921, until his death; chairman, Committee on Military Affairs (Seventy-second through Seventy-fourth Congresses); declined to be a candidate for renomination in 1936; died in Columbia, S.C., on August 6, 1936; interment in Springwood Cemetery, Greenville, S.C.

MCSWEENEY, MILES BENJAMIN, (1855-1921) — sixty-third state governor (D) of South Carolina, 1899-1903.

He was born in Charleston, the son of Mary and Miles McSweeney.

McSweeney's father died when he was four years old, and he was forced to work at an early age. He was a newsboy, and a clerk in a bookstore. He was the corresponding secretary of the Columbia Typographical Union and, later, was also its president.

McSweeney attended evening school, and earned the Typographical Union of Charleston Scholarship to attend Washington and Lee University in Lexington, Virginia. However, he was unable to complete his studies there because of lack of funds.

McSweeney served in the State militia, first as a staff officer holding the rank of major, and later, as a lieutenant colonel.

McSweeney began publishing the *Guardian* in Ninety- six, South Carolina, in 1877, and published the *Hampton County Guardian* in 1879.

He was a delegate to the Democratic National Convention in 1888, 1896, and 1900, and was chairman of the Hampton County Democratic Committee for ten years.

McSweeney was elected to the South Carolina House of Representatives in 1894, and was elected lieutenant governor of South Carolina, 1897-1899.

After the death of Governor William H. Ellerbe on June 2, 1899, McSweeney became his successor, serving the remainder of Ellerbe's term. He was elected to gubernatorial office in his own right in November 1900. During his administration, the Interstate and West Indian Exposition opened, which was held to promote Charleston's status as a major seaport. Also during his tenure, William D. Crum, a black, was appointed postmaster of Charleston. A controversy surrounded the appointment.

McSweeney left office in January 1903. He died on June 4, 1921 in Charleston, South Carolina.

MEANS, JOHN H., (1812-1862) — thirty-ninth states governor (D) of South Carolina, 1850-1852. He was born in Fairfield District, South Carolina, the son of Sarah Milling and Thomas Means. Means attended Mount Zion College in Winnsboro, South Carolina, and graduated from South Carolina College in 1832. After settling in Fairfield, he became a planter.

Means was an advocate to Calhoun's doctrine of secession and supported organization of the State's military; he was a brigadier-general in the South Carolina militia. At the close of the Mexican War, when secession was an issue, he became one of the leaders in supporting separate State action. In the Nashville Convention of 1850, acts were passed in the South Carolina Legislature calling a State convention and providing delegates to another Southern congress.

Means was elected governor of South Carolina in December 1850. During his administration, $350,000 was appropriated for the purpose of arming the State, putting it in a position for defense, and reestablishing brigade encampments for mobilizing the militia. Although the convention for separate State action voted overwhelmingly for immediate secession, a statewide election resulted in citizens opposing such action without support of the rest of the South.

Means tried for re-election to gubernatorial office at the end of his term in 1852, but was defeated in an overwhelming victory by the conservatives.

During the Civil War, Means served as a colonel in the 17th South Carolina Regiment, Confederate States Army, and was killed by a shell fragment on August 29, 1862, at the Second Battle of Bull Run in Virginia. He was married to Sarah Rebecca Stark in January 1833. The couple had two children.

MIDDLETON, ARTHUR, (1742-1787) — - was a statesman and soldier who represented South Carolina in the signing of the Declaration of Independence, and defended the new state in the Revolutionary War.

Middleton was born on June 26, 1742, at Middleton Place, a farm on the Ashley River near Charleston, South

Carolina. The farm was the property of his mother, the former Mary Williams, and part of the large estate owned by his father, Henry Middleton, one of the largest landowners in South Carolina. Young Middleton was educated at Harrow and Westminster schools, and graduated from Cambridge. On April 14, 1757 he was admitted to the Middle Temple to read law, where he served until 1763. He traveled through Europe then sailed home to find his family situation completely different. His mother had given birth to three new daughters, making a total of 12 children in the family, then died on January 9, 1761. His father married Maria Henrietta, the daughter of Lieutenant-Governor William Bull. Arthur himself married Mary Izard in 1764, less than a year after returning to America.

As a member of a prominent Southern family, Middleton was expected to serve in politics. He became a justice of the peace in 1764, like his father had been before him, and he was elected to the colonial House of Assembly. In that position he served on the committee to correspond with the colonial agent in London. In 1768 he resigned from politics and took his wife to London, where his son Henry was born. The family traveled through southern Europe, then in September of 1771 returned to South Carolina and settled in Middleton Place, which Middleton had inherited.

The next year Middleton was elected to the House of Assembly and became one of the leaders of the American Party in South Carolina. In the days that lead to the Revolutionary War his father resigned his seat in the commons house and became a leader of the opposition to the British policy. Henry Middleton was a conservative at heart, and he hoped that through moderate resistance Britain would be compelled to make reasonable changes. Arthur, however, supported more radical change. He helped raise 1,000 guineas to support colonial resistance. He served as a member of the first Provincial congress, on the general committee, and on the secret committee of five. He also served on a special committee investigating rumors that the British were instigating an insurrection among the slaves in the American colonies.

After the arrival of the news of the battle of Lexington Middleton continued to help in the revolution, serving as a member of the first Council of Safety, which held the executive power of South Carolina. In the second Provincial Congress he served on the Council of Safety again and urged for the preparation of Charleston Harbor against attack. He was a leader in the extreme party and advocated excommunication of all those who refused to sign the Association, and all but encouraged activities such as the tarring and feathering of Loyalists. He also proposed that the Provincial Congress take over the estates of those who fled the colony rather than support the revolution. On February 11, 1776 Middleton was appointed to the committee of eleven to prepare a constitution for South Carolina. A few days later his father, weary of battling the radicals ready to go to war to break from Great Britain, stepped down from his seat on the Continental Congress, and the position was offered to Arthur. He chose to stay in South Carolina until the colony's constitution was adopted and a new government was in place, then he traveled north in May. Before he left, he and the secret committee of five arranged and directed the actions of the three parties of citizens who seized the powder and weapons from the public storehouses on the night of April 21, 1776. Middleton claimed his seat on in the Continental Congress May 20, and was present for the signing of the Declaration Independence.

In January 1777 Middleton was reelected to the Congress and he continued serving until October of that year. He was reelected again for the next three years, but declined the positions. He was also chosen as governor of South Carolina, but he declined that position as well.

In 1780 Middleton abandoned his life of farmer and statesman to serve in the militia, defending Charleston. His homestead was on the British line of march, and although the buildings were spared, his valuable collection of paintings were destroyed. He was taken as a political prisoner during the capture of the city, and was sent to St. Augustine and later confined on the Jersey prison ship. He was exchanged in July 1781, and he presented his credentials to the Continental Congress on September 24. He was reelected by the Jacksonborough Assembly, and served until the end of the war.

After the war Middleton went back to Middleton Place, to repair the damages and plant again. He served as a state senator and was instrumental in restoring the state after the Revolution. He became a member of the racing club and the hunting club of St. George's parish, and was an original trustee of the College of Charleston. He died at Goose Creek January 1, 1787, survived by his wife and eight of their nine children. His son Henry later became the governor of South Carolina, and another son, John Izard, an important author.

MIDDLETON, HENRY, (1770-1846) — eighteenth state governor (D-R) of South Carolina, 1810-1812.

He was born in London, England, the oldest son of Mary and Arthur Middleton. His father was a signer of the Declaration of Independence.

Middleton was educated by a private tutor. When his father died in 1787, he inherited Middleton Place on the Ashley River near Charleston, as well as estates in Newport, Rhode Island, and a large fortune.

In 1802, Middleton was elected to the South Carolina House of Representatives, serving in this office through 1810. He then became a member of the State Senate.

In December 1810, he was elected governor of South Carolina. During his administration, a free school system was instituted for indigent children, and the Bank of South Carolina was incorporated. Demands for war with Great Britain were strong throughout the state during his term. Three notable South Carolinians, John C. Calhoun, Langdon Cheves, and William Loudes, were elected in 1811 and sent to the national capital. They took the lead in calling for war, Calhoun writing the final bill. South Carolina responded by raising 5,000 men for the effort.

After his term ended, Middleton served in the U.S. Congress from 1815 to 1819. He was then U.S. Minister to Russia from 1820 to 1830. During the nullification controversy of the 1830s, he was a leader of the Union Party of South Carolina, and was vice president of the 1830 Union Convention.

Middleton was married to Mary Helen Hering. The couple had six sons and four daughters. He died in Charleston, South Carolina in June 1846, and was accorded a public funeral with full military honors.

MILES, WILLIAM PORCHER, (1822-1899) — a U.S. Representative from South Carolina; born in Charleston, S.C., July 4, 1822; attended Wellington School in Charleston and was graduated from Charleston College in 1842; studied law; was admitted to the bar and commenced practice in Charleston; mayor of Charleston 1855-1857; elected as a Democrat to the Thirtyfifth and Thirty-sixth Congresses and served from March 4, 1857, until his retirement in December 1860; member of the Confederate Provisional Congress in Montgomery, Ala., in February 1861; Member of the Confederate Congress from February 1862 to March 1864; colonel on the staff of General Beauregard; president of the University of South Carolina at Columbia 1880-1882; died in Burnside, La., on May 11, 1899; Union Cemetery, Union, Monroe County,

MILLER, STEPHEN DECATUR, (1787-1838) — a U.S. Representative and a Senator from South Carolina; born in Waxhaw settlement, Lancaster District, S.C., May 8, 1787; studied under a private tutor; graduated from South Carolina College at Columbia in 1808; studied law; was admitted to the bar and commenced practice in Sumterville in 1811; elected to the Fourteenth Congress to fill the vacancy caused by the resignation of William Mayrant; reelected to the Fifteenth Congress and served from January 2, 1817, to March 3, 1819; resumed the practice of his profession; member, State senate 1822-1828; Governor of South Carolina 1828-1830; elected as a Nullifier to the United States Senate and served from March 4, 1831, until March 2, 1833, when he resigned due to ill health; delegate to the South Carolina nullification conventions in 1832 and 1833; engaged in cotton planting in Mississippi in 1835; died in Raymond, Hinds County, Miss., March 8, 1838.

MILLER, THOMAS EZEKIEL, (1849-1938) — a U.S. Representative from South Carolina; born in Ferrebeville-Beaufort County, S.C., June 17, 1849; moved with his parents to Charleston, S.C., in 1851; attended the public schools in Charleston, S.C., and in Hudson, N.Y.; employed as a newsboy on a railroad; was graduated from Lincoln University, Chester County, Pa., in 1872; moved to Grahamville, S.C., and served as school commissioner of Beaufort County in 1872; member of the State house of representatives in 1874-1880, 1886-1887, and 1894- 1896; studied law; was admitted to the bar in 1875 and practiced law in Beaufort, S.C.; member of the State executive committee 1878- 1880; served in the State senate in 1880; successfully contested as a Republican the election of William Elliott to the Fifty- first Congress and served from September 24, 1890, to March 3, 1891; unsuccessful candidate for reelection in 1890 to the Fifty- second Congress; again a member of the State house of representatives in 1894; member of the State constitutional convention in 1895; president of the State college in Orangeburg, S.C., from 1896 until 1911, when he resigned; retired from active pursuits in 1911 and lived in Charleston, S.C., until 1923, when he moved to Philadelphia, Pa.; in 1934 returned to Charleston, S.C., where he resided until his death there on April 8, 1938; interment in Brotherhood Cemetery.

MITCHELL, THOMAS ROTHMALER, (1738-1837) — a U.S. Representative from South Carolina; born in Georgetown, Georgetown County, S.C., in May 1783; was graduated from Harvard University in 1802; studied law; was admitted to the bar in 1808 and commenced practice in Georgetown, S.C.; member of state house of representatives, 1809 and 1814-1819; elected to the Seventeenth Congress (March 4, 1821-March 3, 1823); unsuccessful candidate for reelection in 1822 to the Eighteenth Congress; elected to the Nineteenth and Twentieth Congresses (March 4, 1825-March 3, 1829); unsuccessful candidate for reelection in 1828 to the Twenty-first Congress; elected as a Jacksonian to the Twenty-second Congress (March 4, 1831- March 3, 1833);

unsuccessful candidate for reelection in 1832 to the Twenty-third Congress; died in Georgetown, S.C., November 2, 1837.

MOORE, THOMAS, (1759-1822) — a U.S. Representative from South Carolina; born in Spartanburg District, S.C., in 1759; served in the Revolutionary War, taking part in the Battle of Cowpens at the age of sixteen; member of South Carolina house of repre sentatives, 1794-1799; brigadier general in the War of 1812; engaged in planting; was one of the founders of the first high school in Spartanburg District; elected as a Republican to the Seventh and to the five succeeding Congresses (March 4, 1801- March 3, 1813); elected to the Fourteenth Congress (March 4, 1815-March 3, 1817); resumed his agricultural pursuits; died near Moores Station, Spartanburg County, S.C., on July 11, 1822; interment in Moore's Burying Ground.

MOSES, FRANKLIN J., (1838-1906) — fiftiety state governor (R) of South Carolina, 1872-1874.

He was born in Sumter County, South Carolina, the son of Jane McLelland and Franklin J. Moses, a wealthy lawyer and planter.

Moses received his education in private schools. He attended South Carolina College in 1855, but withdrew before completing his courses. He studied law and was admitted to the South Carolina Bar.

Moses was appointed private secretary to South Carolina Governor Francis J. Pickens in December 1860. He was editor of the *Sumter News* from 1866 to 1867.

During the latter part of the Civil War, Moses was appointed a colonel in the Confederate militia. In 1866, he was a delegate to the South Carolina Convention called to endorse President Andrew Johnson. He was elected to the South Carolina House of Representatives in 1867. He served simultaneously as Speaker of the South Carolina House of Representatives, an Adjunct Inspector General of the armed forces of the State, and a trustee of the State University.

While he was in the Legislature, Moses was charged with numerous offenses, including accepting bribes, issuing frauduent pay certificates, misappropriation of funds, and an immoral private life. Nonetheless, he was nominated for governor of South Carolina in the Republican State Convention of 1872. A small faction withdrew and nominated Reuben Tomlinson, who ran as an Independent Democrat.

Moses was elected governor of South Carolina in October 1872, having received 69,838 votes to Tomlinson's 36,553. He took office on December 3, 1872.

His administration was replete with scandal. During the second year of his term, the State's printing bill totaled $385,000. The State's credit was precarious, but when Moses called the Legislature into session, it annulled $5,965,000 in recent bonds, and those who held older bonds were forced to accept six percent interest.

A second Taxpayers' Convention was held in February 1874. Members petitioned the United States Congress for relief. Moses was eventually indicted; he avoided arrest by surrounding himself with loyal militia troops, and escaped trial by winning a legal ruling which provided that he could not be prosecuted while governor.

Moses left office in December 1874. In 1875, South Carolina Governor Daniel H. Chamberlain refused him commission as a circuit judge, even though the Legislature had elected him to the post.

Emma Buford Richardson, married to Moses since December 1859, filed for divorce in 1878. His career continued steadily downward. Bankrupt and without friends, he reduced himself to poverty and drug addiction. Later, he moved to Winthrop, Massachusetts, and became moderator of the town meeting and editor of the local newspaper. He was convicted of petty theft and fraud several times, and was sentenced to three years in the Massachusetts State Prison in 1885, but was pardoned in 1887 by Governor Ames on the grounds that he did not have long to live. Moses died in December 1906, and was buried in Winthrop, Massachusetts.

MOTTE, ISAAC, (1783-1795) — a Delegate from South Carolina; born in Charleston, S.C., December 8, 1738; appointed ensign in His Majesty's Sixtieth Royal American Regiment, December 19, 1756, and promoted to lieutenant

April 15, 1759; served in Canada in the French and Indian War in 1756; resigned and returned to Charleston in 1766; member of the house of commons in 1772; delegate to the provincial congresses of 1774, 1775, and 1776; during the Revolution was commissioned lieutenant colonel of the Second South Carolina (Continental) Regiment June 17, 1775, and was promoted to the rank of colonel September 16, 1776; resigned on election to the privy council in 1779; elected to the assembly from Charleston in 1779; Member of the Continental Congress 1780-1782; delegate to the State convention that ratified the Federal Constitution on May 23, 1788; appointed naval officer for the port of Charleston by General Washington; died in Charleston, S.C., May 8, 1795; interment in St. Philip's Churchyard.

MOULTRIE, WILLIAM, (1731-1805) — sixth and ninth state governor of South Carolina, 1785-1787 and 1792-1794. In his second term, he declared the Federalist party.

He was born in England. His father immigrated to Charleston, South Carolina in 1733, where Moultrie was raised and educated during his early years.

As an adult, Moultrie first distinguished himself by commanding a light infantry division in the regiment of Colonel James Grant, in an expedition of the province against the Cherokee Indians. The renowned Francis Marion was a lieutenant in the same regiment at the time.

In 1775, he became a member of the South Carolina Provincial Congress from the parish of St. Helena, which met in Charleston. After an appointment as colonel in the 2nd South Carolina Infantry, he immediately sought to provide protection for the city. When the troops took possession of Fort Johnson, on James Island, the position was supported by a neighboring camp and battery. Moultrie devised a flag to be used for signaling, and this became known as the first American flag displayed in South Carolina. Its blue color was adapted from the clothing of the State troops, and the crescent which appeared in the right hand corner was taken from a badge worn in the caps of two regiments who garrisoned the fort. A battery was erected at Haddrell's Point under Moultrie's supervision. And, in March of that year, he took command of the fort in process of erection on Sullivan's Island.

In June 1776, the British fleet, under command of Admiral Sir Peter Parker, brought from New York the forces of Sir Henry Clinton, and an attack on the city began. The fortifications commanded by Moultrie bore the brunt of the attack. Although the fleet used cannons to attack the fort, the distance of 350 yards made the shots inneffective in destroying their mark--they sunk into the soft palmetto logs of which the fort was constructed.

The American fire, however, hit the fleet solidly. Although Moultrie had scanty ammunition, he directed his men to single out the British flagship, the *Bristol*. That night, the British admiral finally drew off his ships, and Charleston was safe from further attacks from the English for nearly three years.

In recognition of his defense of Sullivan's Island, the Continental Congress made Moultrie a brigadier-general of the regular army. The palmetto, prominently displayed on the official seal of the State, is a lasting tribute to Moultrie's victory.

His position was primary in the few military operations carried out in the province prior to Charleston's capture by British troops under Sir Henry Clinton in May 1780. He defended Beaufort, South Carolina against a British force under Colonel Gardner in February 1779. In April of the same year, he slowed the advance of General Augustine Prevost toward Charleston until the city was placed in condition for defense. He assisted in the attack of Prevost at John's Island in the Stono River, and the general fell back before General Lincoln's forces. He also took part in the ill-fated siege of Savannah, by the Americans, in 1779.

Moultrie was commandant of Charleston when it surrendered to the British, and was a prisoner on parole from 1779 to February 1792, when he was "regularly exchanged with a number of other Americans, by composition, for Lieutenant General Burgoyne of the British forces, and late a prisoner of war to the United States of America." During the interval, he was offered command of a British regiment in Jamaica, West Indies, if he would desert the

American cause. He refused , stating that he would not part with his integrity.

After being freed from parole, Moultrie visited the camps of Marion and Greene, and was overjoyed to learn of the evacuation of the British from Charleston. He was made a major-general by the U.S. Congress.

Moultrie was elected governor of South Carolina in 1785, and was again elected to the office in 1794. After his second term ended, he occupied his time preparing and issuing *Memoirs of the American Revolution so far as it Related to the States of North and South Carolina and Georgia*, (New York, 1802), a repository of original documents, with brief comments from the writer.

Moultrie died in Charleston, South Carolina in September 1805.

MOWRER, PAUL SCOTT, (1887-1971) — war correspondent and poet who was born in Bloomington, Illinois, and traveled all over the world.

Born July 14, 1887 to Rufus and Nellie (Scott) Mowrer, he started reporting for the *Chicago Daily News* in 1905. He attended the University of Michigan from 1906 to 1908, but he did not complete his education. Between 1907 and 1910 he took the opportunity to become a Paris correspondent, and in the meantime also married Winifred Adams, on May 8, 1909. He wrote for the allied armies during the first Balkan War, then was assigned to the French General Headquarters in 1914, organizing and directing the *Chicago Daily News* war service. He stayed until the end of the war, then was part of the *Chicago Daily News* Peace Conference Bureau. In April, 1918 Mowrer was Awarded the Legion of Honor at the French General Headquarters. He stayed in Europe covering the Moroccan campaigns in the Riff, and working as a general correspondent, political analyst, and head of the European Service. In 1928 he won a Pulitzer Prize for his work as a correspondent, and won the Sigma Delta Chi foreign correspondent's award in 1932. In 1933, just before he returned to the states, Mowrer was promoted to officer of the French General Headquarters. Upon his return he was named associate editor of the *Chicago Daily News*, then was quickly promoted to editor-in-chief, were he stayed for nine years. Just before retiring from newpapers in 1945 he worked for one year as European editor for the *New York Post*. In 1941 he was given an honorary LL.D. from the University of Michigan.

While working as a correspondent Mowrer was inspired to write poetry. Published collections included *Hours of France*, (1918), *The Good Comrade*, (1923), and after returning to the U.S. he wrote *Poems Between Wars*, (1941). After leaving the newspaper business he wrote numerous other works, including *On Going to Live in New Hampshire* (1953), *And Let the Glory Go* (1955), *Fifi* (1956), *Twenty-One and Sixty- Five* (1958), *The Mothering Land* (1960), *High Mountain Pond* (1962), *School for Diplomats* (1964), *This Teeming Earth* (1965), *Island Ireland* (1966), and finally, *The Poems of Paul Scott Mowrer* (1918-1966). He was editor of the *Golden Quill Anthology*, along with Clarence E. Farrar from 1966 to 1970. He was also a contributor to the *Atlantic*, *L'Illustration*, and *Writer's Digest*, among other publications. In 1961 and 1962 he was awarded the Lyric Poetry Award for traditional poetry.

Mowrer wrote books other than poetry as well, including *Balkanized Europe* (1921), *Our Foreign Affairs* (1924), his autobiography, *The House of Europe* (1945), *Six Plays*, (1968), and he edited *A Choice of French Poems* (1969). Mowrer died in Beaufort, South Carolina, April 4, 1971. He and his wife had three children.

N

NAPIER, JOHN LIGHT, (1947-1986) — a U.S. Representative from South Carolina; born in Blenheim, Marlboro County, S.C., May 16, 1947; attended the public schools; A.B., Davidson College, Davidson, N.C., 1969; J.D., University of South Carolina, Colum bia, 1972; served in the United States Army Reserve, first lieutenant, 1969-1977; admitted to the South Carolina Bar in 1972; legislative assistant to United States Senator Strom Thurmond and minority counsel, United States Senate Subcommittee on Administrative Practice and Procedure, 1972-1973; minority counsel and professional staff member, United States Senate Committee on Veterans' Affairs, 1973-1976; chief legislative assistant and legal counsel to Senator Strom Thurmond, 1976-1978; chief minority counsel, United States Senate Committee on Official Conduct, 1977; private practice of law in Bennettsville, S.C., 1978-1980; elected as a Republican to the Ninety-seventh Congress (January 3, 1981-January 3, 1983); unsuccessful candidate for reelection in 1982; returned to the private practice of law in Bennettsville, 1983-1986; appointed by President Reagan as judge, United States Claims Court, September 11, 1986; is a resident of Bennettsville, S.C., and Arlington, Va.

NESBITT, WILSON, (?-1861) — a U.S. Representative from South Carolina; resided in Spartanburg, Spartanburg County, S.C.; attended the common schools and was a student at South Carolina College (now the University of South Carolina) at Columbia in 1805 and 1806; engaged in agricultural pursuits and conducted an iron foundry; justice of quorum of Spartanburg County in 1810; member of the State house of representatives 1810-1814; elected as a Republican to the Fifteenth Congress (March 4, 1817-March 3, 1819); moved to Alabama; died in Montgomery, Ala., May 13, 1861; interment in Oakwood Cemetery.

NICHOLLS, SAMUEL JONES, (1885-1937) — a U.S. Representative from South Carolina; born in Srartanburg, Spartanburg County, S.C., May 7, 1885; attended Bingham Military Institute, Asheville, N.C., Wofford College, Spartanburg, S.C., Virginia Polytechnic Institute, Blacksburg, Va., and the law department of the University of Chicago; was admitted to the bar in 1906 and commenced practice in Spartanburg; city attorney of Spartanburg and prosecuting attorney of Spartanburg County since 1907; member of the State house of representatives tives1907-1908; served by special appointment as circuit judge and as associate justice of the supreme court of South Carolina; organized and was captain for three years of Company I, First Regiment, South Carolina National Guard Infantry; elected as a Democrat to the Sixty-fourth Congress to fill the vacancy caused by the resignation of Joseph T. Johnson; reelected to the Sixty-fifth and Sixty-sixth Congresses and served from September 14, 1915, to March 3, 1921; declined to be a candidate for renomination in 1920; resumed the practice of law in Spartanburg, S.C., until his death there on November 23, 1937; interment in West Oakwood Cemetery.

NOBLE, PATRICK, (1787-1840) — thirty-second state governor (D) of South Carolina, 1838-1840.

He was born in Abbeville District, South Carolina, the son of Catherline Calhoun and Major Alexander Noble.

Noble attended Dr. Moses Waddel's School in Willington and graduated from the College of New Jersey, Princeton, in 1806. After returning to South Carolina, he studied law under his cousin, John C. Calhoun, and was admitted to the South Carolina Bar in 1809. He served in the First Brigade of the South Carolina Militia in 1813-1814.

Noble was elected to the House of Representatives in South Carolina in 1814. While he held his seat, he was aide to Governor Andrew Pickens from 1817 to 1819, and was Speaker of the House from 1820 to 1824. He became lieutenant-governor of South Carolina in 1830, holding the office until 1832. He was again a member of the State Legislature from 1833 to 1836 and, in 1835, was also Commissioner for Railroad between Charleston, South Carolina and Cincinnati, Ohio. He was elected to the South Carolina Senate for a two-year term, serving 1836-1838, and also was chosen its president.

Noble was elected governor of South Carolina in 1838. During his term, continued efforts were made to resolve differences between "Nullifiers" and "Unionists." Of far greater importance at this time, however, were the effects of the Panic of 1837 on the State's banks; in October 1839, the banks of Charleston were forced for a second time to suspend specie payment. Also during Noble's administration, a great agricultural convention was held in Columbia, a movement which led to the forming of district or county agricultural societies and contributed to the State's supremacy in rice and cotton cultivation.

Noble died while still in office, April 7, 1840. He was married to Elizabeth Bonneau Pickins in 1816.

NORTON, JAMES, (1843-1920) — a U.S. Representative from South Carolina; born near Mullins, Marion County, S.C., October 8, 1843; pursued an academic course; left school in 1861 to enter the Confederate Army; served throughout the Civil War in the Army of Northern Virginia; after the war reentered school, but did not finish the regular course; teacher in the public schools 1866-1870; engaged in agricultural pursuits and merchandising; elected county school commissioner in 1870 and reelected in 1872; member of the State house of representatives tivesin 1886, 1887, 1890, and 1891; assistant comptroller general of the State of South Carolina 1890-1894; comptroller lergeneral of the State from 1894 until 1897, when he resigned; elected as a Democrat to the Fifty- fifth Congress to fill the vacancy caused by the resignation of John L. McLaurin; reelected to the Fifty-sixth Congress and served from December 6, 1897, to March 3, 1901; was not a candi date for reelection in 1900 to the Fifty-seventh Congress; resumed agricultural pursuits and also engaged in the real estate business; again a member of the State house of representatives in 1907-1908; died in Mullins, S.C., October 14, 1920; interment in Miller's Churchyard.

NOTT, ABRAHAM, (1768-1830) — a U.S. Representative from South Carolina; born in Saybrook, Middlesex County, Conn., February 5, 1768; educated in early life by a private teacher; was graduated from Yale College in 1787; moved in 1788 to McIntosh County, Ga., where he was employed as a private tutor for one year; moved to Camden, S.C., in 1789; studied law; was admitted to the bar in 1791 and commenced practice in Union, S.C.; member of State house of representatives, 1796-1797; elected as a Federalist to the Sixth Congress (March 4, 1799- March 3, 1801); resumed the practice of his profession at Columbia, S.C., in 1804; elected a member of the board of trustees of South Carolina University in 1805; intendant of Columbia in 1807; elected judge of the circuit court in 1810 and served until his death; president of the court of appeals in

1824; died in Fairfield, S.C., June 19, 1830; interment in the First Presbyterian Churchyard, Columbia, S.C.

O

O'CONNOR, MICHAEL PATRICK, (1831-1881) — a U.S. Representative from South Carolina; born in Beaufort, Beaufort County, S.C., September 29, 1831; attended the public schools and was graduated from St. John's College, Fordham, N.Y., in 1850; studied law; was admitted to the bar in 1854 and commenced practice in Charleston, S.C.; member of the State house of representatives 1858-1866; served in the Civil War as a lieutenant in the Lafayette Artillery; delegate to the Democratic National Conventions in 1872 and 1876; unsuccessful candidate for election in 1874 to the Forty-fourth and in 1876 to the Forty- fifth Congresses; elected as a Democrat to the Forty-sixth Congress (March 4, 1879-March 3, 1881); received credentials as a Member-elect to the Forty-seventh Congress, but died, pending a contest by Edmund W.M. Mackey (which subsequently resulted successfully for the contestant), in Charleston, S.C., April 26, 1881; interment in St. Lawrence Cemetery.

ORR, JAMES LAWRENCE, (1822-1873) — forty-eighth state governor (Provisional) of South Carolina, 1865-1868.
    He was born in Craytonville, Pendleton District, South Carolina, the son of Martha McCann and Christopher Orr.

    Orr was educated in public schools, and attended the University of Virginia in 1839. He studied law in the office of Joseph N. Whitner in South Carolina, was admitted to the South Carolina Bar in 1843, and began a private law practice. He became editor of the *Anderson Gazette* for two years.
    Orr was elected to the South Carolina House of Representatives in 1844, and served through 1848. He became a member of the United States House of Representa-

tives in 1849, and kept his seat until 1859. He was elected Speaker of the House in 1857-1858.

When the Southern Rights Convention met in Charleston, South Carolina in 1851, Orr was an active member. He was also a delegate at the Democratic National Convention in 1856 and 1860, and a member of the South Carolina Secession in 1860. In 1861, he was one of three commissioners sent to Washington, D.C. to negotiate the surrender of federal forts at Charleston.

Orr was opposed to the withdrawal of South Carolina from the Union, but when secession became imminent, he retained his loyalty to the State and joined the cause. At the start of the Civil War, he organized Orr's Regiment of Rifles for service in the Confederate Army. He became a member of the Confederate States Provisional Congress in 1861 and, from 1861 through 1865, was a member of the Confederate States Senate.

In 1865, at the close of the war, Orr was elected Special Commissioner and sent to speak with President Andrew Johnson to secure establishment of a provisional government for South Carolina. He was also a member of the South Carolina Constitutional Convention in 1865.

After the adoption of the new Constitution in September 1865, Orr was elected governor of South Carolina by popular vote, and was sworn into office on November 29. During his administration, he urged the people to give to the blacks a qualified suffrage, convinced that if the State did not act upon the issue, the Federal government would intervene with a universal suffrage act. His position was, however, strongly opposed.

Despite efforts at moderation, the newly-elected South Carolina senators and congressmen were denied their seats in the the United States Congress by Radical Republicans, and the State was placed under military control. Although a semblance of civil government was maintained, South Carolina remained under Reconstruction Acts from March 1867 to July 1868.

Another constitutional convention was called in January 1868. After adoption of the new Constitution, elections were held on April 14, and Robert K. Scott replaced Orr as chief executive of the State on July 9, 1868.

After his term, Orr later served as Judge of the Eighth South Carolina Judicial Circuit from 1868-1870. He was a member of the Republican State Convention in 1872, and a delegate to the Republican National Convention the same year. President Ulysses S. Grant appointed him United States Minister to Russia in December 1872.

Orr died in St. Petersburg, Russia in May 1873, and was buried in the Presbyterian Cemetery in Anderson. He was married in 1844 to Mary Jane Marshall.

OSCEOLA, (1804-1838) — was a Seminole Indian chief.

Born among the Creek Indians on the Tallapoosa River in Georgia in about 1804, Osceola was also known as Powell. He was the son of William Powell, an English trader. His mother was the daughter of an Indian chief. However, others considered him to be of pure Native American ancestry.

Osceola moved to the Florida Territory with his mother and is believed to have fought with the Indians against General Andrew Jackson in the first phase of the Seminole wars while he was still in his teens. His opposition to efforts to move the Seminole westward under treaty is recorded as early as 1832 when he opposed the Treaty of Paynes Landing. On April 22, 1835, when the Seminole chiefs silently refused to acknowledge the treaty, Osceola was said to have angrily thrust his knife through the document in protest. He was arrested and imprisoned for the incident, but escaped by feigning a change of heart. He then led a band of young braves in the murder of a Seminole chief who had agreed to the arrangement. In 1835, while on a visit to Fort King, his wife, the daughter of a fugitive slave, was stolen as a slave. Osceola demanded that the United States Indian agent, General Wiley Thompson, assist in her return, and was reported to have used threatening language. He was imprisoned for six days. Six months later he avenged himself by killing General Thompson and four others outside of the fort. This began the second Seminole war.

Osceola, although not a chief, established himself as the dominant military leader of the Seminoles. Hiding the women and children of the tribe deep in the Everglades, he harassed the United States troops for two years with brilliant guerilla tactics. Osceola's skill caused the United States officer in command, General Thomas S. Jesup, to be severely criticized for his ineffectiveness. Enraged, General Jesup tricked Osceola and several of his followers into coming out of the Everglades into St. Augustine in October 1837 under a flag of truce. When the Indians entered the compound they were arrested and imprisoned despite public protests.

Osceola later moved to Fort Moultrie, near Charleston, South Carolina, where he died, possibly of poison or mistreatment on January 30, 1838. Following his death, the Seminole Wars continued for several more years and resulted in the extermination of most of the tribe.

OVERSTREET, JAMES, (1773-1822) — a U.S. Representative from South Carolina; born near Barnwell Court House, Barnwell District, S.C., February 11, 1773; attended the common schools; studied law; was admitted to the bar in 1798 and commenced practice in Barnwell District; member, State house of repre sentatives, 1808-1813; elected to the Sixteenth and Seventeenth Congresses and served from March 4, 1819, until his death May 24, 1822, at China Grove, Rowan County, N.C., while en route to his home from Washington, D.C.; interment in Savitz Cemetery at Mount Zion Reformed Church, China Grove, N.C.

P

PARKER, JOHN, (1759-1832) — a Delegate from South Carolina; born in Charleston, S.C., June 24, 1759; attended school in Charleston, S.C., and later in England; was graduated from the Middle Temple, London, England; returned to South Carolina; was admitted to the bar in 1785 and commenced practice in Charleston, S.C.; also engaged in the cultivation of rice on his plantation near there; Member of the Continental Congress 1786-1788; resided at Charleston and also on his estates, "Hayes" and "Cedar Grove," and engaged in their cultivation; died near

Charleston, S.C., April 20, 1832; inter ment in the family burying ground on the "Hayes" estate in St. James' Parish, Goose Creek, near Charleston, S.C.

PATTERSON, ELIZABETH J., (1939-   ) — daughter of Olin D. Johnston), a U.S. Representative from South Carolina; born Elizabeth Johnston in Columbia, S.C., November 18, 1939; attended public schools in Kensington, Md., and Spartanburg, S.C.; B.A., Columbia College, Columbia, S.C., 1961; graduate study, Uni versity of South Carolina, 1961-1962; recruiting officer for the Peace Corps, 1962-1964; recruiting officer for VISTA, 1965-1967; director of a Head Start program, 1967-1968; staff assistant for U.S. Representative James R. Mann, 1969-1970; served on the Spartanburg County Council, 1975-1976; South Carolina senate, 1979-1986; elected as a Democrat to the One Hundredth Congress through th One Hundred Third Congresses; is a resident of Spartanburg, S.C.

PATTERSON, JAMES O'HANLON, (1857-1911) — a Representative from South Carolina; born in Barnwell, Barnwell County, S.C., June 25, 1857; attended private schools in Barnwell, S.C., and Augusta, Ga.; studied law; was admitted to the bar in 1886 and commenced practice in Barnwell, S.C.; probate judge of Barnwell County 1888-1892; member of the State house of representatives 1899-1904; elected as a Democrat to the Fifty- ninth, Sixtieth, and Sixty-first Congresses (March 4, 1905-March 3, 1911); resumed the practice of his profession in Barnwell, S.C., where he died on October 25, 1911; interment in the Episcopal Cemetery.

PATTERSON, JOHN JAMES, (1830-1912) — a U.S. Senator from South Carolina; born in Waterloo, Juniata County, Pa., August 8, 1830; attended the common schools and graduated from Jefferson College, Canonsburg, Pa., in 1848; engaged in newspaper work; Publisher of the Juniata Sentinel in 1852 and became editor and part owner of the Harrisburg Telegraph in 1853; engaged in banking; member, State house of representatives 1854-1856; during the Civil War served in the Union Army as a captain in the Fifteenth United States Volunteer Infantry; unsuccessful candidate for election in 1862 to the Thirtyeighth Congress; engaged in banking 1863-1869; moved to Columbia, S.C., in 1869 and engaged in railroad construction; elected as a Republican to the United States Senate from South Carolina and served from March 4, 1873, to March 3, 1879; was not a candidate for reelection to the Senate; chairman, Committee on Education and Labor (Fortyfourth Congress), Committee on Territories (Forty- fifth Congress); resided in Washington, D.C., and engaged in various financial enterprises; moved to Mifflintown, Juniata County, Pa., in 1886; engaged in the construction of electric railways and electric lighting plants; died in Mifflintown, Pa., September 28, 1912; interment in Westminster Presbyterian Cemetery.

PEACE, ROGER CRAFT, (1899-1968) — a U.S. Senator from South Carolina; born in Greenville, Greenville County, S.C., May 19, 1899; attended the public schools and graduated from Furman University, Greenville, S.C., in 1919; newspaper reporter, sports editor, editor, business manager, and publisher in Greenville, S.C.; during the First World War served as an instructor in the United States Army at Camp Perry in 1918; colonel on the Governor's staff 1930-1934; trustee of Furman University 1938- 1948; appointed as a Democrat to the United States Senate to fill the vacancy caused by the death of Alva M. Lumpkin, who had been appointed to fill the vacancy caused by the resignation of James F. Byrnes, and served from August 5, 1941, until November 4, 1941; was not a candidate for election to the vacancy; resumed his career of writing, publishing, and civic activities; at the time of his death was chairman of Multimedia, Inc.; died in Greenville, S.C., August 20, 1968; interment in Springwood Cemetery.

PERRY, BENJAMIN F., (1805-1886) — forty-seventh state governor (D) provisional) of South Carolina, 1865.
He was born in the Pendleton District of South Carolina, the son of Anne Foster and Benjamin Perry.
He received his early education in public schools, and was sent to a Asheville, North Carolina preparatory school

at age 16. After studying law, he was admitted to the State Bar in 1827.

Perry became a journalist, and was editor of the *Greenville Mountaineer* in 1832. In 1850, he founded the *Southern Patriot*, the only Union paper in the State, and was editor of the *Patriot and Mountaineer* from 1855 to 1858.

In 1832, he was a delegate to the Union Convention, and was also a delegate to the Nullification Convention of 1832-1833.

He was elected to the South Carolina House of Representatives in 1836, serving until 1842. He was then elected to the South Carolina Senate from 1844 to 1848, and was also a presidential elector in 1848. In 1849, he was again elected to the State House, keeping his seat until 1860.

Perry took part in the Democratic State Convention in 1852, and the Democratic National Convention in 1860. In the latter convention, his Union views received much negative reaction; however, when the State acted, he gave his full support to the Southern cause. He was appointed a Confederate Commissioner in 1862, a Confederate States District Attorney in 1863, and a Confederate States District Judge in 1864.

He was appointed Provisional Governor of South Carolina by President Andrew Johnson in June 1865. He quickly reappointed all State officials who had been in office at the close of the Civil War, despite severe criticism by radical Republicans. As a result, when the Constitutional Convention met in September 1865, he was able to bring about many important changes for the State. He received approval for the popular election of the governor and presidential electors; equal representation throughout the State based on property and population; the abolishment of the parish system; the popular election of judges for four-year terms; and the ratification of the Thirteenth Amendment to the U.S. Constitution.

Perry declined to run for governor after passage of South Carolina's 1865 Constitution, leaving office on November 20, 1865. He later served as a delegate to the Philadelphia Peace Convention of 1866. He was elected to the United States Senate the same year, but was denied his seat. He was again a delegate to the National Union Convention in 1866, as well as a delegate to the Democratic National Convention in 1868 and 1876.

Perry authored *Reminiscences of Public Men: Sketches of Eminent American Statesmen.* He was married to Elizabeth Frances McCall in April 1837, with whom he had nine children. He died in Greenville, South Carolina in December 1886.

PERRY, WILLIAM HAYNE, (1839-1902) — a U.S. Representative from South Carolina; born in Greenville, Greenville County, S.C., June 9, 1839; attended Greenville Academy, and was graduated from Furman University at Greenville in 1857; attended South Carolina College (now the University of South Carolina) at Columbia, and was graduated from Harvard University in 1859; studied law in Greenville; was admitted to the bar in 1861 and commenced practice in Greenville; served as a private and subsequently as lieutenant in the Confederate Cavalry during the Civil War; resumed the practice of law in Greenville in 1865; member of the State constitutional convention in 1865; member of the State house of representatives tivesin 1865 and 1866; solicitor of the eighth judicial circuit of South Carolina 1868- 1872; served in the State senate 1880-1884; elected as a Democrat to the Forty-ninth, Fiftieth, and Fifty-first Congresses (March 4, 1885-March 3, 1891); declined to be a candidate for renomination in 1890; resumed the practice of law; died at his home, "San Souci," near Greenville, S.C., July 7, 1902; interment in Christ Church Cemetery, Greenville, S.C.

PETERKIN, JULIA, (1880-1961) — author, was born in Laurens, South Carolina on October 31, 1880, the daughter of Julius and Alma Mood. Her father was a doctor, and after her mother passed away, the little girl was raised by a black nurse in the home of her grandparents. She attended public schools and after graduation enrolled in Converse College. Awarded first a B.A. and then a M.A. in 1897 she found work as a teacher after college. She married a rich cotton planter in 1903 and began to help manage her husbands holdings. That work involved supervision of the estate's 450 black workers, and involved her in all facets of their lives. Ms Peterkin also found time to devote herself to various aspects of advanced agriculture and the pursuit of music.

While pursuing weekly music lessons her music teacher suggested she write down some of the plantation stories she had told him. Within a short time she had begun writing and her sketches appeared in the Richmond, Va. *Reviewer*. Northern critics noticed the work and she was published in H.L. Mencken's magazine *Smart Set* in 1922. A collection of these sketches appeared under the title *Green Thursday* in 1924. A series of novels portraying black life struggling against fate quickly followed. *Black April* was published in 1927, *Scarlet Sister Mary* in 1928, *Bright Skin* in 1932, *Roll, Jordan, Roll* in 1933, and *Plantation Christmas* in 1934. Her novel *Scarlet Sister Mary* had received the Pultizer Prize for fiction in 1928, and was produced on Broadway in 1930. She continued her career, writing many short stories and magazine articles. Ms. Peterkin died in Orangeburg, S.C. on August 10, 1961.

PETIGRU, JAMES LOUIS, (1789-1863) — lawyer and political leader, considered by some to be "the greatest private citizen South Carolina has ever produced."

The son of Louise Guy (Gilbert) and William Pettigrew, he was born May 10, 1789 in Abbeville District, South Carolina. His parents were poor, so Petigru started working at an early age, attending school when he could. In 1804 he was able to enter a school operated by Dr. Moses Waddell in Willington, which was very famous at the time. Two years later he entered South Carolina College, paying for his tuition by teaching school in Columbia. He received his A.B. degree in 1809, and taught in St. Luke's Parish and at Beaufort while studying law. It was at about this time he changed his name to Petigru.

He was admitted to the bar in 1812, and although a Federalist he served for a short time in the militia. He moved to Coosawhatchie for a short time, where he was elected solicitor and met and married his wife, Jane Amelia Postell. In 1819 James Hamilton, Jr. offered Petigru a position with his law firm in Charleston, where he quickly gained a strong reputation. In 1822 he was elected attorney general, resigning the position in 1830 to run for the state Senate. He lost the election, but within a few weeks won another election to fill an opening in the lower house.

Petigru vehemently opposed nullification, feeling there was no justification in law, logic or morals. Despite his aversion to politics in general and especially strong disputes, Petigru fought nullification as strongly as he could. He wrote numerous newspaper articles and made uncountable speeches, resulting in his promotion to leader of the Union party. He also opposed the new test oath and won a decision from the court of appeals declaring it unconstitutional. Eventually a compromise on the nullification issue was reached and Petigru left state politics for good at the end of his term. He did serve for two years as the United States district attorney, as a favor to President Fillmore, who could find no other qualified candidates. Petigru was also elected code commissioner in 1859, and retained the position until the Portion of the Code of Statute Law of South Carolina 1860-1862 was completed.

As the passions that separated the North and the South grew more intense Petigru publicly opposed separating from the Union. Mistaking the bells that announced secession for a fire alarm, Petigru said, "I tell you there is a fire; they have this day set a blazing torch to the temple of constitutional liberty, and please God, we shall have no more peace forever." Despite his deep and abiding love for the South and South Carolina Petigru hated everything to do with the Confederate government, and was very public with his disdain. He opposed the Confederate sequestration act in district court. His own home was burned in Charleston, and another home on Sullivan's Island was destroyed during the war as well.

Petigru was considered the leader of the South Carolina bar for forty years, known not only for his knowledge of the law but his deductive reasoning as well. At one point President Lincoln seriously considered him for a Supreme Court position, but in the end Petigru never held a judicial post. He was known for his philanthropy and concern for fellow man, especially those who were poor or oppressed. He died in Charleston March 9, 1863.

PICKENS, ANDREW, (1779-1838) — twenty-first state governor (D-R) of South Carolina, 1816-1818.

He was born in Edgefield County, South Carolina, the son of Rebecca and General Andrew Pickens.

Pickens was a student at the College at New Jersey. During the War of 1812, he was appointed Lieutenant Colonel of the Tenth Infantry. He subsequently commanded the Forty-third Infantry and, in 1814, was appointed to command one of the regiments raised by South Carolina for the defense of Charleston, and fought in the Battle of Lundy's Lane.

Pickens was elected governor of South Carolina in 1816. During his term of office, South Carolina's John C. Calhoun was named Secretary of War of the United States. The State also appointed an engineer to superintend public buildings and oversee civilian and military works, which was the beginning of an extensive internal improvements program. In addition, the price of short-staple cotton on the Charleston market reached thirty- five cents a pound, an all-time high for cotton prices in the antebellum era.

After his term ended, Pickens moved to Alabama and engaged in cotton planting. He was appointed president of the Alabama State Bank by the Legislature, and served as an agent to the Creek Indians in 1820.

Pickens was married to Susan Smith in 1804; the couple had two children. He married a second time to Mary Willing Nelson. He died in Pontotock, Mississippi in July 1838.

PICKENS, FRANCIS W., (1805-1869) — forty-fourth state governor (D) of South Carolina, 1860-1862.

He was born in St. Paul's Parish, Pendleton District, South Carolina, the son of Susannah Smith Wilkinson and Andrew Pickens. His father was the governor of South Carolina from 1816 to 1818. Pickens attended Franklin College in Georgia, and South Carolina College, but withdrew in 1827, his senior year, to study law in Edgefield, South Carolina, under Eldred Simkins. He was admitted to the State Bar in 1828, and established a law practice in Edgefield District in South Carolina.

Pickens was elected to the South Carolina House of Representatives in 1832, serving until 1834, when he was elected to the United States House of Representatives. After leaving his seat in 1843, he was again elected to the State Legislature, serving 1844-1846. Pickens was a member of the Southern Convention in Nashville, Tennessee in 1850; a delegate to the Democratic National Convention in 1856; and the United States Minister to Russia from 1858-1860.

Pickens was elected governor of South Carolina in December 1860. He raised a contingent of 2,158 men during the nullification controversy and, on December 20, six days after his appointment, South Carolina seceded from the Union. Pickens authorized the first action of the Civil War on January 9, 1861, when South Carolina troops on Morris Island fired on the *Star of the West* as it attempted to relieve the Federal Army garrison at Fort Sumter.

South Carolina Legislature established an Executive Council in December 1861, consisting of the governor and four other members, which took over the functions of the chief executive. Pickens protested the move, but the Executive Council was not abolished until the end of his administration in 1862.

After election of his successor, Pickens retired from public life, appearing only once, at the South Carolina Constitutional Convention of 1865, where he urged cooperation of President Andrew Jackson's reconstruction plan.

Pickens wrote a series of anonymous articles for the *Charleston Mercury* during his lifetime, which he penned under the pseudonym of "Sidney."

Pickens was married to Margaret Eliza Simkins, who died in 1842. He married a second time, to Marion Antoinette Dearing, and she also died. In 1858, he married a third time, to Lucy Petway Holcombe. He died in Edgefield, South Carolina in January 1869.

PINCKNEY, CHARLES, (1758-1824) — eighth, eleventh and sixteenth state governor (D-R) of South Carolina, 1789-1792, 1796-1798 and 1806-1808.

He was born in Charleston, South Carolina, the son of Charles and Francis Pinckney. He was second cousin to Thomas Pinckney, who preceded him in the gubernatorial appointment. His father, a lawyer, gained prominence in the State during the American Revolution, and was also president of the South Carolina Convention in January 1775, president of the Senate in 1779, and president of the Council in 1780.

Pinckney was educated in Charleston and went on to study law under his father. In 1779, he was elected to the Legislature. During the fall of Charleston in 1780, Pinckney was captured and made a prisoner of war in St. Augustine.

He became a member of the Continental Congress in 1786, joining Monroe in opposing the relinquishment of the Mississippi. Congress appointed him a member of the committee sent to New Jersey to urge the Legislature of that state to comply with the requisitions of Congress.

As a member of the Convention in 1787, Pinckney drafted and presented a plan for a new constitution. In 1788, he was a member of the South Carolina Convention by which the Federal Constitution was ratified.

Pinckney was elected governor of South Carolina in 1789, and elected for a second term in 1791. He was also president of the Convention in 1790 which adopted a new Constitution for the State. During his administration, all public records were moved from Charleston to the State's new capital of Columbia. The first Assembly met there in January 1790; in June of that year, the new Constitution of the State was ratified.

Pinckney was elected governor of the State once again in 1796. After his term ended, he was appointed to the U. S. Senate and served until his resignation in 1801. An active promoter of Jefferson, he published a series of addresses in his favor under the signature of "A Republican." He also published a second series denouncing the Alien and Sedition Laws. In this campaign, he was opposed to his cousin, Charles Cotesworth Pinckney, who was then a candidate for vice president on the ticket with Adams.

In 1802, Pinckney became U.S. Minister to Spain, and negotiated the treaty by which Spain released all claims to Louisiana. When he returned to Charleston in 1806, he was elected to the State Legislature, and was again elected governor of South Carolina. During this term, the right of suffrage was accorded by the Legislature to all white citizens, without requiring a property qualification. When his third gubernatorial term ended, he was elected to the Legislature in 1810, and again in 1812.

After a short retirement from public life, he was again elected to Congress, and served through the 15th Congress, 1817- 1819.

His last act of public life was a speech against the Missouri Compromise. Pinckney published a pamphlet in which he advocated the election of Monroe over Crawford, and also published an extensive account of his travels through France, Spain, Italy, and Germany.

Pinckney was married to Mary Eleanor Laurens in 1788. The couple had two daughters and one son. He died in Charleston in October 1824.

PINCKNEY, CHARLES COTESWORTH, (1746-1825)
— soldier and statesman, was born in Charleston, South Carolina on February 25, 1746, the son of Charles and Eliza (Lucas) Pinckney. His father was educated in England, practiced law and was made King's counselor and chief justice of South Carolina; he was twice married, his first wife, Elizabeth Lamb, died without children.

Charles Cotesworth Pinckney went to England with his parents at the age of seven, and was educated at Westminster school and at Christ Church, Oxford, and read law at the Middle Temple, London, also attending the law lectures of the famous commentator Blackstone. He traveled in France and Germany and had nine months' training in the Royal Military Academy in Caen, Normandy. Returning to America in 1769, he established himself in Charleston in the practice of law.

In 1775, he was a member of the first Provincial Congress of South Carolina and was appointed by that congress a captain of infantry; he was made a major in December, 1775, and colonel on October 29, 1776. He assisted in the defense of Fort Sullivan on June 28, 1776, joined the Northern army as aide to General Washington and participated in the battles of the Brandywine and Germantown. He was a member of the unsuccessful expedition to Florida in the spring of 1778 and presided over the South Carolina Senate in January 1779.

In the rapid march which saved the city of Charleston from the British under General Augustine Prevost, he displayed great resolution and daring. His regiment formed the second column of the force which invaded Georgia and attacked the lines of Savannah. He commanded Fort Moultrie with a force of 300 men at the time of the second attack on Charleston, in April, 1780, but the British fleet entered the harbor without engaging Fort Moultrie and Colonel Pinckney then returned to the city and helped defend it against the enemy. He urged the rejection of all terms of capitulation and was in favor of continuing hostilities to the end.

When Charleston surrendered, in May of 1780, he became a prisoner of war and was imprisoned for two years. Upon being ordered into closer confinement by his jailers, he wrote to the British commanding officer, "My heart is altogether American, and neither severity, nor favor, nor poverty, nor affluence can ever induce me to swerve from it." In February of 1782, he was exchanged, and was made brigadier-general on November 3, 1783, but had no further opportunity to serve his country in the field as the war was practically at an end. He once again resumed the practice of law, gaining both wealth and prominence.

When the United States Constitution was framed in 1787, he was one of South Carolina's delegates at the convention and he took an active part in the debates. It was on his motion that the clause: "No religious test shall ever be required as a qualification to any office or public trust under the authority of the United States," was put in the Constitution. He moved also to strike out the clause allowing compensation to senators, holding that the Senate should be composed of men of wealth. He was a member of the convention which ratified the Constitution for South Carolina, and of the State Constitutional Convention of 1790.

After the organization of the government he declined successively the places of associate justice of the U.S. Supreme Court in 1791, Secretary of War in 1794, and Secretary of State in 1795. In July, 1796, he accepted the post of U.S. Minister Plenipotentiary to France, resigning the commission of major- general of the South Carolina militia to go abroad. Owing to the strained relations with

France at that time, Pinckney upon arrival in Paris was informed that the Directory would receive no minister from the United States until the grievances of France had been righted, and was reminded of the law which forbade any foreigner to stay more than thirty days in France without permission. He would not be intimidated, however, and left France only when the Directory requested him to withdraw.

He accordingly went to Amsterdam in February, 1797, and soon after, returned to America. Preparations for war were now made by the Congress and three commissioners, Pinckney, John Marshall and Eldridge Gerry, were dispatched to France with authority to consult, negotiate and treat on all claims and differences between the two republics. Upon arrival in Paris the following October, attempts were made to open negotiations wth the Directory, but official recognition was refused them. Talleyrand's secretary assured the commissioners that a gift of money was a necessary preliminary to the negotiations and that a refusal might bring on war. Pinckney is said to have answered, "War be it then; millions for defense, sir, but not a cent for tribute!" Other agents approached them with a proposal that the United States buy certain stock amounting to 32,000,000 florins, which was also rejected by the commissioners and they shortly afterward returned with nothing accomplished.

War with France being imminent, Pinckney was commissioned major-general by President Washington. When his attention was called to the fact that he had been made junior in rank to Alexander Hamilton, whose senior he had been during the Revolutionary War, he replied: "Let us first dispose of our enemies; we shall then have leisure to settle the question of rank." Pinckney was a staunch adherent of the Federalist Party and was its candidate for the vice-presidency of the United States in 1800, and for the presidency in 1804 and 1808. He was the third president-general of the order of the Cincinnati, and for fifteen years prior to his death was president of the Charleston Bible Society. He was a trustee of the College of South Carolina and in 1801, was first president of the board.

He was twice married, to Sarah Middleton with whom he had three daughters, and Mary Stead, a descendant of

Sir Nathaniel Johnson, one of the proprietary governors of Carolina. Pinckney was a true patriot, and a man of wide influence. Charles Chauncey said of him: "His love of honor was greater than his love of power, and deeper than his love of self." He died in Charleston, South Carolina on August 16, 1825.

PINCKNEY, THOMAS, (1750-1828) — seventh state governor of South Carolina, 1787-1789.

He was born in Charleston, South Carolina, the son of Elizabeth and Charles Pinckney. His father, a laywer, served as chief justice of the colony in 1752-53.

Pinckney received his education in England, at Westminster and Oxford. He went on to study law in the Inner Temple and was admitted as a barrister. In 1774, he returned to Charleston and was admitted to the State Bar.

In June 1775, Pinckney was made first lieutenant in one of the regiments raised in South Carolina, later rising to the rank of major. He was aide to General Lincoln in the command of the Southern army in 1778, acting in that capacity again to Count D'Estaing at the siege of Savannah. At the Battle of Camden in August 1780, he was wounded and left for dead on the field; however, after being discovered by the enemy, he was captured and made a prisoner of war in Philadelphia.

Pinckney was elected governor of South Carolina in 1787, serving to restore South Carolina after the ravages of war. During his administration, the Installment Law was passed, and the last installment made on February 20, 1787; this was the final effort by the State to interfere between debtor and creditor.

After declining an offer to become a U.S. district judge for South Carolina in 1789, Pinckney became a member of the Legislature, and drew up the act to establish a court of equity.

Washington appointed him minister to England in 1792. While abroad, he undertook a mission in Spain and negotiated the Treaty of San Lorenzo, by which free navigation was obtained, and the demarcation line of 31 degrees north was established as the boundary between

Spanish possessions in North America and the United States.

Pinckney returned to Charleston in 1796, and served in the 6th Congress, but when the Federalist Party lost power, he retired to private life. In the War of 1812, he was appointed major-general and given charge of the 6th military district, which extended from Virginia to Louisiana.

At the war's end, Pinckney resigned his position and retired once again to private life. He succeeded his brother, Charles Cotesworth, as fourth President-General of the Cincinnati.

Pinckney was married to Elizabeth Brewton, with whom he had two sons and two daughters. He also had a second marriage. He died in Charleston in November 1828.

POINSETT, JOEL ROBERTS, (1779-1851) — a U.S. Representative from South Carolina; born in Charleston, S.C., March 2, 1779; spent his early childhood in England; returned to America in 1788; attended private school at Greenfield Hill, Conn., and later in Wandsworth, near London, England; studied medicine at the University of Edinburgh, Scotland, and attended the military school in Woolwich, England; returned to Charleston, S.C., in 1800; studied law for a few months; traveled extensively in Europe from 1801 to 1809, returning to the United States for short intervals; sent to South America by President Madison in 1809 to investigate the prospects of the revolutionists there in their struggle for independence from Spain; returned to Charleston, S.C., in 1816; member of the State house of representatives 1816-1819; served as president of the board of public works; declined the offer of commissioner to South America by President Monroe; elected to the Seventeenth, Eighteenth, and Nineteenth Congresses and served from March 4, 1821, to March 7, 1825, when he resigned to enter the diplomatic service; Minister to Mexico 1825-1829; member of the State house of representatives, 1830-1831; Secretary of War in the Cabinet of President Van Buren 1837-1841; died near what is now Statesburg, Sumter County, S.C., December 12, 1851; interment in the Church of the Holy Cross (Episcopal) Cemetery.

POLLITZER, ANITA LILY, (1894-1975), feminist, was born in Charleston, South Carolina on October 31, 1894, the daughter of Gustave and Clara Pollitzer. She was a precocious child who could read and write before entering school. Growing up in Charleston she attended local schools and graduated from Memminger High in 1913. The following year she enrolled in Columbia University and three years later graduated with a B.S. degree in art and education. While in college she became interested in the women's movement and joined the National Women's Party. Within a few months of graduation she was a paid lobbyist for the NWP, busy with a schedule of travel, organizing, and speaking on behalf of women's issues. By 1920 she had made significant contributions to the ratification of the nineteenth amendment (women's vote).

She married in 1928 and with her husband's encouragement continued her work for women's rights. This effort included the right of American women who had married foreign nationals to keep their citizenship, equal pay scales for both sexes, and the vote for women in various European countries. At the end of World War II she took part in the founding of the United Nations and ensured that women's equality was guaranteed in that charter. Also in 1945 she became president of the National Women's Party, a post she held until 1949. During the 1950's and 1960's she maintained her efforts for the Equal Rights Amendment, only retiring a few years before her death in 1975.

POLLOCK, WILLIAM PEGUES, (1870-1922) — a U.S. Senator from South Carolina; born near Cheraw, Chesterfield County, S.C., December 9, 1870; attended private and public schools and the University of South Carolina at Columbia; graduated from the law department of that university in 1891; served as clerk on the Committee on the District of Columbia in the House of Representatives 1891-1893; was admitted to the bar in 1893 and commenced practice in Cheraw, S.C.; also engaged in agricultural pursuits; member, State house of representatives tives1894-1898; presidential elector on the Democratic Ticket in 1900; elected to the State house of representatives in 1902, 1904, and 1906; unsuccessful candidate for election to the Sixty-second Congress; elected as a Democrat to the United States Senate to fill the vacancy caused by the death of Benjamin R. Tillman and served from November 6, 1918, to March 3, 1919; chairman, Committee on National Banks (Sixty-fifth Congress); resumed the practice of law in Cheraw, S.C., and died there June 2, 1922; interment in St. David's Cemetery.

PULITZER, JOSEPH, (1847-1911) — publisher of the St. Louis Post-Dispatch and the New York Evening World, Pulitzer maintained high standards of accuracy and excellence during the heyday of yellow journalism. After his death, his will provided for the establishment of the Pulitzer Prize, which honors the best in journalism, letters, and music.

Pulitzer was born April 10, 1847 in Mako, Hungary. After receiving his education in Budapest he emigrated to the United States, where he served in the Union army. After his discharge in 1865 Pulitzer held numerous odd jobs, then fell into the world of journalism as a reporter for the St. Louis Westliche Post, a German-language daily. He later became managing editor and part- owner. Pulitzer also became active in politics and was considered a leader in the Liberal Republican movement. He ran for a seat in the Missouri legislature and won, even though he was only 22, officially too young to become a member of state body. He took part in the disappointing campaign of Horace Greeley in 1872, which hurt him politically, and resulting in his joining the Democratic party. In 1874 he was a delegate to the Missouri state Constitutional Convention. In 1874 he started studying law and he bought the dying Staats-Zeitung, a St. Louis newspaper. He made money on the deal by selling the paper's Associated Press subscription to the St. Louis Daily Globe.

After two years of study Pulitzer was admitted to the District of Columbia bar, but the journalism bug had already bitten him hard, and he chose to relinquish his law career. He purchased the bankrupt St. Louis Dispatch in 1878 and merged it with The Evening Post, establishing the St. Louis Post-Dispatch in 1880. Editorially he criticized soft money, high tariffs, and, of course, corrupt politicians. In 1880 Pulitzer was also a delegate to the

Democratic National Convention and a member of the platform committee from Missouri.

The Post-Dispatch was successful for awhile, but a scandal involving the chief editorial writer hit the paper financially, and Pulitzer went looking for another paper to invest in. He found it in the New York World, which he bought in 1883. This purchase put Pulitzer in the middle of big-time journalism, competing with William Randolph Hearst's New York Morning Journal. Pulitzer fought back by sticking to his principals, which included supporting the Democratic Party and the rights of the working class. He briefly tried his hand at politics again in 1885, winning a seat in the House of Representatives, but he resigned soon after the election because of journalistic duties.

From then on Pulitzer stayed close to journalism. In 1887 he founded the New York Evening World, later adding a Sunday edition. That same year his eyesight began failing, and he gave up management of his papers, although he continued as editor until 1890. When Hearst's "yellow journalism" style became a serious threat however, Pulitzer came back to lead his paper. The World maintained its reputation for intelligent journalism, with accurate reporting, political independence, and fearlessness in the face of corrupt politicians.

In 1903 Pulitzer made a decision about his estate, and willed one million dollars to the Columbia College School of Journalism, agreeing to give an additional one million once the school was operating successfully. He also established the Pulitzer Prize, which continues to be the most coveted award in journalism, fiction, and music. Pulitzer died October 29, 1911, in Charleston, South Carolina. The first Pulitzer Prizes were awarded in 1917. Pulitzer's oldest son took over the publishing and editing of the St. Louis Post-Dispatch, a position he maintained until he death in 1955, and the World and Evening World were sold to the Scripps-Howard chain in 1931.

R

RAGSDALE, JAMES WILLARD, (1872-1919) — a U.S. Representative from South Carolina; born in Timmonsville- Florence County, S.C., December 14, 1872; attended the public schools; employed in a railroad office at Wilmington, N.C., for several years; attended the University of South Carolina at Columbia; studied law; was admitted to the bar in 1898 and commenced practice in Florence, Florence County, S.C.; engaged in agricultural pursuits and banking; trustee of the South Carolina Industrial School; member of the State house of representatives tives1899-1900; member of the State senate 1902-1904; unsuccessful candidate for attorney general of South Carolina and for election in 1910 to the Sixty-second Congress; elected as a Democrat to the Sixty-third and to the three succeeding Congresses and served from March 4, 1913, until his death in Washington, D.C., July 23, 1919; interment in Mount Hope Cemetery, Florence, S.C.

RAINEY, JOSEPH HAYNE, (1832-1887) — a U.S. Representative from South Carolina; born in Georgetown, Georgetown County, S.C., June 21, 1832; received a limited schooling; followed the trade of barber until 1862, when upon being forced to work on the Confederate fortifications in Charleston, S.C., he escaped to the West Indies and remained there until the close of the war; delegate to the State constitutional convention in 1868; member of the State senate in 1870 but resigned; elected as a Republican to the Forty-first Congress to fill the vacancy caused by the action of the House of Representatives in declaring the seat of B. Franklin Whittemore vacant and was the first black to be elected to the House of Representatives; reelected to the Forty-second and to the three succeeding Congresses and served from December 12, 1870, to March 3, 1879; appointed internal-revenue agent of South Carolina on May 22, 1879, and served until July 15, 1881, when he resigned; engaged in banking and the brokerage business in Washington, D.C.;

retired from all business activities in 1886, returned to Georgetown, S.C., and died there August 2, 1887; interment in the Baptist Cemetery.

RANSIER, ALONZO JACOB, (1834-1882) — a U.S. Representative from South Carolina; born in Charleston, S.C., January 3, 1834; received a limited schooling; employed as shipping clerk in 1850; member of a convention of the Friends of Equal Rights at Charleston in 1865 and was deputed to present the memorial there framed to Congress; member, State house of representatives,atives 1868-1869; member of the State constitutional convention in 1868 and 1869; Lieutenant Governor of South Carolina in 1870; president of the Southern States Convention at Columbia in 1871; delegate to the Republican National Convention in 1872; elected as a Republican to the Forty-third Congress (March 4, 1873-March 3, 1875); United States internal-revenue collector for the second district of South Carolina in 1875 and 1876; died in Charleston, S.C., on August 17, 1882; interment in Unity Friendship Cemetery.

RAVENEL, ARTHUR, JR., (1927-   ) — a U.S. Representative from South Carolina; born in Charleston, S.C., March 29, 1927; B.S., College of Charleston, 1950; served in the U.S. Marine Corps, 1945-1946; realtor and general contractor; member, South Carolina State house of representatives, 1953-1958; South Carolina State senate, 1980-1986; elected as a Republican to the One Hundredth Congress through the one hundred third Congresses; is a resident of Mount Pleasant, S.C.

READ, JACOB, (1752-1816) — a Delegate and a U.S. Senator from South Carolina; born at "Hobcaw" plantation in Christ Church Parish, near Charleston, S.C., in 1752; completed preparatory studies; studied law and was admitted to the bar; studied in England 1773-1776; joined other Americans in London in 1774 in a petition against the Boston port bill; returned to the United States and served South Carolina in various military and civil capacities during the Revolutionary War; sent with other Americans as a prisoner of the British to St. Augustine

1780-1781; member, State assembly 1782, and of the privy council 1783; Member of the Continental Congress 1783-1785; member, South Carolina house of representatives and served as speaker; elected as a Federalist to the United States Senate and served from March 4, 1795, to March 3, 1801; unsuccessful candidate for reelection; served as President pro tempore of the Senate during the Fifth Congress; died in Charleston, S.C., July 17, 1816; interment in the family cemetery at "Hobcaw," in Christ Church Parish, near Charleston, S.C.

RHETT, ROBERT BARNWELL, (1800-1876) — a Representative and a U.S. Senator from South Carolina; born Robert Barnwell Smith in Beaufort, S.C., December 21, 1800; completed preparatory studies; studied law; was admitted to the bar and commenced prac tice in Beaufort in 1824; elected to the State house of repre sentatives for St. Bartholomew's Parish in 1826, 1828, 1830, and 1832; elected attorney general of South Carolina in 1832; elected as a Democrat to the Twenty-fifth and to the five succeeding Congresses (March 4, 1837-March 3, 1849); changed his name to Robert Barnwell Rhett in 1838; member of the Nashville convention in 1850; elected as a Democrat to the United States Senate to fill the vacancy caused by the death of John C. Calhoun and served from December 18, 1850, until his resignation effective May 7, 1852; delegate to the South Carolina secession convention in 1860; delegate to the Confederate Provisional Congress in 1861; chairman of the committee which reported the constitution of the Confederate States; moved to St. James Parish, La., in 1867; died in St. James Parish, La., on September 14, 1876; interment in Magnolia Cemetery, Charleston, S.C.

RICHARDS, JAMES PRIOLEAU, (1894-1979) — a U.S. Representative from South Carolina; born in Liberty Hill, Kershaw County, S.C., August 31, 1894; attended the county schools and Clemson College, Clemson, S.C.; during the First World War served overseas as a private, corporal, sergeant, and second lieutenant in the Trench Mortar Battery, Headquarters Company, One Hundred and Eighteenth Regiment, Thirtieth Division, 1917-1919; was graduated from the law department of the University of South Carolina at Columbia in 1921; was admitted to the bar the same year and commenced practice in Lancaster, S.C.; judge of the probate court of Lancaster County, S.C., 1923-1933; elected as a Democrat to the Seventy-third and to the eleven succeeding Congresses (March 4, 1933-January 3, 1957); chairman, Committee on Foreign Affairs (Eighty-second and Eighty-fourth Congresses); was not a candidate for reelection in 1956 to the Eighty-fifth Congress; delegate to the Japanese Peace Conference and United States delegate to the United Nations in 1953; special assistant to President Eisenhower, January 1957-January 1958, for the Middle East, with rank of ambassador; resumed the practice of law; resided in Lancaster, S.C., where he died February 21, 1979; interment in Liberty Hill Presbyterian Church Cemetery, Liberty Hill, S. C.

RICHARDS, JOHN GARDINER, (1864-1941) — Seventy-first state governor (D) of South Carolina, 1927-1931.

Born in Liberty Hill, South Carolina on September 11, 1864, the son of Rev. John and Sophie (Edwards) Richards. He attended Bingham Military Institute and was a captain in the Liberty Hill Rifles for fourteen years. He was also member of the South Carolina Military Board for four years, and was a major in the South Carolina Militia, retiring as a lieutenant colonel. He married Elizabeth Coates Workman in 1888. They had eleven children.

Concurrent with his military career, Richards worked as a farmer and was active in railroad business. He was chairman of the Executive National Association of Railways, and president of the Southeastern Association of Railroad Commissioners. Richards served as magistrate from 1892 to 1900. In 1898 he was elected to the South Carolina House of Representatives. He remained there until 1910, serving for ten years on the Ways and Means Committee, part of that time as chairman. After leaving the House, he became South Carolina Railroad Commissioner. He held that post from 1910 to 1918, and from 1922 to 1926. He was also chairman of the board for the South Carolina Railroad Commission for four years.

Richards ran for governor in 1910, 1914 and 1918, but was unsuccessful in each campaign. He was elected twice to the Democratic National Committee. During World War I, he served on the South Carolina Council of Defense. Later, he was South Carolina Tax Commissioner.

In 1926, Richards tried again for the Democratic gubernatorial nomination and was successful. He went on to win in the general election, running without opposition. He was the first governor in South Carolina elected to a four year term, and his administration ended as the Great Depression took hold. Before the stock market crash however, new funding was voted for the construction of state highways. Since he was constitutionally ineligible to seek a second consecutive term, Richards left office in 1931. In the years that followed, he served as chairman of the South Carolina Natural Resources Commission. He died on October 9, 1941.

RICHARDSON, JAMES B., (1770-1836) — fourteenth state governor (D-R) of South Carolina, 1802-1804.

He was born in Clarendon County, South Carolina, the son of Dorothy and General Richard Richardson. He was a trustee of the public schools of Clarendon Orphan Society in 1798, and a trustee of South Carolina College 1801- 1804 and 1809-1813. Elected to the State House of Representatives in 1792, he served in this office until 1802.

Richardson was elected governor of South Carolina in December 1802. During his administration, the State's Legislature repealed all laws against slave traffic; it also outlawed importation from other states of male slaves over fifteen years of age. While he was in office, an attempt was made to reapportion the State Legislature, but it was defeated in the Senate. During this time, South Carolina Federalists founded the *Charleston Courier*, which quickly became a vigorous party newspaper.

After leaving his gubernatorial duties, Richardson served in the House of Representatives for two years. He was then elected a State Senator in 1806, serving in this capacity until 1814. Returning to the House in 1816, he served a final term which ended in 1818.

Richardson was married to Ann Cantey Sinkler in 1791. He died in April 1836 and was buried in St. Mark's Parish churchyard.

RICHARDSON, JOHN PETER, (1801-1864) — thirty-fourth state governor (D) of South Carolina, 1840-1842.

He was born in Hickory Hill, South Carolina, the son of Floride Bonneau Peyre and John Peter Richardson.

He attended Dr. Moses Waddel's School at Willington, and later attended South Carolina College, but withdrew in 1819 during his senior year. After studying law, he was admitted to the South Carolina Bar and began a private law practice in Fulton, South Carolina.

Richardson was elected to the South Carolina House of Representatives in 1825, keeping his seat until 1834. He was a member of the Nullification Convention, 1832-1833. In 1834, he was elected to the South Carolina Senate and served a two-year term. While there, he was involved in debate on the Test Oath Bill with Governor Hamilton, the recognized head of the "Nullification Party." The result of the debate was a compromise which ended the strife within the State. In 1836, he became a member of the United States House of Representatives, holding this office until 1839.

Richardson was elected governor of South Carolina in 1840. He was the first "Unionist" to hold a high State office since 1832, his election symbolizing the resolution of conflicts between "Unionists" and "Nullifiers" within the State. During his term, the economic slump of the State since the Panic of 1837 was an important issue. After suspension of specie payments by some State banks, the State Legislature had enacted a series of laws regulating the banks more closely. Acceptance of these regulations was made a mandatory part of bank charters. The Bank of South Carolina, however, refused to conform, and the question arose as to how much atonomy the banks should have. Placed before the public, the banks won the lower court decisions, but lost in 1844 in the South Carolina Court of Appeals. The bank question occupied a prominent place in South Carolina politics for several years.

Richardson's administration also worked toward the founding of the two military schools--the Arsenal in Columbia, and the Citadel in Charleston--which were consolidated under the general name of the South Carolina Military Academy and, later, the Cidatel Academy in Charleston. From his efforts, Richardson came to be known as the "father" of the institution.

After his tenure as governor, Richardson remained active in State politics for many years. He was a delegate to the Southern Convention, 1850; member of the Southern Rights Convention, 1852; president of the Kansas Association of Sumter District, South Carolina, 1856; member of the South Carolina Secession Convention, 1860-1862; signer of the Ordinance of Secession, 1865; and member of the South Carolina Constitutional Convention, 1865.

Richardson was married to Juliana Augusta Manning Richardson in October 1827. He died in Fulton, South Carolina in January 1869.

RICHARDSON, JOHN PETER, (1831-1899) — fifty-eighth state governor (D) of South Carolina, 1886-1890.

He was born in Clarendon County, South Carolina, the son of Juliana Augusta Manning and John Peter Richardson, who was governor of South Carolina from 1840-1842.

Ricardson received a private education, and graduated from South Carolina College in 1849.

After the start of the Civil War, Richardson enlisted in the Confederate States Army in 1862, and served on the staff of General James Cautey until the end of the conflict. He then became a planter.

Richardson was elected to the South Carolina House of Representatives in 1856, and again in 1860 and 1878. He was a member of the convention which met in 1865 to establish a provisional government for the State, and was elected to the South Carolina House of Representatives under the Constitution of 1865. He served in the South Carolina Senate 1865-1867, and was treasurer of South Carolina from 1878 to 1886.

Richardson was elected governor of South Carolina in November 1886. While he was in office, a major earthquake struck Charleson, causing an estimated $8,000,000 in damage. Also during his administration, the Federal Circuit Court of Appeals validated the will of Thomas G. Clemson, who left funds for the creation of Clemson Agricultural and Mechanical College.

Richardson was re-elected for a second term in November 1888. During his second term, the Farmers' Association emerged as a political force in the State. In January 1890, the "Shell Manifesto," written by Benjamin R. Tillman, called for a Farmers' Association Convention to meet in March. Richardson left the gubernatorial office in December 1890.

Richardson died in Columbia, South Carolina in July 1899.

RICHARDSON, JOHN SMYTHE, (1828-1894) — a U.S. Representative from South Carolina; born on the Bloomhill plantation, near Sumter, Sumter County, S.C., February 29, 1828; pursued an academic course in Cokesbury, S.C., and was graduated from South Carolina College (now the University of South Caroli na) at Columbia in 1850; studied law; was admitted to the bar in 1852 and began practice in Sumter, S.C.; during the Civil War entered the Confederate Army as a captain of Infantry; later promoted to adjutant of the Twenty-third Regiment, South Carolina Infantry, and served until the close of the war in 1865; member of the State house of representatives 1865-1867; appointed agent of the State of South Carolina in 1866 to apply for and receive the land script donated to South Carolina by Congress; delegate to the Democratic National Convention in 1876; elected as a Democrat to the Forty-sixth and Forty-seventh Congresses (March 4, 1879-March 3, 1883); master in equity for Sumter County 1884-1893; died at his country home, "Shadyside," near Sumter, S.C., February 24, 1894; interment in Sumter Cemetery.

RICHARDSON, ROBERT CLINTON, (1935-   ) — is considered one of baseball's most durable and dependable players.

Born in Sumter, South Carolina on August 19, 1935, Robert Richardson attended the University of South Carolina, Clevenger Business College and Columbia Bible College.

Richardson's interest in baseball began early in life. As a elementary and high school student, he played as often as possible, becoming a member of the high school team and the American Legion team during summer vacations. It was while practicing at Riley Park, where a New York Yankee farm team also practiced, that Richardson attracted the attention of Mayo Smith, the manager of the Norfolk (Virginia) team in the Class B Piedmont League. Richardson turned down offers from 11 major league teams to sign with the Yankee organization on June 12, 1953, a few hours after his graduation from high school.

Thus began an exceptional career in baseball. Richardson played with the Yankees from 1955 until 1966. His impressive statistics include hitting .266 in 1412 games with 1432 hits. He had 643 runs, 196 doubles, 37 triples, 34 home runs and 390 RBI. He hit .300 or better twice. His best year was in 1962 when his average was .302. Richardson led the American League in hits in 1962 with 209. He played in the All-Star game in 1957, 1959, and 1962 through 1966. Richardson was a participant in the World Series in 1957, 1958 and 1960 through 1964, where he hit .305 in 36 Series games and batted six runs in the game on October 8, 1960. He collected 13 hits in the seven-game series in 1964 and 11 in the 1960 classic. He also led the American League second basemen in putouts in 1961 and double plays in 1961, 1962 and 1965. Although he was usually a second basemen, he played shortstop on occasion. Among his honors is the Lou Gehrig Memorial Award, presented to him in 1955.

Richardson was considered one of the most durable and dependable American League baseball players. An intensely religious man, Richardson wanted to quit baseball on several occasions to devote himself to some form of Christian service.

He announced his retirement from baseball on September 17, 1966. He worked as an insurance salesman, a youth worker and special scout for the Yankees as well as the baseball coach at the University of South Carolina. He was also active in the Fellowship of Christian Athletes. Richardson married Alice Elizabeth Dobson on June 8, 1956. The couple has two boys.

RILEY, CORINNE BOYD, (1893-1979) — (wife of John Jacob Riley), a U.S. Representative from South Carolina; born in Piedmont, Greenville County, S.C., July 4, 1893; attended the public schools and graduated from Converse College, Spartanburg, S.C., in 1915; taught in the secondary schools of South Carolina for thirteen years, 1915-1937; field representative, South Carolina State Text Book Commission, 1938-1942; associated with Civilian Personnel Office, Shaw Air Force Base, Sumter, S.C., 1942-1944; elected as a Democrat to the Eighty-seventh Congress, by special election, April 10, 1962, to fill the vacancy caused by the death of her husband, John J. Riley, and served from April 10, 1962, to January 3, 1963; was not a candidate for reelection in 1962 to the Eighty-eighth Congress; resided in Sumter, S.C., where she died April 12, 1979; cremated; ashes interred in Sumter Cemetery.

RILEY, JOHN JACOB,, (1895-1962) — (husband of Corinne Boyd Riley) a Representative from South Carolina; born on a farm near Orangeburg, S.C., February 1, 1895; attended the public schools in Orangeburg County; was graduated from Wofford College, Spartanburg, S.C., in 1915; taught in the Orangeburg city schools 1915-1917, and at Clemson (S.C.) Agricultural and Mechanical College in 1917 and 1918; during the First World War served in the United States Navy as a seaman, second class, and as a yeoman, third class, in 1918 and 1919; engaged in the real estate and insurance business in Sumter, S.C., 1919-1945; secretary of a building and loan association 1923-1945; delegate to Democratic State conventions 1928-1944; elected as a Democrat to the Seventy-ninth and Eightieth Congresses (January 3, 1945-January 3, 1949); unsuccessful candidate for renomination in 1948; elected to the Eighty-second and to the five succeeding Congresses and served from January 3, 1951, until his death at Surfside, near Myrtle Beach, S.C., January 1, 1962; interment in Sumter Cemetery, Sumter, S.C.

RILEY, RICHARD WILSON, (1933 -) — is the United States Secretary of Education.

Born in Greenville, South Carolina on January 2, 1933, the son of Edward and Martha (Dixon) Riley. He attended Furman University and received his A.B. degree in 1954. From 1954 until 1956, he served in the United States Navy as an operations officer aboard a minesweep control ship. After service, he returned to school and studied law at the University of South Carolina.

Riley became legal counsel for the United State Senate's Judiciary Subcommittee in 1959. In 1963, he was elected to the South Carolina House of Representatives. He became a member of the state Senate in 1967. In the legislature he advocated judicial reform and local autonomy. In 1970, Riley pleaded for harmony in the face of a federal court order requiring rapid school desegregation. Unlike many parents, who hustled their children into private schools, he left his own children in the public schools during this period.

Riley resigned from the Senate in 1975 to manage Jimmy Carter's presidential campaign in South Carolina. In 1978, after a defeat for the nomination in 1974, he ran for governor on the Democratic ticket and won over Republican Edward Young. He entered office in January of 1979. As governor, Riley supported environmental issues, refusing to allow the Three Mile Island nuclear power plant to dump the radioactive waste from their accident in South Carolina. Instead he encouraged a federal solution to the problem and in 1980, President Carter appointed him to the Nuclear Waste Disposal Council to study the question. In addition, Riley and his wife received an award from conservationists in 1982 when they designed the grounds of the governor's mansion to be hospitable to wildlife.

Also during his term, the State Constitution was amended to allow governors to run for consecutive terms. Riley therefore ran and was reelected to a second term. During his second administration, he continued the environmental work begun previously. In one important respect the Riley administration continued the policies of its predecessors: he maintained South Carolina's efforts to attract high wage jobs, and like governors before him, grappled with difficult problems of nuclear waste disposal. Although he failed to obtain the tax reform measure he had sought in 1983, he succeeded in 1984, putting through a thorough education reform package complete with higher taxes to pay for it. The program included merit pay and pay raises for teachers, a building program, remedial education, and cash bonuses to schools that improved. The bill passed after Riley convinced both business people and voters that the state needed a better educated workforce if it was to enjoy further economic growth. This act, the Education Improvement Act of 1984, was described by a consultant to the Rand Corporation as " the most comprehensive" education reform legislation ever enacted by any state.

Riley has said that his biggest disappointment as a governor was his failure to reform the penal system, and he was sometimes criticized for enacting crime legislation, such as the Prison Reform Act of 1981, the Emergency Powers Act of 1983, and the Omnibus Crime Bill of 1986. These measures were designed to alleviate prison overcrowding. Riley was also criticized for not bringing more industry into the state.

Despite these criticisms, Riley was hailed as one of the nation's best governors. When he retired from office after two terms, his popularity was intact. He reportedly declined an opportunity to run for the United States Senate in 1984.

When he left office in 1987, he helped form the law firm of Nelson, Mullins, Riley and Scarborough with offices in Greenville, Columbia and Myrtle Beach. Following Bill Clinton's electoral victory in the 1992 presidential election, Riley was asked to serve as personal director of the Clinton-Gore transition team, with responsibility for selecting hundreds of sub-cabinet appointees for positions in the Clinton administration.

On December 21, 1992, President-elect Clinton named Riley secretary of education, an appointment that drew bipartisan praise. It was his talent for translating ideas into concrete results that made him an especially attractive candidate for this post. In this position, Riley is expected to work toward upgrading national academic standards and to place more of an emphasis on improving public education than on giving parents incentives to enroll their children in private schools, a policy that found favor with the Bush Administration.

In his first important move as education secretary, in April 1993, Riley, together with Labor Secretary Robert B. Reich, publicly unveiled an education reform package that, if enacted, would set national standards for academic and occupational performance and provide incentives to schools that indicate a willingness to meet them. Earlier, in March, Secretary Riley endorsed race-based scholarships designed to benefit minority students and to correct past discrimination, thus reversing the policy of former assistant secretary Michael Williams of the Bush Administration, who had called such scholarships a form of reverse discrimination. Together with President Clinton, Riley also succeeded in persuading Congress to pass a bill aimed at creating a less costly, streamlined lending system for college students.

Riley married Ann Osteen Yarborough on August 23, 1957. The couple has four children.

RIPLEY, ALEXANDRA, (1934-) — a dyed-in-the-wool southerner and author, chosen to write the sequel to Gone With the Wind.

Born Alexandra Braid on January 8, 1934 in Charleston, South Carolina, Ripley considers herself, above all else, a Southerner. She was her parents only child, her father an insurance salesman and her mother a hospital administrator, then storeowner. "My parents were Old Charleston, but not Great Old Charleston," Ripley once said. "Charleston is so nice, it didn't matter officially who was rich or poor. Those who were rich did their damnedest not to look it, because that meant you didn't lose your money in the Civil War - you were on the wrong side."

Ripley was brought up to be a Southern lady, learning to knit and play piano, not to interrupt, speak unless spoken to, and of course, never to get dirty. She was also not encouraged to read, because "reading wouldn't catch you a husband." Despite this proper upbringing Ripley

was still a little tenacious. As a child she was caught selling tourists directions to Rhett Butler's grave.

Ripley attended grades one through twelve at one of the
most exclusive finishing schools in Charleston, Ashley
Hall, whose alumni includes women such as Barbara Bush.
She was educated in things like proper deportment, sitting
in a hoop skirt, and how to acquire proper posture. "Because of Charleston's isolation and clannishness, I was
fifty years out of date," Ripley said in Life magazine. Students at Ashley Hall were required to walk up and down
stairs while balancing books on their heads. "I still tend
to elevate what I call manners into some sort of quasi-
religion," Ripley has said. "It has nothing to do with
finger bowls, and everything to do with trying not to
trample on other people."

Ripley later chose to continue her education rather than
follow the role that what expected of a young Southern
girl. She attended her first year at Vassar college in
Poughkeepsie, New York with the help of a scholarship
from the Daughters of the Confederacy. Because of her
family's financial situation, Ripley was given the choice
to continue attending college or having a proper debutante
party. It was fully expected she would take the party, but
instead she chose college, and graduated in 1955 with a
B.A. degree in Russian.

Upon graduation Ripley began work in the advertising
department at Life magazine, and later for Air France in
Washington D.C. In 1958 she married Leonard Ripley, a
businessman. The two lived in Florence, Italy, before
moving to New York City. In 1963 they divorced, and
Ripley moved with her two daughters back to Charleston.

Ripley held several odd jobs, including tour guide,
travel agent and underwear buyer, then she took her first
writing job, ghostwriting papers for neurosurgeons. Within
a few years she moved to New York City and worked as a
manuscript reader at a publishing house, and was
promoted to publicity director. She finally decided to
write her own novels after she received a questionnaire
for inclusion in Who's Who of American Women. Of the
moment, she said, "Was that what I wanted my life to be?
A small paragraph in a large reference book? I threw the
questionnaire in the waste basket and submitted my resig-

nation. Like many, many thousands of others, I longed to write, and now I was going to do it and devil take the hindmost."

Ripley returned to the south, Virginia this time, and wrote her first novel in 1972. Her first published attempt was about a female president of the United States, which went nowhere. She attempted other genre, including a mystery, a nonfiction murder account and a ghosted autobiography, all of which failed. In 1981 she published her first historical novel Charleston, dedicated to the loan officer who lent her $500 to help pay the rent. The book was successful, and Ripley discovered historical novels were her niche, immediately starting on her second novel, On Leaving Charleston. Both novels revolved around the heroine Garden Tradd, who lived at Ashley Barony, an estate that "makes Tara look like a toolshed," according to Publisher's Weekly.

Ripley followed these books with a different kind of historical novel, The Time Returns: A Novel of Friends and Mortal Enemies in Fifteenth-Century Florence. The story fictionalized the lives of actual members of a fifteenth-century Florentine family, conveying the culture and life of medieval Italy. By now Ripley had a following for her books, and was working on her third novel, New Orleans Legacy, when the call came from her agent about the possibility of writing a sequel to Gone With the Wind. Legacy was chosen as a Reader Digest Condensed Book selection and a Literary Guild alternate, but this could not compare with the thrill of possibly being chosen to author the sequel of the one book that has been outsold only by the Bible. "My mind told me that it might be an impossible task...my 'Southern-ness' said that was all the reason to do it. I had to accept," Ripley said later. "I was so terrified some Yankee was going to do it."

The sequel itself was a long time coming. Margaret Mitchell, the author of Gone With the Wind, refused to write a sequel to the novel for fear that it would not compare with the first, so she never wrote again. She died in a hit-and-run accident. The classic love story that took place during the bloodiest and most destructive war this nation has ever seen has never gone out of print, staying on the bestseller list for two years after it was first published in 1936, and for five weeks during its golden anniversary in 1986. Margaret Mitchell won a Pulitzer Prize for the effort. It was translated into 27 languages and distributed in 37 countries. The movie was released in 1939 starring Clark Gable and Vivien Leigh. As a motion picture it won ten Academy Awards and is still being shown in some theaters, and is a popular seller on video tape.

It took years for the Mitchell estate to gain the rights to a sequel for the novel. The Mitchell family, represented by two nephews of Margaret Mitchell, had to win the rights to the sequel in a civil suit with MGM, the distributor of the film. In 1984 they finally won those rights, and promptly began interviewing authors. They talked to twelve candidates, including a man, and heard from dozens of other would-be writers, all anxious to continue the story of Scarlet O'Hara. Because of her background and experience with the genre Ripley was finally chosen. The Mitchell family insisted on few rules, such as no graphic sex, homosexuality or miscegenation. Otherwise Ripley had free reign, even to stray outside the story outline she had presented. "They were gentlemen, I am a lady," Ripley later said. "There were no disagreements."

Writing Part Two for such a classic was quite a frightening task, and Ripley was prepared for the worst. She knew that writing any sequel, whether the writing be good or bad, would provoke the wrath of many Gone With the Wind fans, who thought of the book as almost sacred. "I am trying to prepare myself for a universal hatred of what I'm going to do," she said at that time. Many resented the commercial implications of writing such a novel, knowing that the new author and the Mitchell family would profit greatly. Actually, Ripley herself only received a 15 percent share of the book sales and subsidiary rights, plus an advance of about $160,000. The publisher's auction in April of 1988 attracted great attention, with six companies competing seriously for the rights. Warner Books finally won the prize at a cost of $4.94 million. They were especially interested in the book because they were already in the process of releasing Ripley's New Orleans Legacy in paperback in cooperation with the book's hardcover publisher, Macmillan, which had also published Gone With the Wind.

In the meantime, Ripley was absorbed with writing. She researched for 18 months before writing a word of her novel, visiting sites in Atlanta, Charleston, Savannah, Georgia and Ireland, all of which she used in her book. She sifted through historical documents such as train timetables, weather reports, diaries, journals, letters, and old maps to literally trace the footsteps of her characters. "I'm very persnickety," Ripley said. "I need to know whether it's uphill or downhill from the church, even if I don't use it. I need to believe. And therefore I need to know what was playing at the theater, what you could buy at the market." Ripley read Gone With the Wind six times while in the research faze. She copied the first two hundred pages in longhand, "to get the feel of Margaret Mitchell in my wrist," she said. Ripley wrote her own 823- page novel by hand. "I am not machine compatible," she says.

As for the characters, it was Melanie that Ripley admired, not the strong and willful Scarlett. "Melanie was everything I had been taught I wanted to be. She was a lady, and I was taught that if you weren't a lady - and Scarlett wasn't - you weren't going to have a happy ending." Ripley also admired Ashley, who has often been described as a weak. "I often feel, as Ashley did, that the world has changed and left me behind. I get angry when people call him a wimp. He was holding on to a noble ideal. He had great psychic strength." Writing for Rhett Butler may have been Ripley's favorite part. "His dialogue is the way I think— even if I'm not skilled enough to talk like that. He has a lovely sense of self-mockery. Though he's more of a realist then we are, he's romantic— and kind as I would like to be."

Gone With the Wind ends with Scarlett O'Hara alone, determined to win her husband, Rhett Butler, again. In Scarlett, she travels to Charleston, where she tricks her ex-husband into escorting her around town. They have a near-fatal sailing accident that brings them closer together, but Scarlett leaves for Savannah to visit her immigrant Irish family. She sails on to Ireland, which is on the brink of a civil war of it's own. She buys the O'Hara family land, where she raises the daughter Rhett knows nothing about. The Irish civil war was a twist of historic fate that was a lucky break for Ripley. "I like to have my characters react to the drama of history, and the period after the Civil War in America was dull," Ripley said. "I felt like God had given me a gift-wrapped package."

The original editors of the book disagreed, suggesting that Scarlett travel to California instead. "They said that Gone With the Wind was irrelevant to the sequel!" Ripley remembers. "While they didn't come out and say it needed more sex, when they got to the sex scene on the beach following the sailing accident, they wrote 'At last! At last! This is what we need!' ...I was livid...I was murderously angry!" Ripley went on strike for four months, and refused to write another word until she was assigned a new editor. Finally Jeanne Bernkopf was obtained for her, the editor of Kitty Kelley's un-authorized biographies of Frank Sinatra and Nancy Reagan as well as Whirlwind by James Clavell.

Because of the problems with the editor, Scarlett was published a year later than expected, but with no less fanfare. The advance sales numbered nine hundred thousand with five hundred thousand already in bookstores on publication day, September 25, 1991, while two million more books were on sale in eighteen languages in forty different countries. Ripley developed tendinitis and carpal tunnel syndrome signing ten thousand copies during the promotional tour, plus there were television commercials, magazine ads and satellite interviews. On October 13, 1991 Scarlet became number one on the New York Times bestseller list, and Gone With the Wind was number 14. By the end of 1991 the book sold two million copies worldwide and the rights for the television mini-series had been purchased for a figure between $8 and $10 million.

Critics, of course, were less enthusiastic than the fans. Most accused Ripley of watering down Scarlett, making her milder and gentler than her tough but feminine reputation. They also accused her making Rhett too wimpy, and the happy ending was a disappointment. Some said that even if the book were not taken as a sequel, but seen only as a historical romance, it was a disappointment. They did agree, however, that Ripley was meticulously accurate in historical detail.

Ripley took all of the attention and criticism in stride, stating that if she had to do it over again, she would. She continues to live with her second husband, John Graham, a professor at the University of Virginia she married in 1981.

RIVERS, LUCIUS MENDEL, (1905-1970) — a U.S. Representative from South Carolina; born in Gumville, Berkeley County, S.C., September 28, 1905; attended the public schools, the College of Charleston, Charleston, S.C., and the University of South Carolina at Columbia; studied law; was admitted to the bar in 1932 and commenced practice in Charleston, S.C.; member of the State house of representatives 1933-1936; delegate to the Democratic National Convention in 1936; elected as a Democrat to the Seventy-seventh and to the fifteen succeeding Congresses, serving from January 3, 1941, until his death in Birmingham, Ala., December 28, 1970; chairman, Committee on Armed Services (Eighty-ninth through Ninety-first Congresses); interment in St. Stephen Episcopal Church Cemetery, St. Stephen, S.C.

ROBERT, HENRY MARTYN, (1837-1923) — army engineer and author of the definitive book on parliamentary procedure.

Born in Robertville, South Carolina, May 2 1837, he was the fourth of seven children of Rev. Joseph Thomas and Adeline Elizabeth (Lawton) Robert. His family were descendants of the town founder.

Robert was accepted to West Point in 1853, and he showed exceptional skills in mathematics. After graduation he served for one year as assistant professor of natural and experimental philosophy, and also as an instructor in practical military engineering. He was promoted to second lieutenant of engineers December 13, 1858, and for two years was charged with the defense of San Juan Island in the Washington Territory. At that time the island's boundary was in dispute with Great Britain. During the Civil War Robert supervised defense construction for Washington, Philadelphia, and New Bedford, Massachusetts. For his efforts he was promoted twice, up to captain in 1863. He went back to West Point to teach practical military engineering, and he was treasurer for the school between 1865 and 1867. In 1867 he was promoted to major and was sent to the Northwest again, where he supervised harbor and river improvements in Oregon and Washington.

For the next thirty years Robert traveled the country with the Army Corps of Engineers. He worked on three of the great lakes, Superior, Michigan, and Erie, as well as Lake Champlain. He also worked on the St. Lawrence River, the Delaware Bay, their tributaries, and also the 4th and 13th lighthouse districts. In 1883 he was promoted to lieutenant-colonel, and between 1890 and 1891 he was the engineer commissioner of the District of Columbia. Afterward he worked on rivers in Tennessee, on Long Island Sound, and in New York Harbor, then was promoted to full colonel in 1895. Robert served as division engineer of the Northwest and Southwest Divisions and as president of engineering boards for over 30 projects. After the beginning of the Spanish- American War he was named president of the United States board of fortifications. He retired brigadier-general and chief of engineers May 2, 1901. Even after retirement he was called to engineering duties such as designing a sea-wall for Galveston after the devastating tidal wave of 1900, and designing harbor improvements for Frontera, Mexico. He wrote numerous books on engineering, including *The Waterjet as an Aid to Engineering Construction* (1881) and *Analytical and Topical Index to the Reports of the Chief of Engineers* and the *Officers of the Corps of Engineers, United States Army 1866-1879* (1881). A second volume of this book was published in 1889, covering work done to 1887.

Yet what Robert may be best known for is not his contributions to engineering, but his contributions to parliamentary procedure in meetings. When he was about 25 years old Robert was asked to lead a meeting, and he could not find a reference that would help him prepare. After the meeting he decided to write his own manual, which he passed between friends. *The Pocket Manual of Rules of Order* was officially published in 1876 and was revised in 1893 and 1904. The larger volume, *Robert's*

Rules of Order Revised, was printed in 1915. More than a million copies of this book were sold, and it became the criteria for most organizations in the United States. Robert also published *Parliamentary Practice* (1921) and *Parliamentary Law* (1923), both considered standards. Robert married his first wife, Helen M. Thresher, just before the Civil War on December 24, 1860. They had five children, and his son, Henry M. Robert Jr., became a professor of mathematics at the United States Naval Academy. Helen died in 1895, and Robert married again May 8, 1901 to Isabel Livingstone Hoagland. He died May 11, 1923, and was buried in Arlington National Cemetery.

ROBERTSON, THOMAS JAMES, (1823-1897) — a U.S. Senator from South Carolina; born near Winnsboro, Fairfield County, S.C., August 3, 1823; completed preparatory studies and graduated from South Carolina College (now the University of South Carolina) at Columbia in 1843; engaged in planting; member of the Stnte constitutional convention in 1865; upon the readmission of the State of South Carolina to representation in 1868 was elected as a Republican to the United States Senate; reelected in 1871 and served from July 15, 1868, to March 3, 1877; was not a candidate for reelection; chairman, Committee on Manufactures (Forty-second through Fortyfourth Congresses); retired from public life and active business due to ill health; died in Columbia, S.C., October 13, 1897; interment in Elmwood Cemetery.

ROGERS, JAMES, (1895-1873) — a U.S. Representative from South Carolina; born in what is now Goshen Hill Township, Union County, S.C., October 24, 1895; completed preparatory studies and was graduated from South Carolina College (now the University of South Carolina) at Columbia in 1813; studied law; was admitted to the bar and began practice in Yorkville (now York), S.C.; held various local offices; elected as a Jack sonian to the Twenty- fourth Congress (March 4, 1835-March 3, 1837); unsuccessful candidate for reelection in 1836 to the Twenty-fifth Congress; elected as a Democrat to the Twenty-sixth and Twenty-seventh Congresses (March 4, 1839-March 3, 1843); died in South Carolina on December

21, 1873; interment in what was formerly called the Irish Graveyard at Kings Creek A.R.P. Church near Newberry, S.C.

ROPER, DANIEL CALHOUN, (1867-1943) — a conservative at heart, Roper was an influential member of the Democratic party, serving in numerous appointed posts and as a liaison between two presidents and the Southern delegates in Congress.

The only child of John Wesley and Henrietta Virginia (McLaurin) Roper, Daniel Roper came from a long line of southern families. He was a descendant of John Roper, a vestryman of Blisland Parish, Virginia in 1678. His father was a farmer and a Confederate veteran from Richmond County, North Carolina, and he bought the ancestral plantation of his wife in Marlboro County, South Carolina upon their marriage. Roper's mother died before his third birthday, but his father remarried in 1874, with allowed Roper to have to half-brothers and two half-sisters. He attended a one-room elementary school and the high school in Laurinburg, North Carolina, then he entered Wofford College in Spartanburg, South Carolina. He transferred at the end of his sophomore year to Trinity College in Durham, North Carolina, where he received his B.A. degree in 1888. On Christmas Day of the next year he married Lou McKenzie of Gibson, North Carolina, the daughter of an architect, and they had seven children.

Roper tried several professions after leaving college, including farming, teaching school and selling life insurance. During the agrarian upheaval in South Carolina in 1890, Roper joined the Farmer's Alliance and although a Populist at heart, he decided to stay with the Democrats. He was elected to the South Carolina House of Representative in 1892, where one of his most important contributions was the introduction of a prohibition bill. After his term was complete Roper was appointed clerk to the United States Senate Interstate Commerce Committee. In 1897 he left Washington to work as an office manager in New York City, then moved back to Washington as a life insurance agent. In 1900 he was appointed to the Census Bureau as an enumerator of cotton gins, and over the next eleven years he became an expert on foreign and domestic cotton trade. In 1901 he earned his law degree from National University and in 1911 he used his political connections to become a clerk of the House Ways and Means Committee. Because of his knowledge of the cotton industry and his support of tariff revision, he was very popular with the Southern delegates.

Roper's big break came in 1912, when he became active in the campaign to elect Woodrow Wilson. In gratitude, Wilson was given the post of First Assistant Postmaster General. There he was responsible for filling the positions of 60,000 postmasters, left empty by the Republicans. He also worked closely with Franklin D. Roosevelt, another member of the Wilson administration, to rebuild the Democratic party in the northeast. Roper left the Post office in 1916 to work on Wilson's campaign again. In 1917 he was appointed vice-chairman of the United States Tariff Commission, and in September of that year, Commissioner of the Internal Revenue. He was credited by many for the improvement of the administration and collection of income tax. He also administered the narcotics and wartime prohibition laws and created an intelligence unit to investigate tax fraud.

In 1920 Roper left Washington again, this time to serve as President of the Marlin Rockwell Corporation, a manufacturing firm that was undergoing a reorganization. He then returned to Washington to practice law. In 1924 he became involved in William Gibbs McAdoo's bid for the presidency, and at the 1932 Democratic convention he played a significant role in shifting McAdoo's votes to Franklin D. Roosevelt.

In appreciation, Roosevelt appointed Roper to the cabinet position of Secretary of Commerce. Roper became a conservative influence in the administration, cutting the budget of his department and its foreign and domestic programs as part of a program to save money during the Depression. He established a Business Advisory Council to funnel the ideas and feelings of prominent business people to the congress and the President. He was named chairman of the cabinet committee to oversee the National Recovery Administration, but he found it difficult to effect change, as he was often dominated by the administration's head, Hugh Johnson, and other New

Dealers. He still had a great deal of respect and was very important to the Southern leaders in Congress, so he usually worked to bring harmony and balance among different parties, rather than presenting new ideas.

Eventually Roper had enough of the New Dealers' liberal policies and their belief that big business was to blame for the country's woes. When Roosevelt's reorganization plan divested the Commerce Department of several of its units, Roper resigned. In 1939 he went back to government service again, this time to serve as the United States minister to Canada. He held that position for less than one year, then retired, and died of leukemia in Washington April 11, 1943.

ROSEN, ALBERT LEONARD, (1924-   ) — was a professional baseball player and executive.

Born in Spartanburg, South Carolina on February 29, 1924, the son of Louis and Rose (Levine) Rosen, Albert Rosen developed a very early interest in baseball. At the age of 14, he toured Florida with a softball team, and acquired a reputation that won him a scholarship at Florida Military Academy in St. Petersburg in 1939. In the spring of 1941, he met Roger Peckinpaugh, then the manager of the Cleveland Indians. Peckinpaugh suggested that Rosen report to a minor-league team, a farm for Cleveland, at Sumter, South Carolina. After an inauspicious tryout, Rosen was offered $75 a month to play with Thomasville in the North Carolina State League. However, he refused, graduated from the academy and enrolled in the University of Florida.

Rosen attended the University of Florida for one year, then transferred to the University of Miami at Coral Cables. When the United States Navy introduced its V-12 program there in 1942, Rosen became an apprentice seaman. In 1944, he began midshipmen training at Plattsburg, New York and that year received a commission. After amphibious training, he was assigned to the U.S.S. *Procyon*, an attack transport. On D-Day he was at Okinawa in charge of an LCM (Land Craft Mobile). In April of 1946, he was discharged from the Navy.

Following his discharge, Rosen reported to the Indians and was assigned to the Class C team in Pittsfield, Massachusetts at $175 per month. The next year he was promoted to a Class AA team in Oklahoma City. That year he was named the Texas League's player of the year. In the fall of 1947 Rosen played at Yankee Stadium for the Cleveland Indians. He faced pitcher Joe Page, took three swings and went back to the bench. A few more games like that and he was optioned to Kansas City. During that same year, Rosen received a B.B.A. degree from the University of Miami.

After the 1948 season with Kansas City, Rosen was named the American Association's Rookie of the Year. He batted .327, hit 25 home runs, but made 36 errors. When the Cleveland player Don Black was injured, Rosen was brought in for the World Series with the Boston Braves. He was given one chance as a pinch hitter and popped up. In 1949, Rosen went to a minor league team in San Diego. He hit well (.319) and made 16 errors. In 1950, Rosen was offered a permanent position as the Indian's regular third baseman. That year, he led the American League with 37 home runs and made only 15 errors.

Rosen played for the Cleveland Indians until 1956. He hit .285 in 1044 games with 1063 hits. His record includes 603 runs, 165 doubles, 20 triples, 192 home runs and 717 RBI. Rosen hit .300 or better three times, including a high of .336 in 1953. He hit 20 or more homers six times, leading the American League in 1950 with 37 and in 1953 with 43. One of his most memorable games was the All-Star contest in 1954 when he hit two home runs and a single to drive in five runs for an 11 to 9 victory. He played in the World Series in 1948 and 1954.

Rosen retired from baseball in 1956 over a salary dispute. He went on to become an executive with Bache and Company in Cleveland, remaining there until 1973, then was employed at 1st Continental Investment until 1975 and Caesar's Palace until 1977. He was the president of the New York Yankees baseball club from 1977 until 1979; Bally's Park Place from 1979 until 1980; general manager of the Houston Astro baseball club from 1980 until 1985; and the San Francisco Giants.

Rosen was married twice. First to Terese Ann Blumberg in March 1952. He then married Rita Kallman on July 24, 1971. He has three children and three stepchildren.

RUSSELL, DONALD STUART, (1906-   ) — Eighty-third state governor (D) of South Carolina, 1963-1965.

Born in Lafayette Springs, Mississippi on February 22, 1906, the son of Jesse and Lula (Russell) Russell. He attended the University of South Carolina and the University of Michigan in Ann Arbor, and was admitted to the South Carolina Bar in 1928. The following year, he married Virginia Utsey. They had four children.

Russell moved to Spartanburg, South Carolina and established a law practice there in 1930. During World War II, he was a member of the Price Adjustment Board for the U.S. War Department (1942). He was assistant to the director of War Mobilization in 1943. In 1944 he served in the U.S. Army as a major in the Supreme Headquarters of the Allied Forces in Europe. The following year he was deputy director for the Office of War Mobilization Reconversion. He was assistant to the U.S. Secretary of State from 1945 to 1947, and a member of the Committee on the Reorganization of the U.S. Foreign Service in 1954. From 1951 to 1957, he was president of the University of South Carolina.

Russell ran for governor of South Carolina in 1962, and won as an unopposed Democrat in the general election. Desegregation progressed during his term, and the first black students entered Clemson College and the University of South Carolina. When Senator Olin Johnston died in April 1965, Russell resigned the governorship to fill his seat in the U.S. Senate. He remained in the Senate until 1966. From 1967 to 1971, he was a U.S. District Judge. He was appointed a U.S. Circuit Court Judge in 1971.

RUTLEDGE, EDWARD, (1749-1800) — twelth state governor (Federalist) of South Carolina, 1798-1800.

He was born in Charleston, South Carolina, the son of Sarah and John Rutledge. His father emigrated from Ireland in 1735. His brother, John, was the first State governor of South Carolina.

Rutledge was educated in Charleston, afterwards studying law with his brother. He was admitted to the Middle Temple in London in 1767, and returned to Charleston as a barrister in 1773. The Continental Congress in Philadelphia elected him in September 1774, and he was one of the youngest members of that body.

In 1776, Rutledge served on the first Board of War, which provided defense of the country. In September of that year, under the direction of Congress, he went with Franklin and John Adams to Staten Island for an interview with Lord Howe concerning his proposition for peace. Rutledge maintained that nothing short of independence would satisfy the United States.

Rutledge was again elected to the Continental Congress in 1779. He served in the local militia and rose to the rank of lieutenant-colonel in the Charleston battalion of artillery, commanding in this capacity when the British were defeated and driven from Port Royal Island. He was actively involved in the siege of Charleston, and became a prisoner of war at its surrender in 1780. After being transferred to St. Augustine, Florida, he was kept there for eleven months before his release.

In 1781, Rutledge proposed to Washington a combined French and American attack on Charleston. When he returned to the State, he was elected a member of the General Assembly which met at Jacksonborough, Charleston still being in the hands of the British. After the city was restored, Rutledge served on the Privy Council and returned to the practice of law.

Rutledge favored adoption of the Federal Constitution, and was a member of the Constitutional Convention of 1790. He was elected to the Legislature from 1782 to 1798, and was influential in drawing the act which abolished promogeniture and gave an equitable distribution of the real estate of intestates. He opposed the African slave trade.

In May 1791, Rutledge declined a seat on the U.S. Supreme Court which had just become vacant by his brother John, who resigned to become Chief Justice of South Carolina. Rutledge declined on the grounds that he could be of better service to the general government in the State Legislature.

Rutledge was elected governor of South Carolina in December 1798. During his administration, the Legislature established the office of comptroller, and the State was newly divided into districts, counties, and parishes.

Rutledge was married to Henrietta Middleton in 1774. After her death in April 1792, he married a second time, to Mary Shubrick Eveleigh in October 1792. He died while in office in January 1800.

RUTLEDGE, JOHN, (1739-1800) — first president and first and third state governor of South Carolina, 1776-1778 and 1779- 1782.

He was born in Charleston, South Carolina, the son of Sarah Hext and Dr. John Rutledge. His father immigrated from England to Charleston in 1735.

Rutledge completed his early education in Charleston, then went to England to study law. After his admission to the bar, he returned to Charleston in 1761 and began a practice. In 1762, he was elected to the Provincial Assembly, and quickly became a strong voice in opposing what he considered unwarrantable interference of the Royal Governor in matters of election.

In September 1764, Rutledge became Attorney General pro tempore of South Carolina, holding this position until June 1765. He then became a delegate to the Colonial Congress, which had assembled upon passage of the Stamp Act. Although he was the youngest member of the Congress, his strong voice gained a position for the colony never before accorded to it, and he was made chairman of the committee that prepared the memorial and petition to the House of Lords.

He was a delegate to the first Continental Congress in 1774 and, in 1775, joined John Adams in advocating a complete separation from the mother country. Patrick Henry believed him to be the greatest orator in the congressional body.

In March 1776, Rutledge was elected president of South Carolina under the independent constitution. When British forces approached the colony, he rallied 6,000 men and erected Fort Moultrie to protect the State. He refused to ratify the new constitution of South Carolina after the Declaration of Independence was created, and resigned his office in March 1778. However, upon the second invasion of the English in February 1779, he was recalled and, invested with plenary powers, became the first governor of South Carolina.

During the time when the state was being overrun by the enemy, Rutledge's strength held the army together. He requested assistance from Congress, and kept ward over the state until the Battle of Eutaw Springs, when the British were finally defeated. After his gubernatorial term expired, Rutledge was by law ineligible for re-election. He was sent to Congress once again in January 1782. In June, he was chosen to encourage the Southern states to comply with Congress in terminating the war as quickly as possible. He was foremost in opposing the exchange of Lord Cornwallis, and in repealing the resolution to investigate the conduct of General Gates. He supported the the commissioners in framing the treaty with Great Britain, taking an active part in all proceedings until his retirement from the position in 1783.

Rutledge was made Chancellor of South Carolina in 1784 but, in 1785, declined the appointment of judge of the federal court. He was, in 1787, a member of the convention that framed the constitution, and became a strong opponent of the proposition to prevent the importation of slaves into the states.

When the government became organized, Rutledge was appointed first of five associate justices of the Supreme Court. However, he was not present for the first term when the court convened in New York in 1790, and he resigned the office in 1791 to become chief justice of the State.

Upon the retirement of Chief Justice Jay in June 1795, Rutledge was appointed his successor. He presided for a time, but his confirmation was refused by the Senate in December of the same year, primarily because of his attitude toward the Jay Treaty.

Rutledge was married to Elizabeth Grimke. He died on July 18, 1800, and was buried in St. Michael's Churchyard in Charleston.

RUTLEDGE, JOHN, JR., (1766-1819) — (son of John Rutledge and nephew of Edward Rutledge), a U.S. Representative from South Carolina; born in Charleston, S.C., in 1766; received private instruction and also attended school in Charleston and Philadelphia; studied law with his father; was admitted to the bar about 1787 and practiced in Charleston, S.C.; also engaged as a planter; member of the State house of representatives 1788-1794 and in 1811; unsuccessful candidate for election in 1794 to the Fourth Congress; elected as a Federalist to the Fifth, Sixth, and Seventh Congresses (March 4, 1797-March 3, 1803); unsuccessful candidate for election to the Thirteenth Congress; commanded a company of the Twentyeighth Regiment, South Carolina Militia, in 1799; promoted to major and in 1804 succeeded to the command of the regiment and served as its commander in the War of 1812; commanded the Seventh Brigade from 1816 until his death; died in Philadelphia, Pa., September 1, 1819.

S

SAWYER, FREDERICK ADOLPHUS, (1822-1891) — a U.S. Senator from South Carolina; born in Bolton, Worcester County, Mass., December 12, 1822; attended the public schools; graduated from Harvard University in 1844; taught school in New England 1844-1859; took charge of the State normal school at Charleston, S.C., in 1859; returned to the North during the Civil War; returned to Charleston in February 1865 and was active in advancing reconstruction measures; appointed collector of internal revenue in the second South Carolina district 1865; upon the readmission of the State of South Carolina to representation was elected as a Republican to the United States Senate and served from July 16, 1868, to March 3, 1873; chairman, Committee on Education (Forty-first Congress), Committee on Education and Labor (Fortysecond Congress); Assistant Secretary of the Treasury 1873-1874; employed in the United States Coast Survey 1874-1880; special agent of the War Department 1880-1887; conducted a preparatory school in Ithaca, N.Y., and gave private instruction to students in Cornell University; moved to Tennessee and became president of a company at Cumberland Gap to promote the sale of agricultural lands in that vicinity; died suddenly at Shawnee, Tenn., July 31,

1891; interment in "Sawyer Heights," on the property of his land company, near East Cumberland Gap.

SCARBOROUGH, ROBERT BETHEA, (1861-1927) — a U.S. Representative from South Carolina; born in Chesterfield, Chesterfield County, S.C., October 29, 1861; attended the common schools and Mullins (S.C.) Academy; taught school; studied law; was ad mitted to the bar in 1884 and commenced practice in Conway, S.C.; county attorney of Horry County 1885-1893; served as clerk of the county board 1885-1890; member of the South Carolina State senate in 1897 and 1898 and was elected president pro tempore in 1898; Lieutenant Governor of South Carolina in 1899; elected as a Democrat to the Fifty-seventh and Fifty-eighth Congresses (March 4, 1901-March 3, 1905); declined to be a candidate for renomination in 1904 to the Fifty-ninth Congress; resumed the practice of law in Conway, S.C., and was also interested in banking; served as chairman of the board of regents of the South Carolina State Hospital; died in Conway, Horry County, S.C., on November 23, 1927; interment in Lake Side Cemetery.

SCOTT, ROBERT KINGSTON, (1826-1900) — forty-ninth state governor (Conservative) of South Carolina, 1868-1872.

He was born in Armstrong County, Pennsylvania, the son of Jane Hamilton and John Scott.

Scott received his early education in public schools. In 1842, he moved to Stark County, Ohio, and attended Central College for a time. He studied medicine at the Starling Medical College in 1850, then traveled to California and engaged in mining. After a prospecting tour of South America and Mexico, he returned to Ohio and settled in Henry County to practice medicine.

He invested in real estate and, when his investments began to profit, resigned from medical practice. In 1857, he became involved in merchandising, and remained in this capacity until 1846. He then served in the Pennsylvania militia, and was appointed a captain with the First Pennsylvania Infantry. In 1848, he resigned from military duty.

In 1861, at the onset of the Civil War, Governor Dennison of Ohio appointed Scott a major, and instructed him to organize the 68th regiment of Ohio volunteers. On October 3 of that year, he joined General Hurlbut and took part in the Battle of Hatchie River with General Price's army. As a result of his conduct there, he was promoted to a brigade commander.

The army was reorganized, and the 68th became part of the 17th corps. Scott commanded the advance of General Logan's division on the march into Mississippi; during the investment of Atlanta, he was taken prisoner. He managed to escape, but was recaptured and taken to Charleston, where he was exchanged in September 1864. After immediately resuming command of his brigade, he joined General Sherman in his march to the sea.

Scott earned the rank of major-general for good conduct as an officer and, in January 1866, was ordered to relieve General Rufus Saxton as the Assistant Commissioner of the Fieldman's Bureau in South Carolina. When he arrived in Charleston, he found the city in chaos and the militia destitute. He reestablished order, making a strong impression on the people of Charleston for his executive skill and leadership abilities.

In March 1868, when South Carolina adopted its fifth State Constitution, Scott was nominated the Republican candidate for governor. He won a majority of the popular vote and, on July 6, 1868, Major General E.R.S. Canby, then Military Governor of the State, ordered the new-elected legislature to assume authority.

Scott became the governor of South Carolina on July 9, 1868. On the same day, the legislature ratified the Fourteenth Amendment to the United States Constitution, which cleared the way for the resumption of civilian political control.

During his administration, South Carolina remained in a state of great unrest. In 1871, Scott was charged with fraudulent overissue of State bonds, and impeachment proceedings began against him. He was able to defend himself, however, and the charges were dropped.

Scott was re-elected for a second term in October 1870. The previous fraud charges hung over the executive office, however; many South Carolinians believed that they were being governed by a corrupt administration, and turned to the Ku Klux Klan. When Scott was unable to suppress Klan activity, he was forced to call in federal troops. In addition, in May 1871, the Taxpayers' Convention met in Charleston and warned the State legislature against increasing the State debt. Scott left office on December 3, 1872. He opened a real estate office in Columbia, South Carolina, and remained there until 1877, when he left for Henry County, Ohio to avoid possible prosecution. He opened a real estate office there as well. In 1880, he was charged with killing a man; he was acquitted by reason of accidental homicide.

Scott was married to Rebecca J. Lowry, with whom he had two children. He died in April 1900, and was buried in Henry County, Ohio.

SEABROOK, WHITEMARSH BENJAMIN, (1792-1855) — thirty- eighth state governor (D) of South Carolina, 1848-1850.

He was born on Estido Island, South Carolina, the son of Elizabeth Meggett and Benjamin Whitemarsh Seabrook.

Seabrook graduated from the College of New Jersey in 1812; he afterwards studied law and was admitted to the South Carolina Bar, began a practice, and devoted attention to "Gun Bluff," his cotton plantation on Estido Island.

He was a trustee of South Carolina College from 1829-1837, and also president of the South Carolina Agricultural Society for many years. Seabrook represented his district as a member of the South Carolina House of Representatives from 1814-1829, and was a member of the South Carolina Senate from 1829-1834. He was a presidential elector in 1832, and the lieutenant governor of South Carolina from 1834 to 1836.

He was elected governor of South Carolina in December 1848. The slavery expansion issue was of high importance during his administration. After Calhoun's speech on Southern states' rights to permit slavery, the State Legislature passed a law in 1850 to authorize a general election of delegates to a convention of Southern states to consider ways of arresting Northern aggression. A crisis was averted by passage of the Compromise of 1850 by the U.S. Congress; however, the State remained embroiled in secessionist sentiment. After his term expired, Seabrook was a member of the Southern Rights Covention in 1852. He also authored *History of the Cotton Plant*, which was used as a text at Clemson College, the agricultural and industrial college of the State.

Seabrook was married to Margaret Wilkinson Hamilton in February 1815. He died in April 1855 and was buried on his plantation on Estido Island.

SHAW, ROBERT GOULD, (1837-1863) — colonel of the first black regiment from the Union to fight in the Civil War. He was born in Boston, Massachusetts, October 10, 1837 to Francis George and Sarah Blake (Sturgis). He attended Harvard from 1856 to 1859, then dropped out.

Shaw started to pursue a career in accounting, but he cut his career short in April of 1861 when he enlisted in the 7th Regiment. Raised by a family that took their social obligations seriously, Shaw was a strong supporter of the abolitionist crusade. He felt it was his duty to enlist and demonstrate "that a Negro can be made a good soldier." After enlisting he was quickly promoted to second lieutenant of the 2nd Massachusetts Regiment, and was a first lieutenant by July. In August of 1862 Shaw was promoted to captain.

In April of the next year Shaw was named colonel of the first black regiment from the free states, the 54th Massachusetts Regiment. This group had a reputation for being the most dedicated soldiers, even though they were given shoddy equipment, uniforms, and supplies compared to other troops. On July 18, 1863 the regiment truly proved their bravery when they lead the charge on Fort Wagner near Charleston, South Carolina. Many men lost their lives during that battle, including Shaw. Afterward the blacks were buried in a trench near the battleground. As a gesture he felt his son would approve of, Shaw's father did not request that Shaw's body be found and buried elsewhere. A memorial sculpture of Shaw by Saint-Gaudens was erected on the Boston Commons. His story was the inspiration for William Vaughan Moody's "An

Ode in Time of Hesitation" and Peter Burchard's book, *One Gallant Rush: Robert Gould Shaw and His Brave Black Regiment* (1965).

SHELL, GEORGE WASHINGTON, (1831-1899) — a U.S. Representative from South Carolina; born near Laurens, Laurens County, S.C., November 13, 1831; attended the common schools and Laurens Academy; engaged in agricultural pursuits; entered the Confederate Army as a private in April 1861 and served throughout the Civil War, attaining the rank of captain; resumed agricultural pursuits; member of the State Democratic executive committee in 1886 and 1887; chosen president of the State Farmers' Association in 1888; clerk of court of Laurens County 1888-1896; elected as a Democrat to the Fifty-second and Fifty- third Congresses (March 4, 1891- March 3, 1895); chairman, Committee on Ventilation and Acoustics (Fifty-third Congress); was not a candidate for renomination in 1894; retired to his plantation near Laurens, Laurens County, S.C., and died there December 15, 1899; interment in Chestnut Ridge Cemetery.

SHEPPARD, JOHN CALHOUN, (1850-1931) — fifty-seventh state governor (D)/acting) of South Carolina, 1886.

He was born in Edgefield County, South Carolina, the son of Louisa Mobley and James Sheppard.

Sheppard was educated at Bethel Academy. He attended Furman University in Greenville, South Carolina, and went on to study law. After his admittance to the South Carolina Bar in 1871, he became a member of the law firm of Youmans and Sheppard. In 1875, he moved to Columbia and went into partnership with his brother, Orlando.

Sheppard became a member of the South Carolina House of Representatives in 1876, and kept his seat until 1882; he was also the House Speaker from 1877 to 1882. In 1876, he was a delegate to the Democratic National Convention, and was elected lieutenant governor of South Carolina in 1882.

When Governor Hugh H. Thompson resigned from office to become assistant secretary to the U.S. Treasury in

1886, Sheppard succeeded him as chief executive. He assumed office on July 10, 1886, and served out the remaining five months of Thompson's term. During Sheppard's short term, Charleston was struck by an earthquake which left 92 persons dead, and enormous property damage. Sheppard left office after seeking the Democratic nomination and being defeated in November 1886.

He became president of the Edgefield bank of South Carolina in 1890, and was named chairman of the Board of Trustees, Edgefield Male Academy, in 1891. He served as a member of the South Carolina Constitutional Convention in 1895, and was a member of the Board of Pardons.

Sheppard was elected to the South Carolina Senate from 1898 to 1904, again in 1919 to 1920, and was president pro tempore of the body from 1900 to 1904. He was supreme director of the Knights of Honor, 1906-1910, and was president of the South Carolina Bar Association in 1908.

Sheppard was married to Helen Wallace in May 1879, with whom he had seven children. He died in October 1931 in Edgefield, South Carolina.

SHUBRICK, WILLIAM BRANFORD, (1790-1874) — naval officer and commander of the Pacific coast, was born on Bull's island, South Carolina. He briefly attended Harvard in 1805 before enlisting as a midshipman in the Navy in 1806. He fought on the Constellation and the Constitution during the war of 1812, was promoted lieutenant in January 1813, and was placed in command of the Levant following its capture in 1815. During the next three years, he sailed around the globe in the Washington, the first U. S. vessel to do so. He was promoted to commander in 1820, and for the next two decades served in a variety of posts on the east coast until being raised to commander of the Pacific Fleet during the war with Mexico. Under his leadership the navy captured Mazatlan, Guaymas, La Paz, San Blas and other ports. In 1853, he was place in command of a the squadron protecting fisheries on the east coast, one of several navy posts he held on that coast until 1858 when he sailed with a fleet to Paraguay on a successful and highly praised mission to seek reparation on the attack of a U. S. vessel. Despite his ties to the south, he refused to join the Confederates during the Civil War. He retired from the navy in 1861, but remained active in some advisory roles. He died in Washington.

SIMKINS, ELDRED, (1799-1831) — a U.S. Representative from South Carolina; born in Edgefield, S.C., August 30, 1779; attended a private academy at Willington, Abbeville District, S.C., and was graduated from South Carolina College (now the University of South Carolina) at Columbia; attended Litchfield (Conn.) Law School for three years; was admitted to the bar in 1805 and commenced practice in Edgefield, S.C., in 1806; member of the State house of representatives; served in the State senate 1810-1812; Lieutenant Governor of the State 1812-1814; elected as a Republican to the Fifteenth Congress to fill the vacancy caused by the resignation of John C. Calhoun; reelected to the Sixteenth Congress and served from January 24, 1818, to March 3, 1821; chairman, Committee on Public Expenditures (Sixteenth Congress); declined to be a candidate for renomination; again a member of the State hcuse of representatives, 1828-1829; resumed the practice of his profession and also engaged in planting; died in Edgefleld, Edgefield County, S.C., November 17, 1831; interment in Cedar Fields, the family burial ground, near S.C.

SIMMS, WILLIAM GILMORE, (1806-1870) — author, was born in Charleston, South Carolina on April 17, 1806. He was of Scotch-Irish descent. His father, who had the same name, was a merchant in Charleston who, having failed in business, moved to Tennessee, where he held a commission under Jackson in the war against the Seminoles. His wife, Harriett A.A. Singleton, was of a Virginia family which came early to the state, and in revolutionary times, espoused the Whig side. She died when her second son, William, was in his infancy and the boy was left, in the absence of his father, to the care of his grandmother. When his father went West he wished to take his son, which was resisted, and a lawsuit brought which resulted in the boy remaining in Charleston as he wished.

On account of the difficult financial circumstances of the family, he did not have many early educational advantages, his entire course being confined to the public schools. He developed a passion for literary composition early on, writing verses when only seven years old, and publishing a book, *Monody on General Pinckney*, when only nineteen. He worked as a clerk in a drug and chemical house for some time, and at one time intended to study medicine, but he relinquished this in favor of the study of th law and was admitted to the bar. But before he was twenty- one, he realized that his taste led him in the direction of literary work, and he turned his thoughts in that direction.

His first active engagement was as editor of the Charleston city *Gazette*, in which he also held a proprietor's interest. He took strong sides against the prevailing doctrine of nullification in the publication and although he worked hard, the enterprise proved a failure and he lost what little money he had invested in it. In 1827, he published a volume entitled, *Lyrical and Other Poems*, which was followed the same year by *Early Lays*. The next year he issued another volume, *The Vision of Cortes, Cain, and other Poems*, and in 1830, *The Tricolor, or Three Days of Blood*, a volume of verse in celebration of the French revolution.

Upon the failure of his paper, Simms visited New York, and was introduced to the literary world of the city, where he was warmly received. While in New York, he published, through the Harper's, *Atlantis, a Story of the Sea* which was an imaginative poem written in easy, eloquent verse, interspersed with frequent lyrics. This was the best and longest of his poetic works, and achieved an unusual success. He now devoted himself to fiction, in which line he is best known, and the next year the Harpers published his first story, "Martin Faber, the Story of a Criminal," which was written in an intense passionate style, which commanded public attention at once. This was followed by a long series of stories, which appeared without interruption until a few years before his death.

After the death of his first wife, which occurred shortly after their marriage, and before his visit to New York,
he married the daughter of Mr. Roach, a wealthy planter
of the Banewell district in South Carolina, which placed
him in affluence. He turned his attention to politics, and
was for many years a member of the Legislature, and in
1846, he came within one vote of being elected Lieutenant
Governor of the state. The degree of LL.D. was conferred
on him by the University of Alabama.

During the Civil War he espoused the Southern side,
and he suffered great loss of property when the Federal
troops took possession of Charleston. He spent his time
between his summer residence in Charleston and his plantation, Woodlands, at Midway, where he had a beautiful
home amid the long-leaved pines peculiar to that region,
and where he dispensed a wide hospitality. He was very
helpful to young writers, which made him greatly beloved
by the craft. Edgar Allen Poe pronounced his novels the
best produced in America since Cooper.

In poetry, Simms produced "Donna Florida," a metrical
tale in the Don Juan style, but with nothing vicious in it;
"Grouped Thoughts," "Lays of the Palmetto," "The Cassi-
que of Accabee." In fiction his work might be divided as
follows: revolutionary romances, the principal of which
are the trilogy begun by "The Partisan," "Eutaw," "Guy
Rivers," the first of a series of border tales, and
"Beauchampe," covering the whole period of active warfare in South Carolina, and the careers of the principal
characters engaged; historical romances, among them "The
Yemassee," which is considered his best story; "Pelayo,"
"Count Julien," "The Damsel of Darien," and "Vascon-
celos," preserving the early history and local traditions of
the South; moral and imaginative romances which include
"Martin," "Castle Dismal," and many others. In history,
Simms produced a *History of South Carolina*, *Civil Warfare of the South*, and several biographies of eminent men.

In criticism, Simm's pen covered a wide field. He
edited *Seven Dramas Ascribed to Shakespeare* with notes
and preliminary essays. In periodical literature he was a
liberal contributor, and also founded and conducted
several reviews and magazines, among which may be mentioned, the *Southern Literary Gazette* and the *Southern*

Quarterly Review. His last works were *The Ghost of My Husband* and *War Poetry of the South.* He was forced by ill health to give up writing, and eventually died on June 11, 1870.

SIMPSON, RICHARD FRANKLIN, (1898-1882) — a U.S. Representative from South Carolina; born in Laurens, S.C., March 24, 1898; was graduated from South Carolina College (now the University of South Carolina) at Columbia in 1816; studied law; was admitted to the bar in 1819 and began practice in Pendleton, S.C.; held several local offices; served as major during the Seminole War in 1835; member of the State senate 1835-1841; elected as a Democrat to the Twenty-eighth, Twentyninth, and Thirtieth Congresses (March 4, 1843-March 3, 1849); declined to be a candidate for renomination in 1848; engaged in agricultural pursuits; member of the secession convention in 1860 and signed the ordinance of secession; died in Pendleton, Anderson County, S.C., October 28, 1882; interment in the family cemetery near that city.

SIMPSON, WILLIAM DUNLAP, (1823-1890) — fifty-third state governor (D/acting) of South Carolina, 1879-1880.

He was born in Laurens District, South Carolina, the son of Elizabeth Satterwhite and John M. Simpson.

Simpson attended Laurens Male Academy, and received an A.B. degree from South Carolina College in 1843. He attended Harvard Law School, but withdrew after one session to study law in the office of Henry Young; he was admitted to the South Carolina Bar in 1846.

At the outbreak of the Civil War, Simpson joined he Confederate States Army. He was appointed a major, assigned to the staff of General M.L. Bonham, and helped organize the Fourteenth South Carolina Volunteers. After an promotion to lieutenant colonel in 1862, he resigned his commission in February 1863.

Simpson maintained a private law practice from 1846-1875. In 1854, he was elected to the South Carolina House of Representatives, serving until 1846, and served a second term, 1858 to 1860. He was a member of the South Carolina Senate in 1860, and served until 1863. He was then elected to the Confederate States House of Representatives until 1865. He was a delegate to the Democratic National Convention in 1868, and was elected to the United States Congress the same year, but was refused his seat by the Radical Republicans.

Simpson was voted lieutenant governor of South Carolina in 1876. In February 1879, when Governor Wade Hampton resigned from office, Simpson was sworn in and became governor of South Carolina. During his administration, he worked toward progressive legislation in education, and established the Agricultural Bureau for South Carolina.

Simpson resigned as governor September 1, 1880, to accept an appointment as Chief Justice of the South Carolina Supreme Court. He held this position until his death.

Simpson was married to Jane Elizabeth Young in March 1847, with whom he had eight children. He died in Columbia, South Carolina in December 1890.

SIMS, ALEXANDER DROMGOOLE, (1803-1848) — (nephew of George Coke Dromgoole), a U.S. Representative from South Carolina; born near Randals Ordinary, Brunswick County, Va., June 12, 1803; attended the rural schools of his native county and at the age of sixteen entered the University of North Carolina at Chapel Hill; was graduated from Union College, Schenectady, N.Y., in 1823; read law with General Dromgoole in Brunswick County, Va., and later was admitted to practice; moved to South Carolina in 1826 and settled in Darlington; assumed charge of Darlington (S.C.) Academy in 1827; was admitted to the bar of South Carolina in 1829 and practiced in Darlington; also engaged in literary pursuits; member of the State house of representatives 1840-1843; elected as a Democrat to the Twenty-ninth and Thirtieth Congresses and served from March 4, 1845, until his death; had been reelected in 1848 to the Thirty-first Congress; died in Kingstree, Williamsburg County, S.C., November 22, 1848; interment in First Baptist Cemetery, Darlington, Darlington County, S.C.

SIMS, HUGO SHERIDAN, JR., (1921-   ) — a U.S. Representative from South Carolina; born in Orangeburg, S.C., October 14, 1921; attended the public schools; graduated from Wofford College, Spar tanburg, S.C., in 1941; editor of the Times and Democrat, daily newspaper, Orangeburg, S.C., in 1941 and 1942; enlisted in the United States Army as a private in April 1942; commissioned a captain in November 1944 and commanded Company A, Five Hundred and First Parachute Infantry, One Hundred and First Airborne Division; discharged in October 1945 after serving overseas from January 1944 to September 1945; awarded the Distinguished Service Cross and Silver Star; graduated from the law school of the University of South Carolina at Columbia in 1947; was admitted to the bar August 28, 1947, and commenced the practice of law in Orangeburg, S.C.; member of the State house of rep resentatives in 1947 and 1948; elected as a Democrat to the Eighty-first Congress (January 3, 1949-January 3, 1951); unsuccessful candidate for renomination in 1950; reentered the Army on January 3, 1951, as a captain and served until December 1951; resumed the practice of law from 1951 until 1965; president of Management and Investment Corporation, 1965-1983; is a resident of Orangeburg, S.C.

SIMS, JAMES MARION, (1813-1883) — an early gynecologist who established the first woman's hospital in New York City.

Born in Lancaster County, South Carolina January 25, 1813, Sims was the son of John and Mahala (Mackey) Sims. He graduated from South Carolina College in 1832 and studied medicine with another doctor in his neighborhood, entering Charleston Medical School as soon as it opened. He finished medical school in 1853 at Jefferson Medical College in Philadelphia.

Sims first practiced medicine in Lancaster, South Carolina, near his parents, but he was so effected by the loss of some of his first patients he moved to Mount Meigs, Alabama. He married Eliza Theresa Jones December 21, 1836, and moved to Macon County, Alabama. He relocated again in 1840 to Montgomery, Alabama, where he practiced surgery. Quickly his skills became well known, as he was the only surgeon in the South to correct imbalance of the eye muscles and to treat club-foot. He was thirty years ahead of his time when he wrote several papers and medical journals suggesting that infant lock-jaw could be prevented by allowing newborns to lie comfortably on their sides, rather than placing them in a constrained posture, causing pressure on the base of the brain. His ideas were not accepted by most physicians at the time, but thirty years later a long-term study in Washington D.C. proved that his suspicions were correct.

In 1845 Sims proved to be ahead of his time again, when he developed the silver suture for the treatment of vesico-vaginal fistula. It took three and a half years to develop the procedure, and Sims took patients from all over Alabama into his home while he researched his ideas. The silver suture was later used in many types of surgery, and Sims became famous worldwide for the technique. Also while working on vesico-vaginal fistula Sims developed the duck-bill speculum, also known as the Sims speculum. The use of this instrument elevated the gynecological profession, and Sims took an active interest in the field.

Because of his own health Sims traveled to New York City to seek treatment, and he stayed there as a resident. He demonstrated the silver suture and other treatments successfully, but when he suggested there was a need for a hospital dedicated to women's diseases, he got the cold shoulder. Other doctors and city officials scoffed at the idea, at a time when women's health issues were not taken seriously. Prominent local women did take the idea very seriously though, and they helped to open a temporary hospital in 1855. The facility was so successful that in 1857 the state legislature granted a charter for the Woman's Hospital for the State of New York, and allocated $50,000 for the project. The city council gave an old Potter's Field for the building site. To insure that the new hospital was as modern and practical as possible Sims traveled to Europe to tour examples of hospital architecture, and when he returned he suggested the hospital use the pavilion system, which was implemented.

While in Europe Sims found a positive reception for his demonstrations of the operation for vesico-vaginal fistula.

He was invited to hospitals in London, Paris, Dublin, Brussels, and Edinburgh, always receiving a popular response. In 1862 he and his wife took their nine children to Europe, planning to stay for only a short time. Yet Sims had become so popular there he easily started a practice in Paris, so they decided to stay until the end of the Civil War. They decided to move to London in 1864 for the education of the children. In 1865 Sims wrote *Clinical Notes on Uterine Surgery*, which was published in English, French, and German. This publication described new methods of treatment which once again met with controversy, but within a few years were widely accepted.

In 1868 Sims returned to practice in New York, then in 1870 traveled to Paris again where he established the Anglo-American ambulance corps. He was the first surgeon-in-chief for the corps, treating 1,600 French and 1,000 Germans in the first month. He resigned to return to New York, where the women's hospital was continuing to grow. The first pavilion was completed in 1866, and the second was finished in 1876. Sims was appointed a member of the board of surgeons in 1872, and other surgeons came from miles away to watch him practice his techniques. The board of governors felt it necessary to limit the number of visitors to fifteen for each operation to respect the modesty of the patients, but Sims felt this was an insult to his professionalism. He resigned over the issue in 1874.

Afterward, in 1876, Sims served as president of the American Medical Association, then in 1881 he was president of the American Gynecological Society. In 1881 he was given an honorary degree from Jefferson University in Pennsylvania, and he was even more decorated in Europe. Overseas he was made a knight of the order of Leopold I., made a corresponding fellow of the Royal academy of medicine in Belgium, received the iron cross of Germany, two medals from the Italian government, plus he was decorated by the Spanish and Portuguese. He spent his latter years in Europe, studying accidents during childbirth and sterility. He continued to write for medical journals and make presentations for medical associations. He wrote *Ovariotomy* in 1873 and he wrote his autobiography, *The Story of My Life*, shortly before he died November 13,

1883. His son, Harry Marion Sims, became a surgeon as well, serving in his father's ambulance corps in Europe, then continuing his work in gynecology.

SINGLETON, THOMAS DAY, (?-1833) — a U.S. Representative from South Carolina; born near Kingstree, S.C.; attended the common schools; member, State house of representatives, 1826- 1833; elected as a Nullifier to the Twenty-third Congress and served without having qualified, from March 3, 1833, until his death in Raleigh, N.C., November 25, 1833, while en route to Washington, D.C.; interment in Congressional Cemetery, Washington, D.C.

SMALLS, ROBERT, (1839-1915) — a U.S. Representative from South Carolina; born in Beaufort, S.C., April 5, 1839; moved to Charleston, S.C., in 1851; appointed pilot in the United States Navy and served throughout the Civil War; member of the State constitutional convention in 1868; served in the State house of representatives, 1868-1870; member of the State senate 1870-1874; delegate to the Republican National Convention in 1872 and 1876; elected as a Republican to the Forty-fourth and Forty-fifth Congresses (March 4, 1875-March 3, 1879); unsuccessful candidate for reelection in 1878 to the Fortysixth Congress; successfully contested the election of George D. Tillman to the Forty-seventh Congress and served from July 19, 1882, to March 3, 1883; unsuccessful candidate for reelection in 1882; elected to the Forty-eighth Congress to fill the vacancy caused by the death of Edmund W.M. Mackey; reelected to the Forty-ninth Congress and served from March 18, 1884, to March 3, 1887; unsuccessful for reelection in 1886 to the Fiftieth Congress; collector of the port of Beaufort, S.C., 1897-1913; died in Beaufort, S.C., Feb ruary 22, 1915; interment in the Tabernacle Baptist Church Cemetery.

SMITH, CHARLES A., (1861-1916) — Sixty-sixth state governor (D, acting) of South Carolina, 1915.
Born in Hertford County, North Carolina on January 22, 1861, the son of Joseph and Eva Smith. He attended

Wake Forest University and graduated in 1882. In 1884, he married Fannie Byrd. They had eight children.

Smith worked for many years in the mercantile business and was the owner of the Charles A. Smith Company in Timmonsville. He also worked for the Smith-Williams Company of Lake City; was president of Citizens Bank of Timmonsville; president of the Bank of Lynchburg; and president of the Peoples' Bank of Lamar. In addition he served as president of the Board of Trustees of Furman University, and trustee of Greenville Women's College. He was a member of the State House of Representatives in 1910, and from 1911 to 1915, served as South Carolina's Lieutenant Governor. On January 14, 1915, when Governor Blease resigned his office just five days before the end of his term, Smith became the new State Governor. He served out Blease's term, leaving office on January 19, 1915. The following year, on April 1, Smith died in Baltimore.

SMITH, ELLISON DURANT, (1864-1944) — a U.S. Senator from South Carolina; born in Lynchburg, Sumter (now Lee) County, S.C., August 1, 1864; attended the private and public schools of Lynchburg, Stewart's School at Charleston, S.C., and the University of South Carolina at Columbia; graduated from Wofford College at Spartanburg, S.C., in 1889; member, State house of representatives 1896-1900; unsuccessful candidate for the United States Congress 1901; engaged in mercantile and agricultural pursuits; one of the principal figures in the organization of the Southern Cotton Association in 1905; field agent and general organizer in the cotton protective movement 1905-1908 and became known as "Cotton Ed"; elected as a Democrat to the United States Senate in 1908; reelected in 1914, 1920, 1926, 1932, and again in 1938, and served from March 4, 1909, until his death; unsuccessful candidate for renomination in 1944; chairman, Committee on Transportation Routes to the Seaboard (Sixty-second Congress), Committee on Immigration (Sixty-third through Sixty- fifth Congresses), Committee on Interstate Commerce (Sixty-fifth and Sixty-eighth Congresses), Committee on Con servation of Natural Resources (Sixty-sixth Congress), Committee on Agriculture and

Forestry (Seventy-third through Seventy-eighth Congresses); died in Lynchburg, S.C., on November 17, 1944; interment in St. Lukes Cemetery.

SMITH, O'BRIEN, (1756-1811) — a U.S. Representative from South Carolina; born in Ireland about 1756; came to South Carolina following the Revolutionary War, taking the oath of allegiance to the Government of the United States July 31, 1784; member of the State assembly, 1791-1799; served in the State senate in 1803; elected as a Republican to the Ninth Congress (March 4, 1805-March 3, 1807); died April 27, 1811; interment in the burial ground of the colonial Chapel of Ease of St. Bartholomew's Parish, Colleton County, near Jacksonboro, S.C.

SMITH, WILLIAM, (1762-1840) — a U.S. Senator from South Carolina; born around 1762, probably in North Carolina; attended several private academies; studied law and was admitted to the bar in 1784; settled in Pinckneyville, S.C., and later in Yorkville (now York), S.C., and practiced law; also was engaged as a planter; member, State senate 1802-1808, and served as president of that body 1806-1808; judge of the South Carolina Circuit Court 1808-1816; elected December 4, 1816, as a Republican to the United States Senate to fill the vacancy caused by the resignation of John Taylor; on the same day was elected for the term commencing March 4, 1817, and served from December 4, 1816, to March 3, 1823; unsuccessful candidate for reelection; chairman, Committee on the Judiciary (Sixteenth and Seventeenth Congresses); member, State house of representatives 1824-1825; again elected to the United States Senate to fill the vacancy caused by the death of John Gaillard and served from November 29, 1826, to March 3, 1831; unsuccessful candidate for reelection in 1830; chairman, Committee on Private Land Claims (Twentieth Congress); member, State senate 1831-1832; moved to Louisiana in 1832, and to a farm near Huntsville, Madison County, Ala., in 1833; member, Alabama house of representatives atives1836-1840; declined the appointment of Associate Justice of the Supreme Court of the United States tendered by President

Andrew Jackson in 1829 and 1836; presidential elector on the Democratic ticket in 1836; died at his estate "Calhoun Place," on the Maysville Pike, near Huntsville, Ala., June 26, 1840; interment in the family burial ground on the estate; reinterment in Maple Hill Cemetery, Huntsville, Ala.

SMITH, WILLIAM LOUGHTON, (1758-1812) — a U.S. Representative from South Carolina; born in Charleston, S.C., in 1758; attended prepara tory schools in England 1770-1774; studied law in the Middle Temple at London, England, in 1774; pursued higher studies in Geneva 1774-1778; returned to Charleston, S.C., in 1783; was admitted to the bar in 1784 and commenced practice in Charleston; engaged in agricultural pursuits on his estate near Charleston; member of the privy council in 1784; member of the State house of representatives 1787-1788; warden of the city of Charleston in 1786; elected to the First, Second and Third Congresses and elected as a Federalist to the Fourth and Fifth Congresses and served from March 4, 1789, until July 10, 1797, when he resigned; chairman, Committee on Elections (Third Congress), Committee on Ways and Means (Fourth and Fifth Congresses); appointed United States Minister to Portugal and Spain on July 10, 1797, and served until September 9, 1801, when he took leave of absence;- commissioned Minister to the Ottoman Porte on February 11, 1799, but did not reach that court; returned to Charleston; unsuccessful Federalist candidate for election in 1804, 1806, and 1808 to the Ninth, Tenth, and Eleventh Congresses; lieutenant in the State militia in 1808; again a member of the State house of representatives in 1808; president of the Santee Canal Co.; vice president of the Charles ton Library Society and of the St. Cecilia Society; died in Charleston, S.C., December 19, 1812; interment in St. Philip's Churchyard.

SNYDER, JOHN WESLEY, (1896-1985) — a successful banker and financier, Snyder was a wartime friend of Harry S. Truman, who served in several appointed federal positions in Truman's administration.

Born June 21, 1896 in Jonesboro, Arkansas, Snyder was the son of Jerre Hartwell Snyder, a druggist, and Ellen (Hatcher) Snyder. He graduated from Jonesboro High

School in 1914 and went on to Vanderbilt University in Nashville, Tennessee, but he dropped out after one year. For 18 months he worked with his uncle, Judge E.A. Rolfe, helping with his businesses in farming, banking and timber. Then in the spring of 1917 Snyder decided to enlist in the Army, where he served as caption in the Fifty-seventh Field Artillery Brigade of the Thirty-second ("Red Arrow") Division. Snyder met Captain Harry S. Truman by chance in 1918 when they were both with the AEF in France. Snyder was eventually promoted to full colonel in the Field Artillery Reserve. For several summers after the end of the war he and Truman trained together in the Officers' Reserve Corps at such posts as Fort Riley in Kansas, Fort Sill in Oklahoma, Camp McCoy in Wisconsin, and Fort Ripley in Minnesota.

In civilian life Snyder worked and trained in several banks in Arkansas and Missouri. In 1920 he married Evlyn Cook, and they had one daughter. In 1930 he became the national bank receiver in the Office of the Comptroller of the Currency in Washington, D.C. There he supervised the liquidation of bankrupt financial institutions, keeping very busy during the economic climate of the 1930's. In 1937 Snyder was appointed manager of the St. Louis Loan Agency of the Reconstruction Finance Corporation. Then in 1940, while still maintaining that position, he was appointed assistant to the directors of the Reconstruction Finance Corporation (RFC), and executive vice-president and director of the new Defense Plant Corporation, a subsidiary of the RFC. In this position he was in charge of handling five to eight billion dollars in expenditures for war plant expansion, which he felt should be augmented as quickly as possible. His bold theories of speed at all cost brought him head to head with his superiors, but earned him respect with his colleagues.

On January 1, 1943, Snyder returned to private banking, accepting the position of vice-president of the First National Bank of St. Louis, Missouri. In February of that year he resigned from the Reconstruction Finance Corporation, thus severing all government ties. This did not last long, however, as in April of 1945 Snyder's appointment by President Harry S. Truman for Federal Loan Administrator was approved by Congress. In that position

Snyder became principal advisor on economic and monetary policies to the Truman administration. He was also directly in charge of a large part of the reconversion program, exercising general supervision over subsidiaries such as the Rubber Reserve Company, the Metal Reserve Company, the Defense Plant Corporation, the Defense Supplies Corporation and the Disaster Loan Corporation. In 13 years these agencies approved about 45 billion dollars in loans. Snyder's first act in this post was to consolidate all of these agencies in the interest of economy and efficiency. He then moved forward to improve the efficiency of the government and to become a friend of small banks and businesses by discouraging monopolies in defense industries.

"The defense program is designed to protect a democratic system founded upon private initiative and individual liberty," said Snyder at the time. "Sacrifices of certain privileges will be the only legitimate means to a vital end...(which is) defending our ideal of democracy...and the system of private initiative which is its very foundation. Bankers can...serve as guides in pointing out the way back after difficult days." He emphasized that his agency would not enter into competition with private banks in making loans, but support them in making loans beyond their normal limits, and help them take risks they might not normally be able to take.

In mid-July of 1945 Snyder was promoted from the Federal Loan Agency to the Office of War Mobilization and Reconversion. This agency had just been created in 1943 to organize the most efficient use of natural and industrial resources during wartime, and then later help with the transition back to peace. Snyder quickly learned his new position, and was ready when the Japanese surrendered three weeks after he took his post. He immediately shut down all wartime production of weapons except for what was absolutely necessary, and discontinued all price, distribution and wage controls. As predicted, millions were instantly unemployed, so Snyder pushed Truman to raise unemployment benefits and pass a full employment bill. He advocated a repeal of normal and excess profit taxes and an increase in the minimum wage, with the hope that consumer demand for goods would quickly absorb the sudden increase in unemployment. In 1946, when World War II was over Snyder was named Secretary of the Treasury, where he remained until 1956. He was always a close advisor to President Truman. He was a member of the NATO Council from 1949 to 1953 and was the founder of the Harry S. Truman Scholarship Foundation for careers in public service. He died on Seabrook Island, South Carolina, on October 8, 1945.

SPRATT, JOHN MCKEE, JR., (1942-   ) — a U.S. Representative from South Carolina; born in Charlotte-Mecklenburg County, N.C., November 1, 1942; attended York Elementary School, York, S.C.; graduated fro" York High School, 1960; A.B., Davidson College, Davidson, N.C., 1964; M.A., Marshall Scholar, Oxford University, Oxford, England, 1966; LL.B., Yale Law School, 1969; served, United States Army, 1969- 1971; admitted to the South Carolina bar, 1971 and commenced practice in York; banker; delegate, South Carolina State Democratic convention, 1972-1980; delegate, Democratic National Convention, 1964; elected as a Democrat to the Ninety-eighth and to each succeeding Congresses; is a resident of York, S.C.

STACKHOUSE, ELI THOMAS, (1824-1892) — a U.S. Representative from South Carolina; born in Little Rock, Marion County, S.C., March 27, 1824; attended the common schools; worked on his father's farm; taught school for several years; later engaged in agricultural pursuits; enlisted in the Confederate Army January 9, 1861, and served throughout the Civil War, attaining the rank of colonel of the Eighth Regiment, South Carolina Volunteers; member of the State house of representatives 1863, 1865-1866; member of the first board of trustees of Clemson Agricultural and Mechanical College of South Carolina in 1887; first president of the South Carolina State Farmers' Alliance in 1888; elected as a Democrat to the Fifty-second Congress and served from March 4, 1891, until his death in Washington, D.C., June 14, 1892; interment in Little Rock Cemetery, Little Rock, S.C.

STOKES, JAMES WILLIAM, (1853-1901) — a U.S. Representative from South Carolina; born near Orangeburg, S.C., December 12, 1853; attended the common schools and was graduated from Washington and Lee University, Lexington, Va., in 1876; taught school for twelve years; was graduated in medicine from Vanderbilt University, Nashville, Tenn.; engaged in agricultural pursuits in 1889; president of the State Farmers' Alliance; member of the State senate in 1890; delegate to the Democratic National Convention in 1892; unsuccessful candidate for election in 1892 to the Fifty-third Congress; presented credentials as a Democratic Member-elect to the Fifty-fourth Congress and served from March 4, 1895, to June 1, 1896, when the seat was declared vacant; elected to fill the vacancy thus caused; reelected to the Fifty-fifth, Fifty-sixth, and Fifty-seventh Congresses and served from November 3, 1896, until his death in Orangeburg, Orangeburg County, S.C., July 6, 1901; interment in Sunnyside Cemetery.

STOLL, PHILIP HENRY, (1874-1958) — a U.S. Representative from South Carolina; born in Little Rock, Marion (now Dillon) County, S.C., November 5, 1874; attended the public schools; was graduated from Wofford College, Spartanburg, S.C., in 1897; teacher in the public schools 1897-1901; studied law; was admitted to the bar in 1901 and commenced practice in Kingstree, Williamsburg County, S.C.; member of the State house of representatives 1905-1906; solicitor of the third judicial circuit from 1908 to 1917, when he resigned; chairman of the Democratic county committee and member of the Democratic State committee 1908-1918; commissioned as a major in the Judge Advocate General's Department of the United States Army in 1917; promoted to the rank of lieutenant colonel in 1918 and served throughout the First World War; elected as a Democrat to the Sixty-sixth Congress to fill the vacancy caused by the death of J. Willard Ragsdale; reelected to the Sixty-seventh Congress and served from October 7, 1919, to March 3, 1923; unsuccessful candidate for renomination in 1922; resumed the practice of law; again a member, State house of representatives, 1929-1931; elected as a judge of the third judicial circuit of South Carolina in 1931 and served until December 6, 1946, when he retired; died in Columbia, S.C., October 29, 1958; interment in Williamsburg Presbyterian Cemetery, Kingstree, S.C.

SWEARINGEN, JOHN E(LDRED), (1918-?) — oil company executive, was born on September 7, 1918 in Columbia, South Carolina. He attended the University of South Carolina (starting at the age of sixteen), earning a B.S. degree in 1938. Pursuing his graduate studies in engineering, he enrolled at the Carnegie Institute of Technology, receiving an M.S. degree. In 1939 he went to work as a chemical engineer at Standard Oil Company, and by 1951 had been named a director at one of its subsidiaries, Pan American Petroleum Corporation. Swearingen then returned to the Standard Oil Company in the post of general manager of production, and in 1954, was made vice-president of production. In 1956, he was named executive vice-president, and two years later, became president of Standard Oil.

In order to expand profits, Swearingen instituted sweeping employee cuts and various other changes such as stepping up the production of crude oil, the lack of which, according to Swearingen, contributed to the Standard's inability to keep up with the other oil companies. In a *Forbes* magazine article, the executive pulled no punches in talking about where his company rated in the oil business: "Let's face it. In many respects, this is a second-rate company. This company has just not kept pace with the oil business or with other companies in the past ten years." Between the vast cost-cutting decisions and the expansion of oil refinery production, both in the United States and overseas, Swearingen made Standard Oil a competitive and impressive company that took its place next to the top companies in the oil industry. In 1960 he became Standard's chief executive officer, and five years later became chairman of the board.

Swearingen is married to Bonnie L. Bolding, and the couple have three children.

T

TALBERT, WILLIAM JASPER, (1846-1931) — a U.S. Representative from South Carolina; born near Edgefield, Edgefield County, S.C., October 6, 1846; attended the common schools in Greenwood and Due West Academy at Abbeville, and was graduated from Erskine College, Due West, S.C.; served in the Confederate Army as a private, Company F, Fifth South Carolina Reserves, as a substitute for his father B.M. Talbert, who was discharged December 17, 1862; enlisted at Richmond, Va., September 15, 1864, as a private, Company B, Infantry Regiment, Hampton Legion, South Carolina; engaged in agricultural pursuits near Parksville, McCormick County, S.C.; member of the State house of representatives 1880-1883; served in the State senate 1884-1888; superintendent of the State penitentiary 1891-1893; delegate to the Democratic National Convention in 1892; mayor of Parksville 1895-1900; president of the Democratic State convention in 1899; held various positions in the Farmers' Alliance; elected as a Democrat to the Fifty-third and to the four succeeding Congresses (March 4, 1893-March 3, 1903); was not a candidate for renomination in 1902, but was an unsuccessful candidate in the second primary for the Democratic nomination for Governor in 1902; resumed agricultural pursuits near Parksville, McCormick County, S.C.; moved to McCormick, S.C., in 1927 and lived in retirement until his death in Greenwood, S.C., February 5, 1931; interment in Parksville Cemetery, Parksville, S.C.

TALLON, ROBERT MOONEYHAN, JR. (ROBIN), (1946-) — a Representative from South Carolina; born in Hemingway, Williamsburg County, S.C., August 8, 1946; attended public schools; attended the University of South Carolina, Columbia, 1964-1965; clothing business owner and real estate broker; delegate, White House Conference on Small Business, 1979-1980; elected, South Carolina house of representatives, 1980-1982; elected as a Democrat to the Ninety-eighth Congress (January 3,

1983); and to each succeeding Congresses; is a resident of Florence, S.C.

TAYLOR, JOHN, (1770-1832) — twenty-sixth state governor (D-R) of South Carolina, 1826-1828. He was born in Granby, South Carolina, the son of Ann Wyche and Colonel Thomas Taylor. Taylor received his education at Mount Zion College in Columbia, South Carolina. He further attended Priceton College and, after graduating in 1870, studied law with General Charles Cotesworth Pinckney. He was admitted to the South Carolina Bar in 1793, and practiced law in Columbia for several years.

Taylor was elected to the South Carolina House of Representatives in 1793, serving until 1802, and again in 1804, serving through 1805. In 1806, he became the first Indendant (mayor) of Columbia, and kept this office until 1807. He became a member of the United States House of Representatives in 1807, resigning from this position in 1810. From 1810 until his resignation in 1816, he was a member of the United States Senate. In 1818, he was elected to the South Carolina Senate, and successfully held this office until 1826, when he was defeated for re-election.

Taylor was elected governor of South Carolina in 1826. During his administration, the issue of a protective tariff had grown to major proportions in South Carolina. Mass meetings were held throughout the State to adopt memorials to the national Congress in opposition to protectionism. In December 1827, the State Legislature adopted strong anti-internal improvements resolutions and appointed a committee to report on the "unconstitutional system of protection."

Other changes during Taylor's tenure included chartering the South Carolina Canal and Railroad Company, in 1827, to construct a railway, road, or canal from Charleston to Columbia, Camden, and Hamburg within the state; and the commissioners of free schools reported establishing 892 schools within the State, in which about 9,000 pupils received free instruction.

After leaving the governorship, Taylor served as commissioner for the inspection of bread and flour at Columbia, commissioner for the opening of Broad River, and commissioner of the streets for Columbia.

Taylor was married to Sarah Cantey Chestnut in 1793. The couple had nine children. He died in Columbia in February 1832.

TAYLOR, JOHN, (?-?) — a U.S. Representative from South Carolina; member, State house of representatives, 1802-1805; elected as a Republican to the Fourteenth Congress (March 4, 1815-March 3, 1817); unsuccessful candidate for reelection in 1816 to the Fifteenth Congress and for election in 1820 to the Seventeenth Congress.

TAYLOR, JOHN CLARENCE, (1890-1983) — a U.S. Representative from South Carolina; born in Honea Path, Anderson County, S.C., March 2, 1890; attended the public schools and Fruitland Institute, Hendersonville, N.C.; was graduated from the law department of the University of South Carolina at Columbia in 1919; during the First World War attended the Officers' Training School at Camp Johnston, Fla., in 1918 and was discharged into the Reserves at the end of the war; was admitted to the bar in 1919; engaged in agricultural pursuits; clerk of court and register of deeds for Anderson County, S.C., from 1920 until elected to Congress; elected as a Democrat to the Seventy-third, Seventy-fourth, and Seventy-fifth Congresses (March 4, 1933- January 3, 1939); was an unsuccessful candidate for renomination in 1938 to the Seventy-sixth Congress; resumed his former business pursuits; member, South Carolina State senate, 1951-1954 and 1959-1962; resident of Anderson, S.C., until his death there March 25, 1983; interment in Garden of Memories, Honea Path, S. C.

THOMPSON, HUGH SMITH, (1836-1904) — fifty-sixth state governor (D) of South Carolina, 1882-1886.

He was born in Charleston, South Carolina, the son of Agnes Smith and Henry Tazwell Thompson.

Thompson graduated from The Citadel Academy in 1856. He was a teacher at the Arsenel Academy in Columbia, South Carolina from 1858 to 1861, and served in the Confederate States Army as Captain of Cadets from

1861 to 1865, at which time he was also an instructor at The Citadel.

He became principal of the Columbia Male Academy at the close of the Civil War in 1865, and remained in this position until 1880, and was also the South Carolina superintendent of education from 1877 to 1882. Thompson was elected governor of South Carolina by popular vote in November 1882. During his administration, he proposed a policy of tax reform, rigid economy, and educational development. He was re-elected governor of South Carolina in November 1884, but resigned before the end of his second term to accept an appointment as assistant secretary of the United States Treasury, in July 1886. In 1889, he left his position as assistant secretary to accept an appoinment by President Benjamin Harrison to the United States Civil Service Commission. He held this position until 1892. He was comptroller of the New York Life Insurance Company from 1892 through 1904.

Thompson was married to Elizabeth Anderson in April 1858, with whom he had one child. He died in New York City in November 1904, and was buried in Trinity Churchyard, Columbia, South Carolina.

THOMPSON, WADDY, JR., (1798-1868) — a U.S. Representative from South Carolina; born in Pickensville (now Pickens), Ninety-sixth District, S.C., January 8, 1798; moved to Greenville with his parents in his infancy; received his early education in neighboring schools, and was graduated from South Carolina College (now the University of South Carolina), at Columbia in 1814; studied law; was admitted to the bar in 1819 and began practice in Edgefield, S.C.; moved to Greenville, S.C., and continued the practice of law; member of the State house of representatives, 1826-1829; elected solicitor of the western circuit in 1830; brigadier general of militia in 1832; elected as an Anti-Jacksonian to the Twenty-fourth Congress to fill the vacancy caused by the death of Warren R. Davis; reelected as a Whig to the Twenty-fifth and Twenty-sixth Congresses and served from September 10, 1835, to March 3, 1841; chairman, Committee on Military Affairs (Twenty-sixth Congress); was not a candidate for renomination in 1840; aPpointed Envoy Extraordinary and

Minister Plenipotentiary to Mexico and served from
February 10, 1842, to March 9, 1844; moved to Madison,
Fla., and engaged in cotton planting; appointed solicitor
general of a circuit in 1868; died while on a visit to Tallahassee, Fla., November 23, 1868; interment in the Episcopal Cemetery.

THURMOND, STROM, (1902-) a controversial Governor
and long-time U.S. Senator who has been a member of
four political parties, supported both liberal and conservative ideas, and yet has still survived long enough to become one of the most powerful people in Washington.

Born in Edgefield, South Carolina, on December 5,
1902, Thurmond was the second of six children of John
and Eleanor (Strom) Thurmond. His father was a state
legislator and a political aide to Senator Benjamin R.
("Pitchfork Ben") Tillman. With Tillman's influence John
Thurmond was appointed United States attorney for
western South Carolina, even through there was still controversy over his acquittal for killing one of Tillman's
political opponents in a quarrel. Young Strom learned
much of what he knew of politics by watching Tillman.

Strom Thurmond attended Clemson College, (now
University), receiving his B.S. in agricultural science and
English in 1923. For six years he taught agriculture and
coached high school sports in rural schools around South
Carolina. In 1928 he was appointed superintendent of
education for Edgefield County and he started studying
law at home under his father's guidance. He compressed
three years of education into one, and passed the state bar
exam in 1930, tying the highest score with a Harvard Law
graduate. He left education to join his father's law firm in
Edgefield, Thurmond and Buzhardt, and served as city and
county attorney.

While working as an attorney Thurmond stepped into
politics as well, representing Edgefield County in the state
senate. As a Democrat he supported New Deal programs,
rural electrification and soil conservation. In 1938 he was
chosen by the state legislature to serve as the youngest
circuit judge in South Carolina. Then on December 11,
1941, he took a leave of absence from the bench to join
the army. Since he had been in the reserves for almost 17

years Thurmond was commissioned a lieutenant with the First Army's Eighty-second Airborne Division. On D-Day, 1944, his troop glider crashed behind enemy lines in France. He and other men fought in isolation for two days before they linked with other American forces advancing from Normandy. After the European effort was over, Thurmond went to the Pacific, then was discharged as a lieutenant colonel in 1946. During his years of active service he earned the Purple Heart, the Legion of Merit, the Bronze Star with V, the Bronze Arrowhead, the Distinguished Unit Citation with five battle stars, Croix de Guerre from France, and the cross of the Order of the Crown of Belgium. He continued in the reserves until he retired a major general in 1960.

After returning home Thurmond ran for governor as a Populist. He earned more votes than eleven Democratic candidates in the primary, then won the governor's seat. As a liberal he saw to it that increased funding was provided for health care and education, including black schools. There was more money for libraries, adult education, colleges, universities and school bussing. Thurmond also promoted a fair minimum wage. He led a successful effort to ban the poll tax in South Carolina, and appointed the first black to the state board of medical examiners. He also put all the resources of the state behind the search for a white mob accused of lynching a black man.

However, when President Harry S. Truman integrated the armed forces and called for federal laws against lynching, the poll tax, and racial discrimination in the workplace, Thurmond lead the rallying cry of other Southern governors to protest this perceived threat to state's rights. He and other Southerners strongly disapproved of the Democratic party's civil rights plank, adopted at the Democratic National Convention in 1948. This group decided to form a third party, the States's Rights Party, also called the Dixiecrats. They nominated Thurmond as their Presidential candidate and Governor Fielding L. Wright of Mississippi as Vice-President. They campaigned throughout the south, advocating strong states' rights, segregation, and condemning the Civil Rights movement as Communist. It was their hope that they could win enough electoral votes to throw the election into a deadlock. The party carried four states in the final election: Alabama, Louisiana, Mississippi, and South Carolina. This gave them 39 electoral votes, however, which was not enough to throw the election.

In 1950 Thurmond chose not to run for a second term as governor, but instead ran for Olin D. Johnston's seat in the United States Senate. It was a brutal campaign, and the candidates nearly got in a fistfight over which was more of a segregationist. Thurmond lost the election by 25,000 votes, and he stepped down from his governor's seat in 1951. He went into private law practice again in Aiken, South Carolina, then in 1952 actively supported Republican Dwight D. Eisenhower for president.

On September 1, 1954, U.S. Senator Burnet R. Maybank died, and Thurmond jumped at the chance to take his vacant seat. He decided to run as a Democrat, however, which brought forth the wrath of the state Democratic party, who saw him as a traitor. They chose to support state senator Edgar A. Brown instead, but Thurmond fought back by encouraging the voters of South Carolina to elect him with a write-in vote. He told them this was a fight between the people of South Carolina and the "thirty-one men" who made up the state Democratic committee. The people of South Carolina spoke, and Thurmond became the only United States' senator to win by a write-in vote. His first major battle came when the Supreme Court ruled on segregation in 1954. Thurmond and other Southern senators drafted a Declaration of Constitutional Principles, also known as the "Southern Manifesto," which called the decision a "clear abuse of judicial power." Nineteen senators and 81 representatives signed the document, vowing to resist de-segregation by all lawful means.

Staying true to a unique campaign promise, Thurmond resigned in 1956 in order to run for a full six-year term without the benefit of incumbent status. He won that election, and continued to fight changes in segregation and civil rights laws in Washington. In 1957, Thurmond was dead-set against a proposed civil rights bill, even though the language was weaker than it was originally written, through the work of other Southern leaders. Thurmond called the bill a "vicious weapon to enforce race mixing," and staged a dramatic filibuster that lasted twenty-four hours and eighteen minutes, setting a new record. He left only after the Senate physician threatened to drag him from the chamber. In 1960 Thurmond supported Senator Lyndon B. Johnson for president, but when Johnson chose to share the ticket with John F. Kennedy, Thurmond pulled all inklings of support. He fought the Kennedy administration at every opportunity, calling its' domestic policies radically liberal and socialist, and foreign policies too timid. He wanted the President to forcefully take over Cuba, and would have no part of the nuclear test ban treaty with the Soviet Union, which was ratified in 1963. Even after Lyndon Johnson became President the White House still felt the wrath of Thurmond. He protested every civil rights bill that was proposed, both before and after they were approved. In 1964 he made political history again, breaking from the Democratic party to join the Republicans. "The Democratic party has abandoned the people," he explained. "It has turned its back on the spiritual values and political principles which have brought us the blessings of freedom under God and a bountiful prosperity...The Democratic party has forsaken the people to become the party of minority groups, power-hungry union leaders, political bosses and big businessman looking for government contracts and favors...If the American people permit the Democratic party to return to power, freedom as we have known it in this country is doomed, and individuals will be destined to lives of regulation, control, coercion, intimidation and subversion to a power elite." As a Republican Thurmond supported Senator Barry M. Goldwater of Arizona for president, and his support helped Goldwater win South Carolina, one of the only six states he carried.

In 1965 the passage of the Voting Rights Act changed the South and its politics forever. Thurmond became softer on his segregational ideas, and he started supporting black causes, such as federal funds for black colleges and other black concerns. In 1971 he became the first Southern senator to hire a black staff member. Also in the late sixties Thurmond became a leader to listen to in the Republican party. He supported Richard Nixon for President in 1968 because he felt the alternative, Governor Ronald Reagan of California, was too conservative. "I wasn't too sure after Goldwater was defeated so decisively, being a conservative, that Reagan, another conservative, could quite make it," Thurmond later explained in a Washington Post article. "Whereas Nixon was a little more liberal but yet would be so much better, I felt we stood a better chance to elect Nixon."

Thurmond beat the bushes to get Nixon elected, telling Southerners to ignore third-party candidate George Wallace. He helped Nixon establish strategy, and was instrumental in choosing running-mate. Despite Thurmond's efforts, however, Wallace did win in the South. In 1972 Nixon won in the South, however, and Thurmond began criticizing the administration for deficit spending, high welfare costs, the rapprochement with the People's Republic of China at the expense of Taiwan, and the failure to impose import quotas on textiles. This last point was of special interest to the people of South Carolina. In 1976 Thurmond supported Ronald Reagan for President against incumbent Gerald R. Ford. In 1978 he faced the only serious contention for his own Senate seat ever, from Democrat Charles "Pug" Ravenal. Thurmond pointed to Ravenal's Ivy League education and experience on Wall Street as proof that he could not have the best interest of the south in mind, and Thurmond won again with 56 percent of the vote.

As the 1970's came to a close and the 1980's began, Thurmond became softer on civil rights and harder on crime. In 1976 he helped black lawyer Matthew J. Perry Jr. win an appointment to the United States Court of Military Appeals and sponsored his advancement to the Federal District Court in South Carolina three years later. In 1978 he voted for a constitutional amendment that would grant the predominantly black District of Columbia full voting representation in Congress. And he also supported making Reverend Martin Luther King Jr.'s birthday a federal holiday.

Then in 1981 the Republicans gained the majority in the Senate and Thurmond was made President pro-tem, placing him third in line for the succession of the presidency behind the vice- president and the Speaker of the House. He also became chairman of the Judiciary Committee, and made the enactment of a federal death penalty statute his top priority. He was not able to gain support for a death penalty provision for murder, treason, or kidnapping, but in 1988 he was able to add an amendment to an antidrug bill calling for capital punishment for murder committed during drug trafficking and for the killing of a police officer during the commission of a felony.

Thurmond also presided over most of the confirmation hearings of Reagan Supreme Court nominees, and as senior member of the Armed Services Committee he supported the development of all the major weapons during the 1970's and 80's.

If Thurmond serves out his term to 1997, he will be the oldest person ever to sit on the Senate floor, at the age of 94. He has married twice, first to his former secretary, Jean Crouch in 1947, who died in 1960. They had six children. His second marriage was in 1968 to Nancy Moore, a former Miss South Carolina, 44 years his junior. They have four children together, but separated in 1991. Thurmond is also author of the book, The Faith We Have Not Kept.

TILLMAN, BENJAMIN RYAN, (1847-1918) — fifty-ninth state governor (D) of South Carolina, 1890-1894.

He was born in Edgefield County, South Carolina, the son of Sophia Hancock and Benjamin Ryan Tillman.

Tillman received a private education, and left school in 1864 to join the Confederate States Army. Before he could serve, however, he was stricken with a serious illness that resulted in the loss of his left eye and kept him incapacitated for two years.

He became a farmer in 1868, and worked on a 400 acre estate until 1885. He was a delegate to all Democratic State and National Conventions from 1890 through 1918. He also organized the Farmers' Association.

Tillman was elected governor of South Carolina in November 1890. During his administration, the State Railroad Commission was given the power to fix rates, taxes were made more equitable, and expenditures for public education were increased. The Legislature was reapportioned and congressional districts redrawn to discriminate against blacks.

In 1893, while he was still in office, Tillman founded the Clemson Agricultural and Mechanical College in Fort Hill, South Carolina. Other changes during his term included the limitation of work hours in cotton and woolen factories to 66 hours per week, or 11 hours per day, and approval of a dispensary system for selling liquor.

Tillman was re-elected for a second gubernatorial term in November 1892, and served until December 1894. In the general election of that year, he was elected to the United States Senate, and held his seat until his death in 1918. Tillman was also a member of the 1895 Constitutional Convention, and was chairman of the United States Senate Committee on Naval Affairs during World War I. He founded Winthrop Normal and Industrial College in Rock Hill, South Carolina in 1895.

Tillman was married in 1868 to Sallie Stark, with whom he had seven children. He died in July 1918 and was buried in Ebenezer Cemetery in Trenton.

TILLMAN, GEORGE DIONYSIUS, (1826-1902) — (brother of Benjamin Ryan Tillman), a U.S. Representative from South Carolina; born near Curryton, Edgefield County, S.C., August 21, 1826; pursued an academic course in Penfield, Ga., and in Greenwood, S.C.; attended Harvard University, but did not graduate; studied law; was admitted to the bar in 1848 and commenced practice in Edgefield, S.C.; member of the State house of representatives, 1854-1855 and 1864; enlisted during the Civil War and served in the Third Regiment of South Carolina State troops in 1862; shortly after its disbandment entered the Second Regiment of South Carolina Artillery, in which he served until the close of the war; again a member of the State house of representatives in 1864; member of the State constitutional convention in 1865, held under the reconstruction proclamation of President Johnson; served in the State senate in 1865; unsuccessful candidate for election in 1876 to the Forty-fifth Congress; elected as a Democrat to the Fortysixth Congress (March 4, 1879-March 3, 1881); presented credentials as a Member-elect to the Forty-seventh Congress and served from March 4,

1881, to June 19, 1882, when he was succeeded by Robert Smalls, who contested the election; elected to the Forty-eighth and to the four succeeding Congresses (March 4, 1883-March 3, 1893); chairman, Committee on Patents (Fifty-second Congress); unsuccessful candidate for renomination in 1892; engaged in agricultural pursuits and also as a publicist; member of the State constitutional convention in 1895; unsuccessful candidate for election as Governor of South Carolina in 1898; died in Clarks Hill, McCormick County, S.C., February 2, 1902; interment in the Bethlehem Baptist Church Community Cemetery.

TIMMERMAN, GEORGE BELL, JR., (1912-   ) — Eighty-first state governor (D) of South Carolina, 1955-1959.

Born in Anderson, South Carolina on August 11, 1912, the son of George and Mary (Sullivan) Timmerman. He received his education at The Citadel and at the University of South Carolina where he graduated with an LL.B. degree in 1937. He was admitted to the South Carolina Bar that same year and began a law practice in Lexington, South Carolina. In 1936, he married Helen Miller DuPre.

Timmerman served in the U.S. Naval Reserve during World War II. He was the assistant chief trial attorney for the South Carolina Public Service Authority in 1941. From 1947 to 1955, he was Lieutenant Governor of the State. He was active in Democratic politics, and in 1954, running on the Democratic Party ticket, he won election as governor of South Carolina. He was governor during a time when the Civil Rights Movement began to be felt. The Interstate Commerce Commission came out against segregation on public transportation, the National Association for the Advancement of Colored People (NAACP) threatened to sue for desegregation, and the South Carolina bus segregation law was finally stuck down. Timmerman left the governorship in 1959 at the end of his term. He subsequently was chairman of the South Carolina delegation to the Democratic National Convention of 1956, and in 1964, he served as a Democratic presidential elector.

TIMROD, HENRY, (1828-1867) — considered by many to be the poet laureate of the Confederacy, Timrod never received the fame or appreciation he felt he deserved in his lifetime, dying poor and relatively unknown.

Timrod's father, William Henry, was a bookbinder and locally- popular author who died when Timrod was just ten years old. From his father Timrod seemed to inherit a poetic temperament, and a tendency to be impractical. Timrod's mother, Thyrza Prince, gave Timrod her sensitivity and love of nature. Born December 8, 1828, in Charleston, South Carolina, Timrod was shy and often ill. He was a good student in public schools, where developed his love for writing. After graduation he attended Franklin College (later the University of Georgia) studying the classics. He dropped out after two years, in part because of illness but also because he wanted to get out into the real world. He worked for a short time in the law office of James L. Petigru, but he soon found he was not suited for law, so returned to college hoping to become a professor. He was never offered a position however, so he took a job tutoring children on a South Carolina plantation.

For the next ten years Timrod continued to tutor, and occasionally he published his poetry in periodicals. He sometimes traveled to Charleston to meet with a group of friends also interested in literature, and in 1857 they started their own periodical, *Russell's Magazine.* Even though the writing was considered very good, the magazine did not stay in business for long. In 1860 a collection of Timrod's poems was published for the first time in book form, and they were received favorably. However, the turbulence with the onset of the Civil War made poetry seem trivial, and Timrod's work soon fell into obscurity.

Despite the disappointment, the emotions connected with the war did give Timrod material for his work. In 1861 he wrote the impassioned "Ethnogenesis," about the creation of a new nation. It was followed by a series of war inspired poems, gaining him limited recognition. Poems such as "A Cry to Arms," "Carolina," "Carmen Triumphale," and "Charleston" earned Timrod the informal title of poet laureate of the Confederacy.

Timrod did not enlist during the first year of the war because of ill health, but he did join the Confederate Army March 1, 1862, serving in Company B, 30th South Carolina Regiment. He worked as a clerk in regimental headquarters, and later was assigned to the Confederate Army of the West to serve as a correspondent for the *Charleston Mercury*. He did not adapt to camp life in the west, however, then in December 1862 he began developing tuberculosis and was discharged.

Timrod came home to disappointment, finding that the proposed project of printing an illustrated volume of his works in England had been dropped. This news was extremely disappointing to Timrod, who truly wanted a level of acceptance and even fame for his work. In 1864 he moved to Columbia where he bought a share of the newspaper the *South Carolinian*, and he worked as associate editor. In February of that year he married Kate Goodwin, the true love of his life and inspiration for his poem, "Katie." That same year Timrod's sister married Katie's brother, and 1864 was climaxed on Christmas Eve with the birth of his son, William.

Then soon in 1865 Timrod's world came crashing down. In February Columbia was burned by Sherman's forces and the newspaper was gone, leaving Timrod and his family with no means of support. He was also responsible for his mother, his widowed sister and her children. They resorted to selling most of their possessions and accepting charity. Of the experience Timrod later wrote to a friend, "We have eaten two silver pitchers, one or two dozen silver forks, several sofas, innumerable chairs and a huge bedstead!" To add insult to injury, little William, considered by his father to be "his single rose in a crown of thorns," died in October of that year. It was a loss Timrod never got over. In December he found another job at a newspaper, but after four months he still had not been paid for his work.

Timrod tried in vain to market his poems in the North, and he also tried to establish a girl's school, but with no luck. He landed a job in the governor's office, but the position lasted only a few weeks. He found a temporary respite while visiting a friend in Georgia, and during the visit he wrote a tribute to the Confederates in the Magnolia Cemetery called, "Ode," considered one of his best works. In April he underwent surgery which did not go well, and he died of complications October 6, 1867.

For ten years Timrod's grave went unmarked, while his friends and family tried to market his poems and give him the respect they felt he deserved. In 1873 *The Poems of Henry Timrod* was published, and in 1884 the illustrated version of "Katie" was printed. The Timrod Memorial Association was established in 1898, and they put together a *Memorial Edition*, which created even more interest in Timrod's work. Today Timrod is remembered for his poems of war, and is recognized as one of the great poets of the nineteenth-century South.

TRAPIER, PAUL, (1749-1778) — a Delegate from South Carolina; born in Prince George's Parish, Winyah, near Georgetown, S.C., in 1749; educated in England, where he attended Eton College 1763-1765; admitted pensioner, St. John's College, Cambridge, March 20, 1766; admitted to the Middle Temple, London, February 17, 1767; member of the Provincial Congress and the committee of safety for Georgetown, S.C.; member of the South Carolina general assembly in 1776; justice of the peace in 1776; served in the Revolutionary War as captain of the Georgetown Artillery; elected to the Continental Congress in 1777, but did not attend; died at his home near Georgetown, S.C., on July 8, 1778; interment in the churchyard of Prince George, Winyah, Georgetown, S.C.

TRAVIS, WILLIAM B., (1809-1836) — Texas Revolution soldier, was famous for his last command at the Alamo. He was born to *Mark and Jemima Stallworth Travis* of Red Banks, South Carolina, who moved the family in 1818 to Conecuh County, Alabama. Young Travis attended local schools there, and then began studying law with a judge at Claiborne. Before he was 20, Travis had passed the bar and had set up his own practice. He married one of his former pupils in the school he had taught in, *Rosanna Cato*. The marriage did not work out, however, and in 1831 he left his wife to move to Texas. He settled at Anahuac, a small port at the head of the Trinity River. The following year, the Mexican Revolution began, and

Travis was arrested and jailed by the dictatorial commander of Anahuac, *Colonel Bradburn*. When the townspeople forced *Bradburn* to leave town, Travis was released and moved to San Felipe, an important American settlement in Texas. He became active in the growing "war party" that prepared to fight for Americans' rights against the Mexican governors. He also set up a law office in San Felipe and was made secretary of the *ayuntamiento*. As hostilities between Anglo-Americans and Mexicans grew, Travis was at the forefront of a movement to declare Texan independence from the Mexicans. After San Antonio was captured in 1835, Travis and others brought out a scheme to take Matamoras as well, but that proved impossible, and so he served the Texans as a scout. He was eventually promoted to the rank of lieutenant colonel, and since San Antonio was poorly defended, he was sent to the Alamo to assist *Colonel James* Bowie with his small force of men. Many of them fell ill, including *Bowie*, and Travis was left in command of only about 150 men. Declaring "victory or death!" Travis sent messages for aid, but only a few more soldiers came, and they were grossly outnumbered by the Mexicans who encircled the old mission. Still, over 1,000 Mexican soldiers died in the effort to subdue 180 men.

TROTTI, SAMUEL WILDS, (1810-1856) — a U.S. Representative from South Carolina; born in Barnwell, S.C., July 18, 1810; attended the common schools; was graduated from South Carolina College (now University of South Carolina) at Columbia in 1832; studied law; was admitted to the bar and practiced; served in the Seminole War; member of the State house of representatives,tives 1840-1841, 1852-1855; elected as a Democrat to the Twenty-seventh Congress to fill the vacancy caused by the resignation of Sampson H. Butler and served from December 17, 1842, to March 3, 1843; resumed the practice of law; died in Buckhead, Fairfield District (now county), S.C., June 24, 1856.

TUCKER, STARLING, (1770-1834) — a U.S. Representative from South Carolina; born in Halifax County, N.C., in 1770; moved to Mountain Shoals (now Enoree), S.C.;

received a limited education; held several local offices; member of the State house of representatives;atives elected as a Republican to the Fifteenth Congress; reelected to the Sixteenth through Nineteenth Congresses and reelected as a Jacksonian to the Twentieth and Twentyfirst Congresses (March 4, 1817-March 3, 1831); died in Mountain Shoals (now Enoree), S.C., January 3, 1834; interment in the private burial ground on the family estate west of Enoree, S.C.

TURNER, HENRY MCNEAL, (1834-1915) — was an African American religious leader who advocated the return of blacks to Africa.

Born on February 1, 1834 in Newberry, South Carolina, the son of Hardy and Sarah (Greer) Turner, Henry Turner was born a free man, but worked as a youth with slaves in the cotton field. During this time he taught himself to read and write. He was employed as a janitor in an Abbeville law office for 15 years and the young lawyers in the office assisted him with his studies.

In 1848, Turner joined the Methodist Episcopal Church and was licensed to preach in 1853. He preached throughout the South until 1858, when he joined the African Methodist Episcopal Church and was then transferred to a Baltimore training mission. After studying Latin, Greek and Hebrew at Trinity College, he became pastor of the Israel Church in Washington, D.C. in 1862 and was appointed army chaplain by President Abraham Lincoln in 1863. He was the first black to hold such a position. Turner eventually received a LL.D. degree from the University of Pennsylvania in 1872.

After the Civil War, President Andrew Johnson appointed Turner a chaplain in the regular army and assigned him to the Georgia office of the Freedman's Bureau. Turner soon resigned, however, and turned to recruitment for the African M.E. Church in Georgia. He was also an active Republican Party organizer in that state. Turner was a delegate to the 1868 Georgia Constitutional Convention and was elected to the state legislature in 1868 and 1870. In 1869, President Ulysses S. Grant appointed Turner postmaster in Macon, Georgia and in the years following he also served as a customs inspector in

Savannah. In 1876, Turner became manager of the African M.E. publications in Philadelphia and was elected bishop by the 1880 general conference in St. Louis. He served as bishop for his church in Georgia from 1880 until 1892 and chancellor of the Morris Brown College in Atlanta.

Because Turner had become convinced that African Americans had no chance for equality in the United States, he advocated the return of blacks to Africa, and sponsored an ill-fated colonization attempt to Liberia in 1878.

Pan-African nationalism was his major interest. Turner founded several magazines: *The Southern Christian Recorder* in 1889; *The Voice of Missions* in 1892; and *The Voice of the People* in 1901. He also wrote a number of books, including *The Genius and the Theory of the Methodist Polity* in 1885, and *The Black Man's Doom* in 1896, a criticism of Supreme Court civil rights decisions.

Turner's life exemplified the dilemmas of blacks in 19th- century America. In slave society he was neither slave nor white. Eager to take advantage of his freedom, he could not get a formal education. A politician by nature, he had to be satisfied most of his life with churchmanship. Proclaiming that Africa was the true home of blacks, he could neither persuade many to emigrate nor extract himself from the web of American life. Within his church he gave vigorous leadership, especially during the years just after the Civil War, but he could not convert educated blacks to black nationalism.

Despite these handicaps Turner rose to prominence and power by sheer force of personality. He was a gifted orator and a an energetic worker. His leadership was based on a blunt, astringent style that thrived on controversy. His harsh criticism of American racism won him the admiration of many blacks who were afraid to speak their minds. Most of his following was among the unlettered rural blacks of the South, attracted by his too-simple African emigration scheme and his blistering verbal assaults on middle-class blacks who disagreed with him. But with a politician's instinct for survival, he stayed on good terms with many leading southern whites. Turner's active life spanned the years of emancipation, Reconstruction and the long decade of race relations that followed.

Henry Turner was married four times: Eliza Ann Peacher on August 31, 1856; Martha DeWitt in August 1893; Harriet A. Wayman on August 16, 1900; and Laura Pearle Lemon on December 3, 1907. He died on May 8, 1915.

V

VANDERHORST, ARNOLDUS, (1748-1815) — tenth state governor (Federalist) of South Carolina, 1794-1796.

He was born in Christ Church Parish, South Carolina, the son of Arnoldus and Elizabeth Vanderhorst.

Vanderhorst served in the American Revolution under Francis Marion, attaining the rank of colonel. In 1782, he was elected a senator in the famous Jacksonborough Legislature and, in 1783, was elected a member of the Privy Council of the State. He was Intendent of Charleston in 1785, and again in 1791. In the latter year, he made the address of welcome to President Washington upon his visit to the city.

In 1792, Vanderhorst was elected governor of South Carolina. During his administration, laws were passed abolishing the old British statute, the right of primogeniture, and an equal distribution was granted of the property of intestates. South Carolina citizens were also preoccupied with the controversy surrounding the treaty between Great Britain and the United States, negotiated by John Jay in 1794. The opposition had developed in part because the Jay Treaty made no satisfactory provision for shipment of cotton to England, which was potentially a severe blow to the State's economy.

Many people mistrusted the Federalist Party as a result of the controversy, and Vanderhorst, himself a Federalist, became part of the growing desire by the people for a change in leadership. He was defeated for re-election by Charles Pinckey, a Republican- Democrat, in the 1796 gubernatorial election .

Vanderhorst was married in 1771 to Elizabeth Raver. He died in Charleston in January 1815.

VESEY, DENMARK, (1767?-1822) — a freedman slave leader. First named Telemaque Vesey, little is known about his birthplace and date. He was probably born on the island of St. Thomas in the West Indies around 1767, and it is said he was epileptic. In 1781 he came to be owned by Captain John Vesey, a Bermuda slave trader. They traveled to Charleston, South Carolina in 1783. During the 1790s Captain Vesey helped French colonials escape the revolution in Haiti, and through that experience Vesey learned about the power of revolution, and the possibilities in freedom.

In 1800 Vesey won $1,500 in a street lottery, and he bought his freedom for $600. He used the rest of the money to start a carpentry business, which was very successful. A self-taught reader Vesey began preaching, encouraging his black audiences to rebel against slavery, which he felt was against the laws of the Bible. Vesey had several wives and children who were still slaves, and many say he was disturbed by the insults and inferior treatment of blacks.

In the summer of 1822 a rebellion of house servants and artisans in Charleston was planned. It was originally set for July 14, but because of leaks to whites it was moved up to June 16. The uprising was eventually foiled before it could take place, and ten slaves were arrested. All of them claimed that Vesey was their leader. Vesey insisted that he played no part in the plan, saying that as a freedman he had nothing to gain by such action. He said others were accusing him because they were jealous of his freedom. Vesey defended himself in court, but he was unable to convince the witnesses to change their stories. Vesey and five others were hung July 2, 1822, an event which created an even greater hysteria and led to the execution of 30 more blacks, while others were deported. As a result of the incident South Carolina and several other states tightened restrictions on slave and freedmen rights.

W

WADDEL, MOSES, (1770-1840) — educator whose school trained some of the greatest leaders in the early South.

The son of Irish immigrants, Waddel was born July 29, 1770 in Rowan County (now Iredell County), North Carolina. He attended neighborhood schools, and began teaching local youths at age 14. After his family moved to Greene Country, Georgia in 1788 Waddel opened his own school, and then abandoned it to attend Hampton- Sydney College. He graduated in 1791, and began studying theology with a Virginia clergyman. He received his license to preach in the Presbyterian church in 1792 and preached for a short time in Charleston, South Carolina. He left to open a school near Appling, Georgia, known as the Carmel Academy, and he also preached in the Abbeville District, South Carolina, about 50 miles away. It was there that he met and married his first wife, Catherine, who died less than a year after their marriage. In 1800 he married Elizabeth Woodson Pleasants of Halifax County, Virginia. They moved to Vienna, South Carolina and opened another school.

In 1804 they moved to Willington where Waddel opened his most famous school. What started as a two-room log schoolhouse grew into four recitation rooms and a chapel, with log and brick huts surrounding the main building for study areas. Almost four thousand students passed through the school building while Waddel taught there, including many future clergymen, senators, governors, congressmen, judges, and lawyers. Some of the more distinguished students included John C. Calhoun, William H. Crawford, Hugh S. Legare, George McDuffie, A.B. Longstreet, and James L. Petigru. Many of Waddel's students felt that his discipline was severe and almost cruel, but he had the gift of truly inspiring his students to learn.

In 1818 Waddel published the book *Memoirs of the Life of Miss Caroline Elizabeth Smelt*, which was printed in several editions. In 1819 Waddel left his Willington school to become president of Franklin College (later the

University of Georgia). He is often given credit for increasing the student population there and stimulating religious life. He retired in 1829 and died of a stroke July 21, 1840.

WALLACE, ALEXANDER STUART, (1810-1893) — a U.S. Representative from South Carolina; born near York, S.C., December 30, 1810; received a limited schooling; engaged in planting in his native county; member of the State house of representatives, 1852-1855, 1858-1859 and 1865-1866; successfully contested as a Republican the election of William D. Simpson to the Forty-first Congress; reelected to the Forty-second, Forty third, and Forty-fourth Congresses and served from May 27, 1870, to March 3, 1877; chairman, Committee on Revolutionary Claims (Forty-second Congress); unsuccessful candidate for reelection in 1876 to the Forty-fifth Congress; engaged in agricultural pursuits until his death near York, S.C., June 27, 1893; interment in Rose Hill Cemetery, York, S.C.

WALLACE, DANIEL, (1833-1859) — a U.S. Representative from South Carolina; born near Laurens, S.C., May 9, 1801; received a limited schooling; moved to Union County in 1833; major general of State militia; studied law; was admitted to the bar and practiced in Union and Jonesville, Union County, S.C.; also engaged in agricultural pursuits; member of the State house of representatives 1846-1847; elected as a Democrat to the Thirtieth Congress to fill the vacancy caused by the death of James A. Black; reelected to the Thirty-first and Thirtysecond Congresses and served from June 12, 1848, to March 3, 1853; resumed agricultural pursuits; died in Jonesville, S.C., May 13, 1859; interment in Old Presbyterian Cemetery, Union, S.C.

WATSON, ALBERT WILLIAM, (1922-   ) — a U.S. Representative from South Carolina; born in Sumter, S.C., August 30, 1922; attended the public schools of Columbia and North Greenville Junior College; graduated from the University of South Carolina School of Law at Columbia in 1950; commenced practice in Columbia, S.C., in 1951;

during the Second World War served in the United States Army Air Corps as a weather specialist (sergeant) in the Mediterranean Theater of Operations, 1942-1946; served in the State general assembly, 1955-1958 and 1961-1962; national chairman, Voice of Democracy Program, United States Junior Chamber of Commerce, in 1957; elected as a Democrat to the Eighty-eighth and Eighty-ninth Congresses and served from March 4, 1963, until he resigned from the Eighty-ninth Congress, February 1, 1965, after being stripped of seniority by House Democratic Caucus because of his support of the Republican presidential candidate; reelected as a Republican in a special election, June 15, 1965, to fill the vacancy caused by his own resignation; reelected to the Ninetieth and Ninety-first Con gresses and served from June 15, 1965, to January 3, 1971; was not a candidate for reelection in 1970 to the Ninetysecond Congress, but was an unsuccessful candidate for Governor of South Carolina in 1970; served as an administrative law judge, Social Security Administration; is a resident of Columbia, S.C.

WATSON, JOHN BROADUS, (1878-1958) — was the founder of the behaviorist school of psychology.

Born on January 9, 1878 in Greenville, South Carolina, the son of Pickens Butler and Emma K. (Roe) Watson, John Watson received his M.A. from Furman University in Greenville in 1900 and his Ph.D. from the University of Chicago in 1903. He remained at the university where he was an assistant in experimental psychology from 1903 until 1904 and an instructor from 1904 until 1908. This was a period of intensive study and his superiors considered him "both brilliant and tenacious." Watson received an LL.D. degree from Furman University in 1919.

In 1908, Watson became a professor of experimental and comparative psychology at The Johns Hopkins University and remained there for 12 years. His principle contribution was founding the behaviorist school of psychology, whose principles were first formally stated in his paper of 1913, "Psychology as the Behaviorist Views It." Coming into direct opposition to the methods of introspective psychology, which had dominated the field, he based his "psychology of behavior" on extensive experiments at Johns Hopkins, many on animals, using the devices of Edward Lee Thorndike; and he concluded that personality and habits were results of training or conditioning rather than of inborn constitution. Contending that human beings could be trained to do or be anything, he denied the influence of instinct and heredity and stressed the effects of learning and environment.

Watson's books included: *Animal Education*, 1903; *Behavior: An Introduction to Comparative Psychology*, 1914; *Psychology from the Standpoint of a Behaviorist*, 1919; *Behaviorism*, 1925; and *Psychological Care of Infant and Child*, 1928.

In 1920, his divorce from his wife and almost immediate remarriage caused a scandal that forced Watson to resign from his post at Johns Hopkins. He entered the advertising business and became vice president at the J. Walter Thompson Company in New York in 1924. He left that company a few year later to take over as vice president of William Esty & Company. Watson retired in 1945.

Throughout his years in advertising, he continued his scientific work on a part-time basis. In 1923, the Laura Spelam Rockefeller Memorial Fund financed a study of human behavior with Watson as consultant and Mary Cover Jones as director. The results of the study, published as the paper "The Elimination of Children's Fears", discovered that fear responses could be eliminated through a number of outlets. During the next decade, Watson wrote for popular and scientific periodicals on the subject. Psychologists have credited him with starting the movement of observing infant behavior.

John Broadus Watson was married twice. He married Mary Ickes on October 1, 1904. That marriage ended in divorce. He remarried Rosalie Rayner on December 31, 1920. He had four children. He died in New York City on September 25, 1958.

WEST, JOHN CARL, (1922-   ) — Eighty-fifth state governor (D) of South Carolina, 1971-1975.

Born in Camden, South Carolina on August 27, 1922, the son of Sheldon and Mattie (Ratterree) West. He attended The Citadel where he received his A.B. degree in

1942, and the University of South Carolina where he graduated magna cum laude with an LL.B. degree in 1948. He was admitted to the South Carolina Bar in the latter year. During World War II, he served in the U.S. Army, attaining the rank of major. He married Lois Rhome in 1942. They have three children.

From 1946 to 1948, West worked as a part-time instructor of political science at the University of South Carolina. He also began a law practice in Camden, later forming the firm of West, Holland and Furman, with which he remained from 1948 to 1970. In addition, he served on the South Carolina Highway Commission from 1948 to 1952, and in the South Carolina Senate from 1954 to 1966. In 1966, he became Lieutenant Governor. He served until 1970 when he was elected Governor of South Carolina, running on the Democratic ticket. During his administration, some of the racial unrest of the previous years began to diminish. At the University of South Carolina, a black was elected student president for the first time. The Methodist Church, which had segregated congregations, united the black and white services. Other developments included prohibition of the sale of rare and endangered animal species and the State ratification of the Twenty-sixth amendment to the U.S. Constitution. At the end of his term, in 1975, West returned to practice law with the firm of West, Cooper, Bowen and Quinn.

WESTMORELAND, WILLIAM C(HILDS), (1914-) — United States Army officer, was born in Spartanburg County, South Carolina on March 26, 1914. He attended the United States Military Academy at West Point, earning a B.S. degree in 1936, and then continued his studies at Harvard University, taking the Advanced Management Program.

After the start of World War II, Westmoreland served in North Africa and Sicily as commanding officer of the Thirty-fourth Field Artillery Battalion. As part of the D-Day offensive, he landed with the Ninth Infantry Division on Utah Beach in France, and was later named chief of staff of the division. Between 1947 and 1950, Westmoreland served as chief of staff of the Eighty-second Airborne Division, and in the latter year, became an instructor at Command and General Staff College at Fort Leavenworth, Kansas. He served in the same capacity at Army War College, Fort Leavenworth during 1951-52.

During 1952-53, Westmoreland was commander of the 187th Airborne Regimental Combat Team in Korea. From 1955 to 1958, he served as secretary of Army General Staff in Washington, D.C., with his rank being elevated to major general in 1956. Between 1958 and 1960 he was commander of the 101st Airborne Division known as the "Screaming Eagles."

Between 1960 and 1963, Westmoreland was superintendent at West Point. In 1964, after attaining the rank of general, he was assigned as commander of the U.S. Military Assistance Command in Vietnam, where he served until 1968. From 1968 to 1972, Westmoreland was Chief of Staff of the United States Army, and in the latter year he retired from the service.

A highly decorated officer, Westmoreland received such awards as: Legion of Merit with two Oak Leaf Clusters; Bronze Star with Oak Leaf Cluster; and Air Medal with nine Oak Leaf Clusters, along with numerous awards from several different countries. He also received several civilian honors including being named as *Time's* "Man of the Year" in 1965.

Westmoreland experienced some intense controversy in the Vietnam War years after the My Lai incident, during which American soldiers brutalized and killed a number of Vietnamese civilians. The men of Charlie Company, the perpetrators of the atrocities, were only one group out of almost a thousand companies technically under the command of Westmoreland. Although Lieutenant William Calley was court-martialed, many observers were not satisfied and wanted Westmoreland to shoulder the blame. He refused, however, later writing: "Many Americans did not understand that under the Law of the Land (the Uniform Code of Military Justice), the Chief of Staff had no jurisdiction over the Army's court-martial system. That power was vested in the Secretary of the Army, a civilian appointed by the President."

Having kept a journal during those years, he turned a large portion of it into the book *A Soldier Reports,* published in 1976. Critic Norman Hannah, writing in *National Review*, described it as "an account of a generation of staggering military change as reflected in the life and experiences of one of the leading professionals of the period...a soldier who is competent, devoted, straightforward, possessed of patience, and tolerance for the view of others, a man who modestly did his best for his country."

Westmoreland is married to Katherine Stevens Van Deusen and the couple have three children.

WHALEY, RICHARD SMITH, (1874-1951) — a U.S. Representative from South Carolina; born in Charleston, S.C., July 15, 1874; attended the Episcopal High School, Alexandria, Va., and was graduated from the law department of the University of Virginia at Charlottesville in 1897; was admitted to the bar in 1897 and commenced practice in Charleston, S.C.; member of the State house of representatives 1901-1910, 1913; served as speaker 1907-1910 and as speaker pro tempore in 1913; presiding officer of the Democratic State convention in 1910 and of the Democratic city convention in 1911; delegate to the Democratic National Conventions in 1912 and 1920; elected as a Democrat to the Sixty- third Congress to fill the vacancy caused by the death of George S. Legare; reelected to the Sixty-fourth, Sixty-fifth, and Sixty- sixth Congresses and served from April 29, 1913, to March 3, 1921; was not a candidate for renomination in 1920; resumed the practice of law; appointed commissioner of the United States Court of Claims in 1925; appointed judge of the Court of Claims by President Hoover in 1930, and was designated chief justice in 1939; retired as chief justice in 1947; died in Charleston, S.C., November 8, 1951; interment in Magnolia Cemetery.

WHITE, JOSH, (1915-1969) — singer, was born Joshua Daniel White on February 11, 1915 in Greenville, South Carolina. As a young boy he had a job traveling with blind musicians, helping them in their daily needs such as getting them from one place to another, for which he was paid $4 a week. It was then that he began to sing himself, eventually learning the guitar to accompany the spirituals being performed.

Only eleven when he made his first recording, he became known as the "Singing Christian." At about the age of eighteen he recorded a group of spirituals within a two-day period for Columbia Recording Corporation, a job which netted him $100. In addition, White sang with the group, the Southernaires, on their radio show.

White's guitar playing was cut short after a freak accident in which he slashed his right hand on a broken milk bottle. His hand having become paralyzed, he had to support his young family in some other way, and worked as an elevator operator for a time. He later secured a small role as a character named Blind Lemon in the Broadway stage production of *John Henry*, which starred Paul Robeson. Unfortunately the show only ran for seven performances; however, not long after, White recorded two albums, *Chain Gang* and *Southern Exposure*. White continued appearing as a guest on various radio programs, and eventually got his own 15-minute show on WNEW in 1944.

By 1943, White's hand was healed and he began appearing at various nightclubs in New York, such as Cafe Society Downtown, and was a hit with both the patrons and the critics, singing such songs as "Evil-hearted Man," "Strange Fruit," "I Am Going to Move on the Outskirts of Town," and "The Girl With the Delicate Air." A critic for the New York *Herald Tribune* had high praise for the singer, writing: "A terrific showstopper, he had to do about fifteen numbers at the supper show on the night of our visit. Even a broken string on his guitar didn't help him. He repaired the damage on the floor and went on with his work. Josh White is one of the great nightclub acts."

Along with the folk ballads he was known for, White liked to perform what he called "social conscience" ballads, which dealt with the rough times blacks were forced to live because of poor housing, lynching, and Jim Crowism. Very much a black activist at a time when it was almost dangerous to be one, White refused to continue singing such Negro spirituals as "Swing Low Sweet Chariot," among others, because of their connection to "the Negroes' years of slavery and oppression." Describing himself as a "sensitive and proud member of his race,"

White, who had appeared in two movies that he was not proud of, turned down several other movie offers from Hollywood due to the insulting way blacks were portrayed on the screen.

White was invited to play and sing at the White House on three occasions, one of which included the 1940 Presidential inauguration for President Franklin D. Roosevelt, and he also gave several concerts at the Library of Congress. In addition, the singer made a number of successful tours throughout Europe during the 1950's.

White was married to Carol Carr and the couple had four children. He died on September 5, 1969.

WHITTEMORE, BENJAMIN FRANKLIN, (1824-1894) — a U.S. Representative from South Carolina; born in Malden, Middlesex County, Mass., May 18, 1824; attended the public schools of Worcester, and received an academic education at Amherst; engaged in mercantile pursuits until 1859; studied theology and became a minister in the Methodist Episcopal Church of the New England Conference in 1859; during the Civil War served as chaplain of the Fifty-third Regiment, Massachusetts Volunteers, and later with the Thirtieth Regiment, Veteran Volunteers; after the war settled in Darlington, S.C.; delegate to the State constitutional convention in 1867; elected president of the Republican State executive board in 1867; founded the New Era in Darlington; member of the State senate in 1868; delegate to the Republican National Convention in 1868; upon the readmission of South Carolina to representation was elected as a Republican to the Forti eth and Forty-first Congresses and served from July 18, 1868, to February 24, 1870, when he resigned, pending the investigation of his conduct in connection with certain appointments to the United States Military and Naval Academies; censured by the House of Representatives on February 24, 1870, following his resignation; presented credentials of a second election to the same Congress on June 18, 1870, but the House declined to allow him to take his seat; again a member of the State senate in 1877; resigned from the State senate and returned to Massachusetts, settling in Woburn; became a publisher; died in Montvale, Mass., on January 25, 1894; interment in the Salem Street Cemetery, Woburn, Mass.

WILLIAMS, DAVID R., (1776-1830) — twentieth state governor (D-R) of South Carolina, 1814-1816. He was born in Robbin's Neck, South Carolina, the son of Anne and David Williams.

Williams received his early education at Wrentham, Massachusetts, and attended Rhode Island College in 1795. After studying law and being admitted to the bar in Providence, he returned to South Carolina in 1797 and was admitted to the State Bar.

In 1805, Williams was elected to Congress, and served until 1809. After a subsequent election in 1811, he held his seat until 1813. At the onset of the War of 1812, he was appointed a brigadier-general and served until 1814. As chairman of the Committee on Military Affairs, he was responsible for the seacoast, especially Beaufort and Port Royal.

In 1814, Williams was elected governor of South Carolina. A boon in cotton mills began while he was in office. During the war, the price of cotton had risen dramatically because of wartime commercial restrictions, and a number of New Englanders who migrated to South Carolina began developing an extensive system of mills.

After his term, Williams resumed his law practice and was, for several years, the assistant editor of the Charleston *Courier*. He also established cotton, shoe, and hat factories near Sandy Hill, South Carolina, and constructed the first cotton mill in the State.

Williams was married in 1796 to Sarah Power. The couple had two sons. In 1809, he married a second time, to Elizabeth Witherspoon. He died at Lynch's Creek, South Carolina in 1830, and was buried on his plantation near Society Hill, Darlington County.

WILLIAMS, RANSOME JUDSON, (1892-   ) — Seventy-eighth state governor (D) of South Carolina, 1945-1947.

Born in Cope, South Carolina on January 4, 1892, the son of Theophilus and Ida (Williams) Williams. He attended the Medical College of South Carolina. In 1916, he married Virginia Allen. They had two children.

Williams was president of the Delta Drug Company of Myrtle Beach, South Carolina, and later, part owner of a drug store in Mullens. He also worked as a manager for the Jefferson Standard Life Insurance Company in Florence. He began his political career with his election as Mayor of Mullens. From there he went on to become a member of the South Carolina House of Representatives. He was elected Lieutenant Governor and served from 1943 to 1945. In January of the latter year, when Governor Johnston resigned to take a seat in the U.S. Senate, Williams succeeded to the governorship. During his administration, the Forest Fire Protection Act was passed, as was legislation to control the standard weights of containers, to continue the poll tax, and to lower the voting age for registered Democrats. Other developments included establishment of a retirement system for state, county, and city employees, and the formation of a Department of Research, Planning and Development. Williams left office in 1947. He was a trustee of Coker College in Hartsville; chairman of the Board of Trustees of the Medical College of South Carolina; trustee of the University of South Carolina, Columbia; and trustee of the Citadel. He died in January 1970.

WILSON, JOHN LYDE, (1784-1849) — twenty-fourth state governor (D-R) of South Carolina, 1822-1824.

He was born in Marlborough District, South Carolina, son of Mary Lyde and John Wilson.

Wilson was educated at a local academy, studied law, and was admitted to the South Carolina Bar in 1807. He was elected to the State House of Representatives in 1806, and served three terms, 1806-1808, 1812-1814, and 1816-1818. He continued in public office as a member of the South Carolina Senate from 1818- 1822, and was president of that body in 1822.

Wilson was elected governor of South Carolina in 1822. During his term, he strongly rejected the right of the United States Congress to make internal improvements in individual states. This opposition illustrated a growing disillusionment by South Carolina's leaders with nationalist policies, and their growing adherence to the theory of states' rights. Other issues during his tenure included the barring of free blacks from entering the State, and the opening of the Columbia Canal. After his term ended, Wilson returned to the State Senate. He served from 1826-1830, and was a member of the Nullification Convention of 1832-1833. Wilson was married in 1809 to Charlotte Alston. He married a second time, to Rebecca Eden, in 1825. He died in Charleston in February 1849.

WILSON, JOHN, (1773-1828) — a U.S. Representative from South Carolina; born at Wilson's Ferry (now Pelzer), Anderson County, S.C., August 11, 1773; attended the common schools; engaged in agricultural pursuits in Anderson County, near Golden Grove, S.C.; also operated a public ferry across the Saluda River at what is now known as Pelzer; member, State house of representatives, 1812-1817; elected to the Seventeenth, Eighteenth, and Nineteenth Congresses (March 4, 1821-March 3, 1827); unsuccessful candidate for reelection in 1826 to the Twentieth Congress; died at his home near Golden Grove, in Anderson County, S.C., August 13, 1828; interment in the family cemetery on his plantation, which is now a part of the industrial city of Pelzer, S.C.

WILSON, STANYARNE, (1860-1928) — a U.S. Representative from South Carolina; born in Yorkville (now York), S.C., January 10, 1860; attended Kings Mountain Military School and Washington and Lee University, Lexington, Va.; studied law; was admitted to the bar by an act of the legislature in 1880, then being a minor; settled in Spartanburg, Spartanburg County, S.C., in 1881; practiced law and was also interested in cotton manufactures, gold mining, iron works, and agriculture; member of the State house of representatives 1884-1886 and 1890-1892; served in the State senate 1892-1895; member of the State constitutional convention in 1895; elected as a Democrat to the Fifty-fourth, Fifty-fifth, and Fifty-sixth Congresses (March 4, 1895-March 3, 1901); continued the practice of law in Spartanburg, S.C., and later in Richmond, Va., where he moved in 1913; returned to Spartanburg, S.C., in

January 1928, and died there February 14, 1928; interment in Church of the Advent Cemetery.

WILSON, WOODROW, (1856-1924) — was the twenty-eighth president of the United States.

Born on December 28, 1856 in Staunton, Virginia, he was raised primarily in Georgia and the Carolinas. After a year at Davidson College in North Carolina, he went to the College of New Jersey (now Princeton) and graduated in 1879. He studied law briefly at the University of Virgina and then entered into a short and unsuccessful law practice in Atlanta. In 1883, he began graduate studies at The Johns Hopkins University and received a Ph. D. three years later.

For the next decade, Wilson held a number of teaching positions at prominent universities. From 1885 until 1888, he taught history and political economy at Bryn Mawr College. He was on the faculty of Wesleyan University in Connecticut for the following two years, then Wilson returned to Princeton in 1890 to become a professor of juris prudence and political economy.

In 1902, Wilson was elected president of the Princeton University. During his eight years in this office he attempted to revolutionize the atmosphere of Princeton and to create a community of scholars. His two avenues of approach — the preceptorial system and the quadrangle plan — were designed to encourage the growth of close personal contacts between students and teachers and to establish a collection of small communities much like those at Cambridge and Oxford. These strongly democratic ideas roused heated opposition at Princeton, which had long been a club-dominated and class-conscious campus. However, Wilson's ideas were later adopted at many major universities.

By 1910, Wilson had a strong national following and easily won the Democratic nomination for governor of New Jersey as well as the election. He immediately acted upon his campaign promises and actively pushed through the legislature a series of reform measures including a direct primary law and the creation of a public utilities commission.

Wilson was the Democratic presidential candidate in 1912. The Taft-Roosevelt split in the Republican party enabled him to gain the largest electoral college victory up to that time, although he did not win a majority of the popular vote. On the crest of progressive enthusiasm aroused by his "New Freedom" campaign, Wilson began his administration by carrying through a vigorous program of reform legislation, notably the Underwood Tariff in 1913 that, in addition to lowering rates substantially, also included an income tax. Other reforms included the Federal Reserve Act, 1913; the establishment of the Federal Trade Commission, 1914; and the Clayton Antitrust Act, 1914, which besides attacking monopoly, recognized the legality of labor unions and of their use of strikes and boycotts. Wilson worked closely with Congress and, in April of 1913, he made the first presidential address to a joint session of Congress in more than a century.

Wilson faced a number of foreign affair difficulties including the revolution and civil war in Mexico in 1914. By 1915, world attention centered on the European war and Wilson was embroiled in the problems of maintaining and defending the United States' neutrality. When the loss of U.S. lives and property began, particularly after the sinking of the *Lusitania* in May 1915, Wilson protested vigorously. Early in 1916 a halt to such acts was secured and this victory helped Wilson win reelection that year, mainly because he kept the U.S. out of the war.

In 1917, Germany, who had agreed to cease their use of submarine warfare, resumed submarine operations and fragile relations with Germany were broken. On April 2, after several more U.S. ships were lost, Wilson requested a declaration of war against Germany from Congress. He received it four days later.

Throughout World War I, Wilson's role was primarily that of a moral leader and he enjoyed overwhelming public support. His major contribution was his formulation of the Fourteen Points announced in a speech in January of 1918. Among these points were the proposals for freedom of the seas, arms reductions, open diplomacy, trade liberalization, and a general association of nations. Wilson continued to advocate his peace program

throughout 1918. In October of that year, Germany suddenly accepted it as a basis for negotiations. The Allies
had paid little attention to it, but faced with pressure from
Washington and the prospect of shortening the war, they
also accepted it. An armistice was signed on November
11, 1918.

In December, Wilson sailed for the Versailles Peace
Conference. Earlier secret agreements between the Allies
came to light and the idealism of the Fourteen Points
paled before nationalistic fervor. Wilson secured agreement to the League of Nations Covenant, but was forced
to concede on territorial and arms reduction matters. In
July, he returned to the United States with the treaty of
Versailles, which included the League covenant, and set
off on a cross-country speaking tour to promote the treaty.
However, in September he suffered a collapse and was
brought back to the White House where his condition wor-
sened. The Senate, under the leadership of Henry Cabot
Lodge, approved a number of reservations to be added to
the treaty before ratification. Wilson refused to negotiate
the reservations and called on his supporters to defeat the
ratification. On November 19, 1919 and March 19, 1920
the treaty was voted down by the Senate. Wilson's hope of
making the 1920 presidential election a "solemn referen-
dum" on the treaty failed to materialize because he was
too ill to take part in the campaign.

In December, he was awarded the 1919 Nobel Peace
Prize. Following the inauguration of Warren G. Harding,
Wilson retired to a small house in Washington, D.C.,
where he remained largely inactive and out of public life
until his death on February 3, 1924. Wilson was elected to
the Hall of Fame in 1950.

WINN, RICHARD, (1750-1818) — a U.S. Representative
from South Carolina; born in Fauquier County, Va., in
1750; attended the common schools; moved to Georgia
and then to Fairfield County in South Carolina in 1768;
served as a clerk in a countinghouse; engaged in cotton
buying and other mercantile pursuits, and was a land surveyor; entered the Revolutionary Army as a lieutenant and
attained the rank of colonel of State militia;, after the war
was promoted to the rank of major general of militia;

member, State assembly, 1779-1786; appointed superintendent of Indian affairs for the Creek Nation in
1788; elected to the Third Congress and reelected as a
Republican to the Fourth Congress (March 4, 1793- March
3, 1797); elected to the Seventh Congress to fill the
vacancy caused by the resignation of Thomas Sumter;
reelected to the Eighth and to the four succeeding Congresses and served from January 24, 1803, to March 3,
1813; moved to Tennessee in 1813; became a planter, and
continued in the mercantile business until his death on his
plantation at Duck River, Maury County, Tenn., December
19, 1818; interment at Winnsboro, Fairfield County, S.C.

WITHERSPOON, ROBERT, (1767-1837) — great-great-
grandfather of Robert Witherspoon Hemphill), a U.S.
Representative from South Carolina; born near Kingstree,
Williamsburg County, S.C., January 29, 1767; attended
local schools; elected State treasurer in 1800 and served
one term; was a member of the State house of representatives, 1792-1794, 1802- 1804, 1806-1808, 1816-1817;
elected as a Republican to the Eleventh Congress (March
4, 1809-March 3, 1811); declined to be a candidate for
reelection; had large planting interests in Sumter County,
S.C.; opposed the nullification act in 1832; died near
Mayesville, Sumter County, S.C., October 11, 1837; interment in the Salem Brick Church Cemetery.

WOFFORD, THOMAS ALBERT, (1908-1978) — a U.S.
Senator from South Carolina; born in Madden Station,
Laurens County, S.C., September 27, 1908; attended the
public schools; graduated from the University of South
Carolina at Columbia 1928, and from Harvard University
Law School 1931; was admitted to the bar in 1931 and
commenced the practice of law in Greenville, S.C.; assistant solicitor of thirteenth judicial circuit 1935-1936; assistant United States district attorney 1937-1944; member,
board of trustees, Winthrop College 1944- 1956; appointed
as a Democrat, April 5, 1956, to the United States Senate
to fill the vacancy caused by the resignation of Strom
Thurmond and served from April 5, 1956, to November 6,
1956; was not a candidate for election to fill the vacancy;
engaged in the practice of law; member, State senate

1966-1972; changed party affiliation to Republican; resided in Greenville, S.C., where he died February 25, 1978; interment in Woodlawn Memorial Park.

WOODWARD, JOSEPH ADDISON, (1806-1885) — (son of William Woodward), a U.S. Representative from South Carolina; born in Winnsboro, Fairfield County, S.C., on April 11, 1806; received an academic training and was graduated from the University of South Carolina at Columbia; studied law; was admitted to the bar and practiced; member of the State house of representatives, 1834-1835, 1840-1841; elected as a Democrat to the Twenty-eighth and to the four succeeding Congresses (March 4, 1843-March 3, 1853); declined to be a candidate for reelection in 1852 to the Thirty- third Congress; moved to Alabama and resumed the practice of his profession; died in Talladega, Talladega County, Ala., on August 3, 1885; interment in Oak Hill Cemetery.

Y

YARBOROUGH, CALE, (1939-) — popular stock race car driver, known as the master of the 2.5 mile track.

Born March 23, 1939 in Timmonsville, South Carolina, Yarborough first became interested in racing when he built his first Soap Box race car with his father. Although he didn't do very well, Yarborough fell hard and fast for racing. That Labor Day he and his father listened to the radio broadcast of the first Southern 500, which in Yarborough's opinion was the "Indianapolis 500, World Series and the Kentucky Derby all rolled into one." At age eleven Yarborough's father was killed in an airplane accident, which was a great loss to the young boy. He tried to take over as "man of the house" but his mother very competently ran the family's farm, cotton gin and general store.

Yarborough continued to race soapbox, then at age 15 he and some friends rebuilt a 1935 Ford. The car won him a first place on a dirt track in Sumter, South Carolina, and although he didn't know it at the time, it was the beginning of his career. In high school Yarborough excelled in athletics making the all-state team as a fullback and winning the South Carolina Golden Gloves welterweight boxing championship twice. As a youth he was also known for more daring exploits, such as wrestling alligators and catching poisonous snakes. After graduation he was offered several football scholarships and an opportunity to tryout for the Washington Redskins, but he decided to try qualifying for the NASCAR circuit.

Yarborough lied about his age to get his NASCAR license, and in his first race at Darlington, September 2, 1957 he won $100 prize money. Yet the experience taught him that he was not ready to compete with his idols, so he turned to semi-pro football to make his living, and he also helped organize a flying circus. The circus featured daredevil car-rolling and ramp-leaping, but a near-fatal accident convinced Yarborough the circus wasn't for him. He traveled with the rodeo for awhile, then went back to racing, mostly on dirt tracks. He started driving annually in the Grand National, and in five years he earned a total of $535.

In 1961 Yarborough met Betty Jo Thigpen, and he decided to settle down. The couple tried turkey farming, but in two years the couple had lost $30,000, and Yarborough returned to racing. He worked as a handyman for Holman-Moody Racing, a top NASCAR racing shop. For two years he paid his dues sweeping floors and driving a fork-lift. He tried to drive in NASCAR races as often as he could, persuading owners to let him drive their cars. In 1963 he drove in 18 Grand National races, finishing in the top five three times. The next year he raced in 24 Grand Nationals, ending with two top-five finishes. Finally in 1965 Holman-Moody let Yarborough drive an old car, and he was determined that this be the end of his "long apprenticeship." He drove in all 54 races on the circuit that year and won his first Nascar race in Valdosta, Georgia. Yet he nearly lost everything at the Southern 500 that year, when his car rolled during the first turn. He accidentally nudged another car while trying to pass, and his car flew above the three-story bank on the curve. In his autobiography Yarborough remembers the accidents clearly, stating that he tried to brake and steer in mid-air, actions which of course were useless. Fortunately he was unhurt.

In 1966 Ford boycotted the first part of the NASCAR season, and because he drove a Ford Yarborough had to sit out much of the season too. He came back with a vengeance though, winning the Atlanta 500 on April 3, 1967. Later that year he won the Firecracker 500, at Daytona Beach Florida. The year 1968 was one of Yarborough's best, winning the Daytona 500 by one second. He also shattered records while winning the Firecracker 400, clocking an average speed of 167.247 miles per hour. This was not only the best speed recorded on that track, but it was also faster than the record speeds clocked at the Daytona 500 and the Indianapolis 500.

The race that was most important to him that year, however, was the Southern 500. Plan were in the works to re-pave the legendary track, which had been known to throw racecars into flips end-over-end. It was called "the track nobody could tame," and the purse for a win there was $102,000. While Yarborough claims not to have tamed it, he says he "sure got its attention," leading the race for 88 laps. David "The Fox" Pearson posed serious competition, closing in for a near-win, but Yarborough pulled it off, bringing his winning for the year up to $126,066, the highest on NASCAR's Grand National Circuit for big-bore stock cars.

In 1969 Yarborough suffered his first serious accident, hitting an iron wall at 200 miles an hour. He had numerous injuries, including a fractured bone in his back. After his recovery Ford pulled out of NASCAR, so Yarborough joined an Indy car team. As the team's second driver, however, he found the circuit disappointing. In four Indy 500s he finished only once, coming in tenth place.

In 1973 Yarborough teamed with owner Junior Johnson, who was looking for a replacement for Bobby Allison. Johnson and Yarborough dominated NASCAR for the next seven years, winning 49 Grand Nationals, three consecutive Winston Cup championships and $3 million in earnings. 1977 may have been their best year, when Yarborough won his second Winston Cup Championship, raced in all 30 of the Winston Cup Series (winning nine), and pursing a record $431,576 in one season. That year the other drivers voted him the winner of the Olsonite Driver of the Year award, which he also bcame close to winning in 1974 and 1976. "I don't know how the other guys feel about the award," Yarborough said at the time. "To me it's the best single award a driver can receive. It means he's been judged the best among driver of my kind from any organization."

In 1978 Yarborough broke another record, being the first driver to win three straight national stock car championships. Finally in 1980 he decided to slow down a little and spend more time with his family. He left Junior Johnson and signed with Georgia businessman M.C. Anderson, who allowed him to race a reduced season. Yarborough won five races in 1981 and 1982, but Anderson began pressuring him to go back to a thirty-race schedule. Yarborough left Anderson in November 1982 and began racing for industrialist Harry Rainer and the Hardee's food system.

In his first year with the new team Yarborough won his third Daytona 500. He broke the world record during the first qualifying lap, clocking in at 200.503. Near-tragedy struck during the second lap, when his car spun out of control and was totaled. Yarborough was unhurt, but according to the rules his back-up car was not allowed to take the pole position. He came back though, holding second place for the last ten and one-half laps, then pulling out to take the lead. The nexy year, 1984, Yarborough won his forth Daytona 500, the same way he had won it the year before, pulling out from second place. He was the second driver ever to win the Daytona 500 twice in a row, and it was the 79th win of his career, placing him in second for the most wins of any NASCAR driver.

Yarborough won two other races in 1984, then 1985 started bad with mechanical problems. He placed top-five only three times in his first eleven races, but by the end of the season he had won at the Talledega 500 and the Charlotte Motor Speedway. In 1986 Yarborough didn't place first at all, but he did manage to pull out several top-five and top-ten finishes.

Over the years Yarborough has invested much of his
$4.5 million in a number of successful ventures, including
car, tire and motorcycle dealerships, Hardee's restaurants,
dry-cleaning businesses and satellite dishes. In 1987 he
became a race-car owner himself, establishing the Race
Hill Farms organization. He has also tried his hand at
politics, sitting on the Florence County Council from 1972
through 1976.

In a 1974 interview with *Newsday* Yarborough
described the tension and mind-games involved in racing:
"You're driving at an average 200 miles an hour bumper
to bumper around in a tight circle. The temperature inside
the car is 150 degrees and you've been driving almost five
hours...You are strung out on tension, continuously con-
trolling your fear, thereby turning it into what some might
call courage. On one front, you're fighting the track,
watching every ripple, every angle. On another, you're lis-
tening to the scream of your engine, hearing noises that
aren't there, and praying to God you'll hear noises that
are. All this against a psychological race with the man in
front: What will he do when you pass? Is he wearing
down? You run a different race with the man behind and
the one coming up on your side: What are they thinking
and how do they feel?"

YOUNG, EDWARD LUNN, (1920-   ) — a U.S.
Representative from South Carolina; born in Florence,
Florence County, S.C., September 7, 1920; attended the
public schools; B.S., Clemson College, 1941; served in the
United States Army Air Corps as a flghter pilot in South-
west Pacific, 1942-1946; awarded the Distinguished
Flying Cross and the Air Medal with nine oak leaf
clusters; discharged as major in the Reserve; engaged in
farming and real estate; member, State house of representatives,tives 1958- 1960; delegate, South Carolina State
Republican conventions, 1968, 1970; delegate, Republican
National Convention, 1968; elected as a Republican to the
Ninety-third Congress (January 3, 1973-January 3, 1975);
unsuccessful candidate for reelection in 1974, and for
election in 1976 to the Ninety-fifth Congress; unsuccessful candidate for election as Governor of South Carolina

in 1978; unsuccessful candidate for nomination in 1980 to the Ninety-seventh Congress; is a resident of Florence, S.C.

* * *